MARK
& METHOD

MARK
& METHOD

NEW APPROACHES
IN BIBLICAL STUDIES

SECOND EDITION

EDITED BY
JANICE CAPEL ANDERSON
AND STEPHEN D. MOORE

FORTRESS PRESS
MINNEAPOLIS

MARK AND METHOD
New Approaches in Biblical Studies. 2nd Edition

Translations of Bible quotations in chapter 6 are by the author. Unless otherwise indicated, other biblical quotations are either freshly translated by the authors or are from the New Revised Standard Version of the Bible, copyright © 1989 by the Division of Christian Education of the National Council of Churches of Christ in the USA and are used by permission.

Cover and book design: Douglas Schmitz
Book illustration: chapter opening images by Elizabeth Foster (chapters 1–6, 8) and Micah Thompson (chapter 7)

Cover art: A wooden panel painting (ca. 1200) depicts Saint Mark handing a book to a sacred lion-like animal; from the the the St. Michaeliskirche Nave Ceiling, Hildesheim, Lower Saxony, Germany; © Adam Woolfitt/CORBIS.

Page 124: excerpt from "Atta Troll" by Heinrich Heiner, from *The Complete Poems of Heinrich Heine: A Modern English Version*, trans. Hal Draper (Boston: Surkamp/Insel, 1982), 458–59.

Library of Congress Cataloging-in-Publication Data
Mark and method : new approaches in biblical studies / edited by Janice Capel Anderson and Stephen D. Moore. —2nd ed.
    p. cm.
Rev. ed. of: Mark & method.
Includes bibliographical references (p.   ) and index.
ISBN 978-0-8006-3851-1 (alk. paper)
    1. Bible. N.T. Mark—Criticism, interpretation, etc. I. Anderson, Janice Capel, 1952- II. Moore, Stephen D., 1954- III. Mark & method.
BS2585.52M37 2008
226.3'0601—dc22   2007044129

Manufactured in the U.S.A.

CONTRIBUTORS

Janice Capel Anderson is Professor of Philosophy and Religious Studies at the University of Idaho, Moscow, Idaho. She is the author of *Matthew's Narrative Web: Over and Over and Over Again* (Sheffield, UK: Sheffield Academic Press, 1994) and co-edited *New Testament Masculinities* (Atlanta: Society of Biblical Literature, 2003 and Leiden: Brill, 2004); *Pauline Conversations in Context* (New York: Continuum, 2002); and *Taking It Personally: Autobiographical Biblical Criticism, Semeia* 72 (1995). Her essays, "Matthew: Gender and Reading" and "Reading Tabitha: A Feminist Reception History," are reprinted, respectively, in *A Feminist Companion to Matthew* and *A Feminist Companion to the Acts of the Apostles*, now published by Pilgrim Press.

Robert M. Fowler is Professor of Religion at Baldwin-Wallace College, Berea, Ohio. He is the author of *Let the Reader Understand: Reader-Response Criticism and the Gospel of Mark* (Harrisburg, PA: Trinity Press International, 2001) and *Loaves and Fishes: The Function of the Feeding Stories in the Gospel of Mark* (Atlanta: Society of Biblical Literature, 2006). He is a co-author of *The Postmodern Bible* (New Haven: Yale University Press, 1995) and a co-editor of *New Paradigms for Bible Study: The Bible in the Third Millennium* (New York and London: T & T Clark International, 2004).

Tat-siong Benny Liew is Associate Professor of New Testament at the Pacific School of Religion, Berkeley, California. He is the author of *What is Asian American Biblical Hermeneutics? Reading the New Testament* (Honolulu: University of Hawaii Press, 2008) and *Politics of Parousia: Reading Mark Inter(con)textually* (Leiden: Brill, 1999). He is guest editor of *The Bible in Asian America, Semeia* 90–91 (2002). His essay "Margins and (Cutting-)Edges: On the (Il)Legitimacy and Intersections of Race, Ethnicity, and (Post)Colonialism" appears in *Postcolonial Biblical Criticism: Interdisciplinary Intersections* (New York: Continuum, 2005). Another essay "Re-Mark-able Masculinities? Jesus, the Son of Man, or the (Sad) Sum of Manhood" appears in *New Testament Masculinities* (Atlanta: Society of Biblical Literature, 2003).

Elizabeth Struthers Malbon is Professor of Religious Studies at Virginia Polytechnic Institute and State University, Blacksburg, Virginia. She is the author of *Hearing Mark: A Listener's Guide* (Harrisburg, Pa.: Trinity Press International, 2002); *In the Company of Jesus: Characters in Mark's Gospel* (Louisville: Westminster John Knox, 2000); *The Iconography of the Sarcophagus of Junius Bassus: NEOFITVS IIT AD DEVM* (Princeton, N.J.: Princeton University Press, 1990); and *Narrative Space and Mythic Meaning in Mark*

(New York and San Francisco: Harper & Row, 1986. Paperback, Sheffield, UK: Sheffield Academic Press, 1991). She is a co-editor of *Biblical and Humane: A Festschrift for John F. Priest* (Atlanta: Scholars Press, 1996); *The New Literary Criticism and the New Testament* (Sheffield, UK: Sheffield Academic Press, 1994 Paperback ed., Valley Forge: Trinity Press International, 1994); and *Characterization in Biblical Literature, Semeia* 63 (1993).

Stephen D. Moore is Professor of New Testament at The Theological School, Drew University, Madison, New Jersey. He is the author of *Empire and Apocalypse: Postcolonial Studies and New Testament Studies* (Sheffield, UK: Sheffield Phoenix Press, 2006); *God's Beauty Parlor: And Other Queer Spaces in and around the Bible* (Stanford, Calif.: Stanford University Press, 2001); *God's Gym: Divine Male Bodies of the Bible* (Routledge: New York and London, 1996); *Poststructuralism and the New Testament: Derrida and Foucault at the Foot of the Cross* (Minneapolis: Fortress Press, 1994); *Mark and Luke in Poststructuralist Perspectives: Jesus Begins to Write* (New Haven: Yale University Press, 1992); *Literary Criticism and the Gospels: The Theoretical Challenge* (New Haven: Yale University Press, 1989); and a co-author of *The Postmodern Bible* (New Haven: Yale University Press, 1995).

David M. Rhoads is Professor of New Testament at the Lutheran School of Theology, Chicago, Illinois. He is the author of *The Green Congregation Training Manual*, rev. ed. (Web of Creation Publication, 2005); *Reading Mark, Engaging the Gospel* (Minneapolis: Fortress Press, 2004); *Mark as Story: An Introduction to the Narrative of a Gospel* rev. ed. with Joanna Dewey and Donald Michie (Minneapolis: Fortress Press, 1999); *The Challenge of Diversity: The Witness of Paul and the Gospels* (Minneapolis: Fortress Press, 1996); and *Israel in Revolution 6–74 C. E. A Political History of Israel Based on the Writings of Josephus* (Philadelphia: Fortress Press, 1976). He is the editor of *Earth and Word: Classic Sermons on Saving the Planet* (New York: Continuum Press, 2007) and *From Every People and Nation: The Book of Revelation in Intercultural Perspective* (Minneapolis: Fortress Press, 2005).

Abraham Smith is Professor of New Testament at Southern Methodist University, Perkins School of Theology, Dallas, Texas. He is the author of *Comfort One Another: Reconstructing the Rhetoric and Audience of First Thessalonians* (Louisville: Westminster John Knox, 1995); "Commentaries and Reflections on First and Second Thessalonians," in *The New Interpreter's Bible Commentary* (Nashville: Abingdon, 2000); "Paul and African American Biblical Interpretation," in *True to Our Native Land: An African American New Testament Commentary* (Minneapolis: Fortress Press, 2007); "Cultural Studies" in *The Dictionary of Biblical Interpretation* (Nashville: Abingdon, 1999); and "'I Saw the Book Talk': A Cultural Studies Approach to the Ethics of an African American Biblical Hermeneutics," *Semeia* 77 (1997). He is an associate editor of *The New Interpreter's Study Bible* (Nashville: Abingdon Press, 2003) and co-editor of *Slavery in Text and Interpretation, Semeia* 83/84 (1988).

Contents

PREFACE TO THE SECOND EDITION

The purpose of *Mark and Method* is to introduce students and teachers to some of the most exciting contemporary approaches to the interpretation of the Gospels using the Gospel of Mark as a case study. These approaches—narrative criticism, reader-response criticism, deconstruction, feminist criticism, social criticism, cultural studies, and postcolonial criticism—offer a seven-sided prism through which the Gospel is refracted. We hope that students beginning serious study of the biblical texts will be able to benefit from *Mark and Method*, and that it will also hold some surprises for those who are veterans of such study. The book can be used in courses on Mark, the Gospels, biblical hermeneutics, methods of biblical interpretation, New Testament introduction, and the Bible as literature. It can supplement standard introductory textbooks as well as stand on its own. Scholars who are trying to keep abreast of new developments in the field may also find it helpful.

Although each chapter stands on its own, we recommend that those new to Gospel studies read the introductory chapter and the chapter on narrative criticism first. The introductory chapter traces the career of the evangelist Mark through the centuries and locates the approaches covered in this volume within the history of Gospel studies. The chapter on narrative criticism employs concepts such as plot, character, and setting that are likely to be familiar already to most readers and may thus provide a transition into less familiar territory. We also recommend that you have a good modern translation of Mark at your elbow as you read. We have tried to write clearly with a minimum of endnotes and to define our technical terms as we go along. Nonetheless, readers may find our Glossary helpful. A list of further readings pointing to additional resources accompanies each chapter.

Our choice of Mark as the case study for this textbook was not arbitrary. Mark has long been a favorite testing-ground for new methodologies in New Testament studies. This is no doubt due to factors such as Mark's *brevity* (it happens to be the shortest narrative book in the New Testament), Mark's *priority* (it appears to be the first of the canonical Gospels to have been written), and Mark's *literary artistry* (it is now frequently regarded as the most subtle and enigmatic of the Gospels).

The first edition of *Mark and Method*, which appeared in 1992, had its roots in a specific program unit of the Society of Biblical Literature. All five of the contributors to the first edition (Janice Capel Anderson, Robert Fowler, Elizabeth Struthers Malbon, Stephen Moore, and David Rhoads) were members of the SBL Group on the Literary Aspects of the Gospels and Acts. This tightly knit group, generally of around two to three dozen members, met annually through much of the 1980s and 1990s. It was the main forum and "laboratory" within the SBL for the application of literary methods to New Testament narrative. The principal literary methods on which the work of the group centered, especially in its earlier years, were narrative criticism and reader-response criticism. It was to Mark that these methods had first been applied in New Testament studies.[1]

As the years went by, methodological ferment increasingly characterized the work of the Literary Aspects of the Gospels and Acts Group. Once the genie was out of the historical-critical bottle, New Testament literary critics continued to devour extrabiblical literary theory, which increasingly was itself in methodological ferment. Social-scientific criticism, meanwhile, was also charting new pathways in biblical scholarship. Certain members of the Literary Aspects Group had already pursued feminist versions of narrative or reader-response criticisms,[2] and these and other "political" projects continued. Others sought to merge literary with social-scientific approaches. Still others, meanwhile, were launching challenges to both narrative and reader-response criticisms from the direction of the deconstructive criticism that, during the previous decade, had taken the U.S. literary academy by storm.[3] Collectively, the five essays that constituted the first edition of *Mark and Method* (those on narrative, reader-response, deconstructive, feminist, and social criticisms) reflected the methodological horizon of the Literary Aspects Group in this period. They also reflected our conviction that textbooks can play an important role in encouraging both students and teachers to appreciate and experiment with new approaches.

There were other, still more challenging developments fermenting in biblical studies, however, even as the first edition appeared, developments of which its contributors were as yet only dimly aware. Since that time, biblical studies has made significant progress toward becoming a more globally inclusive discipline, no longer in name only but also on the level of methodology. Throughout the Two-Thirds World and within minority communities in the West (particularly in the United States), highly distinctive modes of biblical interpretation have coalesced. These strategies of reading mark an even sharper break with the inherited models of Euro-American biblical scholarship than any of the five methods introduced in the first edition. Especially prominent among these newest modes of exegesis are cultural studies and postcolonial criticism (both of them, however, having their roots in the older tradition of liberation theology). The editors are grateful to Tat-siong Benny Liew and Abraham Smith for consenting to introduce readers of this second edition to these significant new developments in biblical studies and demonstrating the difference they make for our study of Mark.

The contributors to the first edition, meanwhile, have themselves taken the opportunity the second edition affords to update their original chapters. (One contributor, Moore, has seized the opportunity to jettison and replace at least half of his original chapter.) The sixteen years that have passed since the advent of the first edition have seen some of what was once considered novel or "fringe" move into the mainstream of New Testament studies (this is most of all true of narrative criticism). For the next sixteen years, the editors would like nothing better than that more of what still remains on the periphery of Markan studies, and biblical studies more generally, move steadily inside, and, like leaven, begin to transform the entire lump. If this second edition plays even a small role in that transformation, we will be well content.

The debts of gratitude incurred in the preparation of *Mark and Method* now extend back through the years. We wish to thank the American Academy of Religion for a Collaborative Research Grant in 1989–90 that facilitated our initial efforts. We would also like to thank Elizabeth Struthers Malbon, former chairwoman of the Society of Biblical Literature's section on Biblical Criticism and Literary Criticism, who made it possible for us to present portions of our chapters for the first edition to a stimulating and challenging audience at the 1991 annual meeting in Kansas City. We also thank our students and our families who frequently provided jaded critics with fresh perspectives and other much-needed sustenance. We wish to thank Fortress Press's former editorial director Marshall D. Johnson and editors Charles B. Puskas, Pam McClanahan, and Julie Odland for understanding our purposes so well and seeing the first edition through to completion. Last but not least, we are grateful to current Fortress editors Neil Elliott and Jessica Hillstrom for the patience, expertise, and efficiency with which they have shepherded the second edition into print.

Janice Capel Anderson and Stephen D. Moore

1

INTRODUCTION

The Lives of Mark

JANICE CAPEL ANDERSON AND STEPHEN D. MOORE

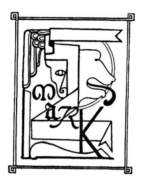

IT IS NOT UNCOMMON FOR A New Testament professor to begin an introductory lecture on the Gospels by asking students, "Have you ever read an entire Gospel straight through? If you have not," the teacher will continue, "you may not realize that each of the four evangelists is a full-fledged author in his own right. Each paints a unique portrait of Jesus." If students are familiar with the Gospels at all, they will likely have read, or heard read, only short passages taken out of their contexts. Here the classroom has parted company with the church. Short passages are read aloud in church services and expounded in sermons. They regularly form the basis for Sunday school lessons. Before hearing that gently accusing voice ("How many of you have ever read a Gospel in one sitting?"), most of us unconsciously combined passages from all four Gospels into a kind of mishmash or harmony.

Tradition, however, is firmly on the side of the student here. As early as the second century of the Common Era, a Syrian Christian named Tatian produced a highly influential harmony of all four Gospels known as the *Diatessaron*. Tatian had his work cut out for him. Hard-to-reconcile details abound in the Gospels. You can quickly establish this by comparing the accounts that the evangelists give of Jesus' resurrection, for example (Matt 28:1-10; Mark 16:1-8; Luke 24:1-12; John 20:1-20), or of Jesus' death (Matt 27:45-56; Mark 15:33-41; Luke 23:44-49; John 19:28-37), transfiguration (Matt 17:1-8; Mark 9:2-8; Luke 9:28-36), or baptism (Matt 3:13-17; Mark 1:9-11; Luke 3:21-22; cf. John 1:24ff.).

Oddly enough, the modern New Testament scholar tends to be someone who seizes gleefully on discrepancies among the four Gospels. Such discrepancies, far from closing the door to understanding, are instead the keys that he or she hopes to use to unlock the particular theological viewpoint of each evangelist. For example, Mark's Jesus dies with a cry of desolation ("My God, my God, why have you forsaken me?"; 15:34) in sharp contrast to Luke's Jesus, who expires on a note of serene confidence ("Father, into your hands I commend my spirit"; 23:46; cf. 23:34, 43). Typically, the scholar will explain this discrepancy with reference both to Mark's theology, which is said to be a theology of the cross, and to Luke's theology, which, among other things, gives particular prominence to prayer. Jesus' cross casts a longer and darker shadow over the Markan landscape than over the Lukan landscape, which helps to explain the bleak manner in which Jesus dies in Mark. And Jesus prays more frequently in Luke's Gospel than in any other, which explains why he dies with a prayer of trust on his lips.

Scholarly preoccupation with the unique theological viewpoint of Mark—or of any evangelist—is a relatively recent development. In the 1950s, the German New Testament scholar Willi Marxsen insisted more emphatically than anyone before him that the evangelist Mark should be viewed as a full-fledged author.[1] The approach that Marxsen pioneered on Mark, and that certain of his colleagues pioneered on Luke and Matthew, came to be known as *redaction criticism*.[2] Mark was said to be a redactor or editor who creatively combined, reworked, and expanded the traditions that he inherited. Marxsen insisted that Mark is "an individual, an author personality who pursues a definite goal with his work."[3] But if Mark was *not* an individual, or even an author in the strict sense of the term, in the period before Marxsen and redaction criticism—a rather lengthy period, to be sure—what then was he? What follows is a highly selective and greatly simplified résumé of the two-thousand-year career of the first evangelist.

HOW MARK BECAME AN AUTHOR

Mark as Peter's Scribe

"Mark" may not have been his real name. At first the Gospels circulated anonymously, it seems. Later, the shortest Gospel came to be titled *Kata Markon*, "(the Gospel) according to Mark." Most likely the name was lifted from certain other texts, also on their way to becoming New Testament texts. These feature a (John) Mark who is associated with Paul and Peter (Acts 12:12, 25; 15:37-39; 2 Tim 4:11; 1 Pet 5:13). By the second century, many Christian leaders were increasingly anxious to keep Gospel authorship in the family. Mark's relationship to Peter is the topic of the earliest "biographical" statement on the evangelist that has come down to us. It is attributed to Papias, Bishop of Hieropolis (in what is now southwestern Turkey). Eusebius (c. 260–340 C.E.), one of the earliest church historians, reports that Papias wrote:

> And the Presbyter used to say this, "Mark became Peter's interpreter and wrote accurately all that he remembered, not, indeed, in order, of the things said or done by the Lord. For he had not heard the Lord, nor had he followed him, but later on, as I said, followed Peter, who used to give teaching as necessity demanded but not making, as it were, an arrangement of the Lord's oracles, so that Mark did nothing wrong in thus writing down single points as he remembered them. For to one thing he gave attention, to leave out nothing of what he had heard and to make no false statements in them."[4]

This early snapshot of Mark presents him as a scribe—an accurate scribe, but one whose talents are otherwise limited. The towering figure of Peter overshadows him. Indeed, Mark is mentioned primarily because he has been enlisted in a battle. Certain second-century Christian groups, struggling for control of the church, want to show that their teaching goes back unerringly to Jesus himself by way of the apostles, the evangelists, and their legitimate successors. Mark has become a link in a chain of authority—although he has not gained any real authority for himself in the process, and certainly not any authority as an independent author or theologian.

Mark as Matthew's Summarizer

If Mark was overshadowed by Peter, on the one hand, he soon came to be overshadowed by Matthew, on the other. St. Augustine is especially associated with the influential view of Mark as Matthew's less illustrious cousin. Writing about 400 C.E., Augustine sought to explain why most of Mark's Gospel also appears in the much longer Gospel of Matthew: "Mark followed him [Matthew] like a slave and seems his summarizer."[5] Partly as a result of Augustine's pronouncement, Mark would labor in Matthew's shadow down to the nineteenth century.

Mark as the Holy Spirit's Writing Instrument

Matthew no less than Mark was eclipsed by the Holy Spirit, the real author of Scripture as far as the church was concerned. So long as the evangelists' pens were in the firm grip of the Holy Spirit, there could be no real contradictions between their accounts. The Spirit was the guarantor not only of the Bible's authority but also of its consistency. Apparent contradictions could always be resolved on some higher, more sublime level. For example, in Matthew, Mark, and Luke, Jesus is tempted in the wilderness soon after his baptism (Matt 4:1-11; Mark 1:12-13; Luke 4:1-13) and cleanses the Temple near the end of his ministry (Matt 21:12-17; Mark 11:15-19; Luke 19:45-48). In John, however, there is no account at all of the temptation, and the Temple cleansing occurs near the *beginning* of Jesus' ministry (2:13-22). Writing about 200 C.E., Origen, a brilliantly inventive Christian theologian and author of the first technical work on Christian interpretation theory, tried to resolve such discrepancies between the Gospels by turning to allegory or spiritual interpretation. The Holy Spirit was not so much concerned with chronology or literal accuracy as with higher meaning: "The truth of these matters must lie in that which is seen by the mind."[6] What Origen's mind sees is that the Temple can represent the church, Judaism, or even the rational soul, which is higher than the body, just as the earthly Jerusalem to which Jesus ascends is higher than Capernaum (see John 2:12-13), a lower region of less dignity.[7] The student of Scripture, "staggered" at finding discrepancies in the Gospel accounts, "will either renounce the attempt to find all the Gospels true . . . or he will accept the four, and will consider that their truth is not to be sought for in the outward and material letter."[8] In addition to solving the problem of contradictions, the authorship of the Holy Spirit and spiritual interpretation also solved the problem of passages that did not seem to make sense or that were offensive when taken literally. Origen gives the example of the devil showing Jesus all the kingdoms of the world from a high mountain during his temptation as a story that should not be taken literally: "Now who but the most superficial reader of a story like this would not laugh at those who think that the kingdoms of the Persians, the Scythians, the Indians, and the Parthians . . . can be seen with the eye of the flesh?"[9]

For Origen, as for legions of other ancient and medieval Christian theologians, scanning Scripture with the eye of the Spirit, "innumerable instances afford nothing more than a fleeting glimpse, a view as through a tiny hole, of a host of most sublime thoughts."[10] But these thoughts are not necessarily those of the biblical writers. Rather, they are those of the Holy Spirit. What the biblical writer seems to be saying on the literal level is less important than what the Holy Spirit means to say on the spiritual level. And if the writer's own limited intentions thereby lessen in interest, so too do the historical circumstances in which he wrote.

Mark would remain the Holy Spirit's stenographer down to the Reformation and beyond. In 1555, John Calvin's *Commentary on a Harmony of the Evangelists* appeared. A crisis of authority in the second-century church had required that Mark sit faithfully at Peter's feet and accurately transcribe Peter's eyewitness testimony, as we have seen. But Calvin has other problems, and whether or not Mark was Peter's scribe is no longer of any great consequence:

Mark is generally supposed to have been the private friend and disciple of Peter. It is even believed that he wrote the Gospel, as it was dictated to him by Peter, and thus merely performed the office of an amanuensis or clerk. But on this subject we need not give ourselves much trouble, for it is of little importance to us, provided only we believe that he is a properly qualified and divinely appointed witness, who committed nothing to writing, but as the Holy Spirit directed him and guided his pen.[11]

The pen would soon be snatched from the Holy Spirit's grasp, however, or at any rate Mark would tighten his grip. The seventeenth and eighteenth centuries saw the advent of the Enlightenment, with its emphasis on reason at the expense of tradition and its emphasis on scientific observation at the expense of divine revelation. "The Gospel under four aspects, but bound together by one Spirit," Irenaeus had pronounced in the second century.[12] But what had held together for so long now threatened to come apart with the irruption of the scientific worldview. The problem of the fourfold Gospel began to elicit radical new solutions.

Mark as Reporter

From Origen to Calvin, commentators had noted that Matthew, Mark, and Luke were strikingly similar to each other but differed markedly from John. In the eighteenth century, the first three Gospels came to be called the Synoptic Gospels: they saw as with (*syn*) one eye (*ōps*). But if they did they were wearing differently tinted spectacles, for there were striking differences among them as well. How could one explain these similarities and differences without recourse to the Holy Spirit? Either all three relied on a common earlier written or oral Gospel, or else they relied on each other. Some scholars still held the view, popularized by Augustine, that Mark abbreviated Matthew. The view that eventually won out, however, and that continues to be the majority view today, was that Mark is the earliest Gospel. Matthew and Luke had used Mark to compose their own Gospels, along with another source called Q. (Much of this scholarship was pioneered in Germany, and Q stood for the German word *Quelle*, meaning "source.") This two-source hypothesis, as it came to be called, attributed passages common to all three Gospels to Mark. Passages that appeared only in Matthew and Luke stemmed from the Q source that they shared in common. To round things out, many scholars spoke of M and L sources to indicate material unique to Matthew or Luke. The quest for the Gospels' sources was called *source criticism*.

What did source criticism mean for our elusive evangelist? It elevated Mark to center stage. If Mark is indeed the earliest Gospel, critics reasoned, was it not likely that Mark preserved the life of Jesus with greater historical accuracy than the other Gospels? Mark's plot became the privileged framework for reconstructions of the ministry of the historical Jesus. Mark appeared to be the most realistic Gospel, the least theological, the least shaped by the needs and concerns of the early Church. This view of the first Gospel and its author was called the Markan hypothesis.

Mark was now thrust into the limelight—not for his theological and authorial creativity, however, but for the lack of it. What was most important about Mark's Gospel was not its author's intentions, or even the text itself, but the text as a window on history. Mark was more a chronicler or reporter than a full-fledged author. Paradoxically, despite his newfound acclaim, Mark was reappointed to the same position that he had begun to occupy in the second century—that of unobtrusive recorder.

Mark as Theologian

Clearly, Mark was overdue for a promotion. In 1901 William Wrede published *The Messianic Secret*. "Exegesis must appreciably modify its previous view of the type of authorship that we have in Mark," Wrede insisted.[13] He added: "Present-day investigation of the Gospels is entirely governed by the idea that Mark in his narrative had more or less clearly before his eyes the actual circumstances of the life of Jesus, even if not without gaps."[14] For Wrede, Mark's narrative reflects the circumstances in which Mark wrote as much as the circumstances of Jesus' ministry. Wrede makes much of Mark 9:9, where Jesus directs his disciples "to tell no one about what they had seen, until after the Son of Man had risen from the dead." Similar injunctions to secrecy occur elsewhere in Mark (1:34, 43-45; 3:12; 5:43; 7:36; 8:26, 30). This pattern arouses Wrede's suspicions. If "Jesus had really kept himself strictly concealed then [his] life would hardly have been worth relating."[15] Moreover, Jesus' trial and execution would then have had nothing to do with his messiahship, for no one would have known of it.[16] For Wrede, the messianic secret is not a historical fact so much as a theological idea, the idea that Jesus became Messiah through his resurrection.[17] However, Jesus' "previous life was only worthy of the Easter morning if the splendour of this day itself shone back upon it."[18] Mark tries to resolve the tension between Jesus' resurrected glory and his earthly existence by asserting that Jesus "really was messiah already on earth"—and he knew it—but he did not yet wish it to be generally known.[19]

Interestingly, the relationship between Jesus' glory and his earthly existence is also a central problem in the Gospel of John. In the scholarly tradition that Wrede was opposing, John and Mark had conveniently been set at opposite poles, the "theologian" among the evangelists at one end, the "historian" at the other end. Wrede's daring thesis was that "Mark too is already very far removed from the actual life of Jesus and is dominated by views of a dogmatic kind. If we look at Mark through a large magnifying-glass, it may well be that we find a type of authorship such as is exhibited in John."[20]

Thanks to Wrede, Mark became not only an author but also a theologian. Still, Mark would have to wait another half-century or so before his talents would be widely recognized. The intervening years would be lean ones for the evangelist.

Mark as Scissors-and-Paste Man

Form criticism of the Gospels rose to prominence in Germany in the period immediately following the First World War. Its aims were twofold: first, to classify the units of tradition of which the Gospels were thought to be composed into appropriate categories or "forms," such as parables, legends, myths, exhortations, proverbs, or controversy stories; and second, to assign each of these units a *Sitz im Leben*, a setting and function in the life of the early Christian communities, such as preaching, teaching, or baptismal ceremony. With the rise of form criticism, Mark became a scissors-and-paste man. Martin Dibelius, one of the pioneers of form criticism, introduced the approach in 1919. In describing the synoptic evangelists he wrote:

> The literary understanding of the Synoptic Gospels begins with recognition of the fact that they are made up of collections of traditional material. Only in the smallest degree are the writers of the Gospels authors; they are in the main collectors, transmitters, editors. Their activity consists in the handling on, grouping and working over the material that has come down to them, and their theological apprehension of the material, insofar as one can speak of an apprehension at all, finds expression only in this secondary and mediated form. Their attitude to their work is far less independent than that of the author of the Fourth Gospel, far less than that of the writer of the Acts of the Apostles.[21]

For Rudolf Bultmann, another major figure associated with form criticism, the theological creativity of the early church was such that the historical Jesus disappears altogether behind the Gospels. But if Jesus vanishes, so do the evangelists—they disappear behind their texts. The Gospels do not "let the personalities of their author appear."[22] *Das Volk*, "the people," the anonymous oral tradition of the early church, becomes the true author of the Gospels. The unity and authority of the Gospels is located in the faith of the early church, not in the Gospels themselves or in their authors.

Mark as Redactor and Author

And so we return to Willi Marxsen, with whom we began. Against the backdrop of statements such as those of Dibelius and Bultmann is situated Marxsen's plea for an appreciation of Mark as "an individual, an author personality who pursues a definite goal with this work."[23] Marxsen bases his case on the relative unity of Mark itself. This unity is no longer a direct effect of divine authorship, as in the precritical period. The unifying power once ascribed to the Holy Spirit is transferred to the evangelist himself.

For Marxsen, form criticism's emphasis on the small traditional units that make up the Gospels fails to explain how "this totally disparate material should finally find its way into the unity of a Gospel."[24] The unity evident in Mark "cannot be understood as the 'termination' of the anonymous transmission of material." Such a process would lead "rather to ultimate 'fragmentation.'" Mark's own contribution to the tradition has "counteracted" its drive toward fragmentation, and this countermovement can be explained only with reference to "an individual, an author personality."[25]

Not for the first time in his career, Mark is dragged into the spotlight and declared superior to his fellow evangelists:

> From the outset, Matthew and Luke had access to a presentation [Mark's] which somehow was already formed. It consisted of an enlarged sketch which formed a unity created by one individual. In addition, Matthew and Luke used anonymous tradition. . . . Mark, on the other hand, has at his disposal only anonymous individual traditions, except for certain complexes and a passion narrative. Mark's achievement in shaping the tradition is thus incomparably greater. As far as we can tell, Mark is the first to bring the individualistic element to the forming and shaping of the tradition.[26]

Mark's preeminence among the evangelists no longer derives from his self-effacement, however. It does not stem from his role as a humble recorder of tradition, as for Papias and Eusebius, or as a fairly reliable chronicler of facts, as for the life of Jesus researchers of the nineteenth century. For Marxsen, Mark is first among the evangelists precisely because he is the most individual and the most creative. He is not only a redactor, but also the most original author of the four.

HOW MARK BECAME A NARRATOR

Mark as Allegorist

Marxsen completed what Wrede had started. With the subsequent popularization of redaction criticism, Mark finally came into his own, no longer eclipsed by Peter, Matthew, or even the Holy Spirit. Nevertheless, Mark's *text* continued to remain in the wings. Redaction criticism was interested in the text only as a means to an end. Marxsen wrote: "The form of the Gospels [i.e., the text] should help us to draw inferences as to the author's point of view and the situation of his community."[27] To see Mark's point of view, to see as he sees, we must look through his text. "First we shall go back behind

Mark," continues Marxsen, "and separate tradition from redaction"[28]—what Mark received from his tradition as distinct from what he added to it. Recall Origen's statement that innumerable instances in Scripture "afford nothing more than a fleeting glimpse, a view as through a tiny hole, of a host of most sublime thoughts,"[29] those of the Holy Spirit. For the redaction critics the Gospel text would likewise afford a glimpse, as through a hole or window, of a host of other thoughts—those of the Gospel writers. Once again a theological notion has gone underground to reemerge in secular guise.

Marxsen's approach to Mark is also reminiscent of patristic and medieval allegory. To read Scripture allegorically was to read it for hidden meanings— meanings metaphorically implied but not expressly stated. Interpreters often identified four levels of meaning in Scripture: the literal, the allegorical, the moral, and the anagogical. This fourfold approach is conveniently summarized in this memory verse common as late as the sixteenth century:

> *The letter shows what God and our fathers did;*
> *The allegory shows us where our faith is hid;*
> *The moral meaning gives us rules of daily life;*
> *The anagogy shows us where we end our strife.*[30]

For example, Jerusalem was literally the historical city, but allegorically it was the church, morally it was the human soul, and anagogically (that is, in terms of the last things) it was the heavenly city.[31] Allegory freed the Gospels to speak to the needs of individuals and the church in ever-changing contexts. It helped to make relevant what, on the surface, seemed irrelevant or downright problematic.

Compare Marxsen's treatment of geographical references in Mark. The wilderness in which John's ministry begins, for example, is not a real place. "We ought not to speculate as to its location," advises Marxsen. Rather, because of the well-established link between the wilderness and Old Testament prophecy, the phrase "in the desert" is introduced in Mark 1:4 merely to qualify "the Baptist as the fulfiller of Old Testament predictive prophecy. Put in exaggerated form, the Baptist would still be the one who appears 'in the wilderness' even if he had never been there in all his life."[32] Similarly for Marxsen, although for more complex reasons, Galilee is not primarily a geographical locale in Mark. Its significance is first and foremost theological.[33]

Indeed, redaction criticism's resemblance to the allegorical method is general and far-reaching. For redaction criticism in the classic German mold, each evangelist's theology assumed its particular form in response to the specific situation in which the evangelist was writing. In retelling the story of Jesus, the evangelist had one foot in the past and the other one firmly in the present. Dimly mirrored in the details of each Gospel narrative, then, are circumstances contemporary with the evangelist that he means to address. The Gospel becomes an "allegory" of the situation that occasioned it.

Theodore Weeden's controversial study of the Markan disciples, *Mark: Traditions in Conflict*, offers an especially striking example of such allegory.[34] Why are Jesus' disciples presented so "negatively" in Mark? Why do they have such difficulty understanding? Why do they fail so miserably (8:32-33; 9:5-6, 18, 32, 33-34; 10:13-14, 35ff.; 14:27-31, 37ff., 50; 16:8)? Weeden's answer is that the disciples in Mark are essentially stand-ins, cardboard cutouts, for Mark's opponents. In attempting to get beyond the literal sense of Mark to unveil its hidden senses, Marxsen, Weeden, and other redaction critics have reactivated the role of the patristic and medieval diviner of allegories.

Mark as Narrator

Another premodern device that has reemerged in a new guise in modern biblical scholarship is the catena. Catenae were collections of authoritative pronouncements on biblical passages and interpretive problems. In the thirteenth century, for example, Thomas Aquinas produced the *Catena Aurea,* which contained opinions from fifty-four Greek and Latin church fathers and other church writers. We no longer appeal to the pronouncements of the church fathers when confronted with a difficult passage of Scripture. We do invoke other authorities, however, especially in our footnotes or endnotes. To write as a scholar is scrupulously to keep track of one's debts to the "fathers" of one's discipline and their less illustrious sons and daughters.

With the passage of time, these debts have grown monstrous. The Gospel texts creak beneath their dreadful weight. Scholars regularly worry that we are losing sight of the texts in a dense forest of commentaries. Then, too, there is the redaction critic's habit of peering over the shoulders of the evangelists while addressing them. The fascination with background is still very strong. Since at least the late 1970s, however, voices have been raised to complain that whereas the Gospels have been endlessly read through, or read around, they have all too seldom been read on their own terms. Isolated at first, these voices have long since swelled into a chorus.

The winds of change have again been blowing in Gospel studies. A review in the *Journal of Biblical Literature* from 1991 serves as a windsock to show the direction of that change. Jack Dean Kingsbury, a well-known Matthean scholar, reviewed the first volume of W. D. Davies and Dale C. Allison's *Critical and Exegetical Commentary on the Gospel according to Saint Matthew.*[35] Increasingly, as Kingsbury notes, biblical commentaries "are assuming encyclopedic proportions"; this one devotes some eight hundred pages to the first seven chapters of Matthew.[36] As such they are predestined to "be consulted on a piecemeal basis" only.[37] By design, this particular commentary "is quintessentially redaction-critical in nature: the steady focus is on questions of tradition history, the situation of Matthew's community, and the intention of Matthew as [the authors] believe this comes to expression in various aspects of his Gospel."[38]

Kingsbury's main objection to Davies and Allison's approach echoed a concern that had been mounting in Gospel studies since the late 1970s, especially in the United States. According to Kingsbury,

> [Davies and Allison] ignore "plot development" in Matthew's Gospel and hence fail totally to convey to the reader any sense of the narrative and dramatic movement of Matthew's Gospel-story. Two consequences flow from this. The first is that the reader often, and sometimes for pages at a time, loses all sense of the fact that any story whatever is being narrated. Or to put it another way, because Davies and Allison pay no attention to plot development, the welter of scholarly observations they make serves not to highlight the story Matthew narrates but to obscure and suppress it. And the second consequence is that in this absence of concern for plot development, the reader gets the distinct impression that Matthew's "theology" becomes the element that Davies and Allison regard as binding the whole of the Gospel together. . . . Without question, one can abstract from Matthew's story a "theology." Still, it dare not happen that recognition of this be permitted to blur the fact that the story Matthew narrates does not turn on "theology" but on "conflict" [e.g., between Jesus and the religious authorities]. Abstracting from Matthew's Gospel-story its "theology" can never be a substitute for analyzing the development of the plot of this story.[39]

Kingsbury, along with many others, argues that an approach that would tear the theology of a Gospel away from its moorings in the evangelist's narrative is necessarily inadequate. A Gospel is not reducible to a set of theological propositions. Redaction criticism seeks to distill the evangelist's overarching theological perspective from his story. For critics such as Kingsbury, however, the Gospels are not simply the vehicles or instruments of a detachable theology. The evangelists are narrative thinkers, narrative theologians. The thought of an evangelist consists in the mediation of an enigmatic set of events centered on Jesus of Nazareth. It transmits those events through emphasizing certain details and repressing others, through plotting, characterization, point of view, and so forth. It renders those events in the form of structured, coherent narrative. To read the Gospels as story, as narrative, is to engage in *narrative criticism.*

HOW MARK LOST HIS GRIP ON THE TEXT

Narrative Criticism and Reader-Response Criticism

Marxsen's case against form criticism began with an appeal to the unity of Mark's creation, as we noted earlier. But Marxsen saw the unity of Mark as residing in the intentions of the evangelist, his overarching theological purpose. For the narrative critics, in contrast, the locus of unity is more in the text itself, in the internal organization of its story world (the artful arrangement of its plot, for example). The author does not vanish from the scene, although his relationship to his creation does become more distant; it is conducted through intermediaries such as the implied author and the narrator, as Elizabeth Struthers Malbon explains in chapter 2.

Narrative criticism easily shades over into a preoccupation with readers and reading. The current interest in the Gospel reader, however, also has its roots in redaction criticism. Once the idea began to take hold that the evangelists were authors as well as collectors, the critic's task became more than ever one of trying to put himself or herself in the position of the original readers or hearers of the Gospels. Implicitly, the task became one of reenacting the roles scripted for these original audiences, of recreating the responses to the story that the evangelist might have anticipated or intended. Therefore, the task was also that of becoming the evangelist's ideal reader by becoming attuned even to the subtle nuances of his intentions. But what if the critic were to take the reading experience as his or her explicit focus and directly examine the complex interaction between story and audience? Then the critic would be fully into the realm of *reader-response criticism,* as Robert M. Fowler explains in chapter 3.

From the vantage point of the present (which is ever precarious), source criticism, form criticism, redaction criticism, and narrative criticism all appear to have "evolved" out of one another. To do redaction criticism on Mark, for example, one must be able to distinguish what Mark contributed from what he inherited, redaction from tradition. Redaction criticism builds on source and form criticism, and frequently narrative criticism and reader-response criticism build on redaction criticism. This bears out the claim of the late Norman Perrin, one of the scholars principally responsible for transplanting redaction criticism from Germany to the United States, that redaction criticism was "mutating" into a true literary criticism.[40] (Actually, it was mutating right before his eyes; two of the contributors to the present volume, Fowler and Anderson, are former students of Perrin's.)

The "author personality" that Willi Marxsen claimed to glimpse behind the Gospel of Mark grew ever more dominant as form criticism gave way to redaction criticism. The advent of narrative criticism has done nothing to retard Mark's personality development. Mark's text assumes an even higher degree of unity and coherence for narrative critics than for redaction critics, as we have seen. Implicitly, the evangelist's masterful purpose, expressed in his narrative creation, remains the ultimate source of that unity. He retains a powerful hold on his text.

Does he retain a corresponding grip on the reader? Is the reader whose responses are the domain of reader-response criticism a puppet in the hands of the evangelist? Or does the reader co-create the meaning of the text together with the evangelist, as Robert Fowler suggests in his chapter? Mark's control over his text appears to weaken once we venture into the territory of reader response. Traditionally, that control has been bound up with the concept of the "author's intention." How has that concept been used in biblical studies? Mary Ann Tolbert explains:

> Modern biblical scholars often tend to use a claim of "authorial intention" to argue for the superiority of their interpretations. . . . And this claim is effective because "authorial intention" is currently accepted by the guild as a conventional criterion of "truthful" research. So, although there may be a variety of texts in the Bible, each text reflects only its own author's intention, thereby giving the illusion, if not in fact the reality, of limitation to the process. The singular Word of God is not restored, but the cacophony is sharply reduced.[41]

In other words, the authority that was once the Holy Spirit's has passed to the biblical authors. Or has it passed instead to those scholars who claim to discern these authors' hidden intentions?

For the form critics, the Gospel of Mark was essentially a community product. The evangelist himself played a modest role as compiler or collector of traditions. With the advent of redaction criticism, the Gospel of Mark was declared the product of a bona fide author. It was a creative retelling of the story of Jesus designed to deliver a forceful message to the community or communities that it originally addressed. With the arrival of literary criticism, Mark's narrative creativity is celebrated still further, and the attempt to reconstruct the situation for which he was writing recedes in importance. During the past half-century or so, then, the author of Mark has emerged into ever sharper focus. Strange to say, however, in the neighboring field of secular literary studies (and hence down the hall from the Religious Studies Department—in the English Department, say, or the French Department), the figure of the author in general has receded steadily into the background over the same period. In this respect, biblical studies and literary studies have been like two trains traveling on parallel tracks in opposite directions. In literary studies, an initial preoccupation with the biographies of authors and other background factors gradually gave way in the 1930s and 1940s to the New Criticism, which eventually declared the author's intention irrelevant to the task of interpretation. The New Criticism was gradually superseded in its turn in the 1960s and 1970s by structuralism and deconstruction. In the process, the text slipped out of the author's grasp—and the author slipped on the text and began to dissolve into it.

Deconstruction

Deconstruction began in France in the 1960s as a development in the field of philosophy but entered the United States in the 1970s as a movement in the field of literary studies. Deconstruction is inherently suspicious of the power often attributed to authors to bend the language of texts to their will, to use language only and not be used by it. For deconstruction, language is an extremely slippery, infinitely resourceful element that refuses to limit itself to what its user intends it to say. There is always an unpredictable and uncontrollable excess of meaning that simmers within every text, always ready to spill over, as Stephen Moore explains (and attempts to demonstrate) in chapter 4. In a deconstructive perspective, therefore, Mark himself would be in the powerful grip of something that operates through him and exceeds his abilities to control it, just as he was for the patristic and medieval commentators—although that something is no longer the Holy Spirit.

The question inevitably arises: If interpretation is no longer answerable to the author's intentions, to what does it answer instead? Here again the history of biblical interpretation can be usefully consulted, a history in which the (human) author's intentions have played but a minor role. In Gospel studies, for example, only in the last fifty years or so have the evangelists' intentions come to play a central role, and for nonacademic Bible readers they continue to count for very little. For much of Christian history the arbiter of conflicting interpretations was the so-called rule of faith—what the church had "always and everywhere" taught, as guaranteed by apostolic succession. Interestingly, the erosion of the authority of authors in our time, coupled with the disintegration of the unified literary text brought about largely by deconstruction, has resulted in an unprecedented upsurge of interest in the rules and regulations that govern interpretation. Increasingly, literary critics have shifted their attention to the network of conflicting interests whose complex interaction determines what may and may not be read in(to) a given text in a given period. Rules governing what one may say and the ways in which it may be said permeate academic life at every level, from the undergraduate term paper on Mark to the weightiest scholarly tome. The academy functions like a secularized church in this regard, the rule of faith having been displaced by other rules, notably the rule of fact.

The modern biblical scholar respects the rule of fact. Davies and Allison's massive Matthean commentary, mentioned earlier, for example, aims to be a "disinterested and objective study in biblical criticism."[42] However, the widespread philosophical and political turn in recent literary studies has had the effect of discrediting terms such as *disinterested* and *objective*. As long as the text was viewed as a stable container of meaning—meaning that its author had put into it and that the critic could extract from it—the critic could claim an effaced and neutral role in relation to the text, somewhat like Papias's Mark at Peter's feet. Once the contribution of the reader to the creation of textual meaning came to be emphasized, however, the critic's role took on a rather different aspect.

Reader-response critics have argued that meaning is not something that one extracts from a text, like a nut from its shell or a nugget from a streambed. Meaning occurs not between the covers of a book or between the margins of a page but in the consciousness of the one who reads.[43] Prior to the creative engagement of a reader who "activates" it, the Bible, like any other text, remains a partial or unfinished object. Criticism is an inescapably creative activity. Prior to the interpretive act, there is nothing definitive in the text to be discovered.[44]

But if meaning is in part the creation of the critic, then criticism can never be "disinterested." The disinterested critic is like Mark before redaction criticism—a neutral recorder or compiler. With the shift of attention to the reader, however, the critic, like Marxsen's Mark, comes to be seen as a creative writer in his or her own right. The critic reworks the textual data in the interests of a particular agenda. As deconstructionists in particular see it, criticism is not qualitatively different from literature. Markan criticism becomes an unconscious reenactment of the text it sets out to master. And if, as Moore argues in chapter 4, that text is marked with problematic ideologies, such as anti-Judaism, then the critic must take particular pains not to perpetuate the injustices of the text in interpretively reenacting it. Deconstruction regularly entails reading against the grain of authorial intention, therefore, and in deconstruction's more politicized modes such reading is ethically motivated.

Feminist Criticism

Feminist critics, too, have been acutely aware that scholarship is always "interested" and never neutral. They point out that gender shapes readings of the Gospels, just as it has shaped the Gospels themselves. It is no accident that female characters in the Bible, female imagery for God, and the role of women in the early church became significant areas of investigation for professional biblical scholars only in the late twentieth century. Although we are rediscovering a rich history of women interpreting the Bible, it is only with the relatively recent resurgence of feminist thought and practice that women gained a toehold in the profession. Not all women are feminists, however, and some men embrace feminism. Feminist scholars read Gospel texts from various feminist perspectives. They criticize androcentric (male-centered) and patriarchal interpretations and construct interpretations of their own.[45] They focus less on the perennial problems of the unity of the Gospels and discrepancies between them than on offensive passages, multiple interpretations, and authority. For Jewish and Christian feminists, questions of authority are particularly acute. Which texts belong in the canon? Which interpretations should govern faith and practice? What institutional interests, whether of nation, religious tradition, or academy, are involved? Where is the locus of authority?

From a feminist perspective, whether Mark is an author in his own right or merely a collector is less important than the views of gender relations that the Gospel and its interpreters embody. Religious and nonreligious feminist critics care about how the social construction of gender shaped and shapes lives past and present. Feminists are concerned with the symbolic meanings of gender in the Gospel texts and in the cultures that produced and read them. They are also concerned with the actual behavior of men and women. These concerns unite historical and theological interests prominent since at least the turn of the last century with the more recent approaches described in this book.

A text reflects the culture that produced it, and culture is a "text" to be interpreted. Feminists are aware that gender relations have taken different forms in different historical and cultural circumstances. Race, class, and other factors have given rise to multiple forms and ideologies of oppression as well as multiple forms of female agency and power. If culture is a text, a script, that assigns gender roles to each of its participants, it is also a text that can be rewritten. If gender relations are culturally constructed at least in part, if they are not always and everywhere the same, then they can be reconstructed through a critique of culture. The feminist attempt to situate interpretations culturally (see Janice Capel Anderson's investigation in chapter 5 of the interpretive history of Mark's "Salome" story as well as Tat-siong Benny Liew's analysis of subaltern women in Mark in chapter 6) arises out of a desire to rewrite the scripts of our culture. Feminists seek to write scripts that call for equality, for the celebration of female difference, or for a new world beyond the two.

HOW MARK BECAME INCREASINGLY DISTANT

Social Criticism

The feminist concern to place Mark and his interpreters culturally also finds expression in another relatively new direction in Markan studies, the turn to social history and the social sciences, especially anthropology and sociology. Courses on the Gospels regularly present students with cautions about ethnocentrism (reading the Gospels through the lenses of one's own culture) and anachronism (reading the Gospels through the lenses of one's own time). Social criticism of the Gospels insists that the proper reading lenses are those tinted by the first-century Mediterranean cultures in which these texts took shape. One should avoid being an "ugly American" (or Canadian, Peruvian, or whatever) as one journeys through the Gospel narratives.

Concern for the original historical context is, of course, nothing new in biblical scholarship. Beginning with the revival during the Renaissance of the practice of reading the Bible in the original languages and the cry of *sola scriptura* during the Reformation, church tradition was increasingly placed in question as an adequate resource for interpreting Scripture. Exegesis of the biblical text (reading its meaning *out* of it) as opposed to eisegesis (reading *into* it) became the ideal. With the rise of historical criticism in the eighteenth and nineteenth centuries, scholars began to see the Gospels more and more as artifacts from the past. The Gospels offered windows on an ancient world that grew stranger the longer one peered into it.

For some scholars, the Gospels also represented a primitive or quaint stage in an evolution toward the enlightened European culture of their own day. What such scholars viewed as irrational in the Gospels had to be decoded into acceptable scientific or historical terms. At the beginning of the nineteenth century, for example, the German critic H. E. G. Paulus explained the story of Jesus walking on the water as a result of the disciples' confusion when Jesus walked on a sandbar in a mist, whereas the "miraculous" feedings of the multitudes simply involved the rich sharing with the poor. A later critic, D. F. Strauss, rejected both naturalistic and supernaturalistic interpretations of miracles and other such phenomena in the Gospels; such elements should be understood as myth, the primitive narrative expression of ideas.

The evolutionary and comparative approach was typical of the rise of the social sciences in general. In New Testament studies, the views of myth that this approach entailed have since been criticized for being simplistic and misleading. Some have also argued that the rationalist, evolutionary approach served a hidden theological agenda: the rationality of Christianity would be shown to be independent of the historical accuracy of the New Testament. The primitive presentations and mythic forms of the Gospels, for example, housed eternal truths acceptable to reason. It would fall to a later historical critic, Rudolf Bultmann, to "demythologize" the New Testament for twentieth-century theology. He sought to translate the three-story universe (heaven, earth, Hades/Gehenna) and myths of the New Testament into existentialist expressions about the truth of what it means to live as an authentic human being in this world.[46] Bultmann's emphasis, however, was less on reason than on faith, which he likewise declared to be independent of the historical accuracy of the Gospels. Christian faith was based on the Christ of faith rather than the Jesus of history.

The movement of Europeans into all parts of the globe in the nineteenth century as traders, missionaries, travelers, and colonizers stimulated research not only into contemporary primitive peoples but also into Greco-Roman and Middle Eastern history. Attempts to trace the origins and diffusion of Indo-European folklore fueled attempts in biblical studies to trace the history of the oral traditions that lay behind the Bible. Folklore studies, emerging from the social sciences of the late nineteenth and early twentieth centuries, had a significant impact on the development of form criticism.

The turn of the nineteenth century also saw the rise in Germany of a more encompassing movement called the History of Religions School. Historians such as Hermann Gunkel, Wilhelm Heitmüller, and Wilhelm Bousset insisted that New Testament scholars pay closer attention to the religions of the Hellenistic world, especially Judaism, Gnosticism, and the mystery religions. Christianity was a syncretistic religion, meaning that it combined many elements of preexisting religions, both Hellenistic and "Oriental." Along with religion, other aspects of ancient history and culture would shed light on the Gospels. In the United States, Shirley Jackson Case, F. C. Grant, and the Chicago school produced a number of studies of the social world of the New Testament. These movements can be seen as forerunners of recent social criticism.

However, there are also certain discontinuities between social criticism and historical criticism as traditionally practiced. Today's social historians and scientists are less optimistic than their predecessors that history can be reconstructed "as it actually was." They are also more sensitive to cultural diversity. Seeming parallels between events or symbols from different groups in the Greco-Roman world can be misleading. Phenomena such as miracles or dying and rising gods do not always have the same meaning in different social contexts, and, as the term *social* indicates, there is less concern with the individual or the unique than with the general and the group. (Mark again begins to fade into his community, his tradition, and his culture.)

In chapter 6 David Rhoads identifies five types of social criticism of the Gospels. The first is *social description,* which reconstructs the material culture, customs, and everyday life of the first-century Mediterranean world. The second is *social history,* which attempts to chart sweeping historical changes. It focuses on the history of groups, movements, and institutions rather than individual persons or events. The activities of women and other marginalized groups frequently come to the fore, in marked contrast to earlier historians' focus on Great Men, great battles, and political elites. Frequently, too, social history highlights struggles for power, sometimes from the perspective of liberation theology. A third area is *sociology of knowledge,* which studies the relationship between a group's worldview and its social organization. It seeks to reconstruct a culture's basic assumptions or common sense. It then correlates this information with the culture's social order. In seeking the fit between worldview and social order, sociology of knowledge often homes in on the function of certain beliefs and practices in the maintenance of the group's social equilibrium or stability. It can also document clashes of worldviews and corresponding conflicts in the social order. A fourth type of social scientific work on the Gospels involves the use of models from *cultural anthropology.* Such models organize information about a single culture, such as a culture's family structure. They also enable cross-cultural comparisons. One can construct a model, for example, of a culture's kinship system or family structure and then compare it to those of other cultures. Many New Testament scholars now turn to such models as aids to interpretation. Constructing a model of one's own culture can help one to avoid ethnocentrism in the study of other cultures. Models can help to fill in the gaps created by the limited information we have about the first century. Models developed from the study of current Mediterranean culture, for example, may shed light on ancient Mediterranean culture. The roles of women in an isolated farm community in Greece may shed light on the roles of women in early Christianity. The responses of contemporary sects to the failure of prophecy may shed light on early Christian responses to the delay of Jesus' second coming, and vice versa. Rhoads particularly shows how a cross-cultural model of purity and pollution can shed light on Mark. A fifth type of social criticism is the identification of *social location*. Social location is the position within a social system that a group occupies. One charts social location via the multiple categories that structure a social system. These categories include markers such as ethnicity, economic class, kinship, gender, and political status. Rhoads points to the scholarly practice of constructing the social location of a Gospel's author and likely first-century audience, a practice within the orbit of earlier redaction critics. In order to pursue this, however, social critics sometimes explore the apparent social location of a Gospel's characters. They also may explore the social location of modern readers, who may or may not occupy a social location similar to various Gospel characters or the likely first-century audience. These activities place the social critic more in the orbit of narrative and reader-response critics while maintaining the importance of the difference between then and now, there and here.

In some ways, then, Mark has become an informant for an *ethnography*. An ethnography is the description and interpretation of a culture that an anthropologist produces. The Gospel ethnographer looks for mentions of coins, for example, and clues concerning agricultural or marriage practices. He or she looks for references to political and economic institutions and marks of social status. Key terms and assumptions of Mark's worldview are sought. His symbolic and mythic universe is mapped.

There are, however, complications. A modern ethnographer is typically a "participant-observer" who lives with the group being studied. He or she can ask questions and can question more than one member of the group. "Mark" can no longer be questioned, needless to say, and his community cannot be observed over the course of several years. Furthermore, *he* is only one informant. Archaeology, other texts, and models must fill in the gaps. Moreover, as the term *participant-observer* indicates, the scholar is always a cocreator of meaning.

The twin goals of social criticism of Mark are to understand the first-century Mediterranean world and to understand the Gospel narrative as a first-century hearer or reader might. Social criticism remains the heir of historical criticism and redaction criticism in viewing the text of Mark as a window on the first-century Mediterranean world. Its second goal, that of understanding the Gospel narrative as a first-century hearer or reader might, further suggests the affinities of social criticism with historical criticism and redaction criticism, despite differences and tensions. But what if the critic's goal were instead primarily that of better understanding the Gospel in its *twenty-first* century context? This brings us to *cultural studies*.

THE EVANGELIST AND THE EMPEROR

Cultural Studies

The first thing to note about cultural studies is that it is not a method as such. Rather, it is a critical sensibility or angle of vision that brings previously unrecognized data into focus. In that respect, cultural studies is more like feminist studies than, say, narrative criticism. Feminist scholars employ specific methods, such as narrative criticism or reader-response criticism, as Janice Capel Anderson does in her chapter. Feminist criticism, however, is itself less a method than a critical, ethical, and political sensibility. Cultural studies is likewise multi-methodological in scope, as Abraham Smith's chapter clearly illustrates. He employs a variety of methods including textual criticism, translation studies, narrative criticism, and reception history including the analysis of visual art. He also fruitfully links cultural studies and postcolonial criticism.

What, then, are the unifying characteristics of cultural studies? First, the concept of "culture" that informs and enables cultural studies is a highly distinctive one. Ultimately, it has its roots in a complex twentieth-century shift from an elite concept of culture as "the best that has been thought or said." This might be labeled an "aesthetic" concept of culture, quintessentially expressed in museum art, classical music, highbrow literature, and other elite products of European civilization. It contrasts with what might be termed an "anthropological" concept of culture. This is an infinitely more expansive notion of culture. It extends to embrace all the minutiae of ordinary, everyday life. But whereas Europeans initially reserved the anthropological concept of culture for "exotic" cultures geographically distant from Europe, eventually it was extended to the everyday lives of Europeans themselves, beginning with working-class Britons. This was the achievement of British cultural studies, beginning in the 1950s. But study of "non-elite" culture did not stop at the borders of Britain. Scholars from around the globe with a stake in issues of culture and identity as well as political change extended the range of cultural studies. Many of these critics also delighted in serious study of popular culture such as rock music and television. As Smith points out, in North America critics such as bell hooks and Cornel West have played an important role in the developing field of cultural studies. Creative work is ongoing in other places as well, often engaging the intersections of local and global cultural practices and products.

Today, cultural studies is primarily the name for the academic analysis of contemporary popular culture in all its myriad manifestations. It is one of the most visible, influential, and controversial academic developments of recent decades. What form or forms might a cultural studies analysis of the Gospel of Mark take? It might take the form of an investigation of Mark's reception and "recycling" in recent popular culture. It might focus, for example, on such phenomena as *Marked*, a graphic-novel adaptation of Mark that resituates the Gospel in a grim, dystopian near-future.[47]

As Smith's chapter shows, however, cultural studies also provides resources for fresh analyses of Mark's reception in earlier historical periods, and even of its functioning in its original first-century context—or culture. The freshness of the approach arises from the fact that the concept of culture stemming from cultural studies is a more thoroughly politicized one than any concept of culture previously employed in biblical studies. In the cultural studies tradition, culture and *ideology* are inextricably intertwined. Just as every human activity, no matter how mundane, is productive of culture, so too is every human activity expressive of ideology—that is, a related system of beliefs and values. Cultural studies, almost from its beginning, has thus been a form of ideology critique, or ideological analysis, or—to employ the term most commonly used in biblical studies—ideological criticism.[48]

Translated into Markan studies, cultural studies dislodges theology as the privileged object of inquiry, knocking it off the pedestal on which redaction criticism placed it half a century ago. More precisely, perhaps, cultural studies blurs the boundary between theology and ideology. In effect, the latter part of Smith's chapter shows that much of what traditionally would be termed "theological" in Mark entails complex self-positioning in relation to the overarching power, authority—and ideology—of the Roman Empire that ruled the first-century Mediterranean world. It thus becomes possible to appreciate how the "theological" in Mark is also, and perhaps more fundamentally, counter-ideological. The title "Son of God" applied to Jesus in Mark, for instance, not only resonates against the backdrop of the Jewish scriptures in which it is used. It also resonates against Roman imperial propaganda in which "Son of God" is a title conferring honor on Roman emperors living or dead. The title thereby makes a paradoxical counter-emperor of Mark's peasant protagonist, Jesus of Nazareth.

Postcolonial Criticism

If Mark's relationship to Rome is but one of a range of possible foci for cultural studies, it is a central focus for postcolonial criticism of Mark. Postcolonial critics are characteristically interested in the complex collusions and resistances that life under empire inevitably entails. Biblical scholars, however, are relative latecomers to postcolonial analysis. Like cultural studies, postcolonial studies is a sprawling academic phenomenon that has given birth to a massive scholarly literature across a wide range of disciplines. In the interdisciplinary context of postcolonial studies, the term *postcolonial* ordinarily refers not to any ancient phenomenon or practice but rather to the complex geopolitical realities that the mid-twentieth century ushered in. For centuries the great European empires had been busy colonizing the rest of the world, eventually controlling almost the entire globe. Following the Second World War, these empires began to crumble. It was in connection with this dissolution, and with the widespread achievement of independence on the part of former colonies, that the term *postcolonial* was first coined.

It was not until the early 1990s, however, that postcolonial studies fully emerged as an academic enterprise. The context was that of a one-superpower world. The United States had emerged as a new and unprecedented kind of empire, one whose primary means of expansion was globalization, the extension of U.S. economic, cultural, and political power worldwide. Globalization made this empire immeasurably more expansive and efficient than any empire of the past. This is the overarching context—one commonly termed *neocolonial*—within which many biblical scholars are now turning with intensified interest to the topic of empire.

As intimated above, postcolonial criticism within New Testament studies most often takes the form of critical reflection on the relations between early Christianity and the Roman Empire. In the case of Mark (as of most early Christian texts), such reflection is hardly unprecedented. For more than a century, scholars have been attempting to situate Mark squarely in its original historical and sociocultural context. And the Roman Empire has always represented the outer limits of that context. If postcolonial criticism does not represent a first look at Mark and empire, however, it does represent a fresh look. As Tat-siong Benny Liew's chapter makes clear, such analysis now has at its disposal the tools of postcolonial theory and criticism—an extensive, interdisciplinary body of reflection on such interrelated phenomena as empire, imperialism, colonialism, nationalism, postcolonialism, and neocolonialism.

More fundamentally, perhaps, what makes the current intensified preoccupation with Mark and empire genuinely new is a keen interest in the question of whether or to what extent Mark *resists* empire. Throughout its history, Mark has been used more often to prop up empire than to resist it. Mark was produced in the margins of the Roman Empire. When Rome was Christianized under Constantine in the fourth century, however, the margins moved to the center. Jerome's Latin translation of the Bible, completed in the early fifth century, finally fixed a previously fluid and unstable canon. It did so, however, with the support of a new imperial power. The Vulgate (as Jerome's Latin translation came to be known) was the first official Bible of imperial Christianity. Locked in the Vulgate's embrace, the primary function of Mark, as of all its canonical companions, became that of legitimizing the imperial status quo.[49] Even the invention of critical biblical scholarship in post-Enlightenment Europe coincided with the inexorable expansion of the great European empires to their outer limits, their greedy encircling of the globe. The extent to which the emergence of biblical criticism was at least an indirect product of European imperialism has yet to be properly investigated. It is only in recent decades, first through liberation theology and liberationist exegesis and more recently through cultural studies and postcolonial criticism, that biblical scholars have turned in earnest to the task of disentangling Mark and other biblical texts from an imperial embrace that spans the millennia.

"MARK" AND "METHOD"

From Peter's scribe, to a writing instrument in the hand of the Holy Spirit, to a reliable chronicler, to a front for an anonymous Christian community, to an editor and theologian, to a full-fledged author of a unified narrative, to a provoker of reader response, to an embodier of gender ideology, to an ethnographic informant, to a critic of first or twenty-first century cultures and ideologies, to a critic of or collaborator with ancient, modern, or postmodern empires—Mark has had many careers. He has been promoted and demoted more times than we can count. Future bosses, future interpreters, will undoubtedly find many other uses for his invention, his Gospel, and Mark's responsibilities will once again diminish or increase.

What factors have determined Mark's more recent careers? The primary stimuli to new approaches in Gospel studies over the past thirty or forty years have come from extrabiblical literary studies and the social sciences. Of the various methods introduced in this book, none has been so fully integrated into mainstream Gospel studies, arguably, as narrative criticism, most especially in North America, and most obviously in Markan studies.[50] Social criticism and reader-response criticism have each had a less transformative impact on Gospel studies, but a substantial one nonetheless. The influence of feminism on Gospel studies, and New Testament studies more generally, is harder to assess. Certainly, feminist scholars have had an impact, as the number of their published articles and books shows. References to feminist work even show up in introductory textbooks. Yet some still consider feminist work to be merely an interesting sidelight, or too political to produce the "assured" and "objective" results that they see as a hallmark of biblical scholarship. Deconstruction, for its part, has undoubtedly remained peripheral to Gospel studies. It has attracted attention on occasion (hostile attention, in particular!), but has exerted little influence on the ways in which the vast majority of New Testament scholars approach the task of exegesis.[51] Cultural studies and postcolonial criticism, meanwhile, are each very recent arrivals in Gospel studies. Already, however, cultural studies, picking up in part on certain interests of reader-response criticism, is encouraging examination of how the Gospels interact with popular culture—movies, novels, music, the Internet—and political movements. There are also signs that the reinvigorated investigation of empire prompted by postcolonial studies is having a notable impact on Gospel studies, not least Markan studies.[52] Nevertheless, we can expect relatively few New Testament scholars to engage with extrabiblical postcolonial theory and criticism.

Prophecy is not our forte. However, we do expect interpreters to continue to develop new approaches and to forge new careers for the evangelist Mark in the years ahead. Some of these developments may emerge from interdisciplinary study and some from the contexts in which scholars live and work. Contributions of scholars from the Two-Thirds World, for example, continue to grow and promise powerful new insights.

Whatever new developments appear, they will both echo and contest previous ways of looking at Mark, as we have tried to show throughout this introduction. The chapters in this volume also involve such challenges and echoes. The contributors are as passionate about the approaches they describe as they are about Mark. We, too, have our favorite axes to grind. One of our key motivations in writing this textbook was to disseminate our ideas and interests to students and those who teach them. When we were students, textbooks provided our initial contact with biblical scholarship. They excited us and colored our views, sometimes indelibly. Some of us can never read the Hebrew Scriptures without being influenced by the emphasis on the covenant put forward in Bernard Anderson's *Understanding the Old Testament*. Norman Perrin's brief *What Is Redaction Criticism?* unlocked the mysteries of form criticism and redaction criticism for us. As teachers, we have found we have limited time to keep up with all of the developments in New Testament studies. We have learned that there is no better way to come to terms with a new approach than to teach it. So this book is unapologetically for students and teachers.

Finally, in fairness to the students and teachers who read this book, we should say something about ourselves. All of us are middle class and most of us are middle-aged. Smith is African American. Anderson, Fowler, Malbon, Moore, and Rhoads are white. Liew, who is Asian American, was born and raised in Hong Kong. Moore was born and raised in Ireland, received his graduate training there, and identifies as Roman Catholic. The rest of us come out of Protestant traditions and received our graduate training at American graduate schools. Two of us, Anderson and Malbon, teach at American state universities. Liew, Moore, Rhoads, and Smith teach at seminaries, while Fowler teaches at a private college. All of us are card-carrying members of the Society of Biblical Literature. We are members of the critical guild—in other words, overtrained readers who need to unlearn as well as to learn.

We hope that the interplay between our readings will shed light both on Mark and on recent trends in Gospel study. The "method" in our title is somewhat misleading, admittedly. None of us gives you a concise, three-step method to apply to Mark or some other biblical text. Few of the approaches we survey would be comfortable with being handled in quite this fashion. Nonetheless, we hope to stimulate you to bring new questions to the Gospels and to create readings of your own that are richer for having read ours.

FURTHER READING

Adam, A. K. M., ed. *A Handbook of Postmodern Biblical Interpretation*. St. Louis: Chalice, 2000. A mini-encyclopedia of theories (e.g., deconstruction, queer theory), theorists (e.g., Jacques Derrida, Michel Foucault, Julia Kristeva), and topics (e.g., author, culture, historiography, postcolonialism).

————, ed. *Postmodern Interpretations of the Bible: A Reader*. St. Louis: Chalice, 2001. This companion to the *Handbook* consists of exegetical essays that apply a wide range of contemporary methods and theories to biblical texts from both testaments.

Barton, John, ed. *The Cambridge Companion to Biblical Interpretation*. Cambridge: Cambridge University Press, 1998. Part 1 is devoted to introductions to a wide range of methods ("historical-critical approaches," "literary readings of the Bible," "the social world of the Bible," etc.), while part 2 is devoted to surveys of scholarship on biblical books in the modern period.

The Bible and Culture Collective. *The Postmodern Bible*. New Haven, Conn.: Yale University Press, 1995. Essentially an advanced primer on critical method in biblical studies. Contains chapters on reader-response criticism; structuralist and narratological criticism; poststructuralist criticism; rhetorical criticism; psychoanalytic criticism; feminist and womanist criticism; and ideological criticism.

Black, C. Clifton. *Mark: Images of an Apostolic Interpreter*. Columbia: University of South Carolina Press, 1994. Chronicles the changing image of Mark from the second to the twentieth centuries, and from patristic interpretation to modern scholarship. An extremely useful resource.

Bray, Gerald. *Biblical Interpretation: Past and Present*. Downers Grove, Ill.: InterVarsity, 1996. A detailed survey of the history of biblical interpretation from the second century down to the late twentieth century written from an evangelical perspective.

Froelich, Karlfried, ed. and trans. *Biblical Interpretation in the Early Church*. Philadelphia: Fortress Press, 1984. A useful introduction to the history of exegesis in the first four centuries C.E., with translated excerpts from works by Irenaeus, Origen, and other commentators.

Harrington, Daniel J. *What Are They Saying about Mark?* 2d ed. Mahwah, N.J.: Paulist, 2004. A useful overview of recent Markan scholarship.

Hayes, John H., ed. *Dictionary of Biblical Interpretation*. 2 vols. Nashville: Abingdon, 1999. Contains articles on a wide variety of approaches ranging from New Testament redaction criticism to Asian biblical interpretation and womanist biblical interpretation. It also has articles on the interpretation of individual biblical books and interpreters such as Calvin and Dibelius.

Kealy, Seán P., C.S.Sp. *Mark's Gospel: A History of Its Interpretation*. Ramsey, N.J.: Paulist, 1982. An indispensable summary of the history of interpretation of

Mark from the early centuries through 1979. Includes bibliographic references to commentators in each historical period.

McKenzie, Steven L., and Stephen R. Haynes, eds. *To Each Its Own Meaning: An
Introduction to Biblical Criticisms and Their Application.* 2d ed. Louisville:
Westminster John Knox, 1999. Introduces methods old and new. Focuses
on both Hebrew Bible and New Testament. Newer methods featured include
social-scientific criticism; canonical criticism; rhetorical criticism; structural
criticism; narrative criticism; reader-response criticism; poststructuralist
criticism; feminist criticism; and socioeconomic criticism.

Moore, Stephen D. *Literary Criticism and the Gospels: The Theoretical Challenge.*
New Haven: Yale University Press, 1989. Includes chapters on narrative criticism, reader-response criticism, and deconstruction.

Morgan, Robert, with John Barton. *Biblical Interpretation.* Oxford: Oxford University Press, 1988. Includes a survey of the development of historical criticism
during the previous 150 years and of recent developments in the use of social
scientific and literary critical methods for biblical study.

Perrin, Norman. *What Is Redaction Criticism?* Philadelphia: Fortress Press, 1969.
In addition to providing an answer to the title question, this book also does a
good job of describing form criticism and the Markan hypothesis.

Pippin, Tina, Ronald Schleifer, and David Jobling, eds. *The Postmodern Bible
Reader.* Oxford: Blackwell, 2001. A companion to *The Postmodern Bible* (see
above), this is an anthology of twenty previously published essays or book
excerpts, most of them readings of biblical texts by major theorists, critics,
or theologians.

Porter, Stanley E. *Handbook to the Exegesis of the New Testament.* Leiden: Brill,
2002. At 638 pages, a detailed primer on method. Includes chapters on textual criticism; source, form, and redaction criticisms; discourse analysis; rhetorical and narratological criticisms; literary criticism; ideological criticisms,
liberation criticisms, and womanist and feminist criticisms; social-scientific
criticism; and canonical criticism.

Rhoads, David. *Reading Mark, Engaging the Gospel.* Minneapolis: Fortress Press,
2004. Combines narrative criticism and reader-response criticism with
social-scientific criticism.

Schildgen, Brenda Deen. *Power and Prejudice: The Reception of the Gospel of Mark.*
Detroit: Wayne State University Press, 1999. A history of Markan interpretation with a thesis to argue. Schildgen contends that each new phase of Mark's
reception is an indicator of new historical forces at work in the world.

Telford, William R. *The Theology of the Gospel of Mark.* Cambridge: Cambridge University Press, 1999. Essentially an exercise in redaction criticism. In addition
to outlining Mark's theology in detail, however, Telford also systematically
compares it to the theologies of every other major New Testament writer.

Yarchin, William. *History of Biblical Interpretation: A Reader*. Peabody, Mass.: Hendrickson, 2004. Thirty-four chapters introduce the most significant methods of biblical interpretation from 150 B.C.E. to the present and the most prominent scholars who exemplify them. Each chapter also contains a sample text that demonstrates a representative scholar's mode of interpretation.

Yee, Gale A., ed. *Judges and Method: New Approaches in Biblical Studies*. 2d ed. Minneapolis: Fortress Press, 2007. The companion volume to the present one. The original edition contained essays on two methods not covered in *Mark and Method*, namely, structural criticism and ideological criticism. This expanded second edition includes added essays on gender criticism, cultural criticism, and postcolonial criticism.

2

NARRATIVE CRITICISM

How Does the Story Mean?

ELIZABETH STRUTHERS MALBON

THE QUESTIONS WE ASK OF THE TEXTS we read are as important as the answers we are led to. Most readers of the New Testament for almost two thousand years have asked religious questions. What does the text mean? What does it mean to me? To us? To our faith and our lives? The answers have reflected not only the different individual readers but also broader cultural shifts. The time and place of the readers or communities of readers have influenced their answers. What other types of questions have been asked by New Testament readers—especially scholarly readers?

Since the nineteenth century, most New Testament scholars have asked, What *did* the text mean? What did it mean in its original context? For its author? To its first hearers or readers? Chapter 1 discusses three chief ways the question, What *did* the text mean? has been asked: source criticism, form criticism, and redaction criticism. Source, form, and redaction criticism might seem to be asking literary questions. Source criticism was first called literary criticism because it approached Matthew, Mark, and Luke as literary documents. However, source criticism is a search for literary sources and relationships in history. Which Gospel was written first? Which Gospel was the historical source for the others? These questions are primarily histori-cal. Form criticism is concerned with the literary form of the small stories. However, form criticism is a search for the sources behind the sources in history. What do the individual stories tell us about the history of the earli-est churches? What may we attribute to the historical Jesus? Redaction criti-cism certainly has literary aspects. As the study of the theological motivation of the editing of earlier traditions, it is concerned with the Gospels as liter-ary wholes. However, redaction criticism is a search for the theology of the churches of the Gospel writers in history. What *did* the text mean? To ask *what* did the text mean is to seek referential meaning. The text's meaning is found in what it refers to—what it refers to other than and outside itself.

In the past three decades, an increasing number of biblical scholars (especially in the United States) have been asking a different question: *How* does the text mean? This question is literary; it represents a search for inter-nal meaning rather than external (or referential) meaning. How do various literary patterns enable the text to communicate meaning to its hearers and readers? How do the interrelated characters, settings, and actions of the plot contribute to a narrative's meaning for a reader? The move from historical to literary questions represents a paradigm shift in biblical studies. A paradigm gives us our basic way of understanding things. When there is a paradigm shift, we are challenged to think of the old and familiar in a new way. The writer of Mark is no longer a cut-and-paste editor but an author with control over the story he narrates. The Jesus of Mark is no longer a shadowy his-torical personage but a lively character. Galilee and Jerusalem are no longer simply geographical references but settings for dramatic action. The account of Jesus' passion (suffering and death) is no longer the source of theological doctrine but the culmination of a dramatic and engaging plot.

THE NEW CRITICISM AND STRUCTURALISM

The shift to a literary paradigm by some biblical interpreters echoed a similar and earlier shift among interpreters of secular literature. In the 1940s the New Criticism argued that the key to reading a poem, play, novel, or short story is to be found in the work itself. Historical information about the cul-ture and biographical information about the author were pushed aside as external to the work. The New Criticism must be understood as a reaction to previous literary studies that gave such information primary importance. A similar reaction in biblical studies led many to move from redaction criticism to literary criticism. The final lines of a poem by Archibald MacLeish may be understood almost as a slogan for the New Critics: "A poem should not mean/But be."[1] A critic or reader must not be concerned with a poem's refer-ential meaning, that is, its reference to some external world. She or he must attend to its being, its presence, its metaphoric power. The poem's power to speak to us depends neither on the author's intention nor on the reader's knowledge of the author's circumstances. It depends on the poem itself—its words, its rhythms, its images.

The New Criticism made its initial impact in New Testament studies on interpretations of the sayings and parables of Jesus. The "significance of forceful and imaginative language" in the Synoptic sayings of Jesus was explored by Robert Tannehill.[2] Robert Funk considered "language as event and theology" in parable and letter.[3] Dan Via reflected on the "literary and existential dimension" of the parables.[4] The surprising, challenging, world-shattering potential of the parables was the theme of John Dominic Crossan's work.[5] "A poem should not mean/But be"—and a parable should not refer but impel.

Structuralism is another critical approach that has influenced biblical literary criticism. Structuralism was born in linguistics and grew up in anthropology, literature, and other areas. Central to structuralism are three affirmations about language. First, language is communication. Language as communication involves a sender giving a message to a receiver; literature as communication means an author giving a text to a reader. Redaction critics focus on the sender or author, and reader-response critics (see chapter 3 below) focus on the receiver or reader. Structuralist critics in particular, like literary critics in general, focus on the text. By analogy, structuralist critics note that within a narrative text a "sender" gives an "object" to a "receiver." For example, in a traditional fairy tale, the king gives his daughter in marriage to the most worthy suitor. (Much of the tale works out which suitor is most worthy.) In a synoptic parable, a king gives a feast to—surprisingly—the poor and the outcast. This model of language as communication and narrative as language has been worked out by French structuralist A. J. Greimas.[6]

Second, structuralism stresses that language is a system of signs. No sign has meaning on its own. Signs have meaning in relation to other signs. Analogously, no element of a literary work has meaning in isolation. Everything has meaning as part of a system of relationships. A narrative, that is, a literary work that tells a story, must be read in two ways to disclose its system of relations. It must be read diachronically, that is, "through time," from beginning to end. It must also be read (understood) synchronically, that is, as if everything happened at the "same time." For a synchronic reading, logical categories (good versus evil, order versus chaos, etc.) are more important than chronological categories. The interrelation of parts within a whole is the key. This approach has been worked out by French structural anthropologist Claude Lévi-Strauss and applied in detail to the spatial settings of Mark's Gospel.[7]

Third, structuralism focuses on language as a cultural code. This understanding of language builds on the other two. Through careful analysis of the oppositions expressed in a text, the even more basic oppositions implicitly supporting it are revealed. Daniel Patte, the foremost biblical structuralist, has illustrated this and other aspects of structuralism in relation to Paul's letters and Matthew's Gospel. Patte seeks to uncover the "system of convictions" of Paul and of Matthew.[8]

Both the New Criticism and structuralism focus on the text itself—the language of the text and the text as language. Biblical literary criticism has been influenced by both approaches and shares this focus on the text. The first texts examined in detail by New Testament literary critics were the sayings and parables of Jesus. These short and powerful texts are in some ways comparable to the poems that intrigued the New Critics. The Gospels are the texts most explored by current New Testament literary critics. The Gospels are narratives, stories, in many ways not unlike the myths and folktales that structuralists often analyzed. New Testament literary criticism has become largely narrative criticism, a label employed by biblical critics but not by secular critics. To understand narrative criticism, we must consider the essential elements or aspects of narratives.

NARRATIVE ELEMENTS

The distinction between story and discourse that was highlighted by literary critic Seymour Chatman has proved useful to narrative critics. Story is the *what* of a narrative; discourse is the *how*. Story indicates the content of the narrative, including events, characters, and settings, and their interaction as the plot. Discourse indicates the rhetoric of the narrative, how the story is told. The four canonical Gospels, for example, share a similar (although not identical) story of Jesus, but the discourse of each Gospel is distinctive. The story is where the characters interact; the discourse is where the implied author and implied reader interact. Story and discourse are not really separable. What we have, in Chatman's words, is the story-as-discoursed. It is this about which narrative critics ask, How does the text mean?

The following elements or aspects of narrative (story-as-discoursed), although overlapping, are frequently distinguished by narrative critics: implied author and implied reader, characters, settings, plot, rhetoric. We will look at each in turn.

Implied Author and Implied Reader

The communication model of sender-message-receiver gives narrative critics a framework for approaching texts: author-text-reader. This simple model, however, soon proves inadequate for narrative analysis. Recent literary criticism has taught us to conceive of the author and the reader not as isolated entities but as poles of a continuum of communication. A real author writes a text for a real reader. An implied author, a creation of the real author that is implied in his or her text, presents a narrative to an implied reader, a parallel creation of the real author that is embedded in the text, and a narrator tells a story to a narratee. Of course, within a story a character may narrate another story to another character. This expanded model is often diagramed like this:[9]

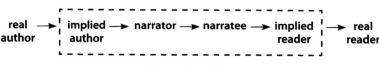

Text or Narrative

Narrative criticism focuses on the narrative, but the implied author and the implied reader are understood as aspects of the narrative in this model. The implied author is a hypothetical construction based on the requirements of knowledge and belief presupposed in the narrative. The same is true of the implied reader. The implied author is the one who would be necessary for this narrative to be told or written. The implied reader is the one who would be necessary for this narrative to be heard or read.

The distinctions between the real and implied author and the real and implied reader are important for narrative critics, who wish to interpret the narrative without reliance on biographical information about the real author and cultural information about the real reader. Of course, basic information about the cultural context is essential to any interpretation. The implied author and implied reader of Mark's Gospel, for example, were literate in *koinē* (common) Greek and knew the Hebrew Bible (later to become the Old Testament for Christians) in the form of its Greek translation in the Septuagint. Narrative critics are eager to know as much as possible about the cultural contexts—especially of ancient works—in order to understand more completely the implied author and the implied reader of the narrative. However, narrative critics are wary of interpretations based on elements external to the narrative—including the intentions (known or supposed) of the real author.

The distinctions between the implied author and the narrator and between the narratee and the implied reader were developed in secular literary criticism for the close analysis of nineteenth- and twentieth-century novels. Ishmael is the narrator of *Moby Dick*, but he is the creation of the implied author. Initially, many narrative critics of the first-century Gospels did not find these distinctions as useful. Many narrative critics observed little or no difference between the implied author and narrator or between the narratee and implied reader of Matthew, Mark, Luke, and John.[10] Thus some narrative critics used the terms *narrator* and *narratee*, while others employed *implied author* and *implied reader*. However, it is important to note, with Mark Allan Powell, that "the narrator and the narratee are not identical with the implied author and the implied reader. They are rhetorical devices, created by the implied author. They are part of the narrative itself, part of the discourse through which the story is told."[11]

The narrator may be characterized in various ways, according to the particular nature of the narrative. The narrators of the Gospels are generally described as omniscient (all-knowing), or omnipresent (present everywhere), or unlimited. The narrator of Mark, for example, is able to narrate events involving any character or group of characters, including Jesus when alone. This narrator knows past, present, and future, as well as the inner thoughts and feelings of the characters. The Markan narrator is also reliable. The narratee may trust him (probably him) as a nondeceptive guide to the action and safely believe that what he foreshadows will be fulfilled. (Even a reliable narrator may be ironic, however.) Some Markan scholars have considered the point of view of the implied narrator of Mark as aligned not only with the points of view of the implied author and the main character, Jesus, but also with the point of view of God.[12] From the point of view of the implied reader or narratee, you can't get any more reliable than that! The narrator begins: "The beginning of the good news of Jesus Christ (Messiah), the Son of God" (1:1). Ten verses later, God concurs, saying to Jesus, "You are my Son" (1:11).

However, the points of view of the Markan Jesus and the Markan narrator are clearly distinguishable. It is the Markan narrator who boldly asserts that Jesus is the Christ, the Son of God (1:1). The Markan Jesus is reticent. Yet the Markan Jesus makes assertions about the Son of Man, about which the narrator is silent, and boldly proclaims the kingdom of God, about which the narrator speaks directly just once, and that after Jesus' death (15:43). There is thus a tension between the Markan narrator who wants to talk about Jesus and the Markan Jesus who wants to talk about God.[13] The implied author, in control of both the Markan Jesus and the narrator, sets up this tension to draw in the implied reader (or audience)—not to resolve the tension but to enable hearing of the story of Jesus in its full complexity and mystery.[14] The interaction of the implied author and the implied reader is part of the discourse. The interaction of the characters is part of the story.

Characters

Characters are an obvious narrative element. A story is about someone—the characters. The actions are carried out by someone—the characters. Narrative analysis of characters is intertwined with narrative analysis of plot. The implied reader of the story-as-discoursed is frequently invited to admire, judge, or identify with the characters. Characters are brought to life for the implied reader by the implied author through narrating words and actions. These words and actions may be those of the character himself or herself, or those of another character, or those of the narrator. A character can be known by what she says and does; a character can be known by what other characters say to or about her and by what they do in relation to or because of her. A character can be known by what the narrator says about him—

including names, epithets, and descriptions—or by what the narrator does in relation to him—including comparative or contrasting juxtapositions with other characters and the unfolding of the plot.

For example, the first mention of Judas Iscariot in Mark, at Jesus' appointing of the twelve, is followed immediately by the narrator's comment, "who betrayed him" (3:19). At the point when Judas's betrayal is being narrated, however, the narrator calls him "Judas Iscariot, who was one of the twelve" (14:10). This is characterization by the narrator's words and *actions*, that is, the ironic placement of these descriptions at moments of greatest contrast. The ironic contrast is extended by the immediate juxtaposition of the story of the unnamed woman who gives up money for Jesus (the anointing woman, 14:3-9) and the story of one of the twelve specially named men who gives up Jesus for money (Judas' betrayal, 14:10-11).

Some narrative critics distinguish characterization by "telling" and characterization by "showing." "Telling" involves the explicit words of a reliable narrator about a character. Anything else is "showing." "Showing" requires more from the narratee and implied reader and is thus more engaging. Most of the characterization in the Gospels is by "showing."

Some narrative critics find it helpful to identify the dominant traits of characters. A trait is a personal quality that persists over time. Sometimes such traits are explicitly named in a narrative. Frequently they are inferred from words and actions, as suggested previously. Some characters are portrayed with only one trait. Others are given a number of traits, or developing traits, or even conflicting traits.

E. M. Forster, novelist and literary critic, called these two types of characters "flat" and "round."[15] The distinction, which is sometimes elaborated, has proved to be extremely helpful for narrative critics. Flat characters are simple and consistent. Some flat characters appear but once, others again and again, but their actions and words are predictable. Round characters are complex or dynamic. They may reveal new aspects of themselves or even change. The distinction between flat and round characters is not the same as the distinction between "minor" and "major" characters. The Jewish leaders are hardly minor characters in Mark, but they are flat. Nor is the flat/round distinction equivalent to negative versus positive. The Jewish leaders in Mark are flat and negative; the anointing woman is flat and positive. The disciples are round and both positive and negative; the Markan Jesus alone is a round, positive character. The flatness or roundness of characters, however, does affect the implied reader's response in praise, judgment, or identification. Round characters elicit identification in a way that flat characters do not.

Just as the points of view of the implied author and the narrator are aligned and take on a positive or negative value, so the point of view of each character or group of characters is given an evaluative point of view by the implied author. Norman Petersen has argued that the two evaluative points of view among Markan characters are "thinking the things of God" and "thinking the things of men."[16] According to Petersen, the implied author, narrator, Jesus, and several minor exemplary characters represent the first (positive) point of view. The Jewish leaders and sometimes the disciples represent the second (negative) one.

New Testament narrative critics are generally aware of the differences in characterization between nineteenth- and twentieth-century psychological novels, for example, and the Gospels. The secular literary theory on which biblical narrative critics so often lean is not particularly supportive at this point. Ways of analyzing characterization in the Gospels are still being developed. Perhaps the current debate about the portrayal of the disciples of Jesus in Mark (Are they "fallible followers" or final failures?) [17] will settle down somewhat as interpreters explore more thoroughly techniques of characterization in use in the ancient world. Vernon Robbins has instructively compared the portrayal of the Markan disciples of Jesus with the portrayal of the disciples of Apollonius of Tyana by Philostratus.[18] I have pointed out that characterization by "types" was conventional in ancient literature, including history writing as well as epic, drama, and other forms. Mark seems to continue this convention by presenting contrasting groups— exemplars to emulate and enemies to eschew. But perhaps Mark challenges this convention as well by presenting fallible followers with whom to identify.[19] More research remains to be done in this area. It may even be that what narrative critics learn about characters internal to the text will have implications for historical critics for whom the Gospels still serve as primary (although layered) sources for the external reconstruction of the historical Jesus. It may be that historical critics assume too much in interpreting literary distinctions or strands in a narrative (e.g., what the character Jesus says about himself versus what other characters and the narrator say about him) as historical layers.[20]

Settings

Characters are the "who" of the narrative; settings are the "where" and "when." The shift from historical questions to literary questions has made a significant impact on the way interpreters think about the spatial and temporal settings of the Gospels.[21] The original questers for the historical Jesus combed the Gospels for information about the geography and chronology of Jesus' ministry. Early redaction critics of Mark argued that its confused geographical references indicate an author writing outside Galilee and Israel, probably in Rome. Later redaction critics speculated that the positive connotations of Galilee in Mark indicate Galilee as the locale of the community for which the Gospel was written.[22] The prediction of the destruction of the Jewish Temple in Mark 13—especially with its cryptic parenthetical phrase, "(let the reader understand)," 13:14—has been cited as evidence that Mark was written prior to 70 C.E. (the date of the Temple's actual destruction by the Romans) *and* as evidence that it was written after 70 C.E.! The spatial and temporal settings of Mark give a clear picture of neither Jesus' time and place in history nor Mark's.

Literary critics, especially narrative critics, interpret these spatial and temporal references internally rather than externally. Together they form the background for the dramatic action of Mark's Gospel. And, in fact, settings often participate in the drama of the narrative. Places and times are rich in connotational, or associative, values, and these values contribute to the meaning of the narrative for the implied reader. For example, the Markan narrator says that Jesus "went up the mountain" (3:13) to appoint the Twelve. Historical critics have searched in vain for a mountain in Galilee. But for the implied author and implied reader, who know their Bible, "the mountain" is where God comes to meet leaders of the people of God. Similarly, "the sea" is where God manifests divine power, and "the wilderness" is where God manifests divine care in miraculously feeding the people of God. Thus the implied reader is shown (not told) that Jesus' power over the sea (4:35-41; 6:45-52) and miraculous feedings in the wilderness (6:31-44; 8:1-10) are divine manifestations.

Markan temporal settings also contribute significantly to the implied reader's appreciation of the narrative. Some temporal references are clearly allusive or symbolic. Jesus' testing in the wilderness for forty days (1:13) is an allusion to Israel's forty years of testing in the wilderness during the Exodus. The twelve years of age of Jairus's daughter and the twelve years of suffering of the hemorrhaging woman intensify the Jewish flavor of the interwoven stories (5:21-43). Twelve is a number symbolic of Israel, with its twelve tribes.

In other cases the implied author uses temporal markers to pace the unfolding of the story. The first several chapters of Mark are peppered with the Greek adverb *euthys*, "immediately" (in English translation this is clearer in the RSV than in the NRSV). The Markan Jesus rushes around—from baptism in the Jordan, to testing in the wilderness, to preaching and exorcising a demon in the Capernaum synagogue, to healing in Simon's house, to healing throughout Galilee. The Markan Jesus' first words tell of the urgency of the present time: "The time is fulfilled, and the kingdom of God has come near; repent, and believe in the good news" (1:15). The Markan narrator's first series of scenes *shows* this urgency. Immediately Jesus acts; immediately the implied reader is to respond.[23]

The pace of the Markan story-as-discoursed is dramatically different in the passion narrative, the story of Jesus' suffering and death. Everything slows down. Story time for the first ten chapters is months and months, perhaps a year. Story time for the last six chapters is about a week. Moreover, everything becomes more specific. Instead of the "in those days" or "in the morning" of the first ten chapters, we now read "two days before the Passover and the festival of Unleavened Bread" (14:1) or "nine o'clock in the morning" (15:25, "the third hour [or watch]," RSV). The same specificity occurs spatially. Instead of "in the house," we find "at Bethany in the house of Simon the leper . . . at the table" (14:3). A modern-day analogy would be a filmmaker's skillful use of slow-motion photography to suggest the profound significance of a climaxing series of scenes. The more detailed setting of scenes in time and space of the Markan passion narrative is the implied author's plea to the implied reader: slow down; take this in; to understand anything of the story, you must understand this. It is another form of urgency.

Spatial and temporal settings need to be mapped out in correlation with the plot of the narrative, just as characters need to be interpreted in terms of their roles in the plot. For the implied author and the implied reader, the elements of narrative—characters, settings, plot, rhetoric—are essentially integrated.

Plot

The plot is the "what" and the "why" of the narrative. What happens? Why? Then what happens? Why? These are questions of the plot. Biblical critic Norman Petersen presents a fruitful distinction between Mark's "narrative world" and Mark's "plotted time." The "narrative world is comprised of all events described or referred to in the narrative, but in their causal and logical sequence." The "plotting of this world is to be seen in the ways its components have been selected and arranged in a sequence of narrated incidents."[24] Events are not always plotted in the narrative in the order in which they would occur in the narrative world. The changes from narrative world to the plotted time of the narrative are part of the implied author's discourse with the implied reader.

Gérard Genette, a literary theorist, has worked out an intricate system for discussing the order, duration, and frequency of events in the plotted narrative.[25] An event may be narrated *after* its logical order in the narrative world (*analepsis*). An event may be narrated *before* its logical order in the narrative world (*prolepsis*). And, of course, events may occur in the same order in both. An event may be narrated with a longer, shorter, or equal duration in comparison with its duration in the narrative world. An event that occurs once in the narrative world may be narrated once or more than once. Changes in order, duration, and frequency are ways the implied author has of leading the implied reader through the story-as-discoursed to an interpretation.

Markan examples will clarify these distinctions. The three passion predictions that the Markan Jesus makes to his disciples (8:31; 9:31; 10:33) point proleptically to what will occur later—but still within the narrative. The Markan Jesus' prediction, echoed by the young man at the empty tomb (14:28; 16:7), that he will go before his disciples to Galilee, points proleptically to an event that is not narrated within the story-as-discoursed. The implied reader, however, has been cued to presume its occurrence in the narrative world (see, e.g., 13:9-13). This narrative technique contributes to the often-noted open ending of Mark's Gospel. A short but surprising and significant analepsis is narrated at 15:40-41. The Markan Jesus' twelve disciples have fled; he is crucified, bereft of their presence. But at the cross "there were also women looking on from a distance." Three are named, but "many other women" are mentioned. At this crucial point the narrator tells the narratee that these women used to follow Jesus and minister to him in Galilee. *Follow* and *minister to* are discipleship words in Mark. So the implied reader learns at the last hour that Jesus had other followers, women followers, from the first. Moreover, these surprising followers stay to the last—although at a distance. Three of them are there at the empty tomb as well.

Conflict is the key to the Markan plot. As Markan characterization does not depend on psychological development within the characters, so the plot does not turn on high suspense and complicated intrigue among the characters. The plot moves by conflicts between groups of characters, or, rather, between God or Jesus and groups of characters. There are multiple conflicts, along several dimensions. The kingdom of God is in conflict with all other claims to power and authority. Jesus is in conflict with demons and unclean spirits. Jesus and the Jewish authorities are in continuing conflict over issues of authority and interpretation of the Law (Torah). Jesus and the disciples are in conflict over what it means to be the Messiah and thus what it means to follow him. All the conflicts have to do with power and authority. Where do ultimate power and authority lie? How should human power and authority be exercised? But all the conflicts are not the same. The disciples, for example, are not portrayed and evaluated by the implied author in the same way as the Jewish leaders are. And, of course, the Markan Jesus responds to the disciples quite differently from how he reacts to the other groups with whom he comes into conflict.

Thus, the elements of narrative include the five Ws one might expect in the first paragraph of a news story: who (characters), where and when (settings), what and why (plot). To the extent that story and discourse can be separated analytically, these three are elements of story. A final narrative element is rhetoric, the how of the story-as-discoursed. Rhetoric refers to how the implied author persuades the implied reader to follow the story. Because narrative criticism (like literary criticism in general) asks *"How* does the text mean?" narrative criticism takes a keen interest in rhetoric.

Rhetoric

Rhetoric is the art of persuasion. Persuasion, of course, works differently in varying contexts. Markan rhetoric is narrative rhetoric. By the way the story is told, the implied author persuades the implied reader first to understand and then to share and extend the story's levels of meaning. Mark's rhetoric is one of juxtaposition—placing scene over against scene in order to elicit comparison, contrast, and insight. This juxtaposition includes repetition, not only of scenes but also of words and phrases; duality (e.g., two similar phrases in immediate succession, or two similar scenes) is widespread. Juxtaposition includes intercalation—splicing one story into another—and framing—placing similar stories as beginning and end of a series. In addition, juxtaposition includes foreshadowing and echoing of words, phrases, and whole events. Echoing and foreshadowing may be intratextual (within the text) or intertextual (between texts). The intertextual echoes heard in Mark's Gospel reverberate with the Septuagint. Symbolism involves the juxtaposition of a literal meaning and a metaphorical one. Irony involves the juxtaposition of an apparent or expected meaning and a deeper or surprising one. Repetition, intercalation, framing, foreshadowing and echoing, symbolism, and irony are favorite Markan rhetorical devices. They are part of the discourse of the narrative. Without the implied author's discourse, the implied reader could not receive the story. The story is never received directly but only as discoursed, only rhetorically.

The interwoven scenes of Jesus' trial before the high priest and Peter's denial (14:53-72) illustrate a number of these rhetorical techniques. The two stories are intercalated. The narrator first tells that Jesus was taken to the high priest (v. 53) and then that Peter followed "at a distance" into the courtyard of the high priest (v. 54). The scene between Jesus and the high priest and other chief priests is played out (vv. 55-65), and then the scene between Peter and the high priest's servant girl and other bystanders is played out (vv. 66-72). The implied reader cannot forget the presence of Peter "warming himself at the fire" (v. 54) all the while Jesus endures the fiery rage of the high priest. Jesus' scene concludes with the guards taunting him to "Prophesy!" (v. 65). Peter's scene concludes with his remembrance of Jesus' prophecy of his denial (v. 72), an ominous echo of the earlier foreshadowing. It is sadly ironic that Peter's noisy denial of his discipleship in order to save his life is narrated almost simultaneously with Jesus' quiet affirmation of his messiahship, although it will lead to his death. The rhetorical juxtaposition of these scenes—characters, words, actions, settings—in the unfolding plot pushes the implied reader not only to judge the two contrasting characters but also to judge himself or herself.

The order of stories or scenes in Mark 8:22—10:52 illustrates the rhetorical devices of repetition, framing, and symbolism. In this section of the narrative, the Markan Jesus three times predicts his passion and resurrection (8:31; 9:31; 10:33). After each prediction, the disciples manifest their limited understanding of serving and suffering as aspects of messiahship and discipleship (8:32-33; 9:32-34, 38; 10:35-41). After each misunderstanding, Jesus renews his teaching on this topic (8:34-38; 9:35-37, 39-50; 10:42-45). Of course, each time Jesus teaches the disciples, the implied author teaches the implied reader. Repetition adds clarity and force.

Around these three three-part scenes (passion prediction units), other scenes (of teaching and healing) are set. Then all these scenes are framed by the only two Markan stories of the healing of blindness. At the beginning of the series, the two-stage healing of blindness at Bethsaida is narrated (8:22-26). At the close, the healing of blind Bartimaeus, who follows Jesus "on the way," is recounted (10:46-52). Blindness and sight are symbolic of misunderstanding and insight. As Jesus healed the blind man of Bethsaida in two stages, so he must teach the disciples in two stages about his messiahship. At Caesarea Philippi, Peter tells that he "sees" Jesus' power and shows that he is "blind" to Jesus' suffering service (8:27-33). As the mighty deeds of chapters 1-8 were the first stage of Jesus' teaching, so the passion prediction units of chapters 8-10 are the second stage. The goal of the journey is for all—disciples and implied readers—to "see" as Bartimaeus does and to follow "on the way."

Understanding the narrative rhetoric is central to the work of the narrative critic because rhetoric is the how of the story's telling and *"How* does the text mean?" is the literary question. Earlier source, form, and redaction critics found Mark's rhetorical style rough and primitive. This judgment may be true at the level of the sentence. (English translations always smooth out Mark's Greek a bit.) But Mark's narrative rhetoric must be appreciated at the level of the scene. In the intriguing juxtaposition of scenes—with their characters, settings, and plot developments—the rhetoric of the Markan Gospel works it persuasive ways with the implied reader.

Narrative criticism compensates for the fragmentation of the text into smaller and smaller units by form and redaction criticism. Even redaction criticism, with its potential to be concerned for the Gospel as a whole, frequently bogs down in ever more meticulous divisions between "tradition" and "redaction"—what Mark received and what he added. Nevertheless, perhaps narrative criticism, in its holistic passion, overcompensates. Deconstructive criticism (see chapter 4 below) compensates for the totalizing effect of narrative criticism—creating a self-consistent unity of the text. Deconstructive criticism may overcompensate as well. But it is good for narrative criticism to be reminded of what it also knows—and often proclaims—of the tensions, gaps, and mysteries of the text itself—and even the text against itself.

Narrative criticism seeks to avoid the "intentional fallacy"[26] of redaction criticism. The narrative critic does not pursue the quest for the real author's intention. Instead, the narrative critic seeks to analyze and appreciate the implied author's effect—that is, the text itself. But what is "the text itself"? Narrative critics affirm that it is the center of a communication process involving author, text, and reader. They (we) focus on the text, partly in reaction to redaction critics' focus on the author, but mostly because we find the text so intriguing.

Reader-response criticism (see chapter 3 below) seeks to avoid the objectivism of narrative criticism—viewing the text as an autonomous object. Reader-response criticism may overcompensate as well. Perhaps narrative criticism's appreciation for the role of the implied reader guards it from the extreme of objectivism. No doubt biblical criticism would benefit greatly from an approach that could—if not simultaneously at least sequentially—keep in view all parts of the communication process: author, text, and reader. Then, "*What did* the text mean?" and "*How does* the text mean?" might contribute more fairly and more fully to the older and enduring question, "What does the text mean—to me—to us?"

NARRATIVE EXAMPLES

I turn now to an extended example of narrative criticism at work in chapters 4–8 of the Gospel of Mark.[27] Such an example should help clarify and integrate the narrative elements. Chapters 4–8 have been chosen because of their rhetorical richness, because they hold together as a subunit within the entire Gospel, and because what Mark does here with these smaller stories is quite distinctive from what Matthew and Luke do with many of the same stories in their Gospels. I could study each narrative element in turn—first characters, then settings, and so on. This type of analysis is often done by narrative critics. But here I look at the interrelated narrative elements as the story unfolds from 4:1 through 8:26, a pattern increasingly frequent within narrative criticism. (Let the reader understand: my implied reader is reading Mark 4–8 along with this chapter.)

Parables on the Sea (4:1-34)

At the beginning of chapter 4, the Markan narrator takes considerable trouble to make sure the narratee locates Jesus at the sea. Within one verse the word *sea* occurs three times and the word *boat* once. The narratee knows from 1:16 that the Sea of Galilee is intended. The setting places Jesus opposite the crowd. Jesus is in the boat on the sea. (The Greek is even more dramatic: "He got into a boat and sat on the sea.") The crowd is beside the sea on the land. Spatial location underlines the differences between characters.

This setting represents a change from the previous scene. The action also changes. Jesus had been healing and exorcising demons; now he is teaching. The Markan Jesus is often said to be teaching or preaching, but few examples are given. Chapter 4, the parable chapter, is an important exception. The narrator's introductory comment, "He began to teach them many things in parables," is followed by Jesus' telling of one parable, that of the sower.

Verse 10 presents a change of characters and thus a new scene. It has proved difficult for real readers to agree on which characters are now assumed by the narrator to be present. It becomes immediately clear that when Jesus was "alone" means when the large crowd had left, not when he was solitary. What does not become immediately clear is who are "those who were around him along with the twelve." If there are two groups (the twelve, the others), they speak as one and Jesus so responds. It seems likely (although this observation is clear only from further analysis throughout the Gospel) that the implied author creates ambiguity about who is hearing Jesus in order to encourage the implied reader to read himself or herself into the story. The implied author, the narrator, and the Markan Jesus have a shared point of view on parabolic teaching, and they simultaneously address the characters, the narratee, and the implied reader. The would-be two groups who are really one (the twelve plus the others) are one over against "those outside."

To those inside has been given (the passive voice suggests "given by God") "the secret [or, better, 'mystery'] of the kingdom of God." For those outside everything "comes in parables." Parables are comparisons or riddles. In understanding parables, those outside are no better off than those to whom the prophet Isaiah spoke: they may hear, but they do not understand. This ironic allusion to Isaiah 6:9-10, which is itself ironic, is an intertextual echo of the Septuagint.

This mysterious little scene about the mystery of the kingdom is followed by the Markan Jesus' allegorical explanation of the parable of the sower. Each element of the parable is taken to represent some element in the larger story of the growth of "the word." "The word" (*logos*) is an early Christian synonym for the gospel, the good news, the message by and about Jesus as the Christ. According to this explanation, the parable of the sower is about improper and proper ways of hearing the word. In its Markan narrative context (parable/insiders and outsiders/explanation), the story of the sower is symbolic of hearing parables as outsiders and as insiders. Insiders receive not only "the mystery" but also an additional explanation.

This twofold pattern, parable plus explanation, seems to be repeated. Verse 21 is a little parable about a lamp; verse 22 is a brief explanation. Verse 24 is a little parable about a measure; verse 25 is a brief explanation. Verse 23, right in the middle, is the echoing refrain: "Let anyone with ears to hear listen!" (cf. 4:9). Next the narrator presents Jesus presenting two slightly longer parables, both about seeds. Neither one is followed by an explanation, but verses 33-34 restate this pattern. To "them" (the outsiders) Jesus spoke the word in parables, "as they were able to hear it." To "his disciples" (and other insiders?) he explained everything privately. As other features in the Markan narrative make even more clear, who is inside and who is outside is not a matter of social status or role but of response to Jesus. "Let anyone with ears to hear listen!"

The final two seed parables offer explicit comparisons to "the kingdom of God." The kingdom of God comes *from God*, not from human effort. It comes in God's time and thus, from a human point of view, it always comes as a surprise. All three seed parables suggest that the best predictor of the kingdom's fulfillment is not its beginning but God's power. But all of these implications are rhetorically shown, not told. Like the characters within the story, the implied readers of the narrative must have ears to hear and eyes to see. One becomes an insider by perceiving and understanding. The Markan Jesus and the Markan implied author recognize all such insight as a mysterious gift.

Mighty Deeds on and by the Sea (4:35—5:43)

The sea continues to be the dominant setting for Markan narrative events from 4:1 through 8:21. When the dominant setting switches to "the way" at 8:27, the plot also takes a turn. Narrative elements frequently echo each other in Mark's narrative. At 4:35 the narrator reports a dramatic event that occurs on the sea. Jesus is already in the boat; the disciples join him, as well as other people in other boats. A windstorm comes up, threatening to fill the boat with water from the waves. Yet Jesus is asleep in the stern. The desperate disciples wake him, saying, "Teacher, do you not care that we are perishing?" Apparently they assume Jesus *could* do something to help—if he just *would*. He does. He "rebukes" the wind, as he had earlier rebuked unclean spirits; and he tells the sea to become still. It does. Jesus also questions the disciples: "Why are you afraid? Have you still no faith?" The disciples—not too surprisingly, "filled with great awe"—question themselves: "Who then is this, that even the wind and the sea obey him?"

The sea scene ends there. No character answers this question. It is forwarded to the implied reader, who shares with the implied author knowledge of the Hebrew Bible in the form of the Septuagint. Psalm 107:23-32 is especially relevant.

> Some went down to the sea in ships,
>   doing business on the mighty waters;
> they saw the deeds of the LORD,
>   his wondrous works in the deep.
> For he commanded and raised the stormy wind,
>   which lifted up the waves of the sea.
> . . . .
> Then they cried to the LORD in their trouble,
>   and he brought them out from their distress;
> he made the storm be still,
>   and the waves of the sea were hushed.
>   Psalm 107:23-25, 28-29

Who then is this, that even the wind and the sea obey him? The Lord God. The Lord Jesus Christ. The power of Jesus the Christ is the power of God. All these affirmations are shown, not told. The fact that the disciples do not explicitly answer their own rhetorical question has more to do with the discourse than with the story. The implied author has the disciples leave the question open for the implied reader. The implied author seems to know that a conclusion the implied reader must work to arrive at will be held more strongly. The narrative rhetoric is persuasive.

Despite the storm, Jesus and the disciples arrive on "the other side of the sea" at "the country of the Gerasenes." Historical interpreters, perhaps beginning with Matthew, who substitutes the name Gadarenes (Matt 8:28), have had difficulty locating such a place. But from a narrative critical point of view, the country of the Gerasenes is Gentile territory opposite Jewish Galilee. If the implied reader does not know that narrative fact from the name, he or she will surely know it from the great herd of swine found there. Since Jewish law classifies the pig as an unclean animal, one unfit for humans or God, primarily Jewish areas do not support large herds of swine. The casting out of a legion of demons from the Gerasene man, who had lived as a wild man among the tombs, is the Markan Jesus' first healing of a Gentile. When the exorcised demons enter the swine, as they had requested, and the swine rush to their deaths in the sea, the Gentile region seems to be purged of evil and made ready for Jesus' preaching of the good news. (There is likely also an anti-colonial jab at the legion of pig-eating Roman soldiers in the area.) Jesus tells the healed Gerasene to go home and tell how much "the Lord" has done for him. Instead, the man goes throughout the "ten (Greek) cities" of the region, the Decapolis, proclaiming "how much Jesus had done for him." Who then is the Lord? The scene ends with all marveling.

The sea, however, still orients the scenes and the movements of the plot. At 5:21 the narrator tells that Jesus crossed "again in the boat to the other side," where a great crowd gathered about him "by the sea." For any implied reader who might be confused about which side of the sea is now "the other side," the implied author again gives a second indication: Jairus, one of the rulers of the synagogue, appears. No synagogues are needed where herds of swine are kept. Back in Jewish Galilee, Jesus heals his own people again. Two healing stories are intercalated: the raising of Jairus's daughter and the healing of the hemorrhaging woman. A third indication of the Jewishness of the setting is the repeated number twelve: a twelve-year flow of blood, a twelve-year old girl. As was mentioned above, twelve is symbolic of the twelve tribes and thus of Israel.

The intercalation is done very naturally. At times it has even been taken literally and historically rather than narratively and rhetorically. Because the woman interrupted Jesus on his way to Jairus's house, Jairus's daughter died. Here intercalation, the inserting of one story into another, is an integral part of the plot. But Markan intercalation is always for interpretive purposes. The framing story is to be interpreted in light of the inside story, and vice versa. Both suppliants have extreme needs. Jairus's daughter is "at the point of death," and then dead; the woman has spent everything she had on medical treatment, only to grow worse. In addition, both suppliants have extreme faith. The woman believes that Jesus' power is so great that merely touching the hem of his garment can heal her; Jairus, with Jesus' encouragement, believes that even if his daughter is dead Jesus' power can enable her to live again. Both the twelve-year-old daughter and the twelve-year suffering woman are reintegrated into life and health, family and society. Whether because of her debilitating illness itself, and her consequent inability to bear children, or, as some interpreters would argue, because her continual hemorrhaging made her ritually "unclean," the woman may have been as isolated socially as Jairus's daughter was separated physically by death. The child becomes again a daughter to her father, and the woman is recognized again as a "daughter" (5:34) of Israel.

At the close of the raising of Jairus's daughter, and thus of the two intercalated healing stories, the narrator adds—not too surprisingly—"at this they were overcome with amazement." But the next addition is surprising: "[And] he strictly ordered them that no one should know this. . . ." Impossible! The commotion, weeping, and wailing mentioned in verse 38 were, in effect, the first phase of the girl's funeral. It would be more than a little difficult not to say something to the mourners. As is frequently the case, what cannot be taken literally can be meaningful at another level. Redaction critics labeled Jesus' command to secrecy here and elsewhere "the messianic secret" and interpreted it in terms of Mark's editing of tradition to meet the needs of his community. Narrative critics see it as a plot device that calls attention to the complexity of the image of messiahship in the Markan Gospel. If Jairus told all that he knew about Jesus, he would tell *only* that Jesus was powerful beyond imagining. For the implied author of Mark that statement would be a half truth; the other half, developed in the other half of Mark's Gospel and equally beyond imagining, is that Jesus is committed to using that power only for service, even in the face of suffering and death. At 5:43 the implied reader knows more than Jairus knows, but not yet the whole truth. Jesus' charge to keep quiet his powerful deed is another way for the implied author to raise the question of his identity. If Lord, if Messiah, what kind of Lord? what kind of Messiah?

Preaching/Rejection/Death (6:1-30)

The event that follows the raising of Jairus's daughter in the plotted narrative suggests another reason for the Markan Jesus' hesitancy in making his mighty deeds known: even a half-truth about his power can be misunderstood. Jesus is rejected in the synagogue in his hometown. His teaching results not only in the astonishment of the people, as it had done earlier, but also in their anger and offense at him. Who does he think he is, anyway? He's just Mary's son (probably a slur, since a male child was normally identified as his father's son). His brothers and sisters are not anything special. Jesus says, "A prophet is not without honor, except in his own country [hometown], and among his own kin, and in his own house" (6:4, RSV). The implied reader says, "Jesus is a prophet."

The Markan Jesus' response to this rejection is threefold: (1) to heal whomever he can, limited, it would seem, by the people's unbelief; (2) to move on to other villages and teach; (3) and to send out the Twelve on a mission of their own. Jesus commissions the twelve, two by two, to go out to preach and exorcise unclean spirits, just as he had been doing. He charges them not to rely on their own provisions ("no bread, no bag, no money") but on the hospitality of others. He warns them that they will be rejected, just as he has been. They go and carry out their double mission of preaching and healing.

While the Twelve are gone, as it were, the narrator tells another story, one about John the Baptizer. This is an intercalation, and it is arranged for interpretive purposes, not just for the convenience of the plot. The link is King Herod's learning about how Jesus' name had become known. What does Herod think about this famous Jesus? Others may think he is Elijah or a prophet, but Herod, apparently feeling the pangs of guilt, thinks Jesus is John the Baptizer raised to life again. For Herod, Jesus raises again the trauma of John's beheading.

In 1:14, passing reference is made by the narrator to the "handing over" (Greek, *paradidonai*) of John the Baptizer: "Now after John was arrested, Jesus came to Galilee, proclaiming the good news of God. . . ." John preached and was rejected. Jesus is preaching. Nothing more is said about John's arrest until 6:14-29, at which point Jesus has been rejected and the Twelve are preaching. John's imprisonment and beheading at the command of Herod is told in a lively and detailed narrative flashback or analepsis. As this story within a story closes with John's death, Jesus' disciples return from a successful preaching tour. (They are sent out as "the twelve" [6:7], but they return as "the apostles" [6:30]. *Apostles* means the "ones sent out.") The Markan narrative rhetoric discloses a parallelism between the preaching, being rejected and "handed over," and death of John, Jesus, and the disciples. At chapter 6 John is dead, Jesus is rejected, and the disciples are preaching. What will happen to Jesus next? What will happen to the disciples?

Mighty Deeds by and on the Sea (6:31-56)

Jesus is concerned for his "apostles"; he takes them away from the crowd by boat to a wilderness place. But Jesus' attempt to find the leisure to eat with his disciples leads, ironically, to the work of teaching and feeding the crowd. Jesus teaches the great multitude that awaits him in the hoped-for deserted place because "they were like sheep without a shepherd." This echo of a common image of aimlessness from the Hebrew Bible (e.g., Num 27:17; 1 Kgs 22:17; Ezek 34:5) alerts the implied reader to the Jewishness of the setting.

The story of the multiplication of the loaves and the fishes and the feeding of the five thousand is filled with dialogue between Jesus and the disciples. "Send the crowd away to get food." "No, you feed them." "How can we feed them?" "Start with what you've got." The miraculous meal in the wilderness echoes God's provision of manna in the wilderness, but it also foreshadows for the implied reader the eucharistic meal. The four verbs "took," "blessed," "broke," and "gave" (6:41) are repeated in the narration of the Last Supper (14:22), which models (actually is modeled after) the Eucharist. As is appropriate for meals that God hosts, everyone eats and is satisfied, *and* twelve baskets full of leftovers are collected. The number twelve reminds the implied reader (symbolically) that the recipients are Jews. The surplus of bread outshines the miracle of the manna, in which nothing extra could remain, except for use on the Sabbath (Exod 16:13-30).

"Immediately" Jesus sends the disciples off by boat again, not to some nearby deserted place this time, but to Bethsaida, a city on the other (Gentile) side of the sea. Jesus dismisses the crowd and goes "up on the mountain" to pray. Which mountain? A mountain by the lakeshore in Galilee? No, the mountain where all of God's prophets communicate with God. The narrator's use of the contrast between land and sea to contrast characters at 6:47 is reminiscent of 4:1. "[And] when evening came, the boat was out on the sea, and he was alone on the land." The disciples are unable to complete their mission to "go on ahead" of Jesus to Gentile Bethsaida. The wind is against them. Then they think they see a ghost passing by them, walking on the water. The implied reader knows it is Jesus yet is able to understand their terror. Jesus' words are another intertextual echo from Exodus: "I am" (usually translated "It is I"). God said "I am" to Moses from the burning bush (Exod 3:14). Who then is this? It does not surprise the implied reader that the wind ceases.

The narrator's next comment, the conclusion to this scene, does surprise. "And they [the disciples] were utterly astounded, for they did not understand about the loaves, but their hearts were hardened" (6:51b-52). Why doesn't the narrator say, "They did not understand about the wind or the walking on water"? What do the loaves have to do with the sea? And why are so many images from Exodus being stacked up here? Bread in the wilderness, walking on (through) the sea, "I am"—and now hardened hearts. The passive voice ("their hearts were hardened") suggests that the disciples' hearts, like Pharaoh's, were hardened by God so that God's overall purpose for the people of God could be worked out. The implied reader must keep reading!

Surprising closings and openings of scenes are becoming the norm. From the cryptic reference to hardened hearts, the implied reader moves not to an anticipated arrival at Bethsaida on the east but to a surprising landing at Gennesaret, still on the west. In the midst of so many other amazing narrative events, one would not have been shocked to read of a successful, even miraculous, crossing to Bethsaida once Jesus entered the boat. But Jewish Gennesaret it is, where a narrative summary of Jesus' ministry of healing is presented. People bring the sick to him from everywhere; as many as touch even the fringe of his cloak are made well. The faith and healing of the hemorrhaging woman echoes for the implied reader. By the sea Jesus feeds five thousand; on the sea Jesus walks; by the sea Jesus heals many. Jesus has authority over the sea—and quite a bit more.

Conflict over Jewish Law (7:1-23)

Authority is the issue in the next series of scenes. Jesus' antagonists are "the Pharisees and some of the scribes who had come from Jerusalem" (7:1). Pharisees and scribes were the chief antagonists of the Markan Jesus in a series of five controversy stories narrated earlier (2:1—3:6). The "scribes who came down from Jerusalem" appeared earlier as ones accusing Jesus of being possessed by Beelzebul, the prince of demons (3:22-30). Jerusalem itself, which has a high positive connotation in traditional Judaism, has a negative connotation in the Gospel of Mark. So, when Pharisees and Jerusalem scribes gather together to Jesus, the implied reader anticipates conflict. And conflict there surely is.

The conflict is triggered by the failure of Jesus' disciples to observe the Jewish (and particularly Pharisaic) regulations about ritual handwashing before meals. The implied author finds it necessary to explain this "tradition of the elders" in a parenthetical aside for any implied reader who may be unfamiliar with it. Because at other times the implied author assumes the implied reader is quite familiar with the Hebrew Bible (in Greek translation), a mixed group of Jewish and Gentile implied readers may be indicated, or implied readers who are familiar with Jewish *Scripture* but not Jewish *tradition* may be assumed. In the explanatory aside, the Pharisees and all the Jews are "they."

The conflict is expressed more in monologue than in dialogue. The Markan narrator's telling is one-sided from the start. The Pharisees and scribes get one question, "Why do your disciples not live according to the tradition of the elders, but eat with defiled hands?" Even that question has been elaborately anticipated by the narrator (7:2-4). Jesus gets two paragraphs of direct defense and counterattack. Jesus turns a statement from the prophet Isaiah against his antagonists. The Isaiah passage underlines what is at stake here for the Markan Jesus: divine commandment versus human tradition. As an example of this opposition, Jesus suggests the disparity between one of the Ten Commandments, "Honor your father and your mother," and the traditional use (and abuse) of *Corban. Corban* refers to money or property that was verbally "offered" or "dedicated" to God, that is, withdrawn from ordinary use. Although the money was not handed over directly to the Temple treasury, it was not required to be used for care of one's parents. The "tradition of the elders" that may momentarily sound honorable on the lips of the Pharisees and scribes is clearly condemned when it is reclassified by Jesus as "human tradition" in opposition to "divine commandment." Jesus appeals to a higher authority—Scripture—and one that his antagonists themselves profess to honor. His antagonists are silenced.

A change of scene occurs with the entrance of a new group of characters. Jesus calls the crowd to himself again and opens with these words: "Listen to me, all of you, and understand." The words echo similar uses of "listen" and "understand" in chapter 4, the parable chapter, and, indeed, these words introduce a parable here. It is a very brief parable (comparison or riddle) about defilement being caused by what comes out of people, not by what goes into them. Because the previous scene concerned the "defiled hands" of the disciples, the topic continues despite the change of scene.

This pattern occurs again immediately (7:17): a change of scene without a change of topic, a third scene concerned with defilement. There is a spatial change: Jesus enters a house. The narrator had not commented on his location earlier; it was presumably out-of-doors. There is a shift in characters: Jesus leaves the crowd. Then his disciples ask him about the parable. The presence of the disciples was not mentioned at the narration of the parable. The implied author does not make everything explicit; thus what is made explicit becomes all the more important.

The shift from Jesus' public teaching of the crowd to his private teaching of the disciples occurs throughout the Markan narrative. It occurs in chapter 4: parable to the crowd, explanation of the parable to the disciples (and "those who were around him"). Frequently, as in chapter 7, this character shift is paralleled by a spatial shift: from out-of-doors or an unspecified location to in "the house."

Chapter 7 also echoes chapter 4 in the introduction of Jesus' explanation of the parable by questioning the disciples' lack of understanding (7:18; 4:13). Only when characters to whom the Markan Jesus is willing to give additional teaching misunderstand does the Markan implied author have an opportunity to give additional teaching to the implied reader. And here the narrator goes beyond Jesus! Jesus says that persons are not defiled by anything that enters their stomachs and passes through their digestive systems. The immediate implication is that persons are not defiled by dirt from unwashed hands. But the narrator notes, parenthetically: "(Thus be declared all foods clean.)" (As the implied reader is aware, observing clean and unclean foods was one of the more obvious ways Jews were distinct from Gentiles.) Then Jesus says that persons are defiled by evil thoughts that come out of their hearts. The riddle is solved. The implicit is explicit.

Contact with Gentiles (7:24—8:10)

"[And] from there he set out and went away to. . . ." From where? Where have we been? the implied reader might well ask. The topic was defilement, and the antagonists were Pharisees and scribes, so the territory must have been Jewish; that is where they would be. In fact, the last landfall was Gennesaret. "[And] from there he set out and went away to the region of Tyre [and Sidon]" (7:24). These place names indicate quite a change. Tyre and Sidon are in the ancient land of Phoenicia, the Roman province of Syria, as far north as the Markan narrative reaches and definitely Gentile territory. But the Markan narrator likes to make sure the narratee follows. The second indication of the Gentile setting of the scene is the double description of the woman who seeks Jesus' help: "a Gentile [a Greek], of Syrophoenician origin."

The narrator explains that Jesus' intention in going north was not to seek out more crowds to heal. "[And] he entered a house and did not want anyone to know he was there. Yet he could not escape notice" (7:24b). The fact that the Syrophoenician woman seeks out the secluded Jesus is just the first indication of her persistence on behalf of her demon-possessed daughter. The Markan Jesus rebuffs her initial request, and he does so with a powerful and degrading metaphor. "Let the children be fed first, for it is not fair to take the children's food [bread] and throw it to the dogs." The children are Israel. She is the dog, and she yaps right back! Two can play at metaphors. "Sir, even the dogs under the table eat the children's crumbs." She has him. She has risked a second rebuke and won her daughter's health. "For this saying [word, *logos*]" (7:29, RSV), Jesus says, you may go home to a healed child, a healed Gentile child. (Jesus, too, seems to have experienced healing.)

The story of the Syrophoenician demoniac is not the first story of a Gentile healed by Jesus in Mark. (This fact interests form critics and bothers redaction critics, who say that it would make more sense if it were the first Gentile healing.) Even as the story echoes the healing of the Gerasene demoniac, it has a certain freshness. It explains more fully the outreach of Jesus' healing power. The Markan Jesus is not opposed to giving additional explanations—even in actions.

The next spatial shift is perhaps the most confusing one in the entire Markan narrative. "Then he returned from the region of Tyre, and went by way of Sidon towards the Sea of Galilee, in the region of the Decapolis" (7:31). Sidon is north of Tyre, and the region of the Decapolis is east of the Sea of Galilee. So Jesus went north to return south, through the east. The implied author seems less concerned with the logic of the travel route and more concerned with the nature of the destinations: Tyre, Sidon, the Decapolis. Gentile place names are accumulated for emphasis. The deaf-mute who is healed is also a Gentile.

The healing is, for Mark's Gospel, a particularly physical one (touching, spitting), but the techniques are common to healers in the Greco-Roman world. The man is healed privately, away from the multitude, and Jesus charges those who know of it to tell no one. But the charge backfires: "the more he ordered them, the more zealously they proclaimed it" (7:36). Astonishment beyond measure is the end result of this encounter with one who "makes the deaf to hear and the mute to speak."

Two stories of Gentile healings have followed the three-scene discussion of defilement. Maybe it is not just all *foods* that the Markan implied author thinks Jesus has declared clean. That possibility is strengthened by the next story: the feeding of the four thousand. The feeding stories resound with the loudest and clearest intratextual echoes of the Markan narrative. Their overall similarities set off their significant differences. The five thousand are fed somewhere on the west (Jewish) side of the sea. The four thousand are fed somewhere on the east (Gentile) side of the sea. (There have been no place references since the mention of the Decapolis.) In the former case, the Markan Jesus' compassion is linked to the people being like sheep without a shepherd, an image from the Hebrew Bible. In the latter case, Jesus' compassion is linked to their hunger, a universal human problem. In the former case, twelve baskets of leftovers are collected; in the latter case, seven. As twelve is a number symbolic of the Jews, so seven is a number symbolic of "the nations," the Gentiles. (In Acts 6, at the instigation of the "Hellenists," seven deacons are chosen to assist the twelve apostles.)

The allusions—backward to the manna of the Exodus and forward to the bread of the last supper and the Eucharist—remain constant between the two feeding stories. What is added is that such bread is for Gentiles as well as for Jews. Jesus heals and feeds his own; that would be story enough. But Jesus also heals and feeds outsiders. That action takes some explaining; it is harder to understand.

Signs and Seeing (8:11-26)

After dismissing the four thousand, Jesus "immediately" gets into a boat with his disciples and goes to the district of Dalmanutha. The location of such a place is no longer known, although it is generally thought to be in Galilee on the sea. Will the Markan narrator give a second clue about the setting? Yes! "The Pharisees came and began to argue with him . . ." (8:11). The implied reader knows the journey has returned to Galilee. Just before his departure from Galilee to Gentile Tyre and Sidon, Jesus was arguing with the Pharisees. Now on his return from the Gentile Decapolis, Jesus and the Pharisees pick up where they left off. If Jesus has so much authority, surely he can produce a sign from heaven, that is, from God, for the Pharisees. Something clear and explicit would be nice. Jesus sighs. No such sign will be given—to them or to "this generation." In Mark's Gospel, Jesus performs mighty deeds (dynameis) but not signs (sēmeia). (Contrast John's Gospel.) To ask for a sign is to demand that divine power be present on one's own terms rather than to perceive it wherever it manifests itself. So Jesus leaves the Pharisees. He gets into the boat again and departs "to the other side."

Yet the next scene is not on "the other side" but on the sea itself. It is the third scene carried out on the sea in Mark's narrative: first, calming the sea; second, walking on the sea; third, a conversation in the boat on the sea. This dialogue is not just another conversation between Jesus and the disciples. It is a careful, symbolic drawing together of themes that have been developed since 4:1. The implied reader's ears ring with echoes: the sea, the boat, loaves of bread, hardened hearts, eyes that do not see, ears that do not hear, five thousand, twelve baskets, four thousand, seven baskets, understand? So many things have happened, and then happened again in a different setting. Jesus tells a parable to all, and then explains it to some. Jesus heals and feeds at home, and then far beyond. There is much to hear and see, to perceive and understand.

As the disciples did not answer their own rhetorical question at 4:41, "Who then is this, that even the wind and the sea obey him?" so they do not answer Jesus' rhetorical question at 8:21, "Do you not yet understand?" The beneficiary of both silences is the implied reader, the one for whom the story is being told. To hear only the silence of the disciples and not also the rhetoric of the implied author is to try to read the story without the discourse. Narrative is always story-as-discoursed. Markan rhetorical discourse relies on juxtaposition: item, item, item; comparison, contrast, insight. The implied reader must make the connections—and *may*—because neither the characters nor the narrator make them explicit. Sea, boat, bread, twelve, seven. Do *you* not yet understand?

The conclusion of a large section of Mark (4:1—8:21) with Jesus' questioning of the disciples (8:14-21) suggests that Jesus' disciples are distinguished from his opponents not by possessing the right answers but by being possessed by the right question: not "Why does he not perform a sign from heaven?" (see 8:11), but "Who then is this . . . ?" (4:41). Jesus responds to opponents and followers with both questions and answers: "Why does this generation ask for a sign?" (8:12). "Truly I tell you, no sign will be given to this generation" (8:12). "Do you not yet understand?" (8:21). "I am" (6:50). "I will go before you to Galilee" (14:28; cf. 16:7). Some interpreters—including redaction, narrative, and reader-response critics—see the misunderstanding (or incomprehension) of the disciples as central to Mark 4–8. Others, including the present author, see as a central thrust of these chapters the search for understanding—understanding of who Jesus is and thus of what following him entails. The disciples embody that search, that ongoing process. Like Mark's Gospel itself (its opening line is, "The beginning of the good news . . ."), the search for understanding does not come to a decisive end in the Markan narrative. But neither the Markan narrator nor the Markan Jesus (nor his messenger at the empty tomb) gives up on the disciples. In this action, too, the implied reader is asked to follow.

"[And] they came to Bethsaida" (8:22). Bethsaida! Because of the significance of the sea conversation, a real reader, at least, and perhaps the implied reader as well, could almost forget about crossing the sea and surely about Bethsaida. Many scenes back—after feeding the five thousand and before walking on the sea—Jesus had tried to send the disciples across the sea before him to Gentile Bethsaida. They never made it on their own. And now Jesus has led them there, led them to the Gentiles by an elaborate detour, through an additional explanation, as a second chance to see and hear the given mystery. The detour involved starting from the familiar (healings at Gennesaret, 6:53-56), arguing against the conventional (the tradition of the elders, 7:1-23), responding to the "other" (Syrophoenician women and deaf mute in the Decapolis, 7:24-37), feeding all who are hungry (feeding the four thousand, 8:1-10), departing from those who demand divine presence on their own terms (Pharisees requesting a sign, 8:11-13), and questioning those who travel alongside (conversation with the disciples on the sea, 8:14-21). So they came at last to Bethsaida, and at Bethsaida the blind see, even if by stages.

Several echoes of the healing of the deaf mute in the Decapolis are heard in the story of the healing of the blind man of Bethsaida. Both suppliants are Gentiles and suffer from communicative disorders. Both persons are healed away from the crowd. Jesus even leads the blind man out of the village. Both stories involve physical healing techniques: applying spittle or saliva to the affected body part and touching with the fingers or hands. Both accounts conclude with Jesus' admonition not to make the healing known. Jesus tells the once-blind man not even to go into the village. The distinctive aspect of the healing of the blind man of Bethsaida—not only in Mark but in all the Gospels—is a healing process of two stages. Blindness and sight are frequently used symbolically in the ancient (and contemporary!) world. The two-stage transition from one to the other increases the symbolic possibilities.

The two-stage healing of the blind man outside Bethsaida is almost universally recognized as a pivotal scene in the Markan Gospel. It is generally linked symbolically with the two scenes that follow it: the "confession" of Peter (8:27-30) and Jesus' first passion prediction (8:31-33). Peter "sees" that Jesus is the Messiah, the Christ. But he fails to "see" that, as the Christ, Jesus must suffer. To heal Peter (and perhaps the implied reader) of that blindness will require a second stage, the second half of Mark's Gospel. The narrative clearly supports this reading.

But the two-stage healing of blindness is a transitional scene, and it also has symbolic links with the scenes that precede it. Jesus has been working in two stages all along: parables and explanations, Jewish healings and Gentile healings, Jewish feeding and Gentile feeding. The duality of the Markan Jesus' technique reflects the twofoldness of the Markan implied author's convictions: Jesus is Messiah for both Jews and Gentiles; Jesus is Messiah of power and suffering service. To see that is to see everything clearly.

CONCLUSION

The implied author of Mark is a storyteller—and a masterful one. For this reason, narrative criticism seems an especially appropriate approach to reading and interpreting the Gospel of Mark. Narrative critics seek to learn more about *how* the story means, that is, how the implied author uses characters, settings, plot, and rhetoric to communicate meaning. If such study can help us align ourselves with the implied reader, our own roles as real readers—and re-readers—of Mark will surely be enriched. We will look intently—and see.

FURTHER READING

General

Chatman, Seymour. *Story and Discourse: Narrative Structure in Fiction and Film.* Ithaca, N.Y.: Cornell University Press, 1978. A classic presentation of the elements of "story" and "discourse" that has been widely influential in biblical narrative criticism; includes thorough discussions of plot, setting, characters, implied author, types of narrators (covert versus overt), and point of view, with examples drawn from secular literature and film.

Genette, Gérard. *Narrative Discourse: An Essay in Method.* Translated by Jane E. Lewin. Ithaca, N.Y.: Cornell University Press, 1980. An attempt at a comprehensive, systematic theory of narrative and simultaneously a study of Proust's *A la recherché du temps perdu,* which focuses on careful delineations of the order, duration, and frequency of narrated events and the mood and voice of narratives.

Rimmon-Kenan, Shlomith. *Narrative Fiction: Contemporary Poetics.* London and New York: Methuen, 1983. A clear, concise, and very helpful overview of narrative aspects: events, characters, time, characterization, focalization, levels and voices, speech representation, the text and its reading, with examples drawn from various periods and various national literatures.

Biblical

Culpepper, R. Alan. *Anatomy of the Fourth Gospel: A Study in Literary Design.* Philadelphia: Fortress Press, 1983. A thorough and rich reading of the narrative of John's Gospel, exploring, in turn, the narrator and point of view, narrative time, plot, characters, implicit commentary, and the implied reader.

Darr, John A. *On Character Building: The Reader and the Rhetoric of Characterization in Luke-Acts.* Louisville: Westminster John Knox, 1992. Based on literary-critical and reader response critical theory, a careful interpretation of the role of the reader in understanding three representative characters: John the Baptist, the Pharisees, and Herod the Tetrarch; an intriguing example of the contemporary crossover of critical approaches.

Howell, David B. *Matthew's Inclusive Story: A Study in the Narrative Rhetoric of the First Gospel.* Journal for the Study of the New Testament Supplement Series 42. Sheffield: Sheffield Academic Press, 1990. An interesting exploration of plot, point of view (especially of the implied author/narrator), and the implied reader who is "included" in Matthew, as well as a comparison with redaction critical discussions of "salvation history," from the point of view of an eclectic reader-response literary paradigm; like Darr, an example of the contemporary crossover of critical approaches.

Kingsbury, Jack Dean. *Matthew as Story.* 2d ed. Philadelphia: Fortress Press, 1988. A literary critical reading of Matthew with emphasis on the plot or story line of Jesus and the story line of the disciples.

Malbon, Elizabeth Struthers. *Hearing Mark: A Listener's Guide.* Harrisburg, Pa.: Trinity Press International, 2002. A brief narrative critical commentary on Mark, with recognition of the importance of orality as a category of appropriating the Gospel; intended for Christian laity.

Moore, Stephen D. *Literary Criticism and the Gospels: The Theoretical Challenge.* New Haven and London: Yale University Press, 1989. A lively, scholarly critique of narrative criticism and reader-response criticism from the point of view of deconstruction and postmodernism; includes an extensive bibliography.

Powell, Mark Allan. *What Is Narrative Criticism?* Guides to Biblical Scholarship. Minneapolis: Fortress Press, 1990. A clear and inclusive introduction to narrative criticism of the Gospels, moving from a sketch of the relationship of narrative criticism to other critical approaches (biblical and secular) to an overview of narrative elements (story and discourse, events, characters, settings).

Resseguie, James L. *Narrative Criticism of the New Testament: An Introduction.* Grand Rapids: Baker, 2005. A presentation of narrative criticism (in the sense of "close reading") and its elements (rhetoric, setting, character, point of view, plot) with concern for literary definitions; lists or discusses numerous examples from the canonical Gospels (especially John), Paul's letters (also counting 2 Thessalonians, Colossians, Ephesians, and 1 Timothy), and the book of Revelation and includes a bibliography with helpful sub-categories.

Rhoads, David, Joanna Dewey, and Donald Michie. *Mark as Story: An Introduction to the Narrative of a Gospel.* 2d ed. Minneapolis: Fortress Press, 1999. An indispensable and inviting introduction to narrative criticism of Mark, focusing on the narrator, settings, plot, characters, and reader; includes a fresh translation of Mark and appendices of exercises for narrative analysis of Mark.

Smith, Stephen H. *A Lion with Wings: A Narrative-Critical Approach to Mark's Gospel.* Sheffield: Sheffield Academic Press, 1996. An exploration of the major issues of narrative criticism: reader response, characterization, plot, time and space, point of view, and irony; essentially a comprehensive digest of the work that literary critics have done on these areas over the past two or three decades, with applications to Mark.

Stibbe, Mark W. G. *John as Storyteller: Narrative Criticism and the Fourth Gospel.* Society for New Testament Studies Monograph Series 73. Cambridge: Cambridge University Press, 1992. An eclectic integration of literary, theological, structuralist, historical critical, and sociological questions in relation to narrative criticism, resulting in practical criticism, genre criticism, a look at social function, and a narrative-historical approach to John's story, with a detailed application to John 18-19.

Tannehill, Robert C. *The Narrative Unity of Luke-Acts: A Literary Interpretation. Volume 1, The Gospel according to Luke.* Philadelphia: Fortress Press, 1986. An exploration of the narrative and theological unity of Luke, with emphasis on the shifting and developing relationships between Jesus and other individual characters and groups of characters.

3

READER-RESPONSE CRITICISM

Figuring Mark's Reader

ROBERT M. FOWLER

WHAT OR WHO DETERMINES THE MEANING OF MARK?

What is the meaning of the Gospel of Mark? In what direction do we look
to find it? What kind of meaning are we looking for? Is the meaning of the
Gospel the author's conscious intention in writing the text? Is the meaning of
the Gospel whatever it tells us about the historical circumstances in which it
was produced? Can the meaning of the Gospel be as simple as a basic understanding of the language in which it was written? Or is the meaning a more
sophisticated understanding of the way in which the story was constructed,
its plot, characters, and settings?

Take, for example, the two extraordinarily similar episodes of the feeding of the five thousand, in Mark 6:30-44, and the feeding of the four thousand, in Mark 8:1-10. What is the meaning of these two stories? Even if we
agree that their meaning is historical in nature, there would still be several
ways to understand them. Perhaps they serve to report the fact that Jesus fed
two different crowds, on two different occasions, with just a few loaves and

fishes. Perhaps Jesus fed only one crowd on one occasion, but the story was told so often that different versions developed, two of which Mark (accidentally?) includes in his Gospel. Maybe the real significance of the two feeding stories is the historical insight that ancient people generally believed in the powers of holy men and women to manipulate the forces of nature, that Jesus was regarded as such a holy man, and consequently that stories such as these would inevitably be told about him. If the meaning of the stories is taken to be theological instead of historical, other possibilities emerge. Could the feeding stories be symbolic allusions to the Lord's Supper? Still further down that same path, is Mark's Gospel suggesting what John's Gospel clearly does, that Jesus himself is the "bread of life," "the bread that came down from heaven" (John 6:25-59)? Instead of historical or theological meaning, could the meaning of the feeding stories be literary in nature? Do the feeding stories in Mark contribute to the advancement of the plot of the narrative? Do they reveal the character of Jesus or the Twelve? Could the setting of both feeding stories (in the desert, like Moses and the Israelite tribes in Exodus)[1] be the most significant things about the stories?

Whether we take the meaning of Mark to be historical, theological, or literary, all of these approaches focus on the written text. They presume that some kind of meaning is bound to the text, waiting there to be discovered. These approaches take the text of the Gospel of Mark either as a window through which to look out on historical events, theological ideas, or cultural attitudes, or as a self-contained house of mirrors, reflecting internally the grammar, syntax, plot, characters, and settings of the narrative.

All of these perspectives assume that meaning is available in or through the text, independent of the reader. What if we take seriously the role of the reader in determining the meaning of the text? Regardless of whether the text is considered a window or a house of mirrors, does it matter who is doing the looking, and when, where, why, and how they are looking? What if we consider meaning not as a property of the text itself, but rather as a function of the experience of the reader in the act of reading the text? What if, instead of considering meaning as something static, unchanging, and preceding the reading experience, we consider it the dynamic, ever-changing creation of the reader in the act of reading?

A text does not come to us wearing its meaning, like a campaign button, on its lapel. The reader-response critic argues that whatever meaning is and wherever it is found, the reader is ultimately responsible for determining it. In reader-response criticism, meaning is no longer considered a given. It is not something ready-made, buried in the text, just waiting to be uncovered. Rather, it is something produced in the act of reading through the unique interaction of the text and the particular reader doing the reading, at a particular moment, from a particular slant. Instead of "*What* determines the meaning of a text?" reader-response critics prefer the question, "*Who* determines the meaning?" The immediate answer is "the reader," which in turn leads to further questions. When, where, why, and how does the reader read?

Reader-response criticism is only one among many forms of criticism today that advocate a change in our understanding of meaning. A shift is taking place, away from a static, objective meaning bound to the text to a more subjective meaning experienced by the reader in the temporal flow of the reading experience. Some of the other approaches to the Gospel of Mark introduced in this book advocate, to a greater or lesser degree, a similar shift in focus to the reader and the reading experience. Approaches such as feminist, deconstructive, cultural, and postcolonial criticism explicitly focus attention on the reader and the reading experience. They could be described as first cousins of reader-response criticism. Even approaches that claim to be text-centered—narrative criticism, for example—nevertheless talk a great deal about the reader and the experience of reading. Many kinds of biblical and literary criticism today are closely related to reader-response criticism.

WHO IS THE READER AND WHAT HAPPENS IN THE READING EXPERIENCE?

Reader-response critics talk a lot about the reader and the experience of reading, but who is this reader, and what happens when this reader reads? One way to understand the reader of Mark's Gospel is to think of him or her as the average, everyday reader on the street or in the church pew, anyone who picks up the Gospel and reads it for personal enrichment or pleasure. Some reader-response critics like to study the responses of such average readers. Then again, we may prefer to think of the reader of Mark as the informed, expert reader. An expert reader is someone who has received specialized training in order to be able to probe the Gospel more deeply than the average reader. Many reader-response critics are concerned about how informed, expert readers read.

A similar distinction made by the literary critic George Steiner between "the reader" and "the critic" is helpful. What Steiner means by "the reader" is someone who honors, reveres, and "serves" the text she or he is reading. What he means by "the critic" is someone who probes, questions, challenges, and "masters" the text.[2] Both roles are common in the church (laypersons are usually readers and clergy are often critics). They are definitely acted out in the college or seminary classroom (students in introductory biblical studies courses tend to be readers, and their professors tend to be critics). This book was written by critics in the hope that it will help readers to read and to talk about their reading experience more thoughtfully. The critic aims to deepen and enrich the experience of the reader. Some of our readers may even become critics themselves. However, both readers and critics read the Gospel of Mark, so what difference, if any, is there between their reading experiences?

Both the reader and the critic of the Bible have their reading experience shaped by the communities of which they are members. Many average readers of the Bible are members of churches or synagogues that have given them some explicit and much implicit instruction in how to read the Bible "correctly." Depending on the beliefs, presuppositions, and style of the religious community, its members may approach the Bible with a fairly clear idea of what they should find there. People tend to find in the Bible what they have been taught to find there.

Critics also are members of communities that tell them how they ought to read the Bible, but often today these are academic instead of religious communities. Once upon a time, the most rigorous training in how to read the Bible was found only in religious communities. In the United States of the early twenty-first century, however, most expert readers of the Bible receive their training in academic institutions that may or may not have an affiliation with a religious denomination. Such expert readers are typically taught to ask historical and literary questions about the Bible. They may or may not ask the old familiar religious or theological questions. Let us be clear: an expert reader can be a member of a religious community, an academic community, or both. Such a reader has to wear a different hat and behave in a different way when participating in the life of one community or the other. The situation is awkward, but it is a fact of life in American culture today. Many of us regularly get our costumes and behaviors mixed up because we belong to so many communities at once.

What is the difference between the kind of Bible reading taught in religious and academic communities? Generalizations here are risky, but perhaps it would be fair to say that academic communities are generally more committed to open, public dialogue about the Bible than many religious communities. Why? Religious communities are obligated to remain faithful to their founding vision or to their dream of the future. Being religious does not necessarily mean being closed-minded, but religious people do have definite ideas about how life is or how it ought to be. In their common life they attempt to live out of that understanding. If they are Jews or Christians, they will read the Bible in the light of their particular experience of God in their life together. To belong to a religious community is to have a tradition to uphold.

The tradition in the academic world, however, is to question and challenge traditions. In contrast to the duty of a religious community to preserve a precious legacy, the business of an academic community is to challenge old ideas and to generate new ones. Furthermore, these ideas are usually of a different sort than the ones cherished in a religious community. Today, the reading experience of the expert reader of the Bible is typically more intellectual than religious.[3] Although average readers are deeply influenced by the community that has taught them how to read the Bible, nevertheless their reading experiences are frequently personal and private. Such personal experiences can be very powerful to them. Indeed, almost everyone who has learned how to read has had such personally meaningful experiences. However, even the most powerful of private reading experiences is limited, in several ways. For one thing, it often hinges upon personal history or psychology. In such cases, others in the same community may not be able to share the experience, to say nothing of outsiders. Also, everyone's knowledge of the world is limited. Everyone has biases and personal opinions. But average readers are often not aware of their own limitations and biases. Many of the average reader's experiences are based on presuppositions and opinions that have never been questioned or even acknowledged. The average reader may also be limited by having read only a narrow range of literature, perhaps a mere handful of favorite texts. For example, some Christian churches teach their members that the Bible is the only literature a Christian should read, a restriction that most of the authors of the biblical books themselves would probably find unnecessarily severe.

The expert reader, by contrast, believes that to read well one must first read widely and deeply. The more literature and more kinds of literature one has read, the better equipped one is to read with skill and insight. In order to read the Bible well, reading widely outside the Bible helps. Moreover, expert readers try to be constantly aware of the limitations and biases of all readers, most especially their own. One of the best ways to learn about one's limitations and biases in reading is to submit one's reading experience to the scrutiny and criticism of other readers. The community of readers to which one belongs can render great service here. Average readers may challenge each other, but expert readers must do so. They probe, question, and challenge, not only the text they are reading, but other critics as well, thereby gaining greater insight into one another and into the text being read.

The average reader often does not talk about reading at all. To him, reading is such a personal matter that he may feel uncomfortable talking about it. The expert reader, however, talks passionately about reading. Whether we realize it or not, whenever we open ourselves up and talk with other people about our reading experience, we are acting as a critic or expert reader. "The reader" and "the critic" are actually roles that we have all acted out from time to time. When an average reader chooses to talk about his reading experience, he is slipping for a moment into the role of critic. When a critic grows weary of talking about reading, she may relax and just savor reading for a while.

Other characteristics further distinguish the expert reader or critic. Unlike the average reader, who may or may not know about others' reading experiences, the expert reader makes it her business to know what other people have experienced as they have read. The expert reader of Mark, for example, is familiar with the history of the reading of Mark's Gospel, sometimes called its *reception history*, some of which was discussed in chapter 1 above. Consequently, the expert reader is familiar with the problems, questions, and puzzles that generations of readers have encountered. Expert readers are acutely aware that they are participating in age-old conversation—often an argument!—about what happens when we read a particular text. One of the major goals of an introductory course in the Gospels is to introduce beginning students to the Gospels' reception history, so that they, too, may participate in the ongoing conversation.

Critics also talk about imaginary, ideal readers of the texts they discuss. Because expert readers are conscious of participating in a centuries-long history of reading, when they talk about the reader they are often thinking about an imaginary, ideal reader who is familiar with this entire reading history. Critics often write as if they themselves were all-knowing ideal readers, but this pose is always a fiction; no flesh-and-blood reader ever really becomes this imaginary super-reader.

Another kind of ideal reader is the reader or hearer of the story that we can imagine the Gospel of Mark itself suggests. The most common labels for the imaginary reader or listener in the text of Mark are *implied reader* and *narratee*, terms that were already introduced in chapter 2 above. Much reader-response criticism of biblical texts has concentrated on discerning the features of the implied reader or the narratee of each text. Some biblical scholars have argued that this approach might be a fresh, new way to gain historical insights into early Christian readers. In this direction lie all the usual pitfalls of historical research, chief among them the temptation to assume that the ancients were just like us. In his chapter on social criticism, David Rhoads discusses the growing body of knowledge about how different people in first-century Mediterranean cultures were from us. Therefore, we should be cautious in making claims about how first-century readers read or heard Mark's Gospel. Admitting that ultimately the reader whose reading experience one is talking about is really one's own self is probably wiser.

Even if we admit that the implied reader and narratee are our own imaginative constructions, we can still imagine them in a multitude of ways. For example, we can imagine the implied reader or the narratee either as entities suspended in the amber of the ancient text or as lively and dynamic roles recreated and performed anew every time a real reader reads. Some kinds of literary criticism of the Bible discuss the reader in the former, static style, in which meaning is still regarded as something frozen in the text. The reader-response critic, however, emphasizes the reading experience through time. When the reader-response critic discusses the implied reader or narratee, she will return constantly to the question of what happens in the temporal flow of language in the act of reading. There are many illuminating ways of talking about the temporal experience of reading, as we shall now see.

FIGURING OUT THE EXPERIENCE OF READING MARK

All language is based on figures of speech. Words never communicate perfectly to reveal exactly how things *are*. The best we can ever do is to use figures of speech that hint at what things are *like*. It follows that the experience of reading can never be captured fully in words. As we talk about our experience of reading, we can use a variety of metaphors or other figures of speech. In the rest of this chapter I apply several of these metaphors to the experience of reading Mark's Gospel.

These metaphors are tools in the reader-response critic's tool kit. In the sections that follow, I introduce a handful of these tools and demonstrate how to use them on interesting passages in Mark. I need to stress that only a handful of tools are introduced and demonstrated. As the critic gains experience, she will want to collect a more complete kit than I shall discuss here. In addition, I need to stress that I shall not discuss any section of Mark at length, for several reasons. For one thing, verse-by-verse discussions of the entire Gospel are readily available in commentaries on Mark, and there is little need to produce more of that kind of discussion here. Moreover, extended discussions can be dull when the critic acts as if every verse is as weighty as every other verse, and we all know that is not true. To the contrary, we all like to talk about the high points or challenging moments of the reading experience. Reader-response critics like to focus their attention on the pivotal moments in reading that have provoked the most arguments through the years. So, these few tools are introduced to you, and their use only briefly illustrated, to entice you to use them yourself to talk about your experience of reading Mark's Gospel. Add your own tools to the kit and use them on the many passages not discussed in this chapter.

THE TEMPORAL EXPERIENCE OF READING

To talk about the temporal experience of reading requires using images about time. In fact, reader-response critics use a variety of time or movement figures of speech to talk about the "temporal," "kinetic," "dynamic," "flow" of reading. As already suggested, reader-response critics are trying to lay aside images of static, fixed meaning embedded in texts. They favor instead images of dynamic processes that focus on the reader in the act of reading. The "response" in reader-response criticism is always a fluid, shifting response, mutating throughout the time of the reading experience.[4]

Assume that we are reading a sequence of words (or sentences, or episodes, etc.), A, B, C, D, E, and so forth. Our understanding of and attitude toward what we are reading changes at each step along the way.[5] For example, at point A we may have a vague idea of what lies ahead at point C. When we arrive at point C, our suspicions about C may be confirmed, denied, or revised. By the time we reach point E, our attitude toward C may be changed yet again, in retrospect. Or again, point A may appear one way at point A, another way from the vantage point of B, another way at point C, another way at point D, and so forth. In brief, the reading experience, if we stop to think about it, is full of twists and turns, surprises and developments. Our minds change constantly as we read. As our minds change, meaning changes.

Many traditional approaches to interpretation unconsciously hurry past the reading experience in order to get to its conclusion. Discussions of narratives often look back upon the story from the vantage point of the end of the reading experience. The end of reading—moment Z, let us call it—may be a very important moment, but it is just one moment among many. We have all read stories that were so enjoyable that we were sad to finish them. Endings are often anticlimactic, in contrast to the intriguing journey that led up to the ending. Like many things in life, the trip itself is often more interesting than the arrival. This approach does not minimize the importance of the final moment in the reading experience, which may be a moment of illumination or power. However, one of the virtues of reader-response criticism is that it encourages us to take seriously every moment of the reading experience, not just the final moment. Accordingly, all of the metaphors that will be introduced here are "temporal experience of reading" metaphors. They try to do some justice to our journey through the text.

Because reader-response criticism is not primarily interested in historical meaning, the fact that the emphasis on the temporal experience of reading can help us to understand better the experience of first-century audiences of the Gospel may come as a surprise. In antiquity, all reading was done out loud, even when a person read in solitude. A piece of religious literature such as Mark's Gospel would typically have been read aloud or even performed from memory to an assembly of interested listeners. The Gospel would not have been read silently, the way average readers are taught to read today. The written text of the Gospel would not have been scrutinized with a critical eye, the way critics analyze texts today, patiently flipping printed pages back and forth. Rather, the typical first-century experience of the Gospel would have been to hear it performed orally, probably in a continuous recitation and probably from beginning to end. The first encounters with the Gospel were thus temporal experiences of oral performance. Nineteen centuries later, people can still hear portions of Mark read in public worship, but the portions are usually so small that the cumulative effects that are inevitable in an extended reading are lost. A wide gulf separates first-century hearing of the Gospel from the modern silent reading of it. However, reader-response criticism's exploration of the temporal experience of reading is a valuable resource that can deepen our appreciation of the temporal experience of the first-century oral performance of Mark.[6]

LOOKING FORWARD, LOOKING BACK

We have already used one metaphor for the reading experience that is virtually universal: as we read we constantly look forward and look back. That is, as we read we try to anticipate what lies ahead, and we constantly review and reevaluate what we have already read. In order to make maximum sense of what we are reading, the reader must ponder not just the present moment of reading, but how the present moment relates to moments remembered from the past and anticipated in the future.

Writing is hard work, and so is reading. Wolfgang Iser suggests that the reader's toil in constantly reviewing the past and previewing the future is like the original creative struggle of the author in writing the text: "We look forward, we look back, we decide, we change our decisions, we form expectations, we are shocked by their nonfulfillment, we question, we muse, we accept, we reject; this is the dynamic process of recreation."[7]

Consider which of our five senses are evoked by our metaphors. Looking forward and looking back are visual metaphors, playing on the sense of sight. One could just as easily substitute an acoustic metaphor, playing on the sense of hearing: a reader "hears" whispers, faint sounds, or maybe trumpet fanfares of what lies ahead, and reverberating echoes, loud or soft, clear or indistinct, of what has preceded.

What are some good examples of moments in reading the Gospel of Mark where the reader looks forward or back? When considering the temporal experience of reading, we can talk about both small-scale micro-moments in reading or large-scale macro-moments. We shall look at some micro-moments first, the frequent occurrence of "immediately" (*euthys*) and "again" (*palin*) in the discourse of the narrative.

Everyone who has read Mark's Gospel carefully has observed that the author seems to make everything in the story happen "immediately" (the Greek word is *euthys*). Sometimes this word occurs in one sentence after another.

- 1:18 And *immediately* they left their nets and followed him. . . .
- 1:20 And *immediately* he called them. . . .
- 1:21 And *immediately* on the Sabbath he entered the synagogue and taught. . . .
- 1:23 And *immediately* there was in their synagogue a man with an unclean spirit. . . .[8]

The author so overworks this word that embarrassed translators scramble to introduce as much variety as possible in their English translations. They may translate *euthys* as "immediately," "at once," "just as," "just then," "as soon as," or sometimes in frustration they just leave the word out of the translation altogether.

In current literary discussions of Mark, this quirk in the author's writing style is credited with setting a mood of urgency for the actions of the characters in the story being told. Rather than addressing the mood it sets for the action in the story, however, the reader-response critic prefers to ask how the frequent *euthys*es affect the reader. What kind of storytelling strategy is at work here? What does having to negotiate this steady flow of *immediately*s do to the reader?

To do full justice to this question, we would have to examine each individual instance of *immediately*. We would have to ask ourselves how to relate each instance to moments before and after in the reading experience. The reader-response critic will not automatically assume that each *immediately* works the same way. Nevertheless, we might hazard the generalization that the cumulative effect of all the *euthys*es is to drill into the reader that this narrative has a relentless forward thrust. Readers who want to read this narrative must jump on the narrative bandwagon, hold on tight, and be attentive to what lies ahead. *Euthys* never says much about *what* to look forward to; it just reminds us to keep looking forward.

Somewhat like *euthys*, but pointing in the opposite direction, the Greek word *palin* stops us dead in our tracks and demands that we look backward momentarily. In Mark *palin* is usually best translated as "again." Unlike *euthys*, which points forward but vaguely so, *palin* usually points us backward to a fairly certain moment earlier in the reading of the narrative. If we stop to think, usually we can recall the previous moment to which the *palin* is pointing us.[9]

To cite just one example, in Mark 8:1 the narrator introduces a scene that should easily remind the reader of the setting for the earlier episode of the feeding of the five thousand in Mark 6:30-44:

> In those days when there was *again* a great crowd without anything to eat, he called his disciples and said to them, "I have compassion for the crowd, because they have been with me now for three days and have nothing to eat. If I send them away hungry to their homes, they will faint on the way—and some of them have come from a great distance." (8:1-3)[10]

Countless readers have puzzled over why the disciples in Mark seem so dense. When Jesus first invites the disciples to feed a hungry crowd in Mark 6:37, they do not know what to do. They have no understanding of what Jesus is capable of doing to satisfy the needs of the crowd. Any reader, however, is bound to understand better than the disciples, especially after Jesus proceeds to feed five thousand men with just a few loaves and fishes. Mark 8:1-3 reminds the reader of this earlier episode. These verses alert the reader to anticipate a second feeding incident in the episode about to unfold. In contrast to the reader's recollection of the past feeding incident and anticipation of another, in Mark 8:4 the disciples reveal to the reader that they learned nothing from the earlier feeding incident and therefore are oblivious to the possibility that Jesus might do it all over again: "His disciples replied, 'How can one feed these people with bread here in the desert?'" (Mark 8:4). How could they *not* know, the reader may say to herself, given their experience back in Mark 6:30-44? The reader-response critic recognizes here and elsewhere that Mark's Gospel is narrated in such a way that the reader often perceives and understands what characters in the story do not.

The two feeding stories in Mark 6 and 8 are a classic example of the widespread repetition or duality in Mark. What is the meaning of such repetition? Some possible historical solutions to the problem were listed previously. But what if we are not content with any of these possible historical meanings of the dual stories? What if we suspect that the meaning of these stories lies less in ancient history and more in how they strike the reader who must encounter them now in the act of reading? As you might anticipate, the reader-response critic will ask, "What happens when the reader reads seemingly repetitious episodes?" And again, the reader-response critic will want to consider every instance on its own terms because the rhetorical possibilities of repetition (as with any storytelling strategy) are endless. By repetition, the reader's insight into the narrative can be built up or solidified; repetition can also weary us, confuse us, or make us suspicious. Repetition giveth and repetition taketh away. It is always wise to consider each moment of reading on its own merits.

Operating at a slightly wider scope than *euthys* and *palin*, the reader looks forward whenever Jesus predicts something in the story and looks back whenever one of his predictions is fulfilled. In Mark's story Jesus can accurately predict the future. This characteristic of Jesus is so prominent in the story that only with difficulty can we shift our attention away from the *story* to the *discourse*—the way the story is told by the storyteller and received by the reader, as explained in the previous chapter.

Perhaps the boldest predictions uttered in the story are Jesus' three predictions of his impending passion—his suffering and death. These three passion predictions (Mark 8:31; 9:31; 10:32-34) provide the framework around which the central chapters 8–10 are constructed. The three predictions are offered so boldly, so clearly, and above all so frequently that no reader can fail to have his expectations for the rest of the narrative shaped by them. As we read on to the end of the Gospel, the reader can have little doubt about what lies ahead. Once again, the reader experiences an ironic tension between what he understands about the story and what the characters in the story do not understand. No one in the story seems to learn anything from these predictions (see Mark 8:32-33; 9:31-34, 38-39; 10:32, 35-45). The reader, by contrast, cannot help but be educated by these signposts to future moments in the narrative.

Although Jesus issues his predictions boldly, their fulfillment is seldom observed by characters in the story (by contrast, see Luke 24:6-8, 44). Rather, the reader, at the level of the discourse, is left to connect the fulfillment back

to the prediction. A good example may be found in Jesus' trial before the Sanhedrin, the council of chief priests and elders in Jerusalem (Mark 14:53-72).
The entire scene fulfills Jesus' passion predictions, especially the third and
most detailed prediction in 10:32-34. Jesus' tormenters spit upon him, strike
him, and taunt him to "prophesy" (14:65), not realizing that Jesus had "proph-
esied" these very actions. However, the reader cannot help but realize that a
prediction has been fulfilled. Still further along in the same passage, Peter
saves his own life by denying Jesus three times, just as Jesus had said he would
(14:29-31; see also 8:35-38). Apparently Peter's denial is taking place at the
same time that Jesus is being taunted by his tormenters, thus the irony that
several different predictions by Jesus are being fulfilled simultaneously. Peter
eventually remembers that Jesus had predicted his triple betrayal (14:72), a
rare instance of a character in the story making a connection between present fulfillment and past prediction. Only the reader regularly makes the connections between past, present, and future in this narrative. The characters
in the story, with the exception of Jesus, generally do not make these connections. Only the reader can make them, thanks to the resources provided to
the reader alone by the discourse of the narrative.

To sum up, "prediction and fulfillment" has typically been treated as a
function of the character Jesus within the story of Mark's Gospel. The reader-
response critic would rather take prediction and fulfillment as a function of
the experience of reading Mark's Gospel. Prediction and fulfillment is almost
never observed by characters in Mark's story; it is observed frequently by the
reader in the experience of reading Mark's story.

FILLING GAPS

Wolfgang Iser has popularized another metaphor for the reading experience:
as we read, we encounter "gaps" in the narrative that must be "filled."[11] Every
narrative has gaps in it, places where something is missing. Reading is not
only a matter of making sense of what is there in the narrative but also what
is not there. Filling is not the only way to handle a gap. Sometimes we can
construct a simple bridge across the gap, we might be able to jump across it,
or we might exercise prudence by walking around it. The gaps that appear in
the path we walk through the reading experience must be negotiated somehow, but readers often have considerable freedom to handle them as they see
fit. Many of the arguments between readers are over how best to deal with
gaps in the texts we read. As long as there are gaps (which is forever), readers
will argue about how to handle them.

Once again, we can look at some small-scale examples and work our
way up. At the level of grammar and syntax, in Mark's Gospel the subjects
and objects of sentences are unspecified in many places.[12] In such cases the
reader is left to figure out who is who in the sentence. A Greek composition

instructor would probably assign Mark a poor grade in style and grammar for such vagueness. In Mark's defense, however, his unspecified subjects and objects usually present little difficulty to the reader, and sometimes the reader is caught for a moment in a most intriguing ambiguity. Whether the grammatical gap is intriguing or merely awkward, it represents a challenge to the reader that, however minor, must be negotiated before the reading experience can continue. It guarantees the involvement of the reader in the ongoing business of making sense of the story. This kind of gap may not be stylish, but it is often engaging, effective rhetoric.

Although many comments by reader-response critics focus on ideal, hypothetical readers, we know a great deal about how actual readers have negotiated Mark's gaps. Two ancient readers who have left us evidence of their gap filling in Mark are the authors of the Gospels of Matthew and Luke. Most scholars believe that Matthew and Luke produced their Gospels by rewriting Mark's, so their Gospels may be understood as implicit reports of their experiences of reading Mark. Just like us, Matthew and Luke had to steer their way through the discourse of Mark's narrative. We are lucky that they left a record of their response to their experience of reading Mark. If we read Mark's Gospel side by side with Matthew and Luke, we can easily find "gaps" in Mark that have been "filled" by Matthew, Luke, or both.

- Mark 1:14 reads: "Now after John was arrested, Jesus came into Galilee, proclaiming the good news of God." A gap lies here between the arrest of John and the beginning of Jesus' preaching mission in Galilee. What connection, if any, is there between these two events? The storyteller gives us no indication, so the reader is free to imagine all sorts of connections. Without doubt, Matthew felt there had to be a connection, for in Matthew 4:12 we read: "Now when Jesus heard that John had been arrested, he withdrew to Galilee." Exactly *why* Jesus went to Galilee remains unclear, but that he went *because* of John's arrest is clear. Such minimal gap-filling is often sufficient to allow us to continue reading.

- In Mark 3:6 the reader is told that the Pharisees and the Herodians plotted Jesus' death. Then, in 3:7 the reader is told that Jesus withdrew to the Sea of Galilee. Should we construct a bridge between these two comments? Matthew does bridge the gap by stating that Jesus himself "knew" about the plot and (therefore) "withdrew" (Matt 12:15).

- In Mark 3:31-35 Jesus is teaching inside a house. Next thing we know he is teaching alongside the sea (Mark 4:1). How did he suddenly get from one place to the other? Matthew fills the gap, if only slightly: "That same day Jesus went out of the house and sat beside the sea" (Matt 13:1).

- Another equally wrenching gap in Mark's narrative occurs between Mark 6:14-29, the story of the death of John the Baptist, and Mark

6:30-44, the story of the feeding of the five thousand. Mark juxtaposes these two episodes with no transition from one to the other. How the reader is to connect them, if at all, is not indicated. Matthew reworks Mark 6:30 into an explicit transition from one episode to another. In Matthew 14:12 Jesus' disciples go to tell him of John's death, which they do not in Mark, and in Matthew 14:13 Jesus hears their report, which of course he cannot in Mark. As a result, in Matthew's Gospel, Jesus and the Twelve's withdrawal to the wilderness, where the multitude will be fed, is in direct response to the report of John's death. No such connection between the two episodes is suggested by Mark. Mark merely gives us the gap between Mark 6:29 and 6:30, and Matthew's bridge is one reader's reasonable attempt to negotiate the gap. If we do not like Matthew's bridge, we are free to build our own.

The gap-filling by Matthew and Luke is exactly what any reader must do when reading Mark's Gospel. The service the reader-response critic provides is to alert us to what we have always done while reading, but seldom stopped to think about.

Other gaps in Mark's narrative are of larger scope. These gaps occur either in the story or in the discourse of the narrative. To spot such gaps requires recognition that story and discourse need not always go together hand in hand. If he wants to, the storyteller can leave something out of the story; if he wants to, he can leave something out of the discourse. The analogy is imperfect, but imagine yourself watching a movie in which occasionally the picture continues while the sound is turned off, and at other times the picture is blanked out while the sound continues. Some examples may help us appreciate how Mark's Gospel can function occasionally with either story or discourse turned off.

An example of a gap in the discourse may be found in Mark 4, the parable chapter. Historically, the parables of Jesus of Nazareth were surely designed to provoke and intrigue his audiences, for they still provoke and intrigue us today. The challenge of Mark 4 to the reader-response critic is to be sensitive not only to the provocation of Jesus' audience within the story, but at the same time to be attentive to how the parables strike us, the readers, who hear them thanks to the narrator's discourse. Furthermore, if we are open to the possibility that something can happen in the story that is missing from the discourse (and vice versa), then we will be in position to discover how we handle this kind of gap in Mark 4.

Mark 4 begins with the famous parable of the Sower (Mark 4:1-9). Immediately afterward, disciples approach Jesus, asking for help in understanding his parables. His response is perhaps more perplexing than the parables themselves: "And he said to them, 'To you has been given the secret of the kingdom of God, but for those outside, everything comes in parables; in order that "they may indeed look, but not perceive, and may indeed listen, but not understand; so that they may not turn again and be forgiven"'" (Mark 4:11-12). Verse 12, in which Jesus seems to say that he uses parables in order to prevent people from understanding him, has been a source of arguments for generations of readers. I shall deal with it further later, in considering another metaphor for the reading experience. For now, I want to concentrate on Jesus' comment that his listeners have "been given the secret of the kingdom of God."

The reader has a major problem here. If we review the first four chapters of the Gospel, we cannot find the place in the story where the "secret of the kingdom of God" was given to Jesus' followers. Countless expert readers have offered countless suggestions as to when this event happened in the story, but there is no consensus solution to this puzzle. Average and expert readers alike want to believe that if a Gospel refers to a scene or an episode in the story, then surely the storyteller meant to narrate that scene or episode in the discourse of the narrative. In other words, is not the storyteller obliged to make all the action of the story take place on the stage, in front of our eyes? Surely Mark would not make something happen offstage, where the audience can neither see nor hear it?

As soon as the question is put this way, most readers will realize that nothing prevents the storyteller from referring to portions of the story that, for whatever reasons, he chooses not to tell us. An analogy between Mark and a play performed on a stage may be helpful. Perhaps you have seen a play by Shakespeare in which a murder or a battle is announced on the stage after it has supposedly happened offstage, out of our sight and hearing. Similarly in storytelling, omitting from the discourse a portion of the story is a standard technique among skilled storytellers. The "giving of the secret of the kingdom of God" is just such a gap in the discourse of Mark's Gospel. It is an allusion to an episode in the story that the storyteller chooses not to narrate.

Besides large gaps in the discourse of Mark's Gospel, the story also has large gaps. The stage analogy would be the scene that takes place on the stage, seemingly in full view of the characters and the audience, but the characters on stage are utterly oblivious to it; only the audience sees and hears what is happening. In such a case, as far as the characters are concerned, what happens on stage has no bearing on them. For all practical purposes, it happens only for the sake of the audience. That is, in narrative terms, the only thing that is moving forward is the discourse; the progress of the story has momentarily halted.

An example of such a gap in the story is Jesus' cry from the cross in Mark 15:34-35: "At three o'clock Jesus cried out with a loud voice, 'Eloi, Eloi, lema sabachthani?' which means, 'My God, my God, why have you forsaken me?' When some of the bystanders heard it, they said, 'Listen, he is calling for Elijah'" (15:34-35). Jesus cries out to God, using the opening words of Psalm 22. But these words are not in Greek, like the rest of Mark's Gospel—they are in Aramaic! Fortunately for the Greek-speaking implied reader of the

Gospel, the storyteller slips in a translation, which tells us exactly what the otherwise exotic words say: in his forsakenness, Jesus is crying out to God. The characters standing around the cross, however, misunderstand what he is saying. They mistake Jesus' cry as an appeal to the prophet Elijah.

So where is the gap? The gap is opened by the storyteller's parenthetical comment to the reader, which translates Jesus' words for our benefit alone. Without the translation, the Greek-speaking reader might be just as lost as those characters on the stage around the cross, who mistakenly hear Jesus cry to Elijah. They hear the same cry that we do, but whereas we are made to understand it by the storyteller's parenthetical comment, they utterly misunderstand. The storyteller has drawn us into a charmed, inner circle of understanding. The characters in the story, however, are excluded from understanding the story. As far as they are concerned, the story has halted, but without their knowledge. In Mark 15:34-35 no one in the story (except maybe Jesus) understands the story, which is to say that for them Mark 15:34-35 is a gap in the story. Only the reader outside the story understands, not so much the story as the discourse of Mark 15:34-35.

Other figures of speech may be helpful in our quest to appreciate gaps in story and discourse. Aside from the metaphor of gaps, in Mark an opaque veil often seems to have been dropped between the audience receiving the story-teller's discourse and the characters in the story. In Mark 4:11, for instance, the opaque veil seems to favor the disciples while shutting the reader of the Gospel out of the secret of the kingdom of God. In Mark 15:34-35, on the contrary, the reader is the privileged insider while the characters in the story are excluded by a veil that prevents them from understanding what they are seeing and hearing on the stage.

Whether we use the metaphor of the gap or of the veil of exclusion, fundamental here is the distinction between the story and the discourse of a narrative. Distinguishing between story and discourse allows us to recognize the occasional occurrence of story without discourse or discourse without story. (Later we shall see that sometimes story and discourse can work simultaneously but at cross-purposes with each other, for instance in dramatic irony.) In such cases, the reader does not so much fill gaps in the story or the discourse as endure them, or, if the veil metaphor is used, the reader must live and learn through the dropping and lifting of veils. Like so many of our reading experiences, we are so accustomed to negotiating the gaps or enduring the veil that we seldom stop to think about what is happening within us as we read.

RECONSTRUCTION

In recent years finding irony galore in the Gospels has become fashionable among biblical critics. The Gospel writers, critics often suggest, constructed their narratives with a strong ironic twist in order to intrigue their readers. The literary critic Wayne Booth, whose insights into the rhetorical uses of irony have proven to be a rich resource for biblical critics, has inspired many of these discussions.[13]

Booth is fascinated by the process readers go through, first to decide whether an author is being ironic, and second to figure out what the author really means to say if indeed she is using irony. Booth suggests that the process of discerning and deciphering irony can be best described by using the metaphor of "reconstruction."[14] At its most basic, an ironic utterance is one that cannot be taken at face value. The true, intended meaning of the words lies hidden somewhere behind the surface meaning. An ironic utterance is like a wobbly building standing on a shaky foundation—we cannot take it the way it stands, so the reader must dismantle and reconstruct the ironic edifice on a more solid footing. Booth proposes a four-step process for reconstructing the meaning of an irony.

"*Step one.* The reader is required to reject the literal meaning."[15] An ironic utterance is incongruous or inconsistent, either within itself or with something else. This incongruity or inconsistency makes accepting it at face value impossible. So the first step is for the reader to decide that the author does not mean exactly what she says.

"*Step two.* Alternative interpretations or explanations are tried out."[16] If the author does not mean what she says, what could she possibly mean? Did she misspeak? Was she careless? Has she forgotten what she has said or done elsewhere in the narrative? Has she gone mad? What could she possibly be up to?

"*Step three.* A decision must therefore be made about the author's knowledge or beliefs."[17] This step is pivotal. The reader must step back and make a judgment about the author. What does the author really think? Where does she really stand? What are her true convictions and motives? Only with such a judgment in hand can the reader hope to reconstruct what really lies behind the irony.

"*Step four.* Having made a decision about the knowledge or beliefs of the speaker, we can finally choose a new meaning or cluster of meanings with which we can rest secure."[18] This step is the reconstruction proper. Having decided where the author really stands, the reader can dismantle the ironic utterance and reconstruct it. The result is, Booth says, a "stable" new construction of meaning.

Turning to examples, Booth himself discusses a much-discussed instance of irony in Mark, the ironic mockery hurled at Jesus as he hangs dying on the cross:[19]

> Those who passed by derided him, shaking their heads and saying, "Aha! You who would destroy the temple and build it in three days, save yourself, and come down from the cross!" In the same way the chief priests, along

with the scribes, were also mocking him among themselves and saying, "He saved others; he cannot save himself. Let the Messiah, the King of Israel, come down from the cross now, so that we may see and believe." Those who were crucified with him also taunted him. (Mark 15:29-32)

Exploring Booth's four-step process in detail should not be necessary here. Clearly, when Jesus' detractors call him "Messiah" and "King of Israel," they do not mean what they say. These characters do not for a second believe that Jesus is Messiah or King (step one). Indeed, the storyteller himself signals that all those surrounding Jesus are "deriding," "mocking," and "taunting" him (step three). The conclusion is easy to draw: everyone is heaping verbal abuse on a dying man (step four).

Thus far we have identified and reconstructed *verbal irony* in the crucifixion scene. At the same time, however, *dramatic irony* is at work here. As the name suggests, verbal irony is an ironic utterance, such as the words said in mockery at the cross. Dramatic irony is ironic incongruity in situations or events in a narrative. It is a classic technique used by playwrights in dramas written for the stage. In the theater, dramatic irony occurs when the audience recognizes and comprehends an ironic incongruity between what the characters on the stage know or understand and what the audience in the seats knows or understands. In a narrative such as the Gospel of Mark, dramatic irony typically involves an incongruity between what is known or understood by characters at the level of the story and what is known or understood by the reader at the level of discourse.

Although the process of perceiving and fathoming dramatic irony is similar to that for verbal irony, Booth's reconstruction metaphor works better for verbal irony. With verbal irony, we can often reconstruct "what the person really meant to say," and thus arrive at a stable, reconstructed meaning. With dramatic irony, however, the ironic incongruity is one of circumstances and events, not necessarily of words, and once the reader has understood the dramatic irony of circumstances or events, it does not go away. Indeed, once the reader grasps the dramatic irony, its ironic tension may grow in magnitude. Dramatic irony, like verbal irony, needs to be figured out, if not entirely reconstructed, but dramatic irony continues to reverberate even after it has been comprehended.

The dramatic irony in Mark 15:29-32 is that, unknown to the mockers at the foot of the cross, Jesus *really is* the Christ, the King of Israel. Ironically, the words they use to insult him are the truest and best possible description of him (step four). They do not realize this fact, however. Only the reader of the Gospel is in position to understand what the characters in the story do not understand. The entire experience of reading Mark's Gospel up to this point has prepared the reader to see the deeper truth: for the author of this Gospel, Jesus is exactly who the mockers think he is not (step three).

Whereas the verbal irony in the crucifixion scene is openly signaled as such by the storyteller, the accompanying dramatic irony is unannounced. The reader has to recognize and come to terms with it entirely on her own. This irony represents a great challenge to the reader, but it is at the same time a tremendous expression of trust by the author in the reader's ability to figure things out for herself.

Other verbal ironies are found on the lips of characters in the story. In the passion narrative especially, many words spoken by characters are ironic:

- Judas calls Jesus "rabbi" ("my teacher") and kisses him, thereby betraying him (14:45).
- Peter, confronted with being a follower of Jesus, says of Jesus: "I do not know this man you are talking about" (14:71).
- Pilate, speaking to the crowd, asks, "Do you want me to release for you the King of the Jews?" (15:9).
- The execution squad conducts a mock coronation, complete with pretend royal garb and a crown of plaited thorns, and calls out to Jesus, "Hail, King of the Jews!" (15:18).

Earlier in the Gospel, on occasion Jesus himself speaks ironically. In Mark 7:9, for example, Jesus "congratulates" the Pharisees and scribes for setting aside one of God's commandments: "You have a fine way of rejecting the commandment of God in order to keep your tradition!" Given everything that surrounds this comment by Jesus in Mark 7, there is little danger of any reader taking Jesus at face value; he does not intend to congratulate, but rather to condemn the Pharisees and scribes for substituting their own traditions for the commandments of God. The verbal irony in Mark 7:9 is easily recognized and reconstructed.

Other examples of dramatic irony in the Gospel are also numerous. A favorite technique of the storyteller to create ironic tension between the story and the discourse is to narrate two almost identical incidents in which the disciples of Jesus seem to learn absolutely nothing. Wonderful examples of these matched pairs of stories are the stilling of the storm in Mark 4:35-41 and the walking on the water in Mark 6:45-52, the feeding of the five thousand in Mark 6:30-44 and the feeding of the four thousand in 8:1-10, and the two incidents in which Jesus welcomes and embraces children in Mark 9:35-37 and 10:13-16. Let us examine this last pair of episodes:

> He sat down, called the twelve, and said to them, "Whoever wants to be first must be last of all and servant of all." Then he took a little child and put it among them; and taking it in his arms, he said to them, "Whoever welcomes one such child in my name welcomes me, and whoever welcomes me welcomes not me but the one who sent me." (9:35-37)

> People were bringing little children to him in order that he might touch
> them; and the disciples spoke sternly to them. But when Jesus saw this, he
> was indignant and said to them, "Let the little children come to me; do not
> stop them; for it is to such as these that the kingdom of God belongs. Truly
> I tell you, whoever does not receive the kingdom of God as a little child will
> never enter it." And he took them up in his arms, laid his hands on them,
> and blessed them. (10:13-16)

The story content of these two episodes is so similar that the temptation
is to concentrate on that. The reader-response critic will resist that temptation, however, by concentrating on the reader's encounter with the storyteller's discourse.

Unlike the verbal ironies we examined in the passion narrative, no
explicit signals here indicate that anyone is saying something that he does
not really mean. Dramatic irony is typically more subtle than that, and consequently the business of reconstruction is less straightforward. At the level of
the story, the reader easily grasps Jesus' consistent attitude toward children.
Just as clear to the reader is the disciples' persistent and stubborn rejection
of Jesus' example. Here we begin to detect an ironic tension between what is
happening in the story and what we understand about the story thanks to the
narrator's discourse.

The introduction to the first of the two episodes is already unflattering to
the Twelve: they had been discussing among themselves "who was the greatest" (9:34). Such egotism is unlikely to impress the reader favorably, especially
since the reader realizes that the disciples were debating their own great-
ness at the same time that Jesus was trying to instruct them about his own
impending death (9:31). Jesus has death on his mind; the disciples, their own
glory. In that setting Jesus embraces the child as a lesson to the self-centered
disciples that instead of seeking to be great, they should seek to be "last of all
and servant of all" (9:35). Accepting someone as insignificant as a child is like
accepting God himself (9:37). Still, in this first of the two episodes, we may be
willing to give the disciples the benefit of the doubt—perhaps they will learn
their lesson. However, the reader has been instructed that the disciples stand
apart from Jesus in their attitude toward children. Will they do better when a
second opportunity arises?

They do not. The second episode jumps immediately into the issue of
receiving or not receiving children. The disciples want to turn children away.
This makes Jesus angry (10:13-14). He insists, again, that children must be
embraced—the kingdom of God belongs to them (10:14)!

The obtuseness of the disciples is quite remarkable. If we were so inclined,
we could forever offer psychological explanations for the disciples' insensitivity in the story. More important to the reader-response critic, however, is the
observation of how our response to the two episodes is shaped by the way the
storyteller narrates them to us. What allows us to recognize and reconstruct

dramatic irony here? Two observations are key. First, the disciples' obtuseness and self-centeredness is already firmly established for the reader even before the first child-embracing scene unfolds. The alert reader may already be prepared to encounter insensitivity on the part of the Twelve in the first of the two scenes, to say nothing of the second. The second key is that when Jesus repeats his warm embrace of children and the disciples are, if anything, more insensitive than ever, the reader is struck by the insight that the Twelve have learned nothing from their previous encounter with a child. The reader experiences an ironic incongruity between the logical expectation that the Twelve would learn from their past mistakes and the reader's observation that they do not in fact learn a thing. The reconstruction metaphor does not work well here; although the reader may perceive and comprehend this ironic incongruity, the incongruity is not resolved or "reconstructed." Rather, the ironic tension continues to haunt the reader. That the disciples have learned nothing from their experience is solidly established. But, the average reader may ask, "Why have they learned nothing?" And, "What is it that they should have learned?" The expert reader may go a step further and ask, "If the disciples have learned nothing, what has allowed *us* to learn a great deal?" And, "Have we learned all that we should?" A reader-response critic goes still further and observes that average and expert readers alike are dealing with a narrative whose fabric is woven with powerful ironic tensions. All readers of this narrative must work their way through ironic tensions between the story and the discourse. All readers of this narrative are regularly challenged to reconstruct irony, to the extent possible.

Besides describing the reader's encounter with irony, the reconstruction metaphor also helpfully describes many other reading experiences. Whenever the reader has to deal with incongruity or with aspects of the story or the discourse that cannot be accepted at face value, the reconstruction metaphor may help us to describe the experience of dismantling a portion of the narrative in order to reconstruct it on a firmer footing.

THE SELF-CONSUMING ARTIFACT

Our next metaphor for the reading experience comes from one of the classic works of reader-response criticism, Stanley Fish's *Self-Consuming Artifacts*.[20] The title of the book is self-explanatory. Fish is concerned with stories that seem to say something but then take it back, or that do something to us and then undo it, in the course of the reading experience. In fact, Fish does not limit himself to a single metaphor: the text that consumes itself as we read it. Instead, he employs a whole family of similar metaphors. The "self-consuming artifact," he says, is a text that "self-destructs," "self-subverts," "inverts," "undermines," "unbuilds," "reverses," "disappoints," "frustrates," "unsettles," "breaks down," "self-cannibalizes," and so forth.[21] To add my own figures to the collection, some texts operate like a knitting machine that knits but at the same time unravels what it has knitted. When you get to the end of the reading experience, although a lot of knitting has taken place, you may not have a sweater, just loose piles of yarn. Or, the self-consuming literary artifact is like a railroad locomotive and crew who tear up the track behind the locomotive in order to re-lay the track in front so that the locomotive can continue to roll forward. As we read, we often cover ground that we can never revisit, because continuing to read requires that we leave those places behind us, sometimes forever.

Mark's narrative seldom unravels itself to the degree that Fish likes to find in seventeenth-century European literature, but at times it comes close. The examples from Mark that I wish to examine all involve surprising revelations to the reader about aspects of story or discourse that the reader could not have anticipated. The first, Mark 10:17-22, is an episode traditionally labeled the story of "the rich man"—an unfortunate label, as we shall see. At the beginning of this episode, a man approaches Jesus and asks what he must do "to inherit eternal life." We know nothing about the man, so most readers will be inclined to hear him out. The question he asks is significant, and we have no reason to suppose that he is not a sincere seeker. Besides, would we not like to hear for ourselves Jesus' answer to this weighty question? Jesus responds by quizzing the man about his observance of several of the Ten Commandments. The man replies that he has faithfully kept them all. The episode hurries toward its resolution, as Jesus replies: "You lack one thing; go, sell what you own, and give the money to the poor, and you will have treasure in heaven; then come, follow me." Presumably, Jesus' demanding prescription strikes at the heart of the man's question. We cannot imagine how Jesus' words are relevant, however, until we hear the final comment by the storyteller: "When he heard this, he was shocked and went away grieving, *for he had many possessions.*" Only now do we grasp what stands between the man and eternal life: his many possessions. He is a rich man, something we had not known until the last two words of the episode. The story sets us up, encouraging us to think favorably of the man, only to pull the rug out from under us at the end. The traditional title given to the episode is unfortunate because it tips off readers to the punch line, thereby robbing it of its punch. This self-consuming narrative artifact has lost much of its power for generations of readers because everyone knows, or thinks he knows, what the lesson of the story is before ever reading it.

Let us turn to another moment of surprise and reversal in reading, one that still packs considerable punch after all these years. In Mark 14:32-42 Jesus and his disciples visit Gethsemane, where Jesus prays an anguished prayer in anticipation of his death. In 14:34 Jesus tells the disciples how deeply grieved he is by the prospect of death, and he charges them to keep watch while he prays. Next, in 14:35-36 he moves on a little farther, where he prays this prayer: "Abba, Father, for you all things are possible; remove this cup from me; yet, not what I want, but what you want." He returns to the disciples and finds them sleeping (14:37)! Then he issues his famous rebuke of the slumbering disciples ("the spirit is willing, but the flesh is weak"). If the story were not so horrific, it would be slapstick comedy that Jesus pours out his soul to God three times, and then comes and finds the disciples sleeping each time.

The pivotal moment of surprise and reversal in the reading of this passage is the moment when Jesus first returns to find the disciples sleeping (14:37). When Jesus goes on just "a little farther" and prays his prayer, the reader accompanies him, so to speak, and we are allowed to watch Jesus pray and to hear his prayer. We may be too preoccupied with watching and listening to think much about it, but if we were to think about the disciples at that moment, we might just assume that they are watching and listening along with us. However, when we return with Jesus to find the disciples sleeping, we are shocked, just as he is shocked. He assumed they were watching and hearing him. We assumed they were watching and hearing him along with us. Both he and we are surprised and disappointed. The disciples have failed Jesus, but they have also failed us. No one in the story stayed awake and heard the prayer. The only faithful, wide-awake witness to Jesus' prayer is the reader. Only the reader of the storyteller's discourse has fulfilled the role of the faithful follower. The master storyteller craftily knits us into the fabric of his narrative at the same time that he unravels the disciples' role inside the story. Furthermore, he successfully keeps us from recognizing what he is doing until after he has done it, much to our surprise.

The last example we shall examine not only is a good example of a self-consuming artifact—it, too, offers surprise by means of reversal—but also demonstrates other interesting reading experiences, including an encounter with a gap and a challenge to reconstruct irony.

In discussing gaps I already mentioned Mark 4:10-13. I observed that 4:11 reveals a gap in the discourse of the Gospel. There Jesus says that his followers have "been given the secret of the kingdom of God," but the giving of that secret was never narrated. Presumably, the giving of this secret happened in the story, but nevertheless it was omitted from the discourse. However, that is just the beginning of the dance steps this passage puts the reader through. Let us see what happens when we continue to read.

To add further insult to the exclusion of the reader from the secret of the kingdom, 4:11 goes on to state that "for those outside everything is in parables." Apparently, the secret of the kingdom is reserved for insiders only; to outsiders, such as the reader, it is a mysterious puzzle or riddle.[22] A curtain seems to separate the reader from Jesus and his disciples: they are on the privileged side, while we stand on the other side, wondering what we are missing. Lest we despair, however, we need to read on.

Just a few steps down the road, a double reversal springs forth. In 4:13 Jesus turns to the "insiders" of 4:11 and asks them: "Do *you* not under-

stand this parable? How then will you understand all the parables?"[23] The
tables are turned; roles are reversed. The disciples, the insiders of 4:11, are
now revealed to be outsiders, those for whom the parables are riddles. The
reader of the Gospel, the outsider of 4:11, now understands that the disciples do not understand. This insight is not much, but it is enough to make
the reader a modest insider. No longer do we stand on one side of the curtain, wondering what is happening on the other side. Now we realize that
those on the privileged side did not understand what was being given to
them, and they have no advantage over us. Indeed, that we understand at
least this much gives us an advantage over them. The insiders of 4:11 are
revealed in 4:13 to be outsiders; the outsiders of 4:11 discover themselves
in 4:13 to be insiders.

This double reversal in 4:13 encourages us to look back over the preceding verses to reconsider and reevaluate what we have just read. Once we hear
Jesus' sharp rebuke of the disciples in 4:13, we may want to reevaluate his
comment to them back in 4:11 that they are the recipients of the secret of the
kingdom of God. In retrospect, in 4:11 could Jesus have been speaking with
tongue in cheek? Could he have been speaking a verbal irony? His words
might not have sounded ironic when we were at 4:11, but viewed in hindsight
from 4:13, they may have changed in tone.

Our suspicion that 4:11 is ironic may be strengthened as we grapple with a
verse we have avoided so far, the notoriously difficult verse in 4:12. This verse
says that Jesus teaches in parables "so that in seeing, they may see and not
perceive, and in hearing, they may hear and not understand, lest they should
turn and be forgiven."[24] In other words, Jesus uses parables with the express
purpose of keeping people from understanding them. Otherwise they would
turn their lives around and receive forgiveness, and we would not want that,
would we? Of course we would! If taken literally, this is the logic of 4:12, and
it strikes us as absurd. (Thus step 1 in the process of reconstructing irony is
invoked: the literal meaning of 4:12 is nonsense.) But maybe we should not
take it literally (step 3—surely both Mark and his protagonist Jesus want to
have an impact on their respective audiences, so that they will turn their
lives around; see Mark 1:1 and 1:15). Could Jesus be speaking with tongue in
cheek throughout 4:11-12, teasing his disciples (step 2)? Then in 4:13 he gets
serious and levels a severe rebuke at the supposed insiders of 4:11. The result
is an experience of dramatic irony in 4:13, when the reader realizes that the
apparent roles of 4:11 have been reversed (step 4—Mark loves to construct
powerful moments of dramatic irony, and this is one of them).

Altogether in 4:10-13 we experience a gap in the discourse in 4:11, a
strong possibility of verbal irony in 4:11-12, and an experience of a self-
consuming artifact in 4:13. Becoming aware of the double reversal in 4:13
requires looking back to reconstruct what was happening in 4:11-12, and
the result is a powerful moment of dramatic irony. All of the figures for
reading that we have discussed thus far—looking forward, looking back;

gaps; reconstruction; the self-consuming artifact—can be used to help us to understand what happens when we read Mark 4:10-13.

THE RESISTING READER

Our last metaphor for the reading experience is "the resisting reader." This metaphor comes from Judith Fetterley's book by this title, a classic work of feminist reader-response criticism.[25]

Fetterley's specialty is the study of American fiction, which she claims is thoroughly androcentric (male oriented and dominated). The masculine perspective is so pervasive in American literature, and among the teachers of American literature, that women as well as men are indoctrinated "to identify as male" as they read:

> The cultural reality is not the emasculation of men by women but the
> *immasculation* of women by men. As readers and teachers and scholars,
> women are taught to think as men, to identify with a male point of view,
> and to accept as normal and legitimate a male system of values, one of
> whose central principles is misogyny.[26]

Fetterley exposes the sexism and misogyny in standard works of American fiction by male authors such as Nathaniel Hawthorne, Henry James, William Faulkner, Ernest Hemingway, F. Scott Fitzgerald, and Norman Mailer. The female characters in these novels and short stories are routinely victimized by men, often without raising the eyebrows of the male characters in the story. Presumably, the reader is also expected not to raise his (or her?) eyebrows. Such is woman's inevitable (and deserved?) fate, the stories seem to imply. In several stories a female character dies, requiring a male character to suffer nobly *his* loss. If a female reader is not careful, she can easily absorb from these texts and perpetuate the very misogynist attitudes that would rob her of "nothing less than sanity and survival."[27]

Accordingly, Fetterley conceives of her book "as a self-defense survival manual for the woman reader lost in 'the masculine wilderness of the American novel.'"[28] Once the sexism and misogyny of American literature and the American educational system are recognized, a woman can learn to read without giving automatic assent to the sexist indignities of these texts, which the educational system insists she must read. Rather than granting unthinking assent to the text, a woman can become a resisting reader:

> The first act of the feminist critic must be to become a resisting rather than
> assenting reader and, by this refusal to assent, to begin the process of exor-
> cising the male mind that has been implanted in us. The consequence of this
> exorcism is the capacity for what Adrienne Rich describes as re-vision—"the

act of looking back, of seeing with fresh eyes, of entering an old text from a
new critical direction."[29]

Notice how the metaphor of "resisting reading" mutates into the metaphor of "re-vision," which returns us to "looking back," the first metaphor
for reading discussed in this chapter. Resisting reading is practiced not
only by feminist readers as a defensive strategy in the face of misogyny. It
can also be practiced by any reader who finds that resistance, rather than
assent, is the responsible, conscientious course of action in a threatening
situation.

That the Bible itself is full of examples of resisting or re-visionary reading is immensely important. The Israelites would still be in Egypt and the
Exodus would never have happened if they had not resisted the enslaving
words of Pharaoh rather than giving them assent. Christianity would never
have been born if the Jewish followers of the Jewish Jesus had not found in
him good reason to re-vision their Jewish legacy in the light of the gospel.
Today, both Jews and Christians, both women and men, are awakening to
the age-old history of sexism and misogyny, which permeates the Bible and
the religions that revere the Bible. Jews and Christians, women and men,
are only now learning to read the Bible resistantly with regard to what it has
to say about gender roles. At the same time, however, they are also learning
to read resistantly what it seems to say regarding a number of contemporary life-and-death issues, such as war, racism, ethnic and religious strife, the
environment, and economic justice.

Persons professing biblical faith need not be fearful that resisting reading
of the Bible is somehow unfaithful reading. To the contrary, one could argue
that the most faithful reading of all is resisting reading. Some of the noblest
moments in Jewish and Christian history are moments of resistance to offi-
cially approved oppression, injustice, or traditions gone sterile. Therefore,
not only feminist literary critics practice resisting reading. It has been and
will always be practiced by all kinds of people struggling for dignity, justice,
or new relevance for their old traditions.

I want to turn to one passage in Mark where resisting reading can be
practiced at several levels. What follows is not a feminist reading, but I shall
point out some possibilities for a feminist reading of this passage. Also, my
example will not address directly the issues of justice and dignity, but a reader
could easily lead it in that direction, if so inclined. Again, I shall only illustrate briefly the exercise of the metaphor. It is up to you to put it to further
good use.

The passage I want to consider is Mark 16:1-8, the last episode of Mark's
Gospel, the discovery of Jesus' empty tomb.[30] Actually, Mark 16:1-8 was
already read resistantly long ago by the author of the Gospel of Matthew, and
I would like to make the focus of our own reading Matthew's resisting reading of the ending of Mark (Matt 27:62—28:20).

The majority of biblical scholars believe that Matthew composed his Gospel by editing the Gospel of Mark. I share that presumption, but with a crucial difference in language. Rather than talking about Matthew as an editor of Mark, I like to describe him as one of the first known readers of Mark. Matthew's Gospel is a record of Matthew's response to his experience of reading Mark's Gospel. Although Matthew often reads Mark with assent to what Mark is trying to do, frequently Matthew is a resisting reader of Mark.

Resisting reading is adversarial reading. It is reading against the grain of the text. It is reading in conflict with other possible readings of the text. Matthew and Mark are in competition with each other, each of them striving to control how you and I read the story of the empty tomb. Matthew's resisting reading of Mark's empty tomb story has been so successful that we tend to read Matthew's version of the story back into Mark's version. That is, in order to read Mark's empty tomb story, we have to resist the urge to read Matthew's story instead. *We have to read resistantly Matthew's resisting reading of Mark.* Unless we read against the grain of Matthew's Gospel, we cannot really read Mark's Gospel at all, either with or against the grain.

Let us consider some of the features of Matthew's resisting reading of Mark 16:1-8:

- *The guard at the tomb.* In Matthew, a guard is set at the tomb, supposedly to prevent Jesus' disciples from stealing his corpse and dishonestly proclaiming him resurrected from the dead. In Mark, there is no guard. Nothing in Mark's story safeguards against someone telling a rival story about the corpse being stolen.

  Matthew expertly deploys his guard story, placing one piece before Mark's empty tomb story (Matt 27:62-66), one piece in the middle (Matt 28:4), and one piece afterward (Matt 28:11-15). Matthew's *story* of the guard surrounds Mark's empty tomb *story* to resist the illegitimate *story* of the disciples' theft of the dead body, to which Mark's *story* is vulnerable.

- *The women who come to the tomb.* In Matthew, two women, Mary Magdalene and "the other Mary," come to the tomb merely to see it. They succeed. In Mark, three women, Mary Magdalene, Salome, and "Mary the mother of James," come with spices to anoint the body. They gain entrance to the tomb, but they fail to anoint the body.

  In Matthew, the identity of "the other Mary" is unclear. By contrast, "Mary the mother of James" in Mark 16:1 is well known. She is also described as "Mary, the mother of Joses" in Mark 15:47 and as "Mary, the mother of James the younger and of Joses" in Mark 15:40. Because the Gospel has already introduced to us a woman named Mary who has sons named James and Joses (Mark 6:3), it makes sense to conclude that these are all references to the same woman.[31]

This conclusion, however, yields some surprises. The Mary introduced in Mark 6:3, along with her sons James and Joses, is none other than Jesus' own mother. Why does Mark refuse to call her "Mary, the mother of Jesus"?[32] Rather than clarifying who she is, why does Matthew hide her identify completely? Is Matthew posting another guard, this time around the reputation of Jesus' mother and his brothers?

Not only does Matthew mask Mary's identity but also he erases any mention of the women's intention of anointing the body. In Mark, the mention of an anointing may strike us as a dramatic irony. The reader has already heard that an anonymous woman anointed Jesus for his burial (Mark 14:8). When three named (prominent? important?) women come to the tomb to anoint the body, the thoughtful reader may suspect that they are doomed to failure because what they intend to do has already been done. By hiding Mary's identity and by changing the women's purpose from anointing to merely viewing the tomb, Matthew resists several negative implications about the women in Mark 16:1-8.

- *Rolling the stone away from the tomb.* In Matthew, because the women have no need to go inside the tomb, they do not need to have the stone rolled away for them. Nevertheless, the stone is rolled away, before their very eyes (and before the reader's eyes), by an angel from heaven. In Mark, although the women need to gain entry to the tomb, and although they have the foresight to buy spices (before sunrise!), they talk to themselves (and to the reader) about their lack of foresight in recruiting someone to roll the large stone away from the tomb. In spite of their incomplete preparations, they go to the tomb anyway and find the stone already rolled away (Mark 16:3-4).

  Preserving the rolled-away stone is Matthew's one nod of assent to Mark 16:2-5 (Matt 28:2). Otherwise, Matthew so freely adds and subtracts that Mark's story is completely re-visioned. Among the material Matthew subtracts is the question posed by the women in Mark: "Who will roll away the stone for us from the door of the tomb?" (Mark 16:3). This question is an ironic reminder to the reader that Jesus had four brothers (Mark 6:3) who could have helped their mother with funeral observances for their dead brother. He also had twelve male disciples who all said they would never forsake him (14:31). The question by the women in Mark 16:3 accentuates the absence of men who might have accompanied the women in paying their last respects. Are we to contrast the faithlessness of the men with the faithfulness of these three women? Is this a place where a feminist reading of Mark can produce interesting results? We will return to this question later.

  In Mark, the women find the stone already removed. Who removed it, when, how, and why is a mystery. Matthew adds to Mark's material and explodes Mark's mysteries by describing an earthquake and an angel descending from heaven (Matt 28:2-4). Matthew resists Mark's ambiguity and replaces it with a blindingly clear revelation of divine power.

- *The angel.* In Matthew, because "an angel of the Lord" rolls away the stone before our eyes, we have no doubt about when, how, and by whom the stone was removed. (However, the answer to the why question remains unclear.) After flexing its heavenly muscles, the angel sits on the stone, outside the tomb (Matt 28:2). In Mark, there is no "angel." Rather, a mysterious "young man" (*neaniskos* in Greek) is discovered by the women sitting inside the tomb (Mark 16:5).

  In the long history of reading Mark's Gospel, the puzzle of the young man in the empty tomb has been much debated. Frequently, this puzzle is linked to the even more bizarre puzzle of the young man running naked through Gethsemane (14:51-52). Because the word *neaniskos* is used in Mark only in 14:51 and 16:5, and because both young men seem to be distinguished primarily by what they wear or do not wear, one option is to conclude that the two young men are in fact one and the same young man. Even with this much decided, many questions remain. Who is he and what is he about? What could it mean that he is unclothed in 14:52 and resplendently clothed in 16:5?[33] Both *neaniskos* puzzles in Mark remain a mystery.

  And both puzzles are neatly solved by Matthew. The young man of Mark 16:5 is turned into an angel descending from heaven, and the young man of Mark 14:51-52 is completely erased from Matthew's narrative. The ambiguity and mystery associated with both young men in Mark are resisted and resolved in Matthew.

- *The women's report.* In Matthew, the angel instructs the women to go tell the disciples that Jesus has been raised from the dead. "With fear and great joy" (Matt 28:8), they run to fulfill this charge. In Matthew, joy overcomes fear. In Mark, the young man gives similar instructions, but the women run away in "terror and amazement" and say "nothing to anyone, for they were afraid" (16:8). In Mark, fear paralyzes the women into silence. Matthew resists the fear and the silence with which Mark's Gospel ends and re-visions it as joy that must be proclaimed (Matt 28:7, 10, 19-20).

- *Encounters with the risen Jesus.* In Matthew, as the women run to report to the disciples, they encounter the resurrected Jesus himself (Matt 28:9-10). He greets them and repeats the instructions of the angel to tell the disciples. Matthew's Gospel then ends with the famous Great Commission to "make disciples of all nations," a mountaintop encounter between the resurrected Jesus and his rehabilitated disciples (Matt

28:16-20). In Mark, no one encounters the risen Jesus. The mysterious young man says that Jesus has been raised up, but no one in the story experiences it personally. Mark's Gospel ends with no one in the story either witnessing the resurrection of Jesus or reporting it.

Matthew must have been extraordinarily dissatisfied with the way Mark's Gospel ends. In Matthew's resisting reading of the ending of Mark, ironies that cast a doubtful light on the mother, the brothers, and the disciples of Jesus are erased. Puzzles are either resolved or eliminated. Fear is swallowed up by joy, and silence is overcome by proclamation. The absence of Jesus, as well as that of the disciples, is replaced by the glorious appearance of Jesus and a fantastic mountaintop reunion with the disciples. Finally, the mystery of the empty tomb and the ambiguity of the young man are thoroughly clarified with bright beams of heavenly glory.

We could go on and on discussing Matthew's resisting reading of Mark 16:1-8, but this much must suffice. Mark's Gospel is comfortable with offering its reader an abundance of irony, ambiguity, and mystery. Matthew's Gospel is not. Therefore, Matthew's reading of Mark is typically a resisting reading, a reading against the grain of Mark's Gospel. Mark's narrative seems designed to intrigue and perplex the reader. Matthew wants to instruct us, openly and clearly. Matthew likes to tell us what to think; Mark wants us to learn to think for ourselves. Mark can live with the possibility that his narrative might be misunderstood and misappropriated—witness his unguarded and ambiguous empty tomb story, vulnerable to many conflicting interpretations. By contrast, Matthew wants to guard against misunderstanding and misappropriation—witness his carefully guarded tomb story. Given Mark's Gospel, one can easily imagine someone like Matthew coming along to clarify and to straighten out Mark's mysteries; given Matthew's Gospel, it is hard to imagine how someone like Mark could hope to interest anyone in giving up Matthew's clarity in favor of Mark's mysteries. Matthew's Gospel is well designed to outshine Mark's Gospel, which it has done throughout the history of the reading of both Gospels.

Matthew and Mark are not merely different narratives; they are narratives in conflict with each other. Mark 16:1-8 and Matt 27:62—28:20 are competing versions of the same story, all tangled up in each other like a bad knot in a pair of shoelaces. If we wish to read either Gospel apart from the other, first we must untangle them. Most readers unconsciously read the Gospels of Matthew and Mark (along with Luke and John) in their native tangled state, and the clarity and directness of Matthew are typically more appreciated by the average reader than the mystery and ambiguity of Mark. If you want to read Mark, however, you have to resist Matthew's resisting reading of Mark.

If we can read Matthew resistantly, then we can decide whether to read Mark with assent or with resistance. I am not going to attempt a resisting

reading of Mark 16:1-8 here, but one way it might be done is through a feminist reading. I shall point out how this might be done and leave my reader to
explore further the possibilities.

A common feminist reading of Mark 16:1-8 argues that the three women
are worthy models of Christian discipleship. By witnessing the crucifixion
and burial of Jesus and then by visiting the empty tomb, they have succeeded
where the male disciples in the story have all failed.[34] From a feminist perspective, this reading has several attractions. First, it resists and shatters the
dominant assumption throughout two thousand years of Christian experience that the chief witnesses to the resurrection of Jesus were men. Second,
it uncovers a crucial, prestigious role for women in the early church. Third, it
thereby provides encouragement to women today to assume significant roles
in the Christian church.

However, as I indicated before, there are severe problems with this reading of Mark 16:1-8.[35] To read Mark 16:1-8 as a story of the success of the
three women is an unconscious reading of the ending of Matthew back into
Mark. Therefore, it is not a resisting reading at all, but an assenting reading of
Matthew masquerading as a reading of Mark. Matthew grants the women a
positive role in witnessing the resurrection and reporting to the disciples, but
it is a minor role, entirely subservient to the major role of the male disciples,
who are the only ones to appear in Matthew's Great Commission scene (Matt
28:16-20). Because the brothers of Jesus and the twelve disciples are utterly
absent at the end of Mark, the minor success of the women in Matthew can
appear a major success when it is imported into Mark. However, this success
is only an illusion, the result of reading Mark the way Matthew would have
us read it.

If we can resist Matthew's resisting reading of Mark, we can recognize
that the three women in Mark 16:1-8 fail, just as so many others in the story
have failed before them. All is not doom and gloom at the end of Mark, however. Many biblical critics are now recognizing that the ending of Mark, just
like the rest of the Gospel, is mostly concerned to make an impact on the
reader.[36] Mark's Gospel may end without insight and faith among the characters in the story, but that does not mean that the audience of the Gospel has
not been well instructed and deeply moved by the experience of reading the
Gospel. The key to understanding the ending of Mark is not to understand
the women or men in the story, but to understand what is happening in the
women or men reading the story.

Maybe a resisting, feminist reading of Mark 16:1-8 could be constructed,
but it would have to take another shape. Readers recognize today that Mark's
Gospel contains some remarkably positive images of women, such as the
woman with a flow of blood in Mark 5:25-34, the Syrophoenician woman in
Mark 7:24-30, and the woman who anointed Jesus in Mark 14:3-9. Mary Ann
Tolbert takes care to observe that the women just mentioned are all anonymous. By contrast, the three women who come to the tomb are all named,

as if they were prominent and well-known persons, as indeed Jesus' mother surely was. Tolbert suggests that the conspicuous naming of the women at the tomb may be an attempt to criticize "the human desire for fame, glory, status, and authority."[37] Speaking of names, the brothers and disciples of Jesus, whose absence is underlined by the women's question in Mark 16:3, are all prominently named in the course of Mark's narration (Mark 3:16-19; 6:3). What might Mark be suggesting to the reader by leaving unnamed most of the minor but successful women and men characters in the story, while prominently naming major women and men characters who fail?[38] Gender roles may indeed be significant in Mark, but gender in Mark (or anywhere) is always tangled with other weighty issues, such as psychology, race, class, ethics, and politics. Any and all of these issues may need to be considered in a feminist reading of Mark. Furthermore, even the brief introduction to reader-response criticism provided by this chapter is enough to teach us that a feminist reading of Mark 16:1-8 might have to look back and re-vision preceding episodes involving (or not involving) other women (or men) characters, negotiate the gaps in 16:1-8, reconstruct the ironies there, and be open to the possibility that in the end the Gospel of Mark may unravel itself, just as it has so many times before. Reading the ending of Mark resistantly may mean resisting our own desire for neat and simple solutions to the puzzles it presents to us or that we present to it.

The tangled endings of Mark and Matthew illustrate the lesson that the Bible itself is full of adversarial, against-the-grain, resisting reading. Printed side by side in our Bibles, the Gospels appear to be cozy bedfellows, comfortably snoozing in the same bed. Appearances, however, can be deceiving. The Gospels are far more in competition with each other than is commonly suspected. They may share the same bed but, like rambunctious siblings, they tussle over who gets the covers. Self-conscious, self-critical, and honest reading of the Gospels requires us to recognize this conflict and to be willing to jump into the fray ourselves. Moreover, what is true of reading the Gospels is true of the Bible generally: To read the Bible is to participate in a rich, long legacy of resisting reading.

CONCLUSION

Reader-response criticism is a critical practice that helps readers read with greater awareness and self-consciousness. As we become more aware of what we are doing as we read (looking forward, looking back, filling gaps, and so on), we become more aware of our response to our reading experience. Our reading and our response to reading become more thoughtful, more considered, which can lead us to take greater personal responsibility for our reading and our response. Particularly if we practice resisting reading, we can become more self-conscious about our acts of assent and our acts of resistance. Our commitments may deepen and be strengthened. Then again, our commitments may change altogether, if we are wise enough to practice resisting reading on ourselves or if we are lucky enough to have friends who challenge us to change.

Reading and responding to our reading is not optional. The question is, "Do we read with more or less self-consciousness?" "Do we respond with more or less awareness and sensitivity?" Assenting and resisting are not optional. The question is, "To what shall we give our assent?" "What shall we resist?" Reader-response criticism can help us to answer these important questions.

FURTHER READING

Bolt, Peter G. *Jesus' Defeat of Death: Persuading Mark's Early Readers.* Society for New Testament Studies Monograph Series 125. Cambridge: Cambridge University Press, 2003. A study of how Greco-Roman readers would have responded to Mark's healing and exorcism stories.

Booth, Wayne C. *A Rhetoric of Irony.* Chicago: University of Chicago Press, 1974. Classic work on the reader's encounter with irony.

———. *The Rhetoric of Fiction.* 2d ed. Chicago: University of Chicago Press, 1983. Booth's brand of rhetorical criticism is closely related to reader-response criticism and has greatly influenced biblical literary criticism.

Davies, Eryl W. *The Dissenting Reader: Feminist Approaches to the Hebrew Bible.* Aldershot: Ashgate, 2003. An exploration of the role of the resisting or dissenting reader of the Hebrew Bible.

Detweiler, Robert, ed. *Reader Response Approaches to Biblical and Secular Texts. Semeia* 31 (1985). Diverse collection of essays; addresses more biblical than secular texts.

Fetterley, Judith. "Reading about Reading: 'A Jury of Her Peers,' 'The Murders on the Rue Morgue,' and 'The Yellow Wallpaper.'" In *Gender and Reading: Essays on Readers, Texts, and Contexts.* Edited by Elizabeth A. Flynn and Patrocinio P. Schweickart, 147–64. Baltimore and London: Johns Hopkins University Press, 1986. Illuminating discussion of the differences between reading as a man and reading as a woman.

———. *The Resisting Reader: A Feminist Approach to American Fiction.* Bloomington and London: Indiana University Press, 1978. Influential work of feminist reader-response criticism; popularized the image of "resisting reading."

Fish, Stanley E. *Is There a Text in This Class? The Authority of Interpretive Communities.* Cambridge and London: Harvard University Press, 1980. Fish here shifts his focus of attention away from the interactions of text and reader to the influence of "interpretive communities" on how readers read.

———. "Literature in the Reader: Affective Stylistics." *New Literary History* 2 (1970): 123–62. Important discussion of the temporal experience of reading.

————. *Self-Consuming Artifacts: The Experience of Seventeenth-Century Litera-ture*. Berkeley, Los Angeles, and London: University of California Press, 1972. Essays exploring the reading experience alluded to in the title.

Flynn, Elizabeth A., and Patrocinio P. Schweickart, eds. *Gender and Reading: Essays on Readers, Texts, and Contexts*. Baltimore and London: Johns Hopkins University Press, 1986. Important collection of essays from a feminist reader-response perspective.

————. *Reading Sites: Social Difference and Reader Response*. New York: Modern Language Association of America, 2004. Attempts to problematize and enrich the more generic "reader constructs" characteristic of early reader-response criticism by introducing such factors as gender, race, and class.

Fowler, Robert M. *Loaves and Fishes: The Function of the Feeding Stories in the Gospel of Mark*. SBL Dissertation Series 54. Atlanta: Society of Biblical Literature, 2006 [reprint of 1981 edition]. Discusses the irony of the two feeding stories and other matched pairs of stories in Mark. The first explicit application of reader-response criticism to a biblical text.

————. *Let the Reader Understand: Reader-Response Criticism and the Gospel of Mark*. Harrisburg, Pa.: Trinity Press International, 2001 [reprint of 1991 edition]. Describes the major features of reader-response criticism and applies it to the experience of reading the Gospel of Mark.

Iser, Wolfgang. "The Reading Process: A Phenomenological Approach." *New Literary History* 3 (1972): 279–99. Classic discussion of the temporal experience of reading.

————. *The Implied Reader*. Baltimore and London: Johns Hopkins University Press, 1974. Popularized the term "implied reader" in literary criticism.

————. *The Act of Reading: A Theory of Aesthetic Response*. Baltimore and London: Johns Hopkins University Press, 1978. Theoretical discussion of the reading experience.

McKnight, Edgar V., ed. *Reader Perspectives on the New Testament*. Semeia 48 (1989). Essays on biblical texts emphasizing "the reader in the text."

Moore, Stephen D. "Stories of Reading: Doing Gospel Criticism as/with a Reader." Chapter 6 of *Literary Criticism and the Gospels: The Theoretical Challenge*. New Haven and London: Yale University Press, 1989. Excellent survey of the use of reader-response criticism in biblical criticism.

Powell, Mark Allan. *Chasing the Eastern Star: Adventures in Biblical Reader-Response Criticism*. Louisville: Westminster John Knox, 2001. Lively account of the practice of reader-response criticism in biblical studies.

Resseguie, James L. "Reader-Response Criticism and the Synoptic Gospels." *Journal of the American Academy of Religion* 52 (1984): 307–24. Brief discussion of reader-response criticism and an examination of several Gospel texts.

Schildgen, Brenda Deen. *Power and Prejudice: The Reception of the Gospel of Mark*. Detroit: Wayne State University Press, 1999. A survey of the almost two-thousand-year history of the reading of Mark's Gospel.

Suleiman, Susan, and Inge Crosman, eds. *The Reader in the Text: Essays on Audience and Interpretation*. Princeton: Princeton University Press, 1980. Along with the Tompkins volume, one of the two best anthologies available of essays on reader-response criticism. Good bibliography.

Tompkins, Jane P., ed. *Reader-Response Criticism: From Formalism to Post-Structuralism*. London and Baltimore: Johns Hopkins University Press, 1980. Important anthology of reader-response essays. The concluding essay by Tompkins helpfully situates reader-response criticism in the history of criticism. Good bibliography.

Van Iersel, Bas M. F. *Mark: A Reader-Response Commentary*. JSNTSup 164. Sheffield: Sheffield Academic Press, 1998. The fruit of a lifetime of study of the Gospel of Mark.

4

DECONSTRUCTIVE CRITICISM

Turning Mark Inside-Out

STEPHEN D. MOORE

WHAT IS DECONSTRUCTION? Article- or book-length answers to this question already run in their thousands across an astonishing array of fields—modern languages and comparative literature, mainly, but also philosophy, psychology, cultural studies, linguistics, anthropology, political theory, history, legal studies, art theory, architectural theory, film theory, even theology and biblical studies. A colossal body of introductions and applications perch precariously atop the shoulders of a relatively slight but extremely slippery body of "exemplary" deconstructive texts, those of the French philosopher Jacques Derrida (1930–2004) in particular.

Derrida published prolifically over a period of almost four decades. As one might expect, his thought evolved significantly during this period. It is, however, "early" Derrida whom this chapter is primarily designed to introduce. It would be impossible to survey the entire sweep of his thought in a single chapter; but there is another reason also for concentrating on the early work. Quite simply, it is the early work that remains Derrida's most influential.[1] And the most significant element of this early work, it seems to me, is its critique of the tendency, intrinsic to the Western philosophical and theological traditions, to think in terms of binary oppositions, of black-and-white or either/or categories, such as presence/absence, nature/culture, primary/secondary, or male/female. For purposes of this chapter, then, the complex field of deconstruction will be simplified and narrowed to its best-known expression: the dismantling[2] of the hierarchical binary oppositions that not only structure our philosophical and theological reflection, as we shall see, but also our everyday thought processes and hence our everyday world.

The successive stages of this chapter mirror the successive phases of deconstructive criticism, especially in the United States. Although modeled principally on the strategies of reading that Derrida had developed in his philosophical work, the first wave of deconstructive criticism occurred not in the field of philosophy but in that of literary studies. In the 1970s, American deconstruction was primarily preoccupied with the internal workings of literary texts, which is to say with the intricate workings of literary language. Beginning in earnest in the early 1980s, however, U.S. literary studies took a sweeping "political" turn. Legions of critics became intensely interested in the complex relations of literary texts to (other) social and cultural realities, such as gender and sexuality, race and ethnicity, and colonialism and postcolonialism. Deconstructive criticism, again drawing mainly on "early" Derrida, was discovered by many of these critics to be an immensely useful resource for that kind of reading as well. (The development even seems to have influenced Derrida himself. The last two decades of his career were marked by more explicit and sustained engagement with political and ethical issues.) Reflecting this two-stage appropriation of deconstruction, the present chapter will begin by exploring the internal world of Mark's narrative, and end by extrapolating from the workings of that world to reflect on Mark's complex relations to the history of Christian anti-Semitism.

ON THE INSIDE LOOKING IN

Notwithstanding its roots in philosophy, deconstruction is much less an exercise in abstract speculation than a flexible strategy of reading—hence its interest for literary critics and for us. Derrida always wrote best curled up inside some text or other. Rather than begin with an introduction to deconstruction in the abstract and only then turn to Mark, I prefer in this section to climb immediately into Mark and begin to read. I am confident that Mark, of all the Gospels, will carry us quickly into deconstructive territory. Specifically, I begin with a consideration of Mark's enigmatic use of the term "parable." Once we have taken initial stock of its peculiarities, we will pause to ponder some relevant facets of deconstructive theory before proceeding further with our reading.

Between the parable of the sower (4:3-9) and its interpretation (vv. 14-20) is Mark's so-called parable theory. Jesus' disciples quiz him concerning the parables, to which he responds: "To you has been given the *mystērion* [secret, mystery] of the kingdom of God, but for those outside everything is in parables; so that they may indeed see but not perceive, and may indeed hear but not understand; lest they should turn again, and be forgiven" (4:11-12). Contrasted as they are with "those outside" (*ekeinois . . . tois exō*; 4:11), Jesus' disciples must be insiders (cf. 3:31-35). And whereas outsiders are expected to see but not perceive, hear but not understand, insiders are, by implication, expected both to see and to perceive, to hear and to understand. But do they?

Mark's parables discourse ends on a reassuring note: "privately to his own disciples he explained everything" (4:34). Yet Mark's next episode, the calming of the storm, has Jesus rebuking his followers for their lack of faith (4:40). Later, following the first feeding miracle, we read that the disciples "did not understand about the loaves, but their hearts were hardened" (6:52; cf. 3:5). More damaging still is the third boat episode, which elicits the following outburst from Jesus: "Why do you discuss the fact that you have no bread? Do you not yet perceive or understand?" (8:17-18; cf. 7:18; 8:21). Already the disciples, far from modeling insider behavior, are meeting the definition of outsiders set forth in the "parable theory" of 4:11-12: they see but do not perceive, hear but do not understand.

Corresponding to these three scenes of incomprehension are the three misunderstandings that later follow Jesus' three predictions of his suffering and death (8:31; 9:31; 10:33-34). In response to the first prediction, Peter reproves Jesus and is sharply rebuked in turn: "Get behind me, Satan! For you are setting your mind not on divine things but on human things" (8:32-33). Following the second prediction, we learn that the disciples "did not understand the saying, and they were afraid to ask him" (9:32). Afterward they argue among themselves about which of them is the greatest (9:34). Following the third prediction, two of the disciples request seats of honor from Jesus, to which he replies: "You do not know what you are asking" (10:35 ff.). To all this must be added, as climactic scenes in this saga of failed discipleship, Judas's betrayal of Jesus (14:10-11), the other (male) disciples' desertion of him at his arrest (14:50; cf. 15:40-41), Peter's threefold denial of him (14:66-72), and the women disciples' confused flight from the tomb (16:8).

Right to the end of the Gospel, then, the insiders are on the inside looking in, as though they were in fact outside.[3] The secret of the kingdom has indeed been presented to them (4:11), but although they are poised before it they cannot penetrate it. Between seeing and perceiving, hearing and understanding, something intervenes, something that also keeps those whom the Gospel *explicitly* designates outsiders outside, something it calls *parable*: "for those outside everything is in parables." What distinguishes disciples from outsiders is that disciples long to be inside, to *be* the insiders they are said to be.

The obscurity of Jesus' parabolic words and deeds does not suffice to explain the abysmal depths of the disciples' ignorance. When Jesus begins "to teach them that the Son of Man must suffer many things, and be rejected. . .and be killed, and after three days rise again," thereby administering the fatal blow to their faltering understanding, the narrator adds: "And he said this plainly [*parrēsia*]" (8:31-32). It seems that the mystery of the kingdom can meet only with misunderstanding (at least for now), whether parabolic or plain speech be used to express it.

Indeed, all of Jesus' speech and all of his actions in Mark quickly reduce to "parable" once they become vehicles of this mystery. "For those outside everything is in parables"—but everything is equally in parables, it would seem, for those who have "been given the secret of the kingdom of God." Consequently and paradoxically, Jesus' innermost circle of followers in Mark is neither fully inside nor yet fully outside. Like the seed scattered by the sower, Jesus' parabolic speech falls ineffectually on rocky ground, unable to take root in the "hardened" hearts of the disciples. Precisely at this point, however, it begins to take root in certain of the seminal texts and themes of deconstruction. Let us turn aside briefly to examine these texts and themes, after which I shall return to Mark's Jesus and his oddly obtuse disciples.

According to Derrida, Western thought has always been built on binary oppositions: mind/body, nature/culture, presence/absence, primary/secondary, literal/metaphorical, history/fiction, object/representation, inside/outside, content/form, text/interpretation, and so on. The first term in each pair, as Derrida notes, is ordinarily assumed to be superior to the second and is elevated over it. All such hierarchical oppositions are founded on suppression, Derrida argues. The relationship between the two terms is traditionally one of subordination rather than equality.

One hierarchical opposition of particular interest to the "early" Derrida was that of speech versus writing. In the West, the spoken word has almost always been privileged over the written. But what could be more *natural* than to privilege speech? As I speak, my words appear to be one with my thoughts. My meaning appears to be fully present both to my hearer and myself. At such moments, the voice appears to be consciousness itself, presence itself: voice, presence, truth. In the West, speech has almost always been the model not only for every form of presence but also for every form of truth. All the names used to express theological or philosophical fundamentals have ordinarily been inseparable from the idea of presence: *God, being, essence, existence,* and so on—the list is very long. And the element of speech in turn (suitably idealized) has never been far from these fundamental presences. Look no further than orthodox Christian theology: God, the supreme *being,* brought the cosmos into *existence,* and subsequently redeemed it, through God's *Word,* Jesus Christ, who thereby revealed God's *essence* as love.[4]

Writing, in contrast, cut off at its source from the authorizing presence of a speaker, has, at least since the time of Plato, regularly been thought to threaten truth with distortion and mischief. As lifeless written marks in place of present living speech, writing has seemed to be an inferior, if necessary, substitute for speech. An orphan, no sooner born than set adrift, cut loose from the author who gives birth to it, writing seems fated to circulate endlessly, if not from foster home to foster home, then from reader to reader. And the reader can never be sure of properly grasping what the author intended to say. For authors have a way of being absent, even dead, and their intended meaning can no longer be directly intuited or double-checked through question and answer, as in the face-to-face situation of speech. Writing defaces speech.

Derrida's characteristic approach to any hierarchical binary opposition is to problematize—or, more precisely, deconstruct—the clean line customarily drawn between the two terms of the opposition. But to deconstruct a hierarchical opposition is not simply to counter-argue that the term traditionally repressed is in reality the superior term—to argue that writing, for example, extends speech immeasurably and enables infinitely more complex forms of culture to emerge (most recently electronic culture). For to invert an opposition, or stand it on its head, is ultimately to leave it intact and unharmed. The pair writing/speech, writing now reconceived as the superior term, is no less a hierarchical opposition than the pair speech/writing, and deconstruction is, among other things, an experiment in non-hierarchical and non-oppositional thinking.

Faced with a hierarchical binary opposition, therefore, deconstruction attempts instead to demonstrate that the membrane separating the two terms of the opposition is necessarily porous or permeable. Each of the two terms is always surreptitiously overflowing the boundaries assigned to it and leaking into its neighbor. Each term in the opposition is joined to its companion by an intricate network of arteries. In consequence, the line customarily drawn between the two terms is shown to be arbitrary and artificial. It is a cultural, ideological, or political reality but not a natural one. "Like Czechoslovakia and Poland," muses Derrida, "[they] resemble each other, regard each other, separated nonetheless by a frontier all the more mysterious . . . because it is abstract, legal, ideal."[5] But as such it can always be redrawn.

Derrida approaches the border between speech and writing, therefore, by asking, in effect: What if the border has already—or has always already—been crossed? What if the illegal alien were already within? What if speech were already the host of writing?[6] Let us extend the question to Mark: What if Jesus' speech in Mark were inhabited by writing? What if it were haunted, infected, afflicted by it?

Effective speech, as commonly understood, is marked by the presence to the hearer of the speaker's intended meaning. Writing, traditionally, is the errant medium with its meaning cut adrift from the consciousness of its producer. Mark's text perverts this "natural" relationship of speech to writing. Take, for example, Jesus' three passion predictions (8:31; 9:31; 10:33-34).

They can be regarded as some of Jesus' clearer statements in Mark as far as the reader—and the narrator (see 8:32a)—are concerned. They are impossibly obscure, however, as far as Jesus' immediate listeners are concerned. Between speech and hearing, something intrudes. Like a blade it severs the circle of understanding, the intimate circle of exchange ("looking around on those who sat around him in a circle . . . "; 3:34; cf. 4:10) within whose circumference Jesus' voice *should* circulate effortlessly, coupling with the ears of his disciples, breath to flesh and nothing between.

Sliced through, Jesus' speech is unable to reach its mark. It falls to the ground and is picked up wrongly. It is as if Jesus were *writing* instead of *speaking*, as if his disciples were *reading* instead of *listening*. The severing blade can only be re(a)d; it makes no sound. Silently it makes its cut, forcing Jesus to write without a pen. And the blade appears to be wielded by Jesus' own Father, who wills that the disciples' hearts should not yet be impregnated with understanding (cf. 6:52; 8:17-18).[7]

Should not Jesus himself be a father? Traditionally, the (male) speaker is father to his speech. Unlike written words, the spoken word is able to reach its target easily because it has a living father, a father who is present to it, who stands behind it, making sure that its aim is straight. Jesus cannot be such a father to his speech. The blade of his own Father has cut off that possibility, severing the "natural" bond that should exist between thought and voice, meaning and sound.

Jesus must write upon the dark field of his disciples' understanding, although not in luminous letters. Indeed, if the disciples' understanding is dark, it is due to the inky blackness of the letters it must soak up, blue-black letters that release no light. Not only does Jesus "write" in Mark, however; he is himself a species of writing—literally, because we know him only through the written letter. Jesus is a man of letters.

Like Jesus who drifts from misunderstanding to misunderstanding across the surface of Mark's page, writing has always been a wandering outcast, drifting from (mis)reading to (mis)reading. At least since the time of Plato, writing has also been read as an orphan or delinquent:

> Once a thing is put into writing, the composition . . . drifts all over the place, getting into the hands not only of those who understand it, but equally of those who have no business with it; it doesn't know how to address the right people, and not to address the wrong. And when it is ill-treated and unfairly abused it always needs its parents to come to its help.[8]

However, "the specificity of writing [is] intimately bound to the absence of the father," as Derrida observes.[9] The present writer is always absent. The orphaned word must circulate without its parent's protective presence, vulnerable to mishandling and misreading. Without its father, it is, in fact, "nothing but . . . writing."[10]

As letter, Mark's Jesus is "delivered into human hands" (9:31; cf. 10:33). As writing, he is penned to the cross, cut off from his Father ("My God, my God, why have you forsaken me?"; 15:34), and exposed to the casual violence of any reader who happens by ("Those who passed by derided him, shaking their heads and saying, 'Aha!'"; 15:29ff.). As writing, Jesus is crucified, stretched out on the wood, the rack, the reading frame. Mark's Jesus does violate the common law of writing by finally uniting with his Father. But even then his status remains more that of an inscription than of a spoken word (or *logos*), marked as it is by absence ("He has risen; he is not here"; 16:6) and exposure to the accidents of (mis)reading ("they said nothing to anyone, for they were afraid"; 16:8).

Mark's Jesus can therefore be read on the model of the written mark (and what is Jesus in Mark but a series of written marks, a marked man?). But Jesus' status in Mark prefigures Mark's own status. Mark's Jesus is a "writer," himself inscribed in a text, but so inscribed as to prefigure the fate of that text. Mark's own destiny as a writing is foreshadowed in the way it writes up the story of Jesus.

Mark is gradually folding back on itself as we read it. Not only is it a writing about Jesus but also it is a writing about writing. In addition, it is a writing about reading, a writing, which, as it retells the story of Jesus, also foretells the history of (mis)reading that the story will generate. But that is not all.

Reading writings *on* writing by the philosophers Plato and Jean-Jacques Rousseau and the modernist poet Stéphane Mallarmé, Derrida finds that the terms used by each writer to describe writing—*pharmakon* in Plato, *supplement* in Rousseau, *hymen* in Mallarmé—have a contradictory, double sense.[11] To take the simplest example, the Greek word *pharmakon* means *poison*, but it also means *cure*.

What of Mark? Mark is not explicitly about writing, of course, but a speech deeply marked with the traits of writing does figure in it, as we have seen. Interestingly, Mark himself has a term for such speech. He calls it *parabolē* (parable), a term whose peculiarities we must now examine even more closely. And in so doing we return, finally, to Mark's insider/outsider opposition.

Parabolai (parables) in Mark are a partition, screen, or membrane designed to keep insiders on one side, outsiders on the other. Outsiders are those for whom "everything comes in parables," parables that they find incomprehensible (4:11-12). At the same time, *parabolai* rupture that membrane, make it permeable, infect the opposition with contradiction: those who should be on the inside find themselves repeatedly put out by Jesus' parabolic words and deeds. Appointed to allow insiders in and to keep outsiders out, parables unexpectedly begin to threaten *everyone* with exclusion in Mark, even disciples seeking entry. Deranged doormen, parables threaten to make outsiders of us all.

In an early interview, Derrida remarked of the *pharmakon*, the *supplement*, and the *hymen*:

> It has been necessary to analyze, to set to work, *within* the text of the his-
> tory of philosophy, as well as *within* the so-called literary text. . . , certain
> marks . . . that . . . I have called undecidables, . . . that can no longer be
> included within philosophical (binary) opposition, but which, however,
> inhabit philosophical opposition, resisting and disorganizing it, *without
> ever* constituting a third term[12]

—that is to say, without ever neatly resolving the contradiction.

Like *pharmakon* and the other "undecidable marks" that Derrida lifts
from the texts he reads, Mark's *parabolē* refuses to be laid to rest within the
constricting framework of a classic binary opposition—here, that of inside
versus outside. *Parabolē* turns language inside out like a pocket, threatening to empty it of its content(s). *Parabolē* takes a voice that issues from the
intimacy of an inside, from the interiority of a speaker, and turns it into an
unincorporable exteriority. Jesus' voice *should* easily be able to leap the gap
separating it from the ear of the hearer. Too blunt to penetrate the ear, however, it cannot fit inside. "Let anyone with ears to hear listen!" cries Jesus (4:9;
cf. 4:23), but nobody has ears big enough.

Parabolē unsettles speech. It inhabits the oppositions of inside and outside, speech and writing. But it dwells there only to disrupt the order of the
house, rock the foundation in which these oppositions are embedded, and
shake the bed frames so as to keep the interpreters restlessly turning over.
Parabolē positions itself between opposing terms, apparently to pull them
apart, all the while sowing confusion between them.

Parabolē is vicious. It inflicts a grievous wound on common sense, and
takes care to leave it untended. As a cure for ignorance, it always turns out
to be a poison.

Just as there are insiders who are outsiders in Mark, are there also outsiders who are insiders? Jesus is identified as Son (of God), not only by God's
self (1:11; 9:7) and by the narrator (1:1), but also by the demons (3:11; 5:7; cf.
1:24, 34) and by the centurion at the foot of the cross (15:39). But although
the demons do have inside information on Jesus, they can hardly be said to
be insiders. Among the human characters, only the centurion—a Gentile,
an officer in the Roman army of occupation, and the specific officer, moreover, charged with crucifying Jesus, and hence a triple outsider—is permitted
to look inside ("Truly this man was a Son of God!"). The women disciples
do advance steadily toward the inside (15:40-41, 47; 16:1ff.)—until *parabolē*
leaps out to greet them from the interior of the tomb to drive them back
outside: "And they went out and fled from the tomb, for terror and amazement had seized them, and they said nothing to anyone, for they were afraid"
(16:8).

But what of that other woman, the anonymous one, who anoints Jesus
with expensive ointment and receives a prophetic accolade in exchange: "she

has anointed my body beforehand for burial. And truly I tell you, wherever the gospel is preached in the whole world, what she has done will be told in memory of her" (14:8-9)? Does Jesus' explanation of the significance of the anointing reflect the woman's own understanding of the action or is it solely his own? Because the narrator allows no speech to the woman, the answer to that question is ultimately unknowable. And even if Jesus *is* giving voice to the woman's own intentions in anointing him, she has come inside (both literally and metaphorically) only for the duration of this scene, after which she vanishes from sight despite her insight. In short, there are no insiders in Mark who are not at the same time outsiders.

The contradiction prevails until the end and beyond. Mark 16:7 does seem finally to promise the long-deferred establishment of the insiders *as* insiders: "he is going ahead of you to Galilee; there you will see him." But 16:8, the Markan nonending, parablelike in its demolition of conventional expectations,[13] threatens to leave the disciples stranded yet again in a liminal zone that is neither fully inside nor yet fully outside.

INSIDE THE WIRE: MARK AFTER AUSCHWITZ

Thus far we have brought deconstructive strategies of reading to bear on the "internal" world of Mark's narrative. How might these same strategies be harnessed for political or ethical reflection oriented to our contemporary world and Mark's place in relation to it?

Once again we will take as our point of departure the deconstruction of hierarchical binary oppositions. Recall that for Derrida, Western thought has almost always been built on such oppositions, one term in the pair being forcibly elevated over the other. The elevation of speech over writing and presence over absence were among those that intrigued the "early" Derrida. Yet all oppositions are not created equal. "Each pair operates with very different stakes in the world," as the deconstructive literary critic Barbara Johnson once remarked.[14] Johnson was writing at a time when many in her field had turned their attention to a specific series of binary oppositions neglected by the "early" Derrida, but equipped with critical sensibilities honed by reading Derrida. This series included the ubiquitous binaries of *gender*—male/female and masculine/feminine; of *sexuality*—heterosexual/homosexual; and of *race* or *ethnicity*—white/non-white (black, brown, yellow, red). "In a classical philosophical opposition," Derrida had observed, "we are not dealing with the peaceful coexistence of a vis-à-vis [or face-to-face relationship] but rather with a violent hierarchy. One of the two terms governs the other . . . or has the upper hand."[15] But what was the case with philosophical oppositions was even more the case with gender, sexual, and racial/ethnic oppositions. The same strategies used to deconstruct the former set of binaries, therefore, could also be used to deconstruct the latter set.

How might we apply these insights to Mark? The hierarchical oppositions male/female and masculine/feminine are, of course, much in evidence in Mark. They might well be the objects of a deconstructive reading that would complement the many feminist readings of Mark that have been produced, such as that of Janice Capel Anderson in the present volume.[16] It is, however, the central ethnic opposition in Mark that I propose to tackle instead, that of Gentile/Jew. This opposition exists, as we shall see, in a symbiotic relationship with a second opposition, that of Christian/Jew, as well as with the insider/outsider opposition that we have already examined in some detail. And the most promising place to begin is near the end with the centurion's "confession," as it is commonly called, at the foot of the cross (Mark 15:39).

"Truly this man was a Son of God!" exclaims the Roman centurion on seeing the manner in which the crucified "breathed his last." He thereby echoes the estimate of Jesus offered by the Markan narrator at the outset of the narrative (1:1), as well as by assorted supernatural agents during the course of the narrative (God: 1:11; 9:7; demons: 3:11; 5:7; cf. 1:24). Apparently, too, the centurion succeeds in combining the precise two elements, divine sonship/messiahship and crucifixion, that Jesus' disciples, the official insiders, have consistently failed to combine, ever since Jesus first introduced the notion midway through the narrative that the Messiah is destined to suffer and die (8:31-33; 9:30-32; 10:32-45).

What are we to make of the fact that the only human character in Mark seemingly granted full inside access to the mystery of Jesus' identity (Son of God and Crucified One at one and the same time), and hence of God's salvific plan for humankind, is a non-Jew? On arriving inside he is warmly embraced by the narrator and the implied reader.[17] Both of them have been awaiting his arrival since the opening verse of the Gospel ("The beginning of the gospel of Jesus Christ, the Son of God"), the narrator knowingly, the implied reader with ever-increasing anxiety. For prior to 15:39, there simply is no human character in the Markan drama capable of identifying its protagonist as Son of God, much less as crucified Son of God. But the centurion is not just *any* character in Mark on other grounds as well. He is also one of only two non-Jewish Roman characters foregrounded in this Gospel (the other is that other representative of Roman imperial authority in the narrative, the Prefect of Judea, Pontius Pilate).

The hierarchical opposition enshrined in Mark 15:39—Gentile insight over Jewish blindness—is also a hierarchical opposition of Christian over Jew. The utterance attributed to the Gentile centurion is the quintessential Christian confession of the crucified Jesus as Son of God, and it is an utterance of which no Jew in this Gospel is capable, not even Jesus' own Jewish disciples.[18]

Whether implicitly or explicitly, all contemporary critical reflection on the Gentile/Jew and Christian/Jew oppositions in Mark (and, indeed, in any New Testament text) is conducted against the horrific backdrop of what was, in effect, the climactic development in Jewish-Christian relations in Western history. I refer, of course, to Nazi Germany's attempted genocidal solution to "the Jewish question" that resulted in the systematic slaughter of approximately six million Jews in concentration camps between the late 1930s and the mid-1940s. And it is within the general framework of a post-Holocaust reading of Mark that I propose to situate my deconstructive reading of Mark 15:39.[19]

With the centurion's confession in 15:39, the partition between insider and outsider in Mark, which I examined earlier, begins to resemble, or at least anticipate, a specific type of fence—the high barbed-wire fence of a Nazi death camp. There is one notable difference, however. Whereas the purpose of the latter fence was to keep the Jews in, the purpose of the centurion's confession, ordinarily read as the christological climax of Mark's Gospel, would seem to be that of keeping the Jews out. (But keeping the Jews out was, of course, also intrinsic to the Nazi agenda.) Reading Mark with post-Holocaust hindsight, it would appear that by the time the climax in 1930s and 1940s central Europe of the centuries-long history of Christian anti-Semitism occurs (a history precipitated in no small part by the Gospel of Mark itself, as we shall see), the insider/outsider opposition in Mark, with its own climax in the Gentile centurion's christological confession, will have mutated into a double barbed-wire electric fence. This fence will be patrolled by jackbooted storm troopers with submachine guns and snarling guard dogs. And its function will have become that of keeping Jews *out* of the Christian Aryan nation precisely by keeping them *in* the camps (at least until they are led away to the gas chambers and the crematoria).

This, no doubt, is a deeply sinister reading of the insider/outsider opposition in Mark. But Mark is, after all, the Gospel that, as has long been argued, first interprets the destruction of Jerusalem and its temple in 70 C.E. by a Roman army as divine punishment for the rejection of Jesus by the Jewish people, embodied in their leaders. Consider the positioning of the "temple cleansing" incident in Mark (11:15-19), which interrupts the two-part anecdote of Jesus cursing and thereby blasting an unproductive fig tree (11:12-14, 20-22). The reader is invited to extract the not-so-subtle message: the destruction of the unproductive fig tree portends the destruction of the "unproductive" temple (see also 15:38).[20] Mark thereby obliquely signals his conviction that the Roman decimation of Jerusalem that brought the Jewish rebellion against Rome that began in 66 C.E. to a catastrophic climax was an act of divine retribution.

The sandwiched material (fig tree-temple-fig tree) is followed almost immediately by the parable of the vineyard and the tenants (12:1-12). This parable deftly reinforces the message, but also extends it by clearly signaling that it is not only the temple that is slated for destruction. The owner of the vineyard (the owner being God and the vineyard Israel, apparently; cf. Isa 5:1-7) sends various emissaries to the vineyard's tenants, culminating with a "beloved son," who, like the previous messengers, is murdered by the tenants. "What then will the owner of the vineyard do?" the parable asks, only to respond: "He will come and destroy the tenants. . . . [T]hey [the chief priests, the scribes and the elders] realized that he had told this parable against them . . ." (12:9, 12).

But, of course, it is not just the Jewish religious leadership who will be destroyed in the Roman retribution of 70 C.E. The general population of Jerusalem, swollen by large numbers of Judean peasantry seeking refuge from the Roman legions within the walls of the city, will also be slaughtered indiscriminately.[21] And it is this general slaughter that Mark seems implicitly to sanction. The blanket designation of Jews as "Christ killers"—the most insistent slur of Christian anti-Judaism and anti-Semitism through the centuries—and as such divinely sanctioned targets for bloody retribution thus finds implicit expression and "legitimation" in the first narrative Gospel.[22] Long before it mutates into the barbed-wire fence of a Nazi death camp, then, the insider/ outsider opposition in Mark, with its systemic exclusion of Jews from the inside, will have mutated, no less paradoxically, into the besieged walls of Jerusalem. Inside these walls the Jewish outsiders will have been herded en masse to await divinely ordained extermination.

Thus far I have been engaged in meticulously teasing out the implications for Jewish-Christian relations of the insider/outsider opposition in Mark. Think of it as unraveling a knot. Literary texts are typically tied together by particular metaphors.[23] The phrase "for those outside" in Mark 4:11, which, of course, does not refer to being literally outside, is one such unifying metaphor, as we have seen. Deconstruction is characteristically interested in tracing the intricate interlacing of such metaphors with a view to untying them, thereby causing the text to disassemble into its constituent parts, so that its most basic operations are revealed. Thus far, however, my analysis has not penetrated deeply enough, for the insider/outsider opposition in Mark still remains intact despite all our probing. We need to deconstruct that hierarchical opposition more effectively, and the Gentile/Jew and Christian/Jew oppositions that depend on it.

On the face of it, Gentile-Christian insight into the mystery (*mystērion*, 4:11) of the kingdom of God in Mark would indeed seem to be elevated above Jewish blindness to the mystery. On the face of it, too, the *mystery* would seem to be embodied in Mark's paradoxical protagonist Jesus, the *insight* embodied in Mark's proto-Christian Gentile centurion, and the *blindness* embodied in both the Jewish religious leadership and Jesus' own Jewish disciples. Yet the membrane simultaneously separating and joining insight and blindness in Mark, insider and outsider, is extremely porous, as we discovered earlier, and in several different ways.

First and perhaps most obviously, although Mark offers us an ending in which Jesus' male disciples are all still outside (14:50-52, 54, 66-72) and the female disciples sent to bring them inside seemingly fail to deliver the message (16:7-8), he has earlier slipped into Jesus' eschatological discourse (chap.

13) a sneak preview of life on the inside for the male disciples, one in which they will finally overcome their cowardice and witness fearlessly to Jesus and the gospel, even before governors and kings (13:9-11). So are Jews, in the persons of these eventually faithful followers, finally allowed inside in Mark after all? Not altogether, because they "will be beaten in synagogues" as a result of their witness (13:9): being inside with Jesus, then, means being outside the Jewish synagogue—being something other than Jewish, indeed. And once those outside the synagogue eventually ascend to power, as they will most dramatically in the fourth century with the Emperor Constantine's patronage of Christianity and the subsequent Christianizing of the Roman Empire, it is those still inside the synagogue who will be the objects of beating—and much worse. So the eventual attainment of the status of insider, anticipated for Jewish disciples of Jesus in Mark 13, will not be good news either in the long run for Jews or Judaism in general.

The partition separating outsider from insider in Mark, and in post-Holocaust hindsight always threatening to mutate into that barbed-wire electric fence, is, perhaps, more effectively deconstructed by the centurion's "confession" itself. What does the centurion's utterance actually amount to? In declaring the bloody, lacerated corpse dangling on the cross before him to have "truly [been] a Son of God" (*alēthēs houtos ho anthrōpos huios theou ēn*), is he really, in good crypto-Christian fashion, as we have been assuming all along, succeeding spectacularly where Jesus' elite hand-picked disciples have so singularly failed, effortlessly coupling the concepts of divine sonship and dishonorable death where they could not, and thereby giving climactic and definitive expression to Mark's theology of the cross? Or is he merely engaging in grim gallows humor instead, the tone inflecting his "Truly this man was a Son of God" actually being one of scathing sarcasm rather than awed reverence,[24] so that the Greek might better be rendered in colloquial American English by "Some Son of God!" or some equally dismissive phrase.

This alternative reading of the centurion's pronouncement finds support from the immediate context. On this reading, the centurion would simply be parroting the derision of everybody else in the vicinity of the cross, not least the Judean religious leadership with whom his commander, Pontius Pilate, is in cahoots: "Those who passed by derided him. . . . In the same way, the chief priests, along with the scribes, were also mocking him among themselves and saying '. . . Let the Messiah, the King of Israel, come down from the cross now. . . .' Those who were crucified with him also taunted him" (15:29-32).

Thus complicated and counter-read, the centurion's utterance seems to oscillate undecidably between confession and oppression.[25] The centurion has often been seen as a stand-in in the narrative for Mark's Gentile-Christian community.[26] Beyond that, however, he can also be said to be the stand-in for post-Constantinian Christianity—Rome become Christian and Christianity become Rome. Intrinsic to imperial Christianity, most especially to the forms it would assume in Europe during the Middle Ages and beyond, was a systemic disavowal of its Jewish origins: no longer Christianity's mother, Judaism became its constitutive other, and Jews became the victims of some of Christianity's most appalling atrocities. And all of this can be said to be uncannily encoded or "anticipated" in the centurion's pronouncement at the foot of the cross (irrespective of the intentions and limited foresight of the Markan author; for deconstructive readings regularly do tactical end-runs around authorial intentionality). The centurion's cryptic words teeter eternally between crypto-Christian christological confession, on the one hand, and derision and dismissal, on the other—specifically, ethnic derision directed by a Gentile against a Jew (a stance that, again, will reach its historical climax in the Holocaust, so that the Roman military officer overseeing the death-torture of three Jewish subjects shimmers uncertainly in the harsh Judean sunlight and morphs momentarily into an SS officer in a concentration camp).

As such, the centurion's words perfectly capture subsequent Christianity's profound ambivalence toward Judaism—its embrace of a Jewish Jesus interpreted through the lens of Jewish scripture, on the one hand, and its disavowal of its own consequent and ineradicable Jewishness, on the other hand, a rejection that regularly found expression in atrocious acts of violence. A deconstructive reading of the centurion's utterance in Mark would thus always keep its two warring semantic elements—christological confession and anti-Jewish invective—in deliberate tension, and hence ever keep us mindful of how the first is always threatening to mutate into the second.

FURTHER READING

General

Caputo, John D, ed. *Deconstruction in a Nutshell: A Conversation with Jacques Derrida*. New York: Fordham University Press, 1996. The extended conversation with Derrida that forms the book's centerpiece is an excellent introduction to many of the major themes of his later thought.

Derrida, Jacques. *Positions*. Translated by Alan Bass. Chicago: University of Chicago Press, 1981. Three (dense) interviews with Derrida that constitute a common port of entry to his early thought.

Kamuf, Peggy, ed. *A Derrida Reader: Between the Blinds*. New York: Columbia University Press, 1990. Twenty-two selections (essays and book excerpts) from Derrida, each introduced by Kamuf, along with a general introduction.

McQuillan, Martin, ed. *Deconstruction: A Reader*. London and New York: Routledge, 2000. Fifty-nine selections (nine of them from Derrida), organized in such sections as "Philosophy," "Literature," "Culture," "Sexual Difference," "Psychoanalysis," "Politics," and "Ethics."

Norris, Christopher. *Deconstruction: Theory and Practice.* 3d ed. London and New York: Routledge, 2002. Originally published in 1982, this classic introduction to deconstruction inevitably shows its age, although an "afterword" from 1991 and a "postscript" from 2002 attempt to bring it up to date.

Powell, Jim. *Deconstruction for Beginners.* New York: Writers and Readers Publishing, 2003. Deconstruction not only made easy, but even illustrated with cartoons.

Royle, Nicholas, ed. *Deconstructions: A User's Guide.* New York: Palgrave Macmillan, 2000. Includes such essays as "What Is Deconstruction?"; "Deconstruction and Ethics"; "Deconstruction and Feminism"; "Deconstruction and Hermeneutics"; and "Deconstruction and the Postcolonial."

Biblical

Aichele, George. *Jesus Framed.* London and New York: Routledge, 1996. A highly original exegetical work on Mark, whose mode of analysis is informed by Derrida, Roland Barthes, and other poststructuralist thinkers.

The Bible and Culture Collective. *The Postmodern Bible.* New Haven: Yale University Press, 1995. Includes a lengthy chapter on "Poststructuralist Criticism," which in turn contains sections on "Deconstruction and Derrida" and "Deconstruction and Reading."

Derrida, Jacques. "Edmond Jabès and the Question of the Book" in *Writing and Difference,* 64–78. Translated by Alan Bass. Chicago: University of Chicago Press, 1978. Haunting, lyrical meditations on writing, Judaism, and the Bible.

Detweiler, Robert, ed. *Derrida and Biblical Studies. Semeia* 23 (1982). Mainly of interest now for the essay by Derrida that it contains, "Of an Apocalyptic Tone Recently Adopted in Philosophy," which engages the book of Revelation.

Jobling, David, and Stephen D. Moore, eds. *Poststructuralism as Exegesis. Semeia* 54 (1991). Contains Derrida's "Des Tours de Babel" (in English, despite the title), possibly the most accessible of his biblical forays, along with other deconstructive readings of biblical texts, including Mark.

Moore, Stephen D. *Mark and Luke in Poststructuralist Perspectives: Jesus Begins to Write.* New Haven: Yale University Press, 1992. Takes its inspiration primarily from Derrida's *Glas* and other "paraliterary" texts from his middle period.

———. *Poststructuralism and the New Testament: Derrida and Foucault at the Foot of the Cross.* Minneapolis: Fortress Press, 1994. Includes a more detailed introduction to deconstruction than the present essay provides, along with a deconstructive reading of certain interrelated themes in John's Gospel.

Seeley, David. *Deconstructing the New Testament.* Leiden, Netherlands: Brill, 1994. Following an introduction to deconstruction, each chapter deals with a different New Testament author, including Mark.

Smith, James A. *Marks of an Apostle: Deconstruction, Philippians, and Problematizing Pauline Theology.* Atlanta: Society of Biblical Literature, 2005. The most impressive application yet of deconstruction to Pauline studies.

Sherwood, Yvonne, ed. *Derrida's Bible (Reading a Page of Scripture with a Little Help from Derrida)*. New York: Palgrave Macmillan, 2004. Includes sixteen exegetical essays, most of which engage with "later" Derrida, together with an introduction and two response essays.

Twomey, Jay. "Reading Derrida's New Testament: A Critical Appraisal." *Biblical Interpretation* 13 (2005): 274–403. Incisive assessment by a literary critic of Derrida's various forays into the New Testament.

Wilson, Andrew P. *Transfigured: A Derridean Rereading of the Markan Transfiguration*. New York: T&T Clark International, 2007. Argues that the theological sensibilities traditionally brought to bear on the Markan transfiguration have failed to take its measure, and performs an alternative reading.

5

FEMINIST CRITICISM

The Dancing Daughter

JANICE CAPEL ANDERSON

SCHOLARS SOMETIMES COMPARE A GOSPEL to a string of pearls. The pearls are small units of tradition such as parables or miracle stories. The string is editorial material that orders, connects, and interprets the pearls. Each evangelist is an editor or redactor. The way the evangelist chooses and shapes the material reflects his theology and worldview. It also reflects the rhetorical conventions and the historical context he shares with his intended audience.[1] Even when scholars think of an evangelist as an author rather than an editor, they still look for the points of view of the implied author and implied audience, as Elizabeth Struthers Malbon explains in chapter 2. Sometimes they also treat these as clues about the flesh-and-blood author and his likely first-century audience. Are the evangelist and his audience struggling with the aftermath of the fall of Jerusalem in 70 C.E.? Are they familiar with intercalation, the technique of sandwiching one story into another to force the interpreter to read one in the light of the other? Do they view the cross as a humiliating sacrifice or the exaltation of a superhuman being? Each string of pearls, each narrative, is a creation with a unique perspective.

When pressed, scholars admit that their interpretations of the Gospels also reflect their own viewpoints. Their interpretations inevitably reflect their own theological, cultural, rhetorical, and historical environment, their own commitments and experiences. Although they acknowledge it theoretically, scholars often forget this point. Interpreters speak and write as if they can reconstruct history, rhetoric, culture, and theology *as it actually was.* They speak as if they can neatly separate what a text meant from what it means to them. Examination of the history of the interpretation of the Gospels, as described in chapter 1, shows that interpretation is always perspectival.

Feminist critics point out that just as theology, historical circumstances, and literary conventions shape the Gospels and interpretations of the Gospels, gender shapes them as well. Indeed, gender is inextricably bound with theology, rhetoric, culture, and history. It is an important category for historical, literary, social-scientific, theological, and ideological analyses of the Gospels.

What is gender? Gender is the social construction of biological sex. Feminists sometimes use the words *women* and *men* to refer to biological sex and *masculine* and *feminine* to refer to gender. Women and men are born with different sexual organs. Different social groups assign different meanings to these sexual differences. They define what it means to be masculine or feminine and the relationships between genders. In white middle-class American culture, boys play with trucks and girls play with dolls. Males are good at math, women are more verbal. Men enjoy action movies, women like "chick-flicks." This way of putting it, however, presents male and female as two separate and mutually exclusive categories. Another way to think of gender is as a sliding scale between masculine and feminine. It is possible to place oneself or to be placed at various points along the continuum one's culture constructs. But things are even more complex. Multiple, sometimes contradictory meanings are attached to sexual differences. Western culture constructs females as dumb and tricky, virgins and whores, pure and sinful, Mary and Eve. Definitions of gender vary with context and change over time. They do not have a one-to-one correspondence to the behaviors of women and men. The construction of gender also varies with race, ethnicity, class, religion, and other factors. Sojourner Truth, a former slave, pointed this out in 1851. When answering a heckler, she said:

> Dat man ober dar say dat women needs to be helped into carriages, and lifted ober ditches, and to have de best places . . . and ain't I a woman? Look at me! Look at my arm! . . . I have plowed, and planted, and gathered into barns, and no man could head me—and ain't I a woman? I could work as much as any man (when I could get it), and bear de lash as well—and ain't I a woman? I have borne five children and I seen 'em mos all sold off into slavery, and when I cried out with a mother's grief, none but Jesus hear—and ain't I a woman?[2]

FEMINIST BIBLICAL SCHOLARSHIP

Who are the feminist biblical scholars who argue that gender is an important analytic category? I am a feminist New Testament critic. I write as a white American middle-class Presbyterian wife and mother trained in academic historical and literary biblical criticism. Not all feminist biblical critics look like me. Not all of them would describe feminist biblical scholarship the way I do. Each feminist critic is a unique pearl with a unique color and shape formed out of the variables of gender, race, class, sexual orientation, nationality, education, age, religion, and personal experience. Some of us use primarily literary, others historical, social-scientific, theological, or ideological methods. Together we form intertwining strands of pearls, pearls of great price.

The most published feminist critics writing in English in the last thirty to forty years have been white middle-class Euramerican Christian academic women. These include such mothers of recent feminist biblical criticism as Phyllis Bird, Elisabeth Schüssler Fiorenza, and Phyllis Trible, and theologians Rosemary Radford Ruether and Letty Russell. More recently younger scholars of similar backgrounds; African-American womanists[3] like Katie Geneva Cannon, Clarice J. Martin, and Renita Weems; Latina feminists such as Leticia Guardiola-Sáenz, Ada María Isasi-Díaz, and Elsa Tamez; and others from around the globe like Musa W. Dube, Hisako Kinukawa, and Kwok Pui-lan have published feminist criticism and enriched the strands. Alongside Christian feminist academics stand Jewish scholars like Esther Fuchs, Amy-Jill Levine, Adele Reinhartz, and Judith Plaskow; those who embrace Goddess religion, such as Carol Christ and Mary Daly; and those who embrace no particular religion, such as Mieke Bal. Male scholars committed to feminist goals have also begun to publish work influenced by feminism.[4] All of these academics are dialogue partners along with the many nonacademic women and men who live and struggle with the Bible and will sit at the table with us.

What do feminist biblical critics share in common? All of us witness to different forms and degrees of oppression in patriarchal religious institutions, the academy, and societies. Some of us experience multiple oppressions due to gender, sexual preference, religion, nationality, race, and class. The string that threads us together is a commitment to feminism. We define feminism in many ways. We might agree with bell hooks, who calls it "a common resistance to all the different forms of male domination,"[5] and Linda Alcoff, who says it is "the affirmation . . . of our right and our ability to construct, and take responsibility for, our gendered identity, our politics and our choices."[6] We also share a commitment to the significance of the Bible, whether as possessing positive authority, needing exposure as a tool of oppression, or both.

FEMINIST BIBLICAL CRITICS AT WORK

What kinds of biblical scholarship do feminists produce? There is no single model. Our choice of method—historical, literary, social-scientific, ideological—influences our work. So do our religious ties. My account will concentrate on Christian feminist criticism, which focuses on the Christian tradition or sees itself as belonging to that tradition. Feminist biblical scholars who study and/or belong to other traditions share in many of the practices of Christian scholars. However, they have their own particular problems and wrestle with different traditions of interpretation. Questions about the nature of the Christian canon and scriptural authority have particularly concerned Christian feminists. Although in practice we often blend them, one way to view our activities is to see them as two-pronged: a feminist critique and a feminist construction.

Varieties of Feminist Critique

1. *Critique of the androcentric and patriarchal/kyriarchal character of the Hebrew Scriptures and the New Testament*
   By androcentric I mean male-centered, treating males as the universal human norm. Androcentrism is a male-oriented worldview. The male as model defines the female as the same, the opposite, or the complement of the male, the universal human. Often the concept of the female as the "Other," the exception, the anomaly, the lack justifies male domination. In order to define themselves as male, men sometimes define the female as the Other, often as an opposite. They define masculine "strengths" in opposition to feminine "weaknesses." Men also project onto the female what they fear or do not understand in themselves. They define as unimportant, and at the same time fear, women's reproductive and nurturant powers. In Western culture the parallel oppositions male/female, culture/nature, mind/body, reason/emotion, active/passive, good/evil often support dominance. Androcentrism often goes hand in hand with patriarchy. Patriarchy literally means the rule of the father. By patriarchal I mean sanctioning male authority over females and children, especially the authority of males of dominant races and classes. Patriarchy may also involve religious, economic, social, and political processes. Feminist biblical scholar Elisabeth Schüssler Fiorenza has thus coined a new term to capture the nature of multiple systems of domination and subordination involving more than gender alone: "kyriarchy." Kyriarchy comes from the Greek word "lord" or "master," *kyrios,* and the Greek word "rule," *archein.* Schüssler Fiorenza describes an interlocking pyramid involving gender, race, class, age, education, and other factors. In such a pyramid, elite women may have power over non-elite men, but elite males are dominant.[7] Even within patriarchy/kyriarchy, however, all women

have some form of power. Power can mean authority or control. Power can also mean the ability to resist, the ability to accomplish goals, disguised power, or power in certain realms of life. In some societies, for example, women control agriculture.

Many examples illustrate androcentrism and patriarchy/kyriarchy in the Hebrew Bible and the New Testament. God is most often presented as a powerful male. Male figures and authorities dominate the texts. Patrilineal genealogy and the process that leads to a male heir, including a male messiah, structure many of them. Sometimes the androcentric and patriarchal/kyriarchal nature of the texts is obvious. Many passages simply assume that only men are religious or political leaders or that women are property. First Timothy 2:11-15 instructs women to keep silent and have no authority over men because women are the authors of original sin. Other passages are more subtle. Barren women such as Sarah (Genesis 11–23), Hannah (1 Samuel 1), and Elizabeth (Luke 1:5-45) interact with God. However, their barrenness as wives is a reproach, and the stories issue in the birth of sons to ensure the male line. Women like the hemorrhaging woman (Mark 5:25-34) or the Syrophoenician woman (Mark 7:24-30) have faith in Jesus. However, their faith is an exception and contrasts with weak male faith because they are women. If even a woman, how much more a man.

An experiment can help you to understand the androcentric and patriarchal/kyriarchal character of the Gospels and Acts. Read Mark 6:41-44 and Acts 1:15-26—passages that do not deal overtly with male-female relationships—substituting female terms for male terms. How strange and exclusionary the passages now sound.

2. Critique of the androcentric and patriarchal/kyriarchal character of biblical scholarship

Biblical scholarship in the past has been androcentric and patriarchal/kyriarchal in its failure to explore the construction of male and female gender. Its reconstructions of the histories of Israel and the early church have ignored or denied the roles of women. Its literary analyses have ignored or marginalized women characters. Its interpretations have often been sexist. Its research questions and interests often have been those of primary significance to elite males. Its theological concerns have arisen out of male experiences and needs. Why should we consider war more fundamental to the human experience than birth? Why should we consider sin only in terms of overweening pride rather than lack of self-esteem? Biblical scholarship has sometimes served to help institutions oppress women, especially non-elite women. Although the situation has improved in the late twentieth and early twenty-first centuries, problems remain.

Examples of the androcentrism and patriarchy/kyriarchy of biblical scholarship are many. Scholars describe the creation of humans last as the crown of creation, the top of a pyramid establishing human superiority over plant and animal creation in Genesis 1.[8] The creation of woman last in Genesis 2 is sometimes described not as a climax, but as a mark of her inferiority.[9] Many interpreters and translators treat the reference in Rom 16:7 to Andronicus and Junia as a reference to two men. They consider Junia, although a well-known woman's name, as short for Junianus. They find it improbable that the text calls a woman an apostle even though early Christian patristic exegesis thought Junia was a woman.[10] Also in Romans 16 and elsewhere some scholars translate references to a woman as *diakonos* as servant or helper, rather than as deacon as for Paul, Apollos, and others.[11]

Biblical archaeologists often concentrate on large, urban public sites. In the past they were more likely to excavate city walls, palaces, and religious centers. These sites help to reconstruct the life of urban elite males active in public religious and political activities. They are less likely to aid in reconstructing the life of the average person, male or female, except in relationship to that elite.[12]

That biblical scholarship has been androcentric and patriarchal/kyriarchal should not be surprising. For the most part only elite European and American men have practiced it. The field is becoming more diverse, but the overwhelming majority of biblical scholars continue to come from this group.

3. Countering passages that legitimate or have been used to legitimate oppression with counterpassages or liberating interpretations of such passages

Many biblical texts, including Genesis 2–3; 1 Cor 11:3-12; 14:34-36; Eph 5:22-24; 1 Tim 2:9-15; and 1 Pet 3:1-7, have been used to justify the domination of women. There is a long history of women countering these passages with passages they find liberating, such as Genesis 1; Judges 4–5; Gal 3:28; John 4; and Acts 2:16-21 (quoting Joel 2:28-32). First Timothy may forbid women to speak in church, but Acts says women will prophesy.

Feminists have also offered liberating interpretations of passages used to legitimate oppression. Genesis 2 and 3 and 1 Cor 11:3-12 have been frequent sites for such work. They do not read the "curse" against women in Gen 3:16 as God ordaining women's inferior status. Some read it as a description of the results of the Fall violating God's intention for creation, results overcome by Christ (Gal 3:28). Carol Meyers places it in the context of man's toil in Gen 3:17-19 and the harsh environment of ancient Palestine. In order for the group to survive, women had to have many pregnancies. Verse 16 is not about the universal domination of women. Instead, it is about the need to submit to male sexual desire to prevent underpopulation in a very specific historical situation.[13]

Varieties of Feminist Construction

1. *Recovering female images of God and concentrating on stories of women in the text in order to recover images of biblical women, images of agency, and images of victimization*

One of the first projects of the most recent wave of feminist biblical interpreters was the search for female images of God. They found that the Bible pictures God as a mother (Jer 31:15-22; Isa 66:7-14; Job 38:28-29), a pregnant woman (Isa 42:14), a midwife (Ps 22:9), a mistress (Ps 123:2), a woman who searches for a lost coin (Luke 15:1-10), a woman making bread (Matt 13:31-33 = Luke 13:18-21), and as Sophia (wisdom).[14] Phyllis Trible showed how the Hebrew Scriptures connect the wombs of women and the compassion of God. The root *rhm* is the source of the nouns "womb" or "uterus" (*rehem*). The same word in the plural means compassion, mercy, or love (*rahamim*). The womb of God is a metaphor for God's compassion.[15]

Feminists also have written about human women characters. These characters often received short shrift in previous scholarship. The female power and activity of Sarah, Hagar, Ruth, Deborah, Jael, Shiphrah and Puah (the Hebrew midwives in Egypt), Miriam, the woman who anoints Jesus, the Samaritan woman, the Syrophoenician woman, Mary the mother of Jesus, Mary and Martha, the women at the cross and tomb, Lydia, Tabitha, and others have been explored. Although female power and agency remain within an androcentric and patriarchal/kyriarchal context and these stories may serve oppressive ends, many women find them empowering. In constructing female gender as "difference" from male gender, as inferiority and loss, paradoxically androcentrism and patriarchy/kyriarchy witness to female importance and power. This is especially crucial in biblical texts dealing with birth, nursing, and menstruation, activities showing the lack and dependency of men. Often the text and many interpretations create and reflect a division between a female private domestic sphere and a public male sphere (and nature and culture). Feminist exegetes, however, have shown women characters active in the public sphere (Deborah or Prisca), women characters who bring out the importance of the domestic sphere (Mary), and argued for the social construction and explosion of the polarity.

Feminists have also focused on biblical characters who are victims. One important example is Phyllis Trible's *Texts of Terror*. There she recounts the tales of Hagar, Tamar, the concubine from Bethlehem (Judg 19:1-30), and the daughter of Jephthah *in memoriam*. Another important example is Elsa Tamez's interpretation of the story of Hagar, a woman abused by a male and an elite female, Sarah.[16] The stories of women like Hagar (Gen 16; 21:9-21; 25:12-16), the Samaritan woman (John 4), and the poor widow who gives two coins (Mark 12:41-44) disclose multiple oppressions. Religion, social position, ethnic origin, as well as their gender, mark characters as marginal.

2. Reconstruction of the historical and social background of the text with reference to the category of gender: rewriting the histories of Israel and the early church

Scholars have sought to do justice to the roles of women in history as the subjects or makers of history as well as the objects of oppression. Not only women leaders but also the everyday lives of "average" women are matters of concern. Taking as a given the past existence of both men and women, they have sought to give voice to the silenced. However, they have not been content simply to add what they can learn about women to previous interpretations of the biblical past. Feminist historians do not simply "add women and stir."[17] They have begun to rewrite the histories of Israel and the early church. They have begun to reconstruct the roles and relationships of men and women, elite and non-elite, in the history of Israel and the early church. They have also started to write the history of gender ideologies, symbolic conceptions of masculinity and femininity. To do these tasks they have focused not only on the biblical text but also on archaeological data and extracanonical writings. Biblical texts tell us what elite men thought about women and gender. They do not tell us directly what women were actually thinking and doing nor how gender roles operated. Archaeology and extracanonical texts add to the pool of data.

3. Recovering the history of women interpreting the Bible and rewriting the history of interpretation

One of feminist criticism's most exhilarating discoveries is the history of women interpreters of the Bible. This history extends from ancient women, to medieval women, to Reformation and Counter-Reformation women, to nineteenth-century U.S. women such as Sarah and Angelina Grimke, Julia A. J. Foote, Elizabeth Cady Stanton, and Maria W. Stewart, to women from around the globe whose biblical interpretation is appearing today. Women have always interpreted the Bible. Their interpretations are not always found in academic tomes, but rather in letters, diaries, devotional literature, and speeches. Reception history, the scholarly approach that traces the history of how the Bible has been read in a variety of media, now includes the work of women interpreters.[18] Much work still needs to be done in this area.

4. Examining readers' responses: asking how gender and other historical and social variables shape the production of meaning

The previous activity, recovering the history of women interpreting the Bible, is actually a subset of this one. To answer the question, "What difference does it make if a reader is a woman?" interpreters have sought the history of women's interpretations of the Bible to compare to male interpretations.

What difference does it make if a reader of a text is a male or a female, elite or non-elite? As Robert Fowler explained in chapter 3, different inter- preters stress the role of the author, text, reader(s), or context in creating meaning. Reader-response criticism stresses the role of the reader. Some reader-response critics write about the reactions of a first-time reader. Others write about an experienced or even an ideal reader who knows everything there is to know about the text. Some reader-response critics write about a hypothetical reader, others about actual readers, past or pres- ent. Sometimes critics call the various ways to describe the reading process *stories of reading.*

Feminist critics have asked, What difference does it make if the reader actual, ideal, or hypothetical is male or female, feminist or not?[19] They have created two new stories of reading. The first is the story of women reading androcentric and patriarchal/kyriarchal texts. The second is the story of women reading women's writing and/or feminist writing. With the Hebrew and Christian Scriptures, we must deal with the first story. When a woman reads an androcentric/patriarchal/kyriarchal text she is *immasculated,* that is, she reads and identifies as male.[20] This is especially problematic if she is a non-elite woman. Yet, as the reader identifies with the male as universal and dominant, she knows she is a female. She constructs herself as Other.

Feminist biblical criticism documents this process. For example, in read- ing Matthew a woman might identify with Peter, who denies Jesus (Matt 26:33-35, 69-75) but who is also the rock upon which the church is founded (Matt 16:18-19). Peter is a universal model of Christian experience. She sees herself as someone who sometimes fails and denies Jesus, but who also can be a faithful rock. However, in the world of the Matthean text, only males are ruling authorities, rocks. Matthew excludes females and thus her from official authority. She is the Other, the maid in the courtyard to whom Peter lies. He should not fear a mere female servant. She is one of the women at the tomb. She fulfills the female role. She serves the disciples as she restores them as Jesus' brothers to him. She reads as a male who views women as weak and subservient. She also reads as a male in awe of female power. The women do remain at cross and tomb. Mary does give birth outside the normal patriar- chal horizon.

However, that is not the end of this story of reading. Once a woman is aware of immasculation, she can read as a feminist. She recognizes the pro- cesses that are taking place. If she tells a story of reading that emphasizes the power of the text, she can describe how the text constructs gender. She can show what the text does to women and non-elite men and resist its gender ideology in her reading. She can help others do the same. If she tells a story of reading that emphasizes the reader, she can show how women immasculate themselves and how they can create readings in which they are not victims.

Or perhaps a feminist can tell a third story of reading in which she recognizes the roles of both text and readers, male and female. As she reads, she recognizes the text immasculating her and the male reading strategies she uses. She also reads recognizing what the text does not allow or tensions within it. She recognizes what she and other feminists might do with the text. She can resist it, read it against the grain, or transform it for feminist use.

A particularly important question for many religious feminists is how the Bible has empowered women readers and hearers in the past and how it might continue to do so, despite its patriarchy/kyriarchy and androcentrism. Another way to phrase the question is, How have women and non-elite men read or heard the Bible so it has been a source of affirmation and power for them? When a feminist reader reads Matthew, how can she recover the power of identifying with Peter without reading herself as Other?

So far I have been mixing up what it means to be a woman, a female, and a feminist, *and* actual and hypothetical readers. Further, I have not asked what difference it makes if the reader is a black academic North American woman or a Guatemalan peasant woman. Being a woman is a matter of biology. Being a female is a matter of a socially constructed gender. Being a feminist is joining a coalition based on politics; it is a position to act from politically. Other factors complicate all these categories. There is no essence of womanhood or even feminism. When I ask what difference it makes if the reader is a woman or a feminist, I can look at the interpretations of actual women of various races, classes, religions, sexual affiliations, and times. I can trace similarities and differences between them. I can also appeal to the experience of reading as a female or a feminist as a hypothesis. What if a woman or a feminist read this text? How might she respond? When I do this, I must construct what it means to be a woman or a feminist at the same time as I explore the gender ideologies the text constructs.

I agree with Elaine Showalter that when we speak of reading as a woman often what we mean is reading as a feminist.[21] As feminist readers, we appeal to the politics, values, and perspective of a class or coalition. We must. No one can speak for everyone. I can speak and read only as a white middle-class North American heterosexual Christian feminist. Yet we must listen to, speak and read with and on behalf of one another. Although never fully achieved, we share bell hooks's commitment to resist the different forms of male domination and a commitment to respect our sameness and our differences. Admittedly, this view is optimistic. When we use the hypothesis of a feminist reader, we must always remember the challenge Audre Lorde poses: "Some problems we share as women, some we do not. You fear your children will grow up to join the patriarchy and testify against you, we fear our children will be dragged from a car and shot down in the street, and you will turn your backs upon the reasons they are dying."[22]

DOING FEMINIST GOSPEL CRITICISM

How does one begin a feminist analysis of a Gospel? A lot depends on your questions, methods, and goals. Let me suggest four steps that may help. These four steps are especially congenial to literary and some social approaches. They can form, however, a starting point for other approaches as well. They are not the only steps one could or should take.

The first step is to look for male and female gender markers in the text, including descriptions of or prescriptions for gender roles and relationships, as well as analysis of male and female characters. One place to begin is with a concordance, an alphabetical list of words found in a Bible, or an online Bible with word search capabilities.[23] There one can check for all references to gender-related terms such as *girl, woman, widow, boy, son, father, master, sister, mother-in-law, prostitute, virgin, marriage, divorce, heir, birth, baby,* and *nursing.* Note that the Greek word for "woman" (*gynē*) can also mean "wife" and the Greek word for "male-man" (*anēr*) also means "husband." Mark, for example, uses the term *gynē* in 5:25, 33; 6:17, 18; 7:25, 26; 10:2, 7, 11; 12:19, 20, 22, 23; 14:3; 15:40. You may also want to scan the Gospel to compile a list of passages that refer to clothing, hunting, agriculture, barter or sale of goods, food, childcare, battle, athletic competition, religious leadership, or other activities associated in some cultures with gender constructions.

Another strategy that focuses on the text is to analyze male and female characters, including character groups. You can list all the male and female characters who appear in a text and the passages in which they appear. Not only how many times male and female characters surface, but also the content of the scenes in which they appear and their role in the plot are important. For each character ask the following questions and any others you think may be significant: Does the character have a proper name or other form of identification? How old is she or he? What is his or her ethnic, national, or religious identity—Jew, Gentile, Samaritan, Roman? What is the character's occupation? Family status? Economic status? Does the character speak in direct or indirect discourse? Does anyone speak to him or her directly or indirectly? What does the person do as an actor? For what persons is he or she the object of actions? Is any of the narrative presented from his or her point of view within the view of the narrator? In what settings does he or she appear? What times does he or she appear—daytime, night, Sabbath? What is the character's relationship to Jesus?

The activities I have described will help you focus on the text using gender as an analytic category. After this initial investigation, you can describe any patterns that you see. Similarities and differences between genders as well as within genders are important. These activities can give rise to questions you would like to pursue further. The next three steps move outward.

A second step is to determine which passages are sites of interpretive arguments. One group is passages people use to oppress or liberate women. Passages about divorce or church leadership are examples.[24] Another site of arguments is passages scholars call interpretive cruxes. These are points in the text that are perennial puzzles.[25] (See notes 24 and 25 for search strategies.)

In the first case, the argument's focus on gender will be obvious. Examples in the Gospel of Mark are the discussion of divorce and marriage in 10:2-12 and the presence of the women at the cross and tomb in 15:40, 47 and 16:1-8. In the second case, you will have to ask how gender figures into the puzzle. Two of the many interpretive cruxes in Mark are the meaning of the naked young man in 14:51-52 and the ending of the Gospel. What is a young man clothed only in a linen cloth doing in Gethsemane? What is the significance of the linen cloth and of his running away naked? Does the Gospel really end at 16:8 with the women saying nothing to anyone? If it does, why? The answers interpreters give to these questions reveal a lot about Mark's constructions of gender and those of the interpreters, both embedded in their social and historical locations.

A third step is to read several reconstructions of gender ideologies and the actual behaviors of men and women in the ancient Mediterranean world. This would suggest further avenues of investigation.[26]

A fourth step for those interested in the history of interpretation is to look for readings of passages you find interesting. One avenue of investigation is to compare various English translations. Translations are always interpretations. A translator's reading of a passage reveals something about the translator's own view and culture as well as about the text itself. Paraphrases and children's Bibles offer data on popular interpretations. For students with Greek, comparing different manuscripts' readings indicated in the notes that accompany the Greek text can also be interesting. Another avenue is to explore the views of various theologians or figures from religious history. Many works of theologians past and present contain scriptural indexes. Works of male theologians that mainstream religious traditions or scholarship consider important are readily available. Thus, finding out if Augustine or Luther commented on a passage is relatively easy. The works of women interpreters are becoming more accessible (see note 18 for helpful sources). Other avenues are interpretations offered in paintings, plays, movies, novels, letters, diaries, and devotional literature.

These four steps provide a starting point for further work. They can engage the interpreter in active thought about a Gospel and gender. The interpreter then must decide which of the types of feminist biblical criticism in the first section of this chapter to pursue, or whether to forge an entirely new path. Are you trying to discover what the Gospel might tell us about the actual roles of women in early Christian history? Are you trying to place the Gospel's gender ideology in the context of first-century

Mediterranean constructions of gender? Are you trying to show how interpretation of a Gospel has been androcentric and patriarchal/kyriarchal? Do
you want to compare how various modern male and female readers respond
to the Gospel? Do you want to reconstruct how a first-century audience
might have responded?

You must decide which historical, theological, literary, social-scientific,
or ideological methods or models to use. These methods and models can
be those feminists have already developed or adapted. They could also
be those you develop or adapt for feminist purposes. (One of the exciting things about feminist scholarship is that it is open to experiment.)
You can critique or transform any of the other six approaches discussed
in this book. You must subject whatever methods and models you use to
a feminist analysis. You must ask yourself where you stand. You must recognize your historical and social location and political choices. In addition to many kinds of feminist biblical criticism, there are many feminisms,
many theories of feminism. If all of this sounds complicated and hard, it is.
Feminist biblical criticism is a revisioning of the whole critical enterprise.
My recommendation is to start small and to rely on others to share in this
group adventure. One of my contributions follows. I hope you will discuss,
challenge, and extend it.

THE DANCING DAUGHTER[27]

In Mark 6:14-29, King Herod orders the execution of John the Baptist. At
his birthday banquet, Herod responds to his dancing daughter's request
for John's head on a platter, a request prompted by Herodias, her mother.
This story of the dancing daughter embodies a male construction of female
gender. It has been a fertile site for further male constructions. Many theologians and scholars have commented upon it. It serves as the text for the Feast
of the Decollation (beheading) of St. John the Baptist, celebrated on August
29 as part of the Roman Catholic liturgical calendar. It has provoked many
interpretations. A 1912 German monograph contains 200 plates of paintings,
sculptures, stained-glass windows, illuminations, engravings, and other art
drawn from the story. The story also has given rise to numerous folk traditions, poems, plays, novels, films, and operas.[28] Versions of the Strauss opera
based on Oscar Wilde's *Salome* are available on DVD as are various films
inspired by the passage.[29]

Many interpretations of Mark 6:14-29 (= Matt 14:1-12) focus on the
women characters, Herodias and her daughter. Although not named in the
Bible, the daughter is usually called Salome, the name Josephus, the first-
century Hellenistic Jewish historian, gives her in his *Antiquities* (18.5.4).
Herodias and Salome evoke multiple examples of the varied male creation of
woman as Other, as Difference. The German poet Heine offers a particularly

detail of *Herod's Banquet* (1452–1465) by Filippo Lippi
Photo © Alinari/Art Resource, NY

vivid example. In Heine's poem "Atta Troll," the narrator describes a wild
goblin hunt on St. John's Eve. Three great dead women play a prominent
role: the Grecian Diana, the Celtic Abunda, and the Jewish Herodias. They
exude sexuality and violence. Herodias enthralls the narrator. He describes
Herodias and woman as devil and angel:

> Whether she was saint or devil,
> I don't know. With women, never
> Can one know where ends the angel
> And the devil makes his entrance.

On her fevered face lay glowing
All the Orient's enchantment,
And her dress recalled in richness
Olden tales of Scheherazade.
. . . .
And in truth she was a princess,
She was queen of all Judea,
Lovely wife of Herod, she who
Claimed the head of John the Baptist.

For this bloody murder she was
One accursed; a ghost of darkness,
She must, till the Day of judgement,
Ride on with the wild hunt's spirits.

In her hands she holds forever
That bright charger with the head of
John the Baptist, which she kisses—
Yes, she kisses it with ardor.

For she loved him once, this prophet:
It's not written in the Bible,
But the people guard the legend
Of Herodias' bloody passion.

Otherwise there's no explaining
The strange craving by the lady:
Would a woman ask the head of
Any man she does not love?[30]

Some interpreters see Salome as Heine saw Herodias, embodying woman as purveyor of sex and death. Others see her as an innocent young girl used by her corrupt mother. The alternatives are pointedly embodied in the title of an obscure book, *Salome: Virgin or Prostitute?*[31] The author, Blaise Hospodar de Kornitz, wrote the book to reconstruct an historical Salome as innocent daughter and defend her honor.

I will look at this fertile story through the lenses of feminist reader-response criticism. I will examine it for the light it sheds on the gender ideologies—the social and symbolic constructions of gender—of Mark and his interpreters. First, I will show how modern biblical scholarship usually treats the story. Second, I will focus on the story itself and how it gives rise to various responses. Third, I will look at the story against the backdrop of texts from its cultural palette. Finally, I will re-place the story in the context of the Gospel of Mark and its construction of male and female gender.

The Story in Modern Biblical Scholarship

The story of the dancing daughter has been a minor interpretive crux in Markan interpretation. Some scholars want to know how reliable it is as a historical account of the death of John the Baptist. They debate the significance of differences between Mark's account and that of Herod's execution of John in Josephus, the Hellenistic Jewish historian mentioned previously. They also debate the "legendary" character of story elements, that is, which details are historical and which are not. For redaction and narrative critics, the central question is, Why is this episode, a flashback, intercalated or inserted into the mission of the twelve apostles (Mark 6:7-13, 30)? These critics typically give one or more of the following answers:

1. It provides an interlude to mark the period of time the mission took.

2. It foreshadows the fate of Jesus, who like John will be executed and his body put in a tomb (6:29 = 15:5-46).

3. It reinforces John as the prototype of Jesus: John preaches and is delivered up (1:7, 14); Jesus preaches and is delivered up (1:14; 3:19; 9:31; 10:33; 15:1, 10, 15).

4. It serves to remove the blame for John's death from the Roman puppet Herod in the same way the Jewish crowds take responsibility for Jesus' death away from the Roman governor Pilate (15:6-15).

5. It is ironic: it serves to undermine the insider status of the Twelve. The Twelve preach repentance as did John (1:4 = 6:12) and are warned about suffering rejection (6:11). However, in the midst of the successful mission of the Twelve, their failure is foreshadowed. John's disciples bury their master. Jesus' disciples forsake him and flee. An outsider, Joseph of Arimathea, buries Jesus. The stories of the mission and the death of John precede chapters 8-10, where the disciples fail to understand Jesus and his passion predictions.

The Story and Its Readers

Verses 14-20 set the stage for the story of the dancing daughter. In these verses the narrator presents the scene from Herod's perspective as well as his own. The narrator has Herod *focalize;* that is, the narrator tells what Herod hears and knows. He tells the story from Herod's point of view. The narrator also offers four explanatory comments beginning with "for" (*gar* in Greek, 6:14, 17, 18, 20), a typical narrative device in Mark. In these comments the narrator presents Herodias rather than Herod as the ultimate cause of John's death. Still, ambivalence remains: Why does Herod *himself* seize and bind John in prison? Why does he execute John when he does not want to do so?

Why does he believe Jesus is John the Baptist raised from the dead? Verses 14-20 form the opening frame of the story of the banquet, presenting it in a certain light.

The narrator makes the transition from the mission of the Twelve to the episode of Herod, Herodias, and John the Baptist through Herod's focalization, "And King Herod heard [of Jesus]," (6:14a). The narrator then offers the first *gar* comment: "For his [Jesus'] name became known. Some said, 'John the Baptist has been raised from the dead; and therefore acts of power work in him.' But others said that he is Elijah; and others said that he is a prophet like one of the prophets" (6:14b-15).[32] The narrator then returns to Herod's focalization: "But hearing this, Herod said: 'John whom I beheaded, this one was raised . . .'" (6:16).

The narrator then begins a flashback with another *gar* explanation: "For Herod himself sending [representatives] seized John and bound him in prison because of Herodias, the wife/woman (*gynē*) of Philip his brother, because he married her" (6:17). The emphasis lies on Herodias as the cause of Herod's action. Attached to this comment is yet another *gar* comment: "For John said to Herod, 'It is not lawful for you to have the wife/woman of your brother'" (6:18). From the perspective of the implied author, this is a challenge to Herod's honor and the legality of the marriage. There are historical arguments about what actual first-century Roman or Jewish marriage and divorce laws and the practices of the descendants of Herod the Great were. Nonetheless, Mark tells us through a reliable character's speech, reported by the reliable narrator, that the marriage was illegal. Leviticus forbids marriage to one's brother's wife except to raise up sons to him through levirate marriage if he dies without an heir (Lev 18:16; 20:21). In Mark 10:2-12, Jesus interprets Scripture as forbidding divorce of husband by wife and wife by husband. He labels subsequent marriage as adultery. In this light Herod and Herodias are committing adultery. The reader or listener's reaction depends in part upon the norms of kinship, status, marriage, and divorce common in his or her culture and knowledge of norms reflected in the Gospel. It also depends on his or her acceptance of the story's viewpoint. Readers who know Josephus's *Antiquities*—which include most ancient and modern biblical scholars as well as writers such as Flaubert—can interpret the story as a rejection of endogamy, as well as of divorce. Endogamy is the practice of marrying within one's extended family. It preserves or advances the wealth, status, and power of the family and of individuals within the family. Josephus's history tells the reader that endogamy and divorce (permissible under Roman and Jewish law) were frequent among the Herodian dynasty. There we learn, for example, that Herodias was not only the wife of Herod's brother but also niece to both of them. The Herod of our story, Herod Antipas, put away his first wife, a Nabatean princess—this marriage was exogamus, a marriage outside one's family—to marry Herodias. Herodias was the daughter of Aristobulus, son of Herod the Great and Mariammne II. Her two husbands were

Herod Antipas, the son of Herod the Great and Malthace, and Herod (possibly Herod Philip), the son of Herod the Great and Mariammne II. Thus, the two husbands were half brothers.[33] The male and female forms of the same name, Herod and Herodias, emphasize the family ties.

After John's challenge of the marriage, the narrator introduces Herodias as an actor and announces her goal: "Now Herodias had a grudge against him and wished to kill him and could not" (6:19). Whereas more extended comments and inside views of Herod seem designed to win sympathy for Herod, this brief comment presents Herodias unsympathetically as a woman with a grudge. The narrator has already provided the motivation for her grudge in John's challenge. The narrator then offers yet another *gar* comment explaining why Herodias could not kill John. This comment again offers Herod's focalization of events as it describes what Herod knows and hears: "For Herod feared John, knowing him a just and holy man, and kept him safe, and hearing him was perplexed, but he heard him gladly." Herod properly recognizes John and protects him from Herodias. In protecting John, a holy man, Herod protects himself. According to the narrator, Herod as king and husband has control over Herodias's actions. Even queens cannot order an execution independently. However, the queen has some power because Herod must protect John from her. She focuses on the threat John poses rather than respecting or fearing any spiritual authority he possesses. The story of the birthday banquet begins in verses 21-23:

> But an opportune (*eukairou*) day came, when Herod gave a supper for his courtiers, and officers and the chief men of Galilee on his birthday, and the daughter of her/of him, Herodias, entered and danced. She pleased Herod and the ones reclining with him. And the king said to the young girl, "Ask me whatever you wish, and I will give it to you." And he swore to her, "Whatever you ask I will give up to half of my kingdom."

In verse 21 we find Herodias's perspective briefly embedded in the narrator's. The word *eukairou*, "well-timed" or "opportune," shows this. The view, however, is not flattering. The same word appears in 14:11, where Judas seeks an opportunity to betray Jesus. Herodias can use Herod's banquet to achieve her goal, the destruction of John. Women without direct power to achieve their goals may achieve them indirectly. In the patriarchal perspective presented, women's power comes from their ability to please men. The story moves in a progression of verbs. The well-timed day comes, the daughter enters, she dances. Verse 22 complicates the story. It reads differently in various early manuscripts and one can translate it in several ways:

> Entering, his daughter, Herodias, danced. . . .
> Entering, the daughter of Herodias herself, danced. . . .

Either way, because her name is the same or because the text identifies
her as Herodias's daughter, the story associates the young girl with Herodias.
In later verses the narrator identifies Herodias as the girl's mother. But is the
girl Herodias's daughter from her previous marriage or Herod's own birth
daughter? The text does not say.[34]

Whatever her name and exact relationship to Herod, the young girl's dancing elicits Herod's extravagant promise of up to half his kingdom. How does
one understand the girl and her dance? How does one understand Herod and
his guests' pleasure? The guests named are all elite males. Do we have a king
and guests charmed by the innocent dance of his young daughter, the apple
of his eye, or do we have a king and his guests aroused—incestuously in the
king's case—and hypnotized by an erotic dance, a young nubile body offering an apple like Eve? Readers have answered the question in both ways. The
daughter and her dance are not described. They are mirrors in which Herod,
Herodias, and interpreters are reflected.

The answer of a father and guests charmed by the dance of an innocent girl
depends in part on Mark's word for the girl, her subservience to her mother,
and the word Mark uses for the pleasure of the king and his guests. It also
depends on finding the honorable dance of a young girl at a male banquet a
cultural possibility. The Greek word for "young girl" is *korasion*. This is the
diminuitive of the word for "girl," *korē*. The word *korē* also stands for the pupil
or the apple of the eye. *Korasion* is the same word Mark uses to describe Jairus's
twelve-year-old daughter who lives at home in 5:41, 42. It is the word used in
the Septuagint, an early Greek translation of the Hebrew Scriptures, to describe
the future Queen Esther and other beautiful girls, virgins (*parthenika*), who
are gathered to King Artaxerxes's (Ahaseurus in the Hebrew version) harem
as possible brides (Esth 2:2, 3, 7, 8, 9, 12).[35] Further, the girl does not make an
immediate request. She seeks her mother's advice. She retains the child's obedi-
ence and unity with the mother. She reflects her mother's desire. The word for
the pleasure of the king and his guests is *aresen*. According to many interpreters, this word does not refer to sexual pleasure. In the New Testament it refers
to making someone happy, accommodating someone, or doing something that
someone will approve or find pleasant (Mark 6:22 = Matt 14:6; Acts 6:5; Rom
8:8; 15:1-3; Gal 1:10; 1 Cor 7:33, 34; 10:33; 1 Thess 2:4, 15; 4:1; 2 Tim 2:4). Read
in this light, the innocence of the dance is important. For some interpreters, it
allows the end of the story to surprise. The haste of the girl and her demand in
direct speech that Herod *immediately* give her John's head on a platter, as well
as the transfer of the head from the girl to her mother, are shocking.

The construction of the daughter and the dance as innocent, however,
has not been the construction of most scholars. Their answer to the question
of Herod's response and the nature of the dance has been an aroused king and
an erotic dance. Those interested in the historicity of the story see the dance
of a princess at a male banquet as a legendary element scholars must justify.

Vincent Taylor quotes Rawlinson: "It (the dance of Salome) is nevertheless not wholly incredible, however outrageous, to those who know anything of the morals of Oriental courts, or of Herod's family in particular."[36] Such reactions assume first-century elite patriarchal/kyriarchal practices that seclude respectable women and carefully guard the modesty and virginity of daughters, especially royal daughters. The daughter's dance violates this norm. The definition of female it implies is of a being who desires sex and who is a temptation to males. The definition of male it implies is of one who is susceptible to female sexuality and who must protect the females of his family in order to preserve male honor. Women must be trained in the female virtue of shame; otherwise, they will become shameless.

This reaction also shares in the colonial and postcolonial Western male's tendency to view the Oriental, and especially the Oriental woman, as an exotic and often immoral Other. The very use of the term *Orient* invokes Otherness. Orient literally means East, that is, east of Europe. For nineteenth-century Europeans, the term Orient conjured up Middle Eastern bazaars and harems, but also by extension the Far East and even Africa—anything exotic and non-European. Rana Kabbani describes the male European view of the Oriental woman as the Other who attracts and repels:

> The eroticism that the East promised was mysterious and tinged with hints of violence. The Oriental woman was linked, like a primitive goddess, with cycles of the supernatural. Cleopatra possesses knowledge of magic and poisonous prescriptions long before the need for death arises. Scheherazade lives on the edge of the sword, its blade is what her narrative must defeat, its shadow what makes her tale so captivating. Salome's dance is sexual and macabre at once. Her beauty is linked to the darker elements, complicit with the corruption that John the Baptist's words uncover. Her dance is delirium inspiring, and causes the unleashing of evil. Oscar Wilde's interpretation of Salome's murderous desire for Jokanaan's head as the other side of her sexual passion for him indicates the treacherous nature of Eastern sexuality: Salome dances on blood, and kisses the severed head in a frenzy of brutish arousal. . . . The dance became invested with an exhibitionism that fascinated the onlooker: he saw it as a metaphor for the whole East. In the Orientalist paintings of the nineteenth century, it often became a trope for the Orient's abandon, for it seemed to be a dramatically different mode of dancing from its Western counterpart.[37]

In addition to the Othering of the Orient, there is a presumption of the depravity of wealthy royals, the corruption of wealth and power. Often interpreters see a contrast between the ascetic John and the depraved Herodians. Chrysostom (ca. 347–407 C.E.) condemns the royal banquet for its drunkenness and luxury.[38] Calvin (1509–64 C.E.), probably influenced by his view of contemporary royalty, praises John for reproving a king to his face and not "winking" at his faults. He warns those who sit at the tables of kings that although they may not end up watching severed heads made a matter of sport, they may partake of many crimes, at the very least debauchery.[39] Gustave Moreau, a nineteenth-century French Orientalist, paints Salome covered with jewels.[40]

L'Apparition (1876) **by Gustave Moreau**
Photo © Erich Lessing / Art Resource, NY

As one can see from the previous references to Oscar Wilde and the European Orientalist painters, the answer of many men to the question of Herod's reaction and the nature of the dance has been an aroused king and an erotic dance. It is the answer of Flaubert's *Herodias*, Huysman's *Á Rebours*, Mallarmé's *Hérodiade*, Wilde's *Salome*, and Richard Strauss's *Salome*, and that of many paintings, stained-glass windows, sculptures, and carvings. Even children's Bibles portray the dance as erotic:

> Then, on the night of the banquet, the beautiful young Salome, daughter of Herodias, had taken up her beads, her bells and her veils, and she had performed an exquisite dance before all the company. It was late in the evening, and wine flowed freely, and Herod found himself overcome by Salome's charms. In his grandest manner, he proclaimed to her before all his guests, "Ask me for any reward, my dear! I will give you anything in homage to such beauty, even half my kingdom."[41]

Why the imagery of eroticism and excess? The text itself does not describe the dance. The dance does not even take up a whole sentence. One reason is Herod's response of offering up to half his kingdom. The readers can imagine no reason for it unless the young girl and her dance sexually entrance the king. A young virgin is sexually desirable. Herod's pleasure is sexual and corresponds to the pleasure King Artaxerxes finds in the *korasion* Esther. The word for this pleasure in the Septuagint of the book of Esther is the same one that Mark uses. Another justification given for this erotic and excessive imagery is the girl's haste to have the head of John. A third is her request in direct speech to have it on a platter, a detail not suggested by her mother. A fourth is the fact that Herodias uses her daughter to bring about John's death by decapitation. Both Herodias and her daughter speak in their own voices. Their desire for John's death is personally and vividly expressed. The girl serves her mother, however. The narrator makes this clear with the compactly described transfer of the head: "And [the executioner] brought his head on a platter and gave it to the girl, and the girl gave it to her mother" (6:28). There is a strange fascination with the detail of the platter. The head is like food on a platter at a banquet. A fifth reason for the imagery is: like mother, like daughter. The immorality of Herod and Herodias's liaison, which John condemned, marks them and their daughter. Herodias's desire is replicated in her daughter.

Both classes of readings—those that view the daughter and dance as innocent and those that view them as erotic—are male constructions of female gender: Salome, virgin and prostitute; Herodias, mother, procurer, and destroyer. Interpreters construct both readings from Herod's perspective. They also view the events from John's perspective, as condemner of immorality and victim. Herodias is universally condemned; Salome is sometimes seen as innocent. Few, if any, readings view the story from the perspective of the women.

In general terms, what is at play in the text and in readings of it? Conceptions vary, but sex, birth, death, food, and women are symbolic realms often associated in Western culture. Personhood is located in the head, the ruler of the body. To ask for a person's head is to ask for the person's death. The head is also a trope or figure of speech that represents the phallus. In

The Dancer's Reward (1893) by Aubrey Beardsley

patriarchal cultures the phallus often symbolizes male personhood and power. The severing of heads (decapitation or decollation) and castration are figures for each other. Males fear the power of women to control and thereby "castrate" them. Women are the source of life and nourishment as mothers or caregivers. They are a source of sexual pleasure and male identity as lovers, as the object of desire. If there is no Other, there can be no Self. The object of one's desire has control over one. Male orgasm is sometimes compared to dying or to lack of control. Men fear and label as dangerous and mysterious female powers they lack and need. They project upon woman what they fear or do not like in themselves, their own desire and violence. The standard, however, is always male. Women are what men are not, which sometimes takes the form of the oppositions discussed earlier in the chapter. In the context of Mediterranean conceptions of honor and shame, to die in battle at the hands of enemy soldiers is honorable. To be executed or to die at the hands of a woman is a mark of shame. For many Western readers, the ethnicity and class of the women plays an important role in their Otherness. Rich and powerful royal women are more feared and more desired. They are more dangerous than their poorer sisters. Wealthy royal women disturb the ordinary male/female paradigm of superior/inferior. Oriental women in general and Jewish (or Idumean, half-Jewish women as the Herodians were) are doubly Other for white, Gentile, Western males. Even Origen, the third-century theologian who describes the daughter's dance as outwardly innocent, makes her movements an allegorical representation of the behavior of the Jewish people. Like Salome's dance, their behavior seemed according to the law up to the point that the grace of prophecy was taken away from them with the death of John the Baptist. Her dance cannot be a sacred Christian dance because it results in the death of John.[42]

Interpretations of this story split the "female" into depraved mother and innocent or depraved daughter as object of male desire. Herod and John are unified by male power and authority. However, the "male" is split into the deceived Herod and the righteous prophet. Both mother and daughter are feared—and victims. Both king and prophet are victims—and victors. By succeeding in her desire to have John beheaded, Herodias (and her daughter) defeat male/phallic power. However, the victory is only temporary.

There is also a question as to which man is actually rendered powerless, John or Herod. Herod is king, but fears and is puzzled by John. He succumbs to Herodias's wishes and the daughter's charms. Although dead, John retains his power because Herod fears Jesus as a John come back to life (6:14). In an ironic reversal in some interpretations, in death John's head borne on a platter by a woman becomes food, the source of life. John is castrated, feminized, but thus assimilates the female power to give birth and nurture. In the Middle Ages veneration of *Johannisschüsseln*, devotional images of John's head on the platter, was popular in Europe. Herod's banquet foreshadowed the Last Supper, and John's head was a type of the Eucharistic body and blood of Christ.[43] The veneration of John's head on the platter paralleled female imagery of Christ as the source of holy food. Through his death, Christ was the mother of the church on whose breast the faithful can nurse.[44] In a contrary move, in interpretations of the late nineteenth and early twentieth centuries, the food motif turns dark. John's head becomes the fetish of Herodias or Salome, depicted as the thwarted lover of John who could only taste his lips and possess (eat) him when dead.

Cultural Palette: Esther, Judith, Jezebel

Mark 6:14-29 evokes images of woman as deceiver and killer and as source of food and salvation alive in cultural tradition through intertextuality. It evokes images of man as wielder of authority, but susceptible to female charms. *Intertextuality* is the reference to or use of one text by another. The story directly cites the book of Esther.[45] It indirectly calls forth associations with the apocryphal book of Judith and the story of Ahab, Jezebel, and Elijah in 1 Kings 19. Readers often read Mark's story in the light of these other stories.

The strongest tie with Esther comes from King Herod's offer of half his kingdom. This directly echoes King Artaxerxes's (Ahasuerus in Hebrew) repeated offer of half his kingdom to Esther in Esth 5:3, 6-7; 7:2-3. Esther, a beautiful young woman, becomes a candidate for queen after her predecessor, Vashti, an uppity woman, defies the order of the king to appear at a banquet as part of a display of his wealth and power. In the Septuagint, Esther and the other candidates are called *korasia*, the same term used of the dancing daughter in Mark. Esther's goodness and beauty win Artaxerxes, and she becomes queen. Esther, unbeknownst to the court, is a Jew. When her uncle and adopted father, Mordecai, learns about a plot to exterminate the Jews and confiscate their property, he calls upon Esther to prevent it. Although Esther is queen, her position is precarious. She does not want to be deposed, as her predecessor was, or killed. Her strategy is to make herself attractive and invite the king and the Jews' chief enemy, Haman, to a series of intimate banquets in her quarters. The king is pleased with her and makes the extravagant offer. He also is jealous of Haman, who attended the banquets and whom he catches leaning over Esther on her couch. Haman begs for his life, but Artaxerxes thinks he wants to violate the king's wife. Haman is executed.

Here again we have the indirect and cunning power of a wealthy royal woman in the context of sexuality, food, and execution. However, Esther stands in ironic contrast to Herodias and Salome, who split the roles of queen and young woman. Esther brings about the salvation of her people and the death of Israel's enemy rather than the death of God's prophet. Esther's story results in the celebration of Purim, Mark's in the Feast of the Decollation of John the Baptist. Female power, exercised through the ability to please men, is to be celebrated if it serves God and the salvation of God's people. It is tainted if it does not. In Esther the hand of a virtuous woman subverts unjust Gentile male power. In Mark the hand of a corrupt woman makes a martyr of a prophet of Israel. "Salome" is the dark obverse of Esther—Esther's shadow sister. In the Septuagint version of Esther, Esther's prayer emphasizes her abhorrence of the bed of the foreigner and her position as his queen. It also emphasizes that she has not eaten his food. Herodias and Herod, in contrast, serve Rome.

Although not alluded to with a quotation, another biblical story also associates deceit, sexuality, food, the power of woman, male vulnerability, decapitation, and the salvation of Israel. In the apocryphal book of Judith, Assyrians, led by their commander Holofernes, besiege a key Israelite town. Judith, a beautiful, pious, rich, and chaste young widow, saves the day. Accompanied by a maid (protecting her reputation for chastity), she enters the camp of the enemy. Maintaining kosher by not eating the enemies' food, and regularly leaving the enemy camp to pray, Judith uses her sexuality to beguile and kill Holofernes. Holofernes invites her to a banquet for his personal attendants. She brings her own food in a bag. After he falls into a drunken stupor, she beheads him and places his head in her food bag (just as John's head is served up on a platter). The head of Israel's enemy replaces kosher food. She and her maid escape because the Assyrians are familiar with her bag and her departure from the camp to pray. The town is heartened and the enemy disheartened by Holofernes's head. Israel's enemy is defeated "by the hand of a woman" (Jdt 9:10; 13:14; 16:5, echoing Judg 5:24, where Deborah and Jael defeat Israel's enemy Sisera, again in a context where food, sexuality, and death are associated. Jael covers Sisera, feeds him milk, and kills him as he sleeps by driving a tent peg into his head). Judith exults:

> But the Lord Almighty has foiled them
> by the hand of a woman.
> For their mighty one did not fall by the hands of the young men,
> nor did the sons of the Titans strike him down,
> nor did tall giants set upon him;
> but Judith daughter of Merari
> with the beauty of her countenance undid him. . . .
> Her sandal ravished his eyes,
> her beauty captivated his mind,
> and the sword severed his neck! (Jdt 16:5-6, 9, NRSV)

The defeat of the Assyrians is even more remarkable because God uses a woman to accomplish it. The male is susceptible to female charm. Females can use their beauty and power to please against greater male authority and physical strength. Again, the intertextual context is ironic. Judith beheads Israel's enemy, not one of its prophets. However, the food and castration motifs are more prominent than in Esther. Interpreters' tendencies to associate Salome and Judith have been strong. In European painting, sometimes the only way to tell a portrait of Judith with Holofernes's severed head from one of Salome with that of the Baptist is the presence of a sword in the woman's hand.

Margarita Stocker sees Judith and Salome as obverse sides of a male myth of the mysterious female Other: "For Judith with a sword is Judith: Judith with a severed head but no sword slides into Salome. She is the ambiguous Other, assimilating a Salome—whose own function is directly sensual and evil—to a more menacing, because sanctified destroyer."[46] In the history of the reception of the Salome story, we have seen the same kind of dual female nature constructed for Salome herself.

The third intertextual association is between Mark and 1 Kings 18–21 and 2 Kings 9. Mark closely associates John the Baptist with Elijah in 6:14-15 as well as in 9:11-13. Elijah's chief antagonist is Queen Jezebel, a Canaanite, who leads her husband to worship the Baals, rival gods. Jezebel seeks to kill Elijah, although she in unsuccessful. She *is* successful in having Naboth, a faithful Israelite, killed so her husband can possess Naboth's vineyard, the inheritance given by God to Naboth's fathers. God punishes Ahab and Jezebel by cutting off their male descendants. Jezebel is thrown out of a window, trampled by horses, and eaten by dogs. Here we have a royal woman as a deceiver and as a threat to God's prophet. Unlike Esther and Judith, she is not a heroine. As God's opponent, she receives her just deserts.

Later interpreters' visions of the fates of Herodias and Salome, persecutors of the second Elijah, also reflect this concern with just deserts. Josephus recounts Herodias going into exile with her husband after reverses in dealings with Rome. Calvin views this as a proper punishment in his *Commentary on a Harmony of the Evangelists*.[47] Heine has her doomed to join a goblin hunt. Josephus does not recount Salome's death, but the popular male imagination has her falling through the ice up to her neck and dancing in the water until decapitated, committing suicide, or being trampled under the feet of soldiers by Herod's order.[48]

Wily female behavior with sexual overtones or undertones is judged appropriate if the results are approved. Feminine wiles are good if they further God's plans. Despite any human lords, is the woman faithful to the Lord? What the intertextual references to Esther and Judith do is to provide ironic commentary upon the Markan story. Both Esther and Judith as women are marginal and threatened. They personify the position of their people. Their stories are stories of the marginal and weak overcoming strong pagan empires. They succeed because they remain true to God and God to them. Their stories contrast with the stories of the pagan Jezebel and Herodias, who violate God's law and lead their husbands astray. Understood in this context, Mark 6:14-29 is part of the ambiguous portrayal of Rome in Mark. On the one hand, interpreters see a favorable view of Rome. They point to words borrowed from Latin and the shift of the blame for John's death from Herod to Herodias and that of Jesus from Pilate to the Jewish crowds (15:6-15). On the other hand, the unclean spirits cast from

the Gadarene demoniac into the unclean pigs name themselves Legion
(5:1-20), the name for a segment of the Roman army, and Herod is paralleled to the pagan Artaxerxes.

The Story in the Context of the Gospel of Mark

The reason I chose to examine the story of the dancing daughter is that it is
the only story in Mark where a woman is *clearly* a "bad guy." Feminist critics
have praised many women in the Gospel for their initiative and faith despite
their unnamed and doubly marginal status as women who are poor (the
widow who gives her mite, 12:41-44), gentile (the Syrophoenician woman,
7:24-30), or ill (the hemorrhaging woman, 5:25-34). The woman who anoints
Jesus for his burial beforehand (14:3-9) and the women at the cross and tomb
(15:40-41, 47; 16:1-8) have been contrasted favorably with the Twelve, who
misunderstand Jesus and flee.

The story of the dancing daughter extends and complicates the picture of
gender ideology in Mark. Women, like men, are "bad guys" as well as "good
guys." The story highlights the complex and often contradictory character of
symbols and assumptions about female and male gender. It also highlights
the importance of variables like age, ethnicity, and class in constructions of
gender. The named adult royal woman Herodias is presented quite differently
than the unnamed Syrophoenician Gentile woman or the poor unnamed
Israelite woman with her mite. As noted before, there is controversy over
Mark's attitude to Rome. Nonetheless, royal women should be saviors of
Israel and its prophet rather than aligned against them, just as the elite Pharisees and Sadducees should be. Here the cultural palette becomes significant
for interpretation.

The cultural palette also reveals androcentric and patriarchal/kyriarchal
views of women—women's power is in their ability to please men, they bring
blessing and threat to males and to male honor. The position of the *korasion*
is dangerous, and so on—all replicated in Mark. A comparison with the other
Markan story involving a *korasion*, the healing of Jairus's daughter (5:21-24,
35-43) emphasizes these views. Both Jairus's daughter and the dancing daughter are at a dangerous stage from a patriarchal perspective, between childhood
and womanhood. Jesus saves the walking daughter (5:42) from corruption.
The mother's corruption of the dancing daughter leads to the death of John.
In the Jairus story, the daughter and mother are in the traditional cultural
position, unnamed and embedded in Jairus, a synagogue ruler. They appear
in the context of the home. The male healer returns this little daughter to life
because of the faith of her father. Agency is in male hands. The story of Peter's
mother-in-law (1:29-31) is similar. She is unnamed, embedded in a male,
and healed in a house. Perhaps the strongest aspect of patriarchy/kyriarchy
is that, aside from Herodias, no women have positions of official authority
and power, even those Mark implicitly praises. No women preach or heal.

The only powerful woman in Mark is also, after Judas, one of its most reviled villains.

However, there are tensions in this androcentric and patriarchal/kyriarchal perspective. Unnamed women not described as embedded in or protected by male fathers or husbands act boldly and are rewarded by Jesus. The first of these is the woman with the female flow of blood (5:25-34). Jesus calls her "daughter" and praises her faith. Her story is intercalated in the healing of Jairus's daughter. The Syrophoenician woman comes to Jesus in a house and persuades him to heal her daughter, even though she is a Gentile (7:24-30). The poor widow with her mite exceeds the rich in her piety (12:41-44).[49] In the house of Simon the leper, an unnamed woman anoints Jesus with costly oil beforehand for his burial. What she has done is to be remembered wherever the Gospel is proclaimed (14:9). The ambivalence is again seen in 15:40-41. Although it was not mentioned earlier, at the crucifixion, the reader is told about women who had come up with Jesus to Jerusalem and who had followed and served him all along. Above all, Jesus' rejection of traditional family ties introduces tensions. In 3:21, apparently his relations, including his mother, brothers, and sisters, think he is beside himself. Jesus is within a house with listeners encircling him. His family is outside (cf. 4:11). Doing the will of God rather than blood kinship constitutes his family, his brothers, sisters, or mothers. Again, in 6:1-6, he confronts unbelief from those in his native place, his patrimony (*patrida*). They know him as the carpenter, the son of Mary. They know his brothers and sisters. Jesus responds to their being scandalized by him: "A prophet is not unhonored except in his native place (*patridi*) and among his relatives and in his house" (6:4). Again, in 10:29 he speaks of those who have left house or brothers or sisters or mother or father or children or lands, for his sake and for the gospel. They will receive "a hundredfold now in this time, houses and brothers and sisters and mothers and children and lands, with persecutions, and in the age to come eternal life" (10:30). Jesus himself spends much time in houses, the private, domestic sphere, attempting to construct his new family. On one level, for Mark, gender and traditional kinship are irrelevant; on other levels gender *is* relevant and involves hierarchy. Perhaps this is the meaning of the saying that in heaven there will be no marrying or giving in marriage (12:25). As David Rhoads shows in chapter 6, the Markan Jesus breaks some cultural boundaries and transforms and forms others. Mark is full of reversals of insiders and outsiders, rich and poor, the first and the last, male and female. The key Markan distinction is between doing or violating the will of God, being on the side of God or of man (8:33).

What is a feminist Christian reader to make of the Herodias–dancing daughter story in the context of Mark and its interpretation? First, one sees different historical constructions of gender and contradictory constructions even within a single cultural moment. This shows that such constructions are not natural or unchangeable. Second, cultural definitions of female as different, as Other, as marginal, give witness to women's power. The need to assert marginality contradicts the assertion. Women provoke various male fears and desires. In the history of Western interpretation, this statement is true both of Herodias, who quite clearly is a villainess for Mark, and the daughter and the dance, whose sensuality and innocence are ambiguous in Mark. Third, Christian feminists could find an important clue for creating their own reading from the Markan emphasis on food and from medieval readings of the story, which emphasize the daughter bearing the head on a platter and the connection between John's head and the Eucharist.[50]

Food is clearly an important topic in Mark, including the section in which our story occurs. The story of the dancing daughter is intercalated or inserted in the mission of the Twelve. The poverty and proclamation of the Twelve mirror the poverty and proclamation of the prophet John (1:4-6; 6:7-13). However, like Herod and the Pharisees, they do not correctly understand who Jesus is or that their mission will eventually involve shame/castration/martyrdom like that of John and Jesus (13:9ff.). Jairus's daughter, healed, is to be given food (5:43). The disciples are not to take bread with them on their mission (6:8). It will be supplied. John's head becomes food on a platter. When the apostles return, Jesus tells them to feed the male crowd of five thousand (6:34ff.). He supplies the food. A short time later he again feeds a crowd of four thousand despite the disciples' skepticism (8:1-9). Finally, Jesus warns the dense disciples of the leaven of the Pharisees and of Herod, who both misunderstand who Jesus is (8:13-21). The disciples do not see Jesus as a source of food, as the source of bread. At the Last Supper (14:17-25), the Twelve (including the betrayer and the eleven who will flee) eat Jesus' bread (body) and drink his wine (blood), foreshadowed by John's head on the platter, which was recounted as the Twelve went on their mission. Herod's banquet gives way to Jesus' messianic banquet. Jesus, like John, is food.

Here is an answer to why the story of the dancing daughter is intercalated into the mission of the Twelve. Feasting and food link this intercalated episode to the bread of Mark's "sandwich." John, become food, is a type of Jesus, who will soon give his body to be eaten. But Jesus himself, in feeding the multitude, also prefigures his self-giving. As Peter's mother-in-law and the women who follow Jesus *serve* (1:31 and 15:41), so, too, Jesus serves. Jesus' own body is offered as nourishment—like that of a mother. So, too, is John's.

Jesus and John are female. They are sources of food who bleed and feed just as women bleed and feed. This upsets Western gender conventions. If one views this as simply assimilation and usurpation of female difference or even a simple reversal of value poles, it does not empower. It also posits a biological female essence. If, by contrast, we view it as the affirmation of the female body and common humanity along with human particularity— equality that does not destroy difference—it may.

FURTHER READING

Women in Mark and Feminist Interpretation of Mark

Dewey, Joanna. "The Gospel of Mark." Pages 470–509 in *Searching the Scriptures: A Feminist Commentary.* Edited by Elisabeth Schüssler Fiorenza. New York: Crossroad, 1994. Dewey seeks: "to lay bare the androcentrism of the text, noting where and how Mark renders women invisible or subordinate, and to bring out the liberating egalitarian vision of the gospel" (470). As Dewey comments on each section of Mark, she offers both a narrative and a feminist analysis.

Kinukawa, Hisako. *Women and Jesus in Mark: A Japanese Feminist Perspective.* Maryknoll, N.Y.: Orbis, 1994. Kinukawa examines the relationships between women and Jesus in Mark. Her critical scholarship and perspective as a Japanese feminist bring new insights.

Levine, Amy-Jill, ed, with Marianne Blickenstaff. *A Feminist Companion to Mark.* Cleveland: Pilgrim, 2004. Eleven excellent articles on a variety of Markan texts employing a variety of methods. The series of which this volume is a part, Feminist Companion to the New Testament and Early Christian Writings, has many other volumes that also collect useful feminist articles.

Malbon, Elizabeth Struthers. "Fallible Followers: Women and Men in the Gospel of Mark." *Semeia* 28 (1983): 29–48. An important early narrative critical approach.

Mitchell, Joan L. *Beyond Fear and Silence: A Feminist-Literary Reading of Mark.* New York: Continuum, 2001. Mitchell reads the Gospel as a whole from a literary perspective in the light of the question of why the Gospel ends with the women's silence at the empty tomb in Mark 16:8.

Tolbert, Mary Ann. "Mark." Pages 350–62 in *The Women's Bible Commentary.* Expanded edition. Edited by Carol A. Newsom and Sharon H. Ringe. Louisville: Westminster John Knox, 1998. Tolbert introduces the Gospel including the role of women characters, the Greco-Roman context, and Mark as popular literature. In the comment section, she treats "Women among the Healed," "Women as Examples of Faithful Acts," "Women Depicted in a Negative Light," and "Women in the Passion Narrative."

Monographs, Reference Works, and Collections of Feminist Biblical Criticism

Bach, Alice, ed. *Women in the Hebrew Bible: A Reader.* New York: Routledge, 1998. A collection of essays organized in seven categories: "The Social World of Women in Ancient Israel," "Reading Women into Biblical Narratives," "Goddesses and Women of Magic," "Rereading Women in the Bible," "Sexual Politics in the Hebrew Bible," "Feminist Identities in Biblical Interpretation," and "A Case History: Numbers 5:11-31."

Bal, Mieke. *Murder and Difference: Gender, Genre, and Scholarship of Sisera's Death.*
    Bloomington: Indiana University Press, 1988. A literary critic explains how
    different disciplines look at Judges 4 and 5 and how gender is involved in inter-
    pretation. Included here as an example of a postmodern feminist approach.
Bird, Phyllis A., Katherine Doob Sakenfeld, and Sharon H. Ringe, eds. *Reading the
    Bible as Women: Perspectives from Africa, Asia and Latin America. Semeia* 78
    (1997). This thematic journal issue contains readings of biblical texts from
    the perspectives of women from a variety of contexts and several overview
    pieces. Articles treating the Gospels include "Borderless Women and Bor-
    derless Texts: A Cultural Reading of Matthew 15:21-28," by Leticia A. Guar-
    diola-Sáenz; "Reading the Bible 'with' Women in Poor and Marginalized
    Communities in South Africa (Mark 5:21—6:1)," by Malika A. Sibeko and
    Beverley G. Haddad; "Polarity or Partnership? Retelling the Story of Martha
    and Mary from Asian Women's Perspective (Luke 10:38-42)," by Ranjini
    Rebera; and "A Korean Feminist Reading of John 4:1-42," by Jean K. Kim.
Cannon, Katie Geneva, and Elisabeth Schüssler Fiorenza, eds. *Interpretation for
    Liberation. Semeia* 47 (1989). The seven thoughtful essays in this collection
    are by people of color. They all comment in one way or another on the way
    race, class, and gender shape interpretation. Articles which focus on New
    Testament texts include Clarice J. Martin's essay, "A Chamberlain's Journey
    and the Challenge of Interpretation for Liberation," which offers a history
    and critique of scholarship on Acts 8:26-40, and Sheila Brigg's essay, "Can an
    Enslaved God Liberate? Hermeneutical Reflections on Philippians 2:6-11,"
    which explores the uses of analogy.
Dube, Musa W. *Postcolonial Feminist Interpretation of the Bible.* St. Louis: Chalice,
    2000. A sophisticated linking of postcolonial and feminist analysis. Dube
    explains and argues for the linkage. The book includes a striking reading of
    the Canaanite woman story in Matthew 15:21-28. Her criticism of Western
    male and feminist scholarly readings of the story notes their failure to take
    imperialism into account. Her research on and analysis of African Indepen-
    dent Church women's readings illustrates the possibilities of cross-cultural
    reading.
Fiorenza, Elisabeth Schüssler. *In Memory of Her. A Feminist Theological Reconstruc-
    tion of Christian Origins.* New York: Crossroad, 1983. The major work of the
    best-known feminist New Testament critic. The first part of the book focuses
    on hermeneutics or theory of interpretation; the second offers a feminist
    reconstruction of early Christian history.
———. ed. *Searching the Scriptures: A Feminist Introduction.* Volume 1: New York:
    Crossroad, 1993. Volume 2: New York: Crossroad, 1994. Volume 1 has arti-
    cles on the history and contexts of feminist interpretation, hermeneutics, and
    methods. Volume 2 contains commentaries on canonical New Testament
    texts such as the Gospel of Mark and 1 Corinthians, the book of Judith from
    the Apocrypha as well as non-canonical texts such as the Sibylline Oracles
    and the Gospel of Mary Magdalene.

Hayes, John H., ed. *Methods of Biblical Interpretation*. Nashville: Abingdon, 2004. This paperback collection of slightly revised entries from the 1999 *Dictionary of Biblical Interpretation* contains several useful and relevant entries: Ada María Isasi-Díaz on "Mujerista Biblical Interpretation"; Clarice J. Martin on "Womanist Biblical Interpretation"; and Vicki C. Phillips on "Feminist Interpretation." Helpful bibliographies.

Meyers, Carol, Tony Craven, and Ross S. Kraemer, eds. *Women in Scripture: A Dictionary of Named and Unnamed Women in the Hebrew Bible, the Apocryphal/ Deuterocanonical Books, and the New Testament*. Grand Rapids: Eerdmans, 2001. Exactly as the title says, this reference work has entries on named and unnamed women as well as several introductory articles.

Newsome, Carol A., and Sharon H. Ringe, *The Women's Bible Commentary*. Expanded edition. Louisville: Westminster John Knox, 1998. This commentary introduces each book of the Bible (in the Protestant canonical order) and the Apocrypha. It also includes commentary on passages the commentators view as having special significance for women.

Tolbert, Mary Ann, ed. *The Bible and Feminist Hermeneutics. Semeia* 28 (1983). An important collection from the 1980s. Contains four exegetical essays on New Testament texts and two on texts from the Hebrew Scriptures. A concluding essay sharply outlines types of feminist criticism and challenges.

Trible, Phyllis. *God and the Rhetoric of Sexuality*. Philadelphia: Fortress, 1978.
————. *Texts of Terror: Literary-Feminist Reading of Biblical Narratives*. Philadelphia: Fortress, 1984. These two books are by a mother of recent feminist criticism of the Hebrew Scriptures. They involve literary methods. The second is especially accessible to students and others with little familiarity with biblical scholarship. It confronts texts that are very troubling for religious feminists, texts in which women are victims of male violence.

Weems, Renita J. *Just a Sister Away: Understanding the Timeless Connection between Women of Today and Women in the Bible*. New York: Warner Books/Walk Worthy Press, 2005. (Previous edition: *Just a Sister Away: A Womanist Vision of Women's Relationships in the Bible*. San Diego: Luramedia, 1988). Very accessible to beginning students because it was written for group study. Weems approaches a number of biblical passages from a womanist perspective.

Resources on Feminist Thought

Code, Lorraine, ed. *Encyclopedia of Feminist Theories*. London: Routledge, 2000. Entries organized alphabetically include topics of interest to feminists such as "childcare," reviews of feminist thought such as "liberal feminism," and academic approaches such as "anthropology," as well as entries on individual feminists.

Tong, Rosemary. *Feminist Thought: A More Comprehensive Introduction*. 2d ed. Boulder, Colo.: Westview, 1998. Clear introductory textbook. Contains chapters on liberal, radical, Marxist and socialist, psychoanalytic and gender, existentialist, postmodern, multicultural and global, and ecofeminist traditions of feminist thought.

6

SOCIAL CRITICISM

Crossing Boundaries

DAVID RHOADS

THE NEW TESTAMENT WRITINGS WERE PROFOUNDLY social documents. Each writing of the New Testament was deeply embedded in a particular community's culture and history. Each writer shared a common social system with readers/hearers that enabled communication to take place. The writer addressed specific audiences with a distinctive message for a given time, place, and circumstance. As such, the writings of the New Testament were social acts.

Our reading of the New Testament is also a social act. For us, however, reading the New Testament is a cross-cultural experience. The writers of the New Testament were first-century people living in the cultures of the Mediterranean world, while we represent contemporary cultures in the twenty-first century from across the globe. Our languages, customs, economies, political orders, social systems, values, cultural knowledge, and ethos are different from the Mediterranean cultures of the first century. We tend to project our predominantly urban industrial societies back onto writings that are from a preindustrial peasant society. In the West, we read into the writings many of the modern Western cultural assumptions about life—notions

145

of individualism, progress, freedom, class structure, time, mobility, and so on. We have our twenty-first century "cognitive maps" by which we select, sort, and comprehend the material we read in the New Testament. In so doing, however, we can easily misunderstand writings addressed to first-century people.

A text from the first century is like a door, an opening through which to look into another culture, a different world. However, if we look at the door without going through it, we see only how the text fits into the décor in the room on our side of the door. We see the text only in the context of the world we inhabit. Instead, we need to enter in imagination through the door into the world on the other side of the door, in order to see the text in the context of the very different cultures of first-century Palestine and the Roman Empire. The question is: How can we understand the New Testament as a collection of writings from the eastern Mediterranean world of the first century rather than impose meanings we bring to the text from our time and place? The social study of the New Testament offers many resources to address this question.

In recent decades, there has been an explosion of books and articles in the social study of the New Testament. During the last twenty-five years, seminars in scholarly societies have appeared under such titles as "The Social Description of Early Christianity," "Social Sciences and the New Testament," and "The Context Group." All these groups are devoted to sharing and promoting scholarship on the social study of the New Testament. Biblical scholars are eager to understand the society, the culture, and the communities in and behind the New Testament writings.

As a way to describe this emerging social study of the New Testament, I identify five approaches that have emerged: (1) social description, (2) social history, (3) the sociology of knowledge, (4) the use of models from the social sciences, particularly cultural anthropology, and (5) the identification of social location. I will survey these approaches and then illustrate them with a case study on the dynamics of purity and defilement in the Gospel of Mark.

SOCIAL DESCRIPTION

Social description draws upon all the information we have from the ancient world: literature, archeological excavations, art, coins, inscriptions, and so on. Scholars analyze and organize this information to describe every aspect of the social environment of the New Testament in its original setting: occupations, tools, houses, roads, means of travel, money, economic realities, architecture, villages and cities, laws, social classes, patron-client relations, gender roles, markets, clothes, foodstuffs, cooking practices, and so on. Such social description enhances our understanding of the daily cultures and customs in Palestine and in the larger Roman Empire at the time of Jesus and the early Christian movement.

One way to think about social description is to imagine you are the director of a film portraying scenes from the life of Jesus. For example, consider
the story about Jesus healing the man with the withered hand (Mark 3:1-6).
What information do you need in order to make this scene authentic? What
did a synagogue look like? Was it a stoa (porch) in a market area, a free-
standing building, a room in another structure, or simply a gathering of
people? Who went there? How were gender relations configured there? What
did people do there? Did they read from the Torah (the first five books of the
Hebrew Bible)? Was it a papyrus scroll or a parchment book? How did they
dress? What was the Sabbath? What were the practices and the prohibitions
related to the Sabbath at that time? What Sabbath laws were at stake in Jesus
healing the man? How serious were penalties for violation of the Sabbath?
What was the social status of a man with a "withered hand" in that culture?
How did people treat such a person? Who were the Pharisees? How would
they bring charges against Jesus? Why in the end did they not indict him?
Why did they go off to meet with the Herodians? If you were a director stag-
ing such a drama, you would develop a passion for such questions as a means
to comprehend fully this scene in its ancient material and social context.

Understanding such a story is like understanding a joke from another culture. You have to know what ideas and information are being assumed before
you can "get" the meaning of the joke. For example, the Pharisees were watching to indict Jesus because, according to the laws of Israel, it was illegal to
work on the Sabbath and because healing was considered to be work. Such a
situation was serious for several reasons: observing the Sabbath was a solemn
obligation; observing the Sabbath helped to distinguish Judeans from Gentiles
(non-Judeans); and penalties for flagrant offenses could be severe, including
even death.[1] Synagogues were most likely public buildings that also functioned
as courts of law, which is why this setting was so threatening to Jesus. And the
key question is: Why did the Pharisees not indict Jesus when he healed the
man? The reason is that Jesus cleverly evaded indictment by avoiding any real
"work." He does not touch the man or command him to "be healed" but only
tells him to "stretch out the hand!" No wonder the Pharisees went off in frustration to plot with the followers of Herod Antipas to destroy Jesus—because
Herod Antipas alone had the right to carry out capital punishment in Galilee
under the Romans. Such information is essential for readers to "get" the story.

Many fine studies describe the material and social worlds of daily life in
the first century. In so doing, they provide vital means for us to understand
people, events, and stories from that time.

SOCIAL HISTORY

Social historians seek to understand the broad sweep of change in history.
This approach applies a comprehensive knowledge of social description

through time to produce a social history of the period. Biblical scholars seek to answer critical questions of social history in relation to the New Testament and early Christianity. For example: How did Christianity develop in the rural areas of Palestine? How did Christianity develop in the urban areas of the ancient world? How did the Greek culture and the Judean culture inter-relate in the period of Roman domination? What were the social causes and dynamics of the Roman-Judean War of 66 to 70 c.e., and how did this war affect the early Christian movement? Then the question becomes: How do these developments fit into the social movements of the larger Greco-Roman world of that time? Regarding the study of biblical literature, those who take this approach will ask how the Gospel of Mark fits into the social and politi-cal history of the times, much as we might ask the place of Benjamin Frank-lin's *Poor Richard's Almanac* in preindustrial America or the relationship of John Steinbeck's *The Grapes of Wrath* to the Great Depression.

To deal with social history in relation to Mark, we might pose the follow-ing questions: What were the social forces behind the writing of the Gospel of Mark? What political conditions prevailed in that time and place? How did the tragic Roman-Judean War of 66 to 70 c.e. impact the writing of the Gospel? What was Mark's community like, and how did they spread the good news about Jesus? How much did the expectation of an imminent end to the world impel the writing of this Gospel? What social class or classes did the Gospel of Mark address? Were the readers Judeans? If not, how much did they know of or identify with the Judean people? What groups persecuted Mark's community? What was the fate of Mark's community in the context of the Roman Empire? One cannot do a broad social history based on one writ-ing alone; nevertheless, social historians can seek to explain the appearance of Mark's Gospel in the sweep of the social history of the time. Unfortunately, the task is difficult because Mark refers to his own time (a generation after Jesus) only indirectly in the story.

As an illustration, we might ask how the Roman-Judean War of 66 to 70 c.e. affected the writing of Mark's Gospel. In 66 c.e., the Judeans in Israel expelled the Roman troops from Palestine and rallied for independence. Diverse groups from all over Israel joined the war movement—lower class groups resisting economic oppression, sectarian groups fighting for the first-commandment prohibition against any lord but God, and high-priestly groups seeking better terms in the relationship between Judea and Rome. The war ended in disaster for the Judeans. The Romans returned, decimated the countryside, defeated the nation, besieged and destroyed Jerusalem, razed the Temple in 70 c.e., and either killed or took into slavery most Judeans who survived the siege. Writing his Gospel during or just after the war, Mark told a story about events preceding the war. In Mark's narrative, the Judean messiah had already come in the person of Jesus, who preached to his disciples that they should be like servants and not like the leaders of the Gentile nations who lord over people (10:42-45). The leaders of Israel portrayed in Mark's story rejected Jesus and his message. Jesus in turn predicted their downfall and that of the Temple (12:9; 13:2; 14:62). At the trial scenes, the high priests stirred up the crowd to call for Jesus' execution and to choose freedom for Barabbas, a prisoner who had committed murder in an insurrection (15:6-15). When Jesus died, God split the curtain and left the Temple and Israel to destruction (15:38). We can see how Mark wrote this story in part to reveal, from his point of view, what he considered to be the destructive attitudes in Israel that led to the Roman-Judean War. He also showed how the Judean faction of the followers of Jesus differed from other groups in Israel.

With this approach, we can see more clearly how the sociopolitical history of the time shaped the Gospel of Mark. In turn, we can also see how this early Christian writing fit into the broader social history of the Roman period. Traditionally, social historians have focused on the rulers and the wealthy, since written records and archaeological remains are primarily from these elites. Recently, however, some social historians have been reconstructing the past from the perspective of the populace, seeking to unmask the dynamics of oppression, to recover the lives of the poor, outcasts, slaves, and women, and to identify the various counter-imperial movements in the face of Roman hegemony. The writings of the New Testament, including the Gospel of Mark, are prime sources for such social histories.

SOCIOLOGY OF KNOWLEDGE

The sociology of knowledge offers the insight that different cultural worldviews support different social systems. The first aspect of this approach is to reconstruct the worldview—the everyday assumptions—of a given culture or group. The second aspect is to see how this worldview gives legitimacy to and maintains the particular social order of the group that holds such a worldview.

The first facet of the sociology of knowledge deals with what people in a particular culture take for granted in their understanding of the world, their "social construction of reality."[2] Whereas social description focuses on the material realities of a society, sociology of knowledge deals with how that society organizes and interprets those realities. Despite conflicts and differences within societies, there is a general coherence that holds each society together. Each society interprets, organizes, and experiences life in its own way. Each society has sets of common values and customary ways in which people interact. Each society has shared beliefs about time, space, and the meaning of life. All these facets make up the shared assumptions of what a given culture would consider to be "common knowledge." Such beliefs and understandings constitute the fabric of meaning without which a society as such does not exist. People seldom question these assumptions. People are born into this world, grow up in it, and tend to take the world of shared meanings for granted. Of course, the core values of a culture can be subverted and changed. Sociology of knowledge makes us aware of the relativity of cultures and challenges the idea that cultures are fixed.

If we are to understand the first-century cultures and subcultures, we should be aware of the assumptions we make from our own cultures and subcultures. Otherwise, we will unconsciously project them onto our reading of a writing such as Mark's Gospel. To see and judge other societies by our own assumptions is cultural ethnocentrism. The first-century Mediterranean cultures would consider "the way things are" to be quite different from the dominant United States culture—gender roles, social classes, economic dynamics, political power, and so on. For example, many people in the United States may assume that it is good for an individual to "get ahead." However, some cultures, including the peasant cultures of the first century, view individuals who "get ahead" as dishonorable, because "getting ahead" is destructive of the social order—for in a world in which honor and goods are considered to be limited and in short supply, those who gain are at the same time thereby depriving others. Thus, the sociology of knowledge is about the everyday understandings of the world that people in a culture take for granted, what everyone in that culture "knows" to be true. If we are to understand the cultures of the first century, we need to appreciate how their cultures are different from our own.

When children grow up en-culturated into a particular society, sociologists refer to this process as "primary socialization." When people enter another society and take on the basic assumptions of this other culture, sociologists refer to this process as "resocialization at the primary level."[3] Resocialization at the primary level can also occur when a group within a society challenges the core values of that society and embraces other values. Such resocialization in primary assumptions is also a way to understand conversion. The Christian movement arose in particular cultures and led people to change the way they thought about some assumptions of those cultures and to abandon other assumptions. It called them to inhabit the world in a different way, to convert to a social group with different assumptions.[4] Thus, from the perspective of sociology of knowledge, early Christianity offered an alternate world of meaning for those who chose to inhabit it. Reading or hearing a narrative like Mark was a way to enter such a new symbolic universe. We might ask: Which assumptions about life does the author of Mark share with the readers without calling those assumptions into question? Which assumptions does the author challenge and subvert? What new views does the author want the readers to adopt?

Consider, for example, the conception of space and time in the narrative world of Mark's Gospel. Early in the story, the narrator tells us that Jesus saw "the heavens being torn open" and "the Spirit of God coming down upon him" (1:9-11).[5] After this, "a voice from the heavens" addressed Jesus. Immediately, the Spirit drove Jesus to the desert to be "tested by Satan," and "angels" served him (1:12-13). Subsequently, Jesus appeared in Galilee where he "drove out many demons" (1:39). When we combine these and other clues, we see that the author holds a predominantly Israelite conception of the cosmos. There is no notion of a universe infinite in time and space, but a limited and flat earth with a canopy over it, heavens extending from earth up to where God dwells, and Satan dominating an earth populated by angels and demons. Many other elements of the story fill out this spatial picture of the cosmos, such as Jesus' going "up onto a mountain [the lower heavens] to pray" (6:46), the promise to gather disciples "from the four winds" (13:27), and the prophecy that "the Son of Man" would "come on the clouds of heaven" (14:62). The author does not argue for this view of the cosmos but simply assumes that the audience shares the same worldview.

At the same time, Mark wants to change the reader's view of some aspects of the cosmos. Regarding temporal assumptions, Mark wants to convince readers that God's kingdom/rulership over the world has begun with the baptism of Jesus (1:14-15) and that the fulfillment of that kingdom would come before the end of Jesus' generation (9:1; 13:30). Mark also wants people to know that the spatial dynamics of the cosmos have changed. Powers of God that were in heaven are now available on earth for those who have faith. He also wants to convince people to leave their limiting, social space within Israel in order to proclaim the good news to all the Gentile nations—to the ends of the earth.

To ferret out a comprehensive picture of how Mark imagines the world, we might consider his views about nature and history, past and future, laws and customs, the human condition, sin and illness, purity and pollution, death and the afterlife, and so on. By culling details from the narrative, we can put together cultural assumptions the author makes about the world. In this way, we can sort out which primary cultural assumptions the author takes for granted and which primary assumptions the author wishes to challenge and change—such as purity rules, ethical values, and attitudes toward death.

The second facet of the sociology of knowledge correlates such worldviews with particular social organizations. Here sociologists make the argument that a mutual relationship exists between the assumptions of a given culture or group and the social organization of that group. How does the worldview of a group generate, legitimate, and maintain the particular social order of the group? In turn, how does the social order of a group influence the worldview of that group? There is no "necessary" correlation between worldview and social order; nevertheless, efforts to make correlations are illuminating.

For example, Wayne Meeks argues that the worldview or symbolic universe expressed in the Gospel of John supports a certain kind of social group.[6] The Gospel of John portrays Jesus as "the man from heaven" who brings knowledge of God to the world; yet only some people understand him while most people do not grasp his message at all. There is a strong dualism between those of the light and those in the darkness. Such a belief system about Jesus, Meeks argues, supports a small, tight-knit group of people who understand Jesus, but who are isolated and alienated from the general society of people who do not understand. As such, the belief system in the Gospel of John gave religious legitimacy to the group's isolation from the world.

Similarly, in the narrative world of the Gospel of Mark, there is a correlation between the worldview held by Jesus in Mark's story and the social organization of the Jesus movement depicted there. The worldview Jesus teaches his followers involves these assumptions: God's rulership has begun (1:15); followers are to cross boundaries to proclaim the good news to the ends of the earth (13:10, 27); and the mission is urgent because the end of history will come soon (13:5-37). This missionary commitment to spread the good news to all nations before the world ends supports a social organization very different from that of John's Gospel. Instead of fostering a tight-knit group isolated from the world, Mark urges upon his hearers a loose-knit social network based on hospitality as disciples go from place to place proclaiming the gospel (1:17; 6:7-13; 10:29-30).[7] Thus, the sociology of knowledge helps one to see how the group's "knowledge" relates to the social order of that group.

MODELS FROM CULTURAL ANTHROPOLOGY

A fourth area of social study of the New Testament involves the use of models from cultural anthropology. From the study of many cultures, anthropologists formulate models to map the dynamics of a culture and to describe certain phenomena that occur in many cultures. Models deal with such matters as kinship relations, corporate personality, rituals, purity-pollution rules, economic systems, and so on.

A model is a simplified description/abstraction of similar events or phenomena occurring across many cultures or groups. For example, if we draw up a descriptive model of the characteristic dynamics of demonic possession/exorcism from the study of many contemporary cultures in which this phenomenon occurs, then we can use that model to investigate and understand demonic possession better in first-century Israel. The point of using a model is not to fit facts into an abstract paradigm, nor is it to impose models onto first-century realities. Rather, a model serves as a heuristic device to probe and to question, to notice details we might have ignored, and to see connections that explain dynamics and relationships. As such, models are not a tool to research new historical information; rather, they aid in the process of interpretation. Biblical scholars draw on the models of anthropologists whose work is especially helpful in the study of early Christianity. They change and adapt the models to interpret specific historical situations in New Testament times. Models help to overcome ethnocentrism by providing a framework different from our own cultural maps with which to organize and assess information.

For example, Robin Scroggs drew a model from the work of Max Weber and Ernst Troeltsch on the characteristics of religious sects.[8] Scroggs applied the model to the early Christian church to show in what ways it was indeed a typical religious sect. John Gager drew on the work of anthropologist Leon Festinger about religious sects that expected the end of the world.[9] Gager applied the model to the earliest Christians because they expected that Jesus would return within their own generation. Gager argued that when this did not happen the early Christians responded like other such sects; namely, rather than give up their beliefs they actually intensified their missionary activities.

Bruce Malina has made the most comprehensive effort to map the social framework of first-century cultures by using models drawn from the study of modern Mediterranean societies.[10] As such, he interprets the New Testament with models drawn from societies that are in historical and geographical continuity with those of the first-century Mediterranean region. He explicates the following models. In contrast to a social focus on economic gain, first-century Mediterranean people sought above all else to gain honor and to avoid shamefulness. In contrast to a quest for individual freedom, people got their identity from group participation and conformity. In contrast to an assumption that economic acquisition can be unlimited, people held to the peasant experience that all goods are limited and in short supply. In contrast to a quest for equality, there were dominant roles for men and subordinate roles for women. Also, in general, these cultures had a patrilineal kinship system in which kinship is traced through male descent lines. Marriage was endogamous, that is, people married within their own group. Finally, society was organized according to rules related to purity and defilement. Malina's work lays out the dynamics of each of these models and applies them to the New Testament writings. Other scholars have developed cross-cultural models for the study of healing, demonology, social networks, and so on.

Cultural anthropologists may take one of three approaches to analyze a society or group:[11]

1. Models may come from a structural-functionalist approach, which assumes that social forces work together to create a balance. Here the issue is to see how different parts of a society work together to maintain stability. This approach tends to see society in terms of how it preserves the status quo.

2. Models may come from a conflict framework of analysis, which assumes that different parts of society are in conflict with each other. Here the issue is to see how conflicting needs and interests will be worked out. This approach tends to see society in terms of changes that take place in struggles over power and control.

3. Models may come from a symbolic framework of understanding, which focuses on the meanings people assign to social interactions. Here the issue is to discern the symbolic meanings that members of the society share and to determine how those symbols change.

Several scholars have applied models from cultural anthropology to the Gospel of Mark. Vernon Robbins analyzed the social role of the teacher Jesus and his disciples.[12] John Pilch has studied Markan assumptions about the nature of illness, healing, and exorcism.[13] Herman Waetjen employed a model about millenarian sects to highlight the new social order that Jesus announces in his establishment of the kingdom.[14] Jerome Neyrey applied a model from the work of anthropologist Mary Douglas to display the dimensions of purity and defilement in Mark's narrative.[15] I will elaborate this last example in my case study of Mark.

IDENTIFYING SOCIAL LOCATION

The fifth area of the social study of the New Testament is to identify the social location of the original author/audience of a biblical writing. Social location refers to the position in a society shared by a group of people. Locating a group within its particular social system helps to identify the political, economic, religious, and cultural place of that group in society. It also helps to clarify the power dynamics of that group in relation to other groups.

In first-century Israel, for example, one might identify the social location of an individual or a community in terms of such group factors as ethnic identity as Judean or Gentile (non-Judean), gender, sectarian identity (Sadducees, Pharisees, Essenes, revolutionaries), social class, economic class, family of birth, role within the family, priestly or Levitical ancestry, village/region, honor/shame status, purity/impurity, health/disability, among others. Group identities are especially important in light of the fact that, in first-century cultures, people got their identity from their embeddedness in groups.

Given the anonymity of the Gospel of Mark, historians have had to infer a conception of the author from the Gospel itself. Scholars identify the author of Mark variously as Judean Christian or Gentile Christian, dwelling in urban Rome or rooted in rural Syria or Galilee, one of the educated elites or a person from the peasant class, highly trained in literate rhetoric or an untrained storyteller rooted primarily in the oral tradition, and writing before, during, or after the Roman Judean War of 66 to 70 C.E. Because Mark's Gospel is complex, it lends itself to quite divergent reconstructions. In addition to proposing a social location of the author, scholars can also do an assessment of the social location of the characters within Mark's Gospel and, by implication, propose a social location for some likely first-century audiences. The ideological question to ask about the power dynamics of these social locations is this: Whose interests does this writing serve? And whose interests does this writing oppose or marginalize?

Richard Rohrbaugh has offered the most comprehensive analysis of the social location of Mark's author and an implied first-century audience. He identifies Mark's social location within the framework of a pre-industrial, advanced agrarian society, with social classes that included ruling elites (1–2%), retainers or agents of the elites (5%), urban non-elites (3–7%), peasants (75%), unclean and expendables (10%), and no middle class. First, he surveys the social location of the characters in the Gospel. Jesus (as a woodworker), the disciples, and the crowds come from the peasant class. The minor characters who approach Jesus for help come mostly from among the unclean and expendables. The opponents of Jesus are the upper-class elites (the high priests and elders, along with Herod Antipas and Pilate) and their retainers (scribes and Pharisees, Herodians and Roman soldiers).

Based on inferences from his analysis of the characters, Rohrbaugh places Mark's first-century audience predominantly in the rural peasant class of Palestine with opponents among the Judean and Gentile elites and their retainers (with exceptions), with an eagerness to include women, and with a commitment to cross boundaries in order to embrace the unclean and the expendables. As such, Mark's audience participated in an oral, non-literate culture, which embraced the traditions of Israel that favored the people (in contrast to the traditions that favored the elites). The values expressed in Mark's Gospel had limited regard for social honor and kinship loyalties and offered support to the peasants and expendables, namely, to those who suffered the most under Roman imperialism. Rohrbaugh dates Mark's Gospel around the end of the Roman-Judean War (66–70 C.E.), a context in which this audience of Judean peasants, along with some Gentile Christians, incurred opposition from both Judean leaders and Roman overlords (13:9). By implication, the author of Mark also shared the same social location as the audience.

When we ask whose interests Mark's Gospel serves, it is quite clear that it is in solidarity with peasants and expendables along with others who respond favorably to Jesus' activity. At the same time, the Gospel stands against those in power who are in opposition to Jesus and his followers and who seek to marginalize, defame, and oppress them.

In addition to identifying the original social location of Mark's Gospel, it is also important to identify the social location of modern readers, especially as the cultural range of interpreters is extensive and their social identities are quite diverse. Identifying social location clarifies the values, beliefs, commitments, angles of perspective, and limitations that hearers may bring to the act of interpretation. Depicting the social location of interpreters also helps to name the similarities and differences between the ancient contexts of the New Testament writings and the contexts of contemporary readers.[16] For example, most scholarly interpreters come from the middle or upper class of the dominant culture, whereas Mark's audience likely came from the suppressed culture of peasants in a society in which there was no middle class. Conversely, when modern interpreters originate from suppressed or colonized cultures, they may share much in common with the social location of Mark's first century audiences.

Conclusion

The five approaches to the social study of the New Testament outlined above interrelate with and depend upon one another. They may be used together with great profit. In fact, John Elliott has developed a method that combines several social approaches in the service of interpreting a New Testament text, a method he calls Social-Scientific Criticism.[17] Such an approach draws upon social description and models from cultural anthropology to reconstruct the sociopolitical situation of the audience and the author's strategy for dealing with it. This approach works especially well with New Testament letters, in which the author, readers, and social situation are identified directly in the letter. There are, however, many ways to combine these methods with benefit. In the case study that follows, I will draw upon the various approaches outlined above to study one facet of the narrative world of the Gospel of Mark.

A CASE STUDY: PURITY AND BOUNDARIES

In order to illustrate these approaches to the social study of the New Testament, I will analyze the dynamics of purity and defilement *within the narrative world of the Gospel of Mark*. In focusing on the narrative world, I am making no assumptions about whether or not the author of Mark has accurately depicted either the historical Jesus or the historical leaders of Israel. That is a historical issue to be dealt with by other methods. In this study, I am assuming that Mark's Gospel was written by an anonymous author in Galilee or rural Syria around 70 C.E., that his audience shared a social world similar to that of Jesus' time depicted in the narrative, and that he writes in solidarity with the peasant culture of Israel. After briefly introducing purity and defilement in Mark, I describe the social phenomenon of purity and defilement in first-century Israel and then show its relevance to an understanding of the narrative world of Mark. In order to clarify the issues at stake, I then apply models from the symbolic approach to cultural anthropology.

It is important to be aware of several cautions in a study of the narrative world of the Gospel of Mark. In such a study, the interpreter hypothetically adopts the point of view of the Markan narrator and presents the beliefs and values of the narrative as a means to understand it. Without qualification or comment, this procedure can be dangerous, because it tends to normalize and ratify Mark's point of view. In Mark's portrayal, Jesus and the narrator see purity and defilement as oppressive boundaries to be crossed in order to reach those on the margins in need of help. The authorities in the story see purity and defilement as crucial boundaries to guard and protect in order to preserve the nation from the loss of identity and the threat of assimilation into Hellenistic culture and the domination of the Roman Empire. In Mark, the two points of view are expressed as caricatures, so that the hearers see clearly the choices—what they are to choose for and what they are to choose against. Mark takes sides strongly in favor of one approach and against another. It is important to see that this is Mark's point of view, and it is a point of view expressed in a specific, concrete historical circumstance. Further, it is open to ethical evaluation, even as a position taken in the context of the author's own time.

In the narrative world of Mark, Jesus, the disciples, and the authorities are all Judeans in Israel; there are no "Christians" in Mark's narrative. And these Judean groups portrayed in the Markan narrative do not represent later Jewish groups or later Christian groups. The conflict in Mark's narrative world is not between Christians and Jews but between a Judean peasant faction led by Jesus, on the one hand, and the Judean authorities, on the other. As such, the power dynamic expressed in Mark is not between two religions but between subjects and rulers, between peasants and elites, in first-century Israel. Hence, to equate the point of view attributed to Jesus in Mark with *the Christian* point of view is inappropriate and historically inaccurate. To equate the point of view attributed to the authorities in Mark as *the Jewish* point of view is also inappropriate and inaccurate. To absolutize or to universalize insights acquired here—either about the Jesus faction in the story or about the Judean leaders in this story—will lead to discrimination and domination of one group over another, a posture that has been historically so tragic in the history of Christian treatment of Jews. We may learn from this case study of Mark the various dynamics of boundaries and the differing points of view about them as a way to assess boundaries and oppression in our own world. However, our historical circumstances differ, and these circumstances invite us to make our own judgments about which, if any, point of view expressed in the story is the most ethical approach called for in a given contemporary situation.

It is easy to see how this case study relates to several other methodologies presented in this book. First, as I have said, the analysis will focus on the *narrative* world of Mark's Gospel. In so doing, it will not deal with the historical Jesus or with Mark's community, but with the society and the Jesus movement as Mark's *narrative* portrays them. Second, the rhetorical analysis of the Markan impact on its ancient audience is the realm of study of *reader-response* criticism, although the original audiences were gathered communities of *hearers* in an oral culture experiencing performances of Mark. Third, because of the differing roles of males and females in relation to purity, this case study is relevant to *feminist* concerns.[18] Fourth, the power dynamics between the peasant movement and the authorities of Israel over purity and defilement fit into the larger picture of the colonial rule in Israel by the Roman Empire and thereby lends itself well to *postcolonial* biblical analysis. Finally, the dynamics of social location in relation to Mark make it abundantly clear how essential it is to take account of the *cultural location of the interpreter*.

Issues of purity and defilement are not familiar to most contemporary readers. When we read Mark, we come across phenomena that are strange to us. Jesus drives out "unclean spirits" (1:23; 5:2); he "cleanses a leper" (1:40-45); and he "declared all foods clean" (7:19). Pharisees accuse Jesus of "eating with sinners" (2:16), and they accuse the disciples of eating bread with "defiled hands" (7:1-23). These notions of purity and defilement have nothing to do with our modern ideas of sanitation or cleanliness. Rather, they refer to states that are caused by forces capable of making things either "pure" or "defiled," either "holy" or "polluted," either "clean or unclean." What is pure is rooted in the reality of the holiness/purity of God; and what is defiled/polluted is related to what deviates from or stands in opposition to God. When we investigate the Judean society of Palestine in the first-century, we discover that dynamics of purity and defilement pervaded the culture.[19] When we come to understand Mark, we see that the forces that cause purity and the forces that cause defilement relate to many aspects of the story: holiness, spirits, demons, illnesses, graves, corpses, Gentiles (non-Judeans), Sabbath, foods, animals, hearts, and so on. The issues of purity are writ large across the pages of Mark's story.

Social Description and Worldview in First-Century Palestine

In the first century, the Judean nation was a temple state under the control of the Roman Empire.[20] For Judeans living there, religious, political, and economic life centered on the Temple in Jerusalem. This temple was a huge complex that dominated the city. It housed more than two thousand priests at a time. During religious festivals, the Temple teemed with tens of thousands of Judeans from all over the known world. The Judean people believed that God's central dwelling on earth was the inner sanctuary of the temple. God's presence in the temple and the proper worship there would guarantee the prosperity of the people, the productivity of the land, and the security of the nation from foreign domination. Israel was a theocracy, a form of government in which God is considered to be the origin and head of state. Within the nation, the high priests had the political task of leading the nation (within Roman parameters) and of providing proper worship in the temple; the Sanhedrin was the administrative and judicial council; and the Pharisees and scribes were experts in the interpretation of the law or Torah, the five books of Moses. As the people of God, the Judeans believed they were set apart to be holy (that is, dedicated to the Lord), to worship God faithfully, and to follow God's laws.

What gave this whole system coherence was the concept of holiness or purity.[21] Holiness was a core value of the Judeans, as stated (by God) in the law: "You shall be holy, for I the Lord your God am holy" (Lev 19:2). God was holy, and the people were therefore to be holy. Because God was holy, God would not tolerate ritual impurity or flagrant immorality. And God wanted people to worship rightly. The law of Israel therefore dealt with holiness.

The law laid out that which was to be embraced in order to assure holiness and that which was to be avoided in order to prevent defilement. There were two kinds of holiness: moral holiness and ritual holiness. The law contained the moral codes for holy behavior among people in the nation. The law also contained the regulations for the ritual observance of holy times and holy festivals to guarantee prosperous life on the land. As such, the law laid out the regulations for proper worship in the temple. In addition, the law contained the holiness codes designating which animals people were permitted to eat and which animals would defile them, the definitions of leprosy, regulations about avoiding corpses, and so on. Moreover, the law prescribed rituals and sacrifices as means to purge defilement from the land, the temple, and the people. In general, Judeans in Palestine were committed to preserving God's holiness, to preserving their own holiness, and to avoiding defilement. How might they have gone about these commitments?

First, most Judeans were devoted to preserving the holiness of God. They protected God's dwelling in the temple from unclean people and unclean animals and things that were defiled. For example, only priests in a state of purity could enter the temple court to offer sacrifices, and they offered there only animals classified as pure and without blemish. All Israelites were to be in a state of purity when they came to worship in the temple. Otherwise, they would defile the temple. In turn, God might destroy the unclean person who came into God's presence in the temple. If people defiled the sanctuary in a flagrant way, God might withdraw from the sanctuary, thereby removing the protection and the benefits that God's presence there secured for the temple, the people, and the land. Also, the effects of flagrant immorality committed outside the temple—bloodshed (murder), idolatry, and sexual sins (Leviticus 18 and 19 and Numbers 35)—could reach into the temple and defile the sanctuary.

Second, Judeans in Palestine were concerned to preserve the ritual and moral holiness of the people of God. They were concerned for ritual purity. For example, Judeans contracted ritual impurity by childbirth, by touching lepers, through the blood of menstruation, through contact with corpses, and by eating unclean foods, among other things. Much ritual defilement was unavoidable in the normal course of life and was not, in general, considered sinful. Such contact defiled a person for brief periods lasting from one to seven days. Such a state of defilement prohibited people from participation in festivals, certain meals, and temple functions. To deal with this defilement and to restore purity, the law required the defiled person to do ritual washings, endure a waiting period, and/or make an offering to God. In addition to ritual impurity, Judeans guarded against moral defilement. They were to avoid sins of immorality and idolatry, particularly the immorality and idolatry associated with Gentiles. Moral defilement had the force to defile the land and the sanctuary, but it did not make a person ritually impure and was not contagious by contact (except through such things as spit or shared food).[22] Moral impurity was dealt with by rituals of repentance and forgiveness and/or by punishment. By guarding their ritual and moral holiness, the people of Israel could preserve their traditions and avoid assimilation into the larger Hellenistic culture and the Roman imperialism that threatened to overtake their religious traditions.

We can see how Judeans in Palestine organized their world to preserve their holiness. Jerome Neyrey has demonstrated the structures of holiness by reference to "cultural maps" of places, people, things, and times that served to organize Judean life.[23] Although these maps of holiness come from later writings, they nevertheless reflect an earlier time and are helpful in understanding the mentality of holiness that prevailed in the first century.

First, consider the "map of places" from the Mishnah, the early third-century collection of oral commentary on the Torah. It offers a geographical listing (*Kelim* 1.6-9) cited in ascending order of holiness:

1. The land of Israel is holier than any other land. . . .

2. The walled cities of Israel are still more holy. . . .

3. Within the walls of Jerusalem is still more holy. . . .

4. The Temple Mount is still more holy. . . .

5. The rampart is still more holy. . . .

6. The Court of Women is still more holy. . . .

7. The Court of the Israelites is still more holy. . . .

8. The Court of Priests is still more holy. . . .

9. Between the porch and altar is still more holy. . . .

10. The sanctuary is still more holy. . . .

11. The Holy of Holies is still more holy. . . .

Notice that the holy of holies, God's central place of residence on earth, is the holiest place. At all costs, the Judeans must protect this inner sanctuary of the temple from defilement. The degrees of holiness outward from the sanctuary correspond directly with the nearness to or distance from this sanctuary. In this listing, certain people belong in certain spaces. Each group is holy enough to attain their proper place, but not holy enough to penetrate closer to the sanctuary without defiling that place. Notice that the territory of Gentile nations is off the map and not holy at all. In general, the Jews avoided contact with Gentiles because they represented immorality, idolatry, and ritual impurity.

Neyrey also presents the purity map of people from the later Jewish Tosefta (*t. Meg.*), cited in descending order of holiness:

1. High priest

2. Priests

3. Levites

4. Israelites

5. Converts

6. Freed slaves

7. Disqualified priests

8. Temple slaves

9. Bastards

10. Eunuchs

11. Others with physical deformities

Notice how some of these categories of people correlate with places on the geographical map. Only the designated High Priest can enter the holy of holies. Only priests and Levites can enter the Court of the Priests. Only male members of groups five through seven can enter the Court of the Israelites, and so on. Again, the map does not include Gentiles, because they are not holy. Also, the map excludes women from the scheme of holiness. Due to impurity from the blood of menstruation and childbearing, women bore a regular threat of defilement.

Neyrey presents other maps, not only of places but also of things and times. One such list specifies who can marry whom. Another map lists the degrees of defilement attached to people and to things that will defile by contact, such as a leper, the corpse of an unclean animal or human, bodily fluids (such as pus or semen) that are out of place, or persons considered defiled. Another map lists the hierarchy of holy times not to be defiled by certain prohibited behavior, times such as the Sabbath days and the Passover festival.

Holiness/purity was a core value of the society. It was the major concept by which the nation-culture structured and classified everything in its world—people, places, objects, and times. All groups and sects agreed in principle on the importance of purity. However, various Judean sects in Palestine understood purity in different ways, based their view on differing interpretations of Scripture, and they applied the regulations about it in different ways.[24]

1. The sect of the Sadducees included mainly high priests and other aristocrats. They believed that proper worship in the temple was essential to the holiness that preserved the life of the nation. As such, they applied the purity regulations only to life at the temple. Lower priests and Levites needed to be pure only when they took their annual two-week stint of service in the temple. Ordinary Israelites needed to preserve their purity only when they entered the Court of the Israelites to offer sacrifices. Judeans were to offer at the sanctuary only pure, unblemished animals. As Sadducees, the high priests guarded everything and everyone who entered the temple in order to ensure the purity of this holy place.

2. The Pharisees were a group of Judeans who studied the written law and also passed down oral traditions of their interpretations and applications of the law. Like the Sadducees, they applied purity regulations to the temple. However, they went further and applied the purity regulations to all Israelites and to all times, not just when people were at the temple. Pharisees believed that all Israel was a kingdom of priests. Just as priests kept themselves pure while doing service in the temple, so all Judeans should at all times observe purity regulations. Just as the priests performed ritual washings before meals as a removal of defilement from contact with that which was unclean, so all Judeans should wash hands and food and utensils before eating.[25] They should do this in order to cleanse themselves from direct and indirect contact they may have deliberately or inadvertently had with unclean things or people. The Pharisees promoted these measures as a margin or "fence" to protect people from defilement due to contact with Gentiles, such as, for example, may have occurred in the marketplaces.

3. The sect of Essenes had the most stringent purity regulations.[26] Although some Essenes lived in towns and villages, many Essenes had fully withdrawn from the life of the nation and the temple in the second century B.C.E. and established a monastic community at Qumran on the shores of the Dead Sea. They believed that the Maccabean high priests were not legitimate and that they had thus defiled the temple and the whole land by their presence there. In their view, God had withdrawn from the temple because of these violations. So too, the Essenes withdrew. At Qumran, the Essenes carried out the strictest holiness codes as if for the temple. They did so in the conviction that their community was now the surrogate "temple"—the only place holy enough for God to dwell on earth. They saw both ritual and moral impurity as defiling by contact, and they considered all outsiders as unclean. The Essenes offered no sacrifices, but as a community they preserved strict holiness

in order to provide a place in Israel for the presence of God, in the hope that God would soon inaugurate a new order in Israel and the world.

4. Some revolutionaries before and during the Roman-Judean War of 66–70 C.E. held to a strict interpretation of the first commandment against idolatry, arguing that there should be "No Lord but God" over the holy land and the holy people of Israel. Therefore, they rejected any acknowledgement of the Roman Emperor as Lord and they opposed the Roman census of people and property in 6 C.E. With "zeal" for God, they sought to purge the land of the defiling presence and influence of Gentiles. In addition, they opposed the elite Judeans who gave "idolatrous" allegiance to the Roman overlords and who cooperated with them. They believed their own revolutionary actions would cleanse the holy land from its defilement and assure God's support in their commitment to free Israel from imperial domination.

5. Most Judeans in Palestine were peasants who followed the regulations when they went to the temple for festivals. The purity laws applied equally to all Israelites, but not all Israelites were equally able to carry them out. Few peasants had the time or the material resources to carry out the ritual prescriptions of purity that the Pharisees advocated. For the same reasons, many peasant Judeans often disregarded other laws as well, such as the regulations of the Sabbath and the requirements for tithes due the temple. Many Judeans had direct contact with Gentiles in the marketplaces of the cities and indirect contact through Judean tax collectors. The Pharisees maligned as "sinners" (see Mark 2:15-17) those peasant Judeans who ignored the purity laws.

This system of purity as holiness served Israel well throughout its history, preserving a minority culture from absorption into dominant cultures that held political sway over Israel. At the time of Jesus, the culture and religion of the Judeans were threatened by the dominant Greek culture and the imperialism of the Roman Empire. The Judean structures of purity protected the people from these threats of cultural and political domination. By keeping themselves separate from Gentiles, the Judeans maintained the beliefs and practices that comprised their way of life. At the same time, they sought to be an example of moral and ritual holiness for the nations. The Judean nation hoped that eventually the Gentile nations would be drawn to see Jerusalem as a place of justice and true worship.

When we turn to the depiction of Israel in the Gospel of Mark, we see issues of both purity and defilement throughout: the Holy Spirit, cleansing a leper, work on the Sabbath, corpses, exorcism of unclean spirits, Gentiles, sinners, unclean foods, and so on. As portrayed in Mark's story, the leaders of the nation uphold the laws of ritual purity as we have outlined them. By contrast, Jesus makes an onslaught against these purity rules and regulations. In Mark's view, Jesus is indeed holy, for the "Holy Spirit" comes upon Jesus at his baptism (1:10) and he is called "the Holy One of God" (1:24). Nevertheless, Jesus counters the purity rules that preserved the holiness of the nation.

- He encounters "unclean spirits" (1:21-28).

- He touches a leper (1:40-45).

- He heals Simon's mother-in-law on the Sabbath (1:29-31).

- He pardons sinners (2:1-12).

- He calls a tax collector to follow him (2:13-14).

- He eats with tax collectors and sinners (2:15-17).

- His disciples pluck grain on the holy Sabbath (2:23-28).

- He heals an impaired man on the Sabbath (3:1-6).

- He drives unclean spirits from a man at a graveyard in Gentile territory, and they go into a herd of swine (5:1-20).

- He is touched by and heals a woman with a flow of blood (5:25-34).

- He touches the corpse of a little girl (5:35-43).

- His disciples eat bread with unwashed/defiled hands (7:1-15).

- He declares that all foods are clean (7:17-23).

- He heals a Gentile woman in the Gentile land of Tyre (7:24-30).

- He feeds and eats with Gentiles in a desert in Gentile land (8:1-10).

Instead of using purity regulations to protect, the Markan Jesus transgresses the boundaries of purity. Through the agency of the "holy" spirit empowering Jesus, God enters the arena of impurity without regard to the risk of defilement and, by an act of reversal, brings purity to those who are unclean.

In Mark's portrayal, the leaders of the nation protect the boundaries of ritual purity that Jesus violates.

- They accuse Jesus of blasphemy for claiming the right to pardon sins (2:1-12).

- They challenge his eating with tax collectors and sinners (2:15-17).

- They challenge the disciples' plucking grain on the Sabbath (2:23-28).

- They seek charges against Jesus for healing on the Sabbath and they plot to destroy him (3:1-6).

- They say Jesus is possessed by an unclean spirit, not the Holy Spirit (3:22-30).

- They say he drives out demons by the authority of Satan, the ruler of demons (3:22-30).

- They accuse Jesus because his disciples violate the traditions of the elders by eating bread with unwashed (defiled) hands (7:1-15).

- They condemn Jesus to death for blasphemy against God and hand him over to the Roman authorities, who crucify him (14:53-65).

Cultural Anthropology: Models, Explanations, and Insights

What is going on here? How can we make sense of the issues of purity? How do the notions of purity and pollution work? What is the difference in the two approaches to purity between the peasant movement of Jesus and the Judean leaders? How can we unpack the dynamics of Mark's story? To deal with these questions, we can turn to explanations, insights, and models from cultural anthropology.

For example, we can understand better the concepts of purity and pollution/defilement by making use of a model from cultural anthropologist Mary Douglas.[27] In her view, purity represents the notion that there are places for things and things are in their place. That is, people, animals, and things are pure when they have a place in the system and when they are in their proper place. By contrast, pollution represents the notion that some things have no place or that things are out of their place. In this case, people, animals, and things are defiled when they have no place in the system or when they are out of their proper place. Purity and pollution imply, therefore, an ordered classification of people, animals, and things—with corresponding boundaries. Thus, if we observe what a culture considers to be pure and polluted, we can see how that culture gives order to the world.

As Douglas points out, dirt or that which pollutes is "matter out of place."[28] Soil belongs in a garden, but soil does not belong in a house. When soil is in a house, we consider it to be "dirt" because it is out of place. This is an analogy for the whole purity-pollution system. The assumption is that there are "places" for things and for people and for animals and for behaviors—a place for things and things in its place. We have already seen how thoroughly Israel classified people, places, objects, and times in terms of holiness. Holiness/purity occurs when something or someone has a place and is properly in place. Pollution occurs when something or someone is out of place or when something or someone has no place. Purity rules of avoidance and purification are ways of dealing with things and people that are out of place or do not belong. Such regulations serve to make the world conform with the structure of ideas. By keeping the purity rules, people impose order on experience and achieve harmony or consonance between worldview and behavior.

Douglas's analysis of the ancient Hebrew system of purity-pollution illustrates the model clearly. The ancient Hebrew culture as reflected in the book of Leviticus in the Law of Moses is a purity-pollution system based on "holiness." The notion of holiness is rooted in two concepts: wholeness and set-apartness. First, holiness has to do with what is whole. That which is pure/holy is that which conforms wholly to its classification. Now we can see why human beings with "deformities" were considered marginal and unclean and why animals with "blemishes" were considered unclean and were not to be offered at the temple. They were not considered to be whole, and therefore they did not fit wholly within their class. Also, we can see why fish and cattle and doves are clean animals and do not defile people who eat them. These animals fit the Israelite classification of "normal" animals. Conversely, eels (no scales) and pigs (no cloven hooves) and ostriches (do not fly) do not fit the Hebrew classification of normal or whole animals. These animals are therefore not clean and will defile those who eat them.[29] In light of these explanations, we can now understand the list of holy places cited previously and the list of those people who belong in each place. We can see also that Gentiles are to be avoided because there is no place for them in the system.

Second, holiness has to do with things and people that are set apart, things which by virtue of being in their place are kept away from certain other things; that is, things are holy when they are in their place, when they are not where they do not belong. Now we can understand why blood, spit, and semen are unclean. They belong inside the body. When they come out of their place, for example when blood comes out in a menstrual flow, these things are unclean and will defile people. Lepers are unclean because they have boils or breaks in the skin where pus or fluid comes out. Also, we can see how important it was for certain people to stay apart from certain places. No one can enter the Holy of Holies except the High Priest. Women who go beyond their place into the Court of the Priests will defile it. Gentiles are prohibited from entering beyond the outer courts of the temple on penalty of death. Thus, in the Hebrew culture, there was an ordered classification of the world with proper places for people and things. People or things that did not fit the classification or that were out of place were considered to be unclean and capable of making other things unclean.

In Mark's depiction of the Judean nation, the authorities support this system. They maintain boundaries and guard them to protect God's holiness and to protect the Judean culture from assimilation. But in Mark's portrayal, Jesus has a very different Judean approach. Jesus does not reinforce the purity system of the authorities. He crosses boundaries, redraws them, or eliminates them. As a result, he has contact with all types of unclean people and objects.

He goes to places that are out of bounds. He violates holy times. What is the key to this clash between the authorities and Jesus? How can we explain these two very different approaches to purity?

We can get insight into the different approaches of the leaders and Jesus by delineating their differing attitudes toward boundaries. We have already seen the connection between purity and boundaries. In his work on boundaries, Jonathan Z. Smith helps us see the fundamental difference between these two approaches to purity depicted in Mark's Gospel.[30] Smith would argue that the difference between the authorities and Jesus is so dramatic as to represent polar opposites. One approach maintains boundaries and secures holiness by guarding against that which would defile. The other approach crosses boundaries and risks defilement to make what is unclean pure.

The one choice is "the affirmation of one's place" within the order of certain boundaries. Here, "each person is called to dwell in a limited world in which everything has its given place and role to fulfill. To be sacred is to remain in place. To break out, to cross boundaries, is to open the world to the threat of chaos, to commit transgression."[31] In this approach, the leader is one who discerns order and helps people fulfill their roles within that order. We can see that the leaders of Israel in Mark embrace this stance.

The other choice expresses a desire "to be unbounded, to be liberated." In this view, boundaries have become oppressive and restrictive or are simply limiting. Here people do not define themselves "by the degree to which they harmonize themselves and their society to the cosmic patterns of order, but rather to the degree to which they can escape that order."[32] Here, "positive sacred power [is] to be gained from the violation of the given boundaries of the world, from the transcendence of the way things ordinarily are."[33] In this approach, the leader is the one who enables people to escape the bounds. We can see that Jesus and his followers in Mark embrace this stance, not to attain personal freedom but in order to reach outcasts with the blessings of the reign of God.

These stances, Smith argues, are "the two basic existential options" open to human beings. A total worldview is implied in each of these stances. Smith resists giving a higher value to one stance or the other. A great deal may depend on the historical and social circumstances. Order can be creative or oppressive. The transgression of order can be creative or destructive. Yet the two options represent such fundamentally different worldviews that "to change stance is to totally alter one's symbols and to inhabit a different world."[34] Clearly, Mark is biased toward the approach that portrays Jesus as a transgressor of boundaries. Yet to understand Mark's approach, we must see the validity and the difficulties of both stances. The approach of the authorities in Mark could prevent assimilation and/or it could become oppressive. The approach of Jesus could counter the effects of such oppression or it could be recklessly undermining the distinctive traditions and identity of Israel. We must also recognize how distinctive Mark's approach is in comparison with some other New Testament writings. The Gospel of Matthew, for example, presents a mixed approach of both crossing and guarding boundaries, while others, such as the Pastoral Epistles, clearly favor the approach that guards boundaries.

How then can we bring these two different worldviews into sharper focus? To help us, we now turn to another model from the work of Mary Douglas. She argues that the approach of any given culture or group tends to be uniform toward all boundaries. She shows how people in the same culture have a similar attitude toward boundaries at several levels of experience. One can see this "unity of experience" in the attitude toward boundaries at three levels:

1. The social boundaries of the group or culture.

2. The bodily boundaries of persons within the culture.

3. The cosmological boundaries that the people project through their belief systems about God and the world.

Douglas argues that the attitude toward boundaries tends to be the same at each of these three levels. For example, if a society is anxious about what goes in and out of the orifices of the bodily boundary, then this society will probably also guard the social boundary carefully to protect who comes in and who goes out of their social group. Regarding the cosmological level of beliefs in such a society, one would expect to find a dualism with a distinct boundary separating the good from the evil, the holy from the unclean. "Conversely," Douglas says, "if [in another culture] there is no concern to preserve social boundaries, I would not expect to find concern with bodily boundaries."[35] And in such a culture with little concern to guard social boundaries, the beliefs about God and the world will show ambiguity and interaction around the boundary between good and evil.

We can see how the system works when we notice how the view of boundaries in the Judean culture of the first century is the same at the cosmological, bodily, and social levels.

1. *Cosmological boundaries.* At the cosmological level, the dominant motif was the pursuit of holiness by separation from what was considered unclean. There was a boundary set around God to protect God's holiness and to separate God from all that would defile. People were to guard this boundary in order to keep God from withdrawing. On earth, God's central place was the holy of holies in the temple. As we have seen, many boundaries surrounded this holiest place. The cosmic order also included boundaries for people and animals: cosmological lines separated Israel from the Gentile nations, and other lines separated animals into clean and unclean. As we have seen, people were to

guard these boundaries in order to keep what is holy separated from that which defiles.

2. *Bodily boundaries.* Similarly, the skin of the body was considered a boundary to be guarded. The skin makes a person a bounded system. The skin keeps certain things in place inside the body, such as pus, blood, and semen. When out of place, these things were thought to make a person unclean. For example, leprosy was defined as any condition in which fluids, such as pus and blood, seep out of the skin. Similarly, people could guard the skin from unclean things going in from outside the body, for example, by refusing to eat the meat of an unclean animal. Such unclean food taken in from the outside would defile a person. Hence, people guarded the boundary of the body to avoid contact with what was considered unclean, because what comes out of the body as well as unclean things that go into the body would defile people.

3. *Social boundaries.* The boundary of Israel distinguished Judean from Gentile. Only male Judeans who were circumcised (the mark of being Judean) and without blemish were considered pure. Judeans who had contact with Gentiles risked becoming unclean, and intermarriage was strictly prohibited. At the same time, Gentiles who came among Judeans were often considered to be "out of place" in the Judean community and, as we have seen, were prohibited from entering the temple sanctuary on penalty of death. Generally speaking, ancient Judeans guarded the social boundary to keep Judeans in and Gentiles out so as to avoid the influence of Gentile immorality and idolatry.

Of the three levels in this scheme, the most important level was that of the social group. The bodily boundaries and the cosmological order protected and maintained the social boundaries of the group or society. Thus, Douglas notes, "Israel is the boundary that all other boundaries celebrate and that gives them their historical load of meaning."[36] The whole classification system existed in order to protect and sustain the group, especially in the face of cultural/imperial domination. The avoidance of unclean, marginalized Judean people within the nation was a hedge or a fence against the outer boundary that separated Judean from Gentile. Thus, according to Douglas's model, there was a coherence of attitudes toward boundaries at several levels, and the coherence served to reinforce the group's experience of its social boundary.

As we have seen, this system is reflected in the depiction of the authorities in Mark's story. They separate themselves from the unclean in Israel (2:15-17); they guard the holy Sabbath from defilement (2:23—3:6); they guard God from blasphemy (2:1-12; 14:53-65); they guard the temple from unclean people

(11:15-18) and blemished sacrifices (12:32-33); and they guard the body from impure food (7:1-23). By separating themselves from lepers, unclean sinners, and people with unclean spirits and by mandating that people wash hands after going to the markets (7:1-23), the authorities seek to protect the nation by providing an internal hedge against the external boundary leading to contact with the (even more unclean) Gentiles, where there is an even greater risk of defilement. At the same time, by labeling such people as "unclean" and "sinners," they marginalize them within the nation. And when Jesus challenges the boundaries that guard against the unclean within Israel, the authorities seek to discredit Jesus with the people by portraying him as unclean—namely, by claiming that he acts under the authority of Satan and that he himself is possessed by an "unclean spirit" (Beelzebul 3:22-30).[37]

By contrast, the Judean movement of Jesus in Israel, according to Mark's portrayal, illustrates a contrasting attitude toward boundaries, the effort to be "unbounded" in order to overcome obstacles in the service of the kingdom of God. Here we see that happens when people abrogate purity rules, cross boundaries, or redraw them. Whereas the authorities in Mark's story guarded boundaries, Jesus and his followers transgressed boundaries. Whereas the leaders saw boundaries as means of protection, the Jesus movement saw boundaries as oppressive and limiting. Whereas the leaders withdrew from uncleanness, the Jesus movement overcame, ignored, or redefined uncleanness. Whereas the Pharisees avoided contact with that which defiled, Jesus and his disciples sought contact in order to overcome the oppressive and destructive effects of defilement. The leaders had power by staying within the ordered boundaries, whereas the Jesus faction expressed power by crossing boundaries. The Jesus faction, as depicted by Mark, treated boundaries as lines to cross, to redraw, or to eliminate.

In Mark's depiction of the Jesus movement, we see again a consonance, albeit of a very different character, in the attitude toward boundaries at the cosmological, the social, and the bodily levels.

Cosmological Boundaries

Mark's narrative shares the core value of the Judean society in depicting God as holy. The empowering force behind the activity in the kingdom of God in Mark's portrayal is the "Holy Spirit" (1:8-10), and Jesus is the "Holy One of God" (1:24). However, in contrast to the view that people are to attain holiness by separation from the threatening force of impurity, Mark presents the view that people are to overcome uncleanness by spreading wholeness. Here God does not withdraw because of the threat of defilement by contact with the unclean. Rather, God's holiness is an active force that expands and invades in order to overcome uncleanness and to remove it. Thus, in contrast to the view that God is to be protected within the confines of the temple, the Markan God spreads the life-giving power of the kingdom through Jesus and his followers into the world wherever people are receptive to it.

In Mark, God's holiness spreads even into the territory of Satan. Satan is the adversary of God, and Mark refers to the demons under Satan's authority as "unclean spirits." Before the kingdom arrived, the world was Satan's house (3:23-29). Now, however, God breaks out of the confines of heaven, rips apart the boundary between heaven and earth, and sends the Holy Spirit upon Jesus, who then invades Satan's territory (1:9-13). To establish rulership over the world, God crosses into Satan's arena. God sends down the Holy Spirit upon Jesus at his baptism (1:10-11). Immediately, the Spirit drives Jesus to confront Satan in the desert. Through the agency of Jesus, God binds Satan and plunders Satan's house (3:22-30). As such, God reclaims people from the destructiveness of the "unclean spirits" (1:12-13; 5:1-20; 9:14-19) and restores them to community. The "holy" work of God is that which brings life and overcomes the destructive work of Satan (3:4; 9:42-49).

Also, in Mark, God breaks out of the confines of the temple to be available everywhere. The Judean leaders know that God resides on earth in the temple, and they protect God from what is unclean. Jesus condemns the temple as holy space because the leaders use it to set boundaries; and, by their commercial activity in the courts, they prevent Gentiles from worshiping there (11:17). At the death of Jesus, God tears apart the curtain of the sanctuary and breaks out of the confines of the temple sanctuary (15:38). In Mark's portrayal, God therefore leaves the temple in order to spread out over the earth. God leaves the temple and becomes available anywhere on earth to grant blessings and to pardon sins. The temple is no longer needed for rituals and sacrifices because God is now accessible "wherever" people offer prayers of faith and forgiveness (11:20-25).

Furthermore, Mark eliminates the cosmological boundaries that would identify people or things as unclean in and of themselves. For example, Mark eliminates the notion that animals might be unclean in and of themselves, for the Markan Jesus declares all foods clean (7:19). Also, Mark eliminates the notion that Gentiles are to be avoided. Mark rejects the boundary line distinguishing pure Judeans from Gentiles who are ritually and morally unclean. In Mark's view, any Judean or Gentile may be on God's side or against God— based on faith in Jesus' proclamation of the rule of God and on moral behavior rather than on ritual purity (3:29; 7:15). Also, Gentile land is not unclean in and of itself (4:1-20; 7:24—8:10). Furthermore, Mark rejects the interior lines that provided the margin or fence against unclean Judeans within Israel.

Mark's Jesus does not eliminate the boundary line distinguishing God's people from others. He redraws the line exclusively in terms of *moral* behavior rather than *ritual* impurity.[38] He eliminates dietary boundaries and "ritual defilements" that come by external contact with unclean things, but he does not abrogate purity notions altogether. Rather, he redefines the purity/holiness of people and times in terms of faith and moral behavior that the law and the prophets enjoin. The "evil designs" that come out from people in actions—illegal sexual acts, thefts, murder, expressions of greed, malicious acts, and so on—*these* "are the things that defile people" (7:14-23; 12:28-34). This list includes the bloodshed and sexual offenses that traditionally rendered one morally impure. Nevertheless, Jesus expands the range of moral behavior that renders one impure to encompass all behavior that is destructive and dehumanizing of others (see also 3:4; 9:42-48; and 12:28-34). Also in this passage, Jesus considers that the individual alone is rendered impure, not the land or the sanctuary.[39] In the Gospel, Mark addresses moral defilement by means of repentance and forgiveness outside the rituals of the temple. John the Baptist is portrayed as having a ritual that effects forgiveness of sins (1:4-8). Apart from any ritual, Jesus pardons the sins of those who come to him for healing (2:1-12) and who turn to embrace the rule of God (4:12; 11:25).

Those who respond favorably to Jesus and his teaching are on the inside; those who reject him and his teaching are on the outside (3:31-35; 4:10-13). Those who do the will of God as Jesus teaches it are Jesus' "brother and sister and mother," whereas those who do not do the will of God are in opposition to Jesus and are on the outside (3:31-35). In order to give all people an opportunity to be on the inside, the followers of Jesus are to proclaim the inauguration of the kingdom of God to all people, Judean and Gentile alike, without respect to ritual purity or impurity (13:10, 27). Thus, Jesus redraws the line distinguishing God's people without respect to "ritual" purity or impurity.

As portrayed in the narrative, God is spreading holiness throughout Israel and to the ends/margins of the earth (13:27). Followers are also to spread out in order to bring the kingdom of God to Gentile nations (13:10). They are not to be limited by avoiding people or animals or things that are considered unclean by society.

Social Boundaries

The attitude toward social boundaries in Mark's narrative world reveals the same approach—transgressing, overcoming, redrawing, or eliminating. The Jesus movement described in the narrative of Mark is not a stationary community that seeks to protect its boundaries but a network going out from Jesus like branches on a tree: first Jesus, then the disciples he sends out (6:7-13), and then those who receive the disciples by hospitality (9:37) and pass the word on (1:28, 45; 5:20). The people in the network expand in outreach and influence.

Relationships in the network are based on reciprocity between those who proclaim and heal and those who give them hospitality. Jesus offers no provisions for establishing stationary communities—neither ongoing rituals such as baptism nor a repetition of the last supper Jesus had with his disciples, and no directions for communal organization or discipline. Jesus tells disciples to leave their families and property and to receive new familial relations in the hospitality offered them from one village to the next. The person who is at the extremity of the network—one who simply offers a cup of water to someone who bears the name of Christ—is fully part of the network and will receive a reward (9:41). Solidarity in this network is based, therefore, not on relationships in a stationary community, but on the hospitality that followers receive from those who choose to be in solidarity with them as the disciples move from place to place. The solidarity of hospitality is the means by which the disciples receive "houses, brothers, sisters, mothers, children, and fields" (10:28-30). In contrast to a culture that is stationary and that protects itself by maintaining boundaries, the Jesus movement in Mark is a loose-knit network comprised of people who are spreading out and crossing boundaries.

In Mark's portrayal, Jesus and his followers, like God, are "boundary-crossing" figures. They cross the boundaries established by the culture that protect people from ritual uncleanness. Instead of preserving holiness by avoiding contact, the Markan movement spreads holiness by making contact.[40] Instead of avoiding contact with all people outside the group, Jesus' followers give all people the chance to experience the good news of the reign of God (13:10). Instead of defilement as the force that is contagious, holiness is the force that is contagious. In every case, instead of Jesus being defiled by the contact, Jesus makes that which is unclean become clean by spreading purity, forgiveness, exorcism, and healing.

Nor does the Jesus network depicted in Mark guard boundaries to protect those who are inside from those who are outside. The people in the network sow the seeds of the good news everywhere (4:13-20) and exclude no one from the network or from its benefits. Jesus eats with tax collectors and sinners. Jesus heals all who request healing, including a Gentile woman in Tyre (7:24-30). In Gentile territory, he feeds four thousand people who have followed him into the desert (7:31—8:10). The narrative explicitly rejects guarding boundaries by excluding people. At one point, the disciples prevent a man from exorcising a demon in Jesus' name because he "was not following us." In response, Jesus tells them, "Do not stop him . . . for whoever is not against us is for us" (9:38-40). As such, those inside the network are to do nothing to set the limits of the community. Rather, they simply spread the influence of the network. Those outside the network who reject the followers of Jesus are the ones who set the limits of the network by their acts of rejection. Jesus tells the disciples that if others do not welcome them they are to leave that locale and shake the dust off their feet as a witness to the rejection (6:11). However, they do so only to confirm a decision already made by the outsiders rejecting them.

Furthermore, Jesus gives no directions for expulsion from the network. In fact, he strictly prohibits any attempt to dominate or exclude "the little ones who have faith" (9:42). Jesus himself, knowing that one of the Twelve is about to betray him, nevertheless offers the cup to him at the last communal (Passover) meal, and they all drink from it—including Judas (14:23). The Markan Jesus defines the boundary lines that distinguish insiders and outsiders; however, he prohibits the people in the network from guarding these lines. And because followers do not guard or maintain the boundary lines, there is no margin to the boundary. People can get in easily, and once inside, they can be at various levels of commitment or betrayal. This prohibition against guarding boundaries serves to prevent anything or anyone from inhibiting the expansion of the network. It is also in conformity with Jesus' moral injunction not to lord over anyone (10:41-45).

Bodily Boundaries

Similarly, the followers of Jesus do not guard the body against things going in from the outside. Jesus says, "There is nothing from outside that by entering people is able to defile them, because it does not enter into the heart, but goes into the stomach and on out into the latrine." The Markan narrator adds, "—thus he declared all foods clean" (7:17-19). Therefore, there is no need to wash the hands before eating or to protect the body from taking in certain foods or to be concerned about the waste that goes out into the latrine, because Jesus declared all foods to be clean (7:1-23). This attitude toward the bodily boundary replicates the attitude toward the social boundary. As anyone may enter the network without making the group unclean, so anything may go into the body without making it unclean. There is no need to guard the boundaries from what is outside the person or the group.

There are two exceptions to the prohibition against guarding the boundary of the body. In Mark, demons are "unclean spirits" who enter and possess people. Unlike foods, they do not enter the stomach and go on out. Rather, they affect the whole person, including the heart, making faith impossible. To drive out an unclean spirit by the power of the "Holy" Spirit is thereby to render a person clean. Also, people are to guard the bodily boundary against fornication and adultery. Here the focus is not so much on guarding physical boundaries. Rather, the focus is on guarding to ensure that immoral and destructive behavior will not come out from the heart (10:1-12; cf. 7:20-23).

In the Markan worldview, what renders one clean or unclean is the behavior that comes out from the heart. As God spreads the kingdom and as the Jesus movement spreads holiness, so the individual spreads love for God and neighbor outward from the whole heart (12:29-31). However, immoral behavior that goes out from the heart can make that person unclean (7:20-23). Jesus says, "For from inside, from the hearts of people, come the evil designs: fornications, thefts, murders, adulteries, expressions of greed, malicious acts, deceit, licentiousness, envious eye, blasphemy, arrogance, reckless folly. All these evil things come out from inside and defile the person" (7:21-23). Thus, Mark eliminates ritual defilement as a demarcation and draws a line between moral and immoral behavior as that which determines purity or defilement. Mark honors moral behavior coming from the inside rather than guarding against unclean things from the outside.

In the same way, the Markan Jesus gives place to moral behavior over against physical wholeness. Mark shows through the many healings that it is God's will to make people whole. Yet, rather than cause someone else to sin, it is better to cut off one's own hand and to enter the rule of God maimed than to have two hands and be thrown into Gehenna (9:42-49). Thus, the purity that comes from physical wholeness is not a criterion for being acceptable to God; rather, what makes one acceptable is the moral behavior that comes out of the heart. This concern for morality over ritual purity and physical wholeness is evident in the "wise" statement of the scribe that loving God and the neighbor with the "whole" heart is more important than all the "whole" burnt offerings and sacrifices (pure animals without blemish, 12:32-33).

As such, the only maintenance Jesus recommends for the bodily boundary is for followers to do whatever they must do in order not to let harmful actions come out from their own heart. One guards not the body but the heart so that what comes out of the heart is life-giving for others rather than destructive.

Summary

In Mark's narrative, the leaders erected and maintained boundaries to preserve holiness, while Jesus and his disciples spread holiness outwardly—the good news of the kingdom, the power of the Spirit, and the loving deeds that come from within. In Mark's narrative, leaders, especially the Pharisees, guarded boundaries to prevent what was unholy from coming in, while the followers of Jesus overcame boundaries until they should reach the ends of the earth, a goal that Mark considered to be attainable within a generation after the death of Jesus (13:26-31).

We do not know how much Mark's narrative portrayal accurately reflects the historical Jesus or the historical leaders of Israel. What we have seen is the conflict between Jesus and the authorities within the narrative world, how the authorities sought to control his boundary-crossing activities, and how they eventually brought him before the Roman procurator who executed him as a messianic pretender. It is also reasonable to infer that a similar conflict was present between Mark's historical audience and the Judean and Roman authorities—as predicted by Jesus in the story (13:9). Mark's Gospel offered the audience empowerment to cross the boundaries that made them vulnerable in order that they might bring the rule of God to the ends of the earth.

The approach to boundaries in Mark is somewhat unusual, even in early Christianity. Just as there were differing approaches to purity among groups in Judaism, so the early expressions of Christianity differed. For example, many early Christian communities considered baptism to be an important ritual of entrance. Also, both Paul (1 Cor 5:3-5) and Matthew (18:15-18) have procedures for expelling people from a Christian community. Thus, even if Mark depicts Jesus and his followers as a movement of Judeans who were boundary-crossing figures, many early churches, frequently of Gentile make-up, consolidated and organized in order to survive and to prevent assimilation as they spread into the larger Greco-Roman world—often by guarding and maintaining boundaries around the Christian communities. Nevertheless, Mark offers the vision of a radical attitude toward boundaries inspired by the mission to bring the good news of healing and wholeness to those outside the boundaries—to the margins of the earth.

CONCLUSION

The extended example given here illustrates the various approaches presented at the beginning of this chapter.

1. *Social description.* We identified many customs, laws, and practices related to purity and defilement in first-century Palestine.

2. *Social history.* We saw to some extent how the approach to purity in Mark related to the social history of the time. We might also have shown how the conceptions of purity developed in the course of Israel's history and how they related to the social history of the larger Roman world.

3. *Social construction of reality.* We showed "maps" that reveal how the ancient Judeans organized their life together in terms of holiness and defilement. Also, we saw how the Markan Jesus sought to re-socialize followers from their primary enculturation regarding purity, defile-ment, and boundaries. Furthermore, we saw how the Markan attitude toward boundaries supported a social network oriented to mission.

4. *Cultural anthropology.* We employed models to help us interpret the social phenomena and to clarify the different attitudes to purity and boundaries evident in the narrative of Mark's Gospel.

5. *Social Location.* We saw how the peasant location of Jesus within the narrative world and the rhetorical thrust of the Gospel to historical audiences favored the interests of the most vulnerable in society and opposed the Judean and Gentile authorities who marginalized and oppressed them. The efforts of Jesus and his followers to challenge the social order led to persecution and death.

6. *Ethical reflections.* We have cautioned against the unethical use of such a study that would lead to stereotyping, prejudice, or oppression of one group over another group. We also suggested that readers be conscious of the influence of their social location in interpretation. And we encour-aged the use of insights from the conflict in Mark to illuminate the power dynamics of conflicts over boundaries among contemporary groups.

The social study of the first century may seem like an overwhelming task. If you wish to pursue it, begin with one text such as the Gospel of Mark, or even with a single episode within a Gospel. Find something there that puzzles and fascinates you—demons, tax collectors, the temple, fasting, marriage and divorce, leprosy, attitudes to Gentiles, and so on. Then begin to explore this problem with the methods presented here. Many books available on daily life in the first century give extensive social description. Many of the books cited here bring insights from cultural anthropology to bear upon the dynamics of first-century culture. You will discover other resources. Soon you find yourself unraveling a mystery or putting the pieces of a puzzle in place. Then you can go on to the next problem. Soon you find how pieces of the puzzle fit together into a larger picture. You are doing detective work on the first century. Although the task may seem endless, the delight comes from the process of exploration into another world and from the illumination of the biblical stories that results along the way.[41]

FURTHER READING

Blasi, Anthony, Jean Duhaime, and Paul-André Turcotte, eds. *Handbook of Early Christianity: Social Science Approaches.* Walnut Creek, Calif.: Alta Mira, 2002. Large collection of articles on various aspects of the social world of early Christianity.

deSilva, David. *Honor, Patronage, Kinship, and Purity: Unlocking New Testament Culture.* Downers Grove, Ill.: InterVarsity Press, 2000. Analysis of key facets of the first-century cultural context with applications to the New Testament.

Diest, Ferdinand. *The Material Culture of the Bible: An Introduction.* Sheffield: Sheffield Academic Press, 2000. Presents valuable information about the life and times of ancient Hebrew culture.

Elliott, John. *What Is Social Scientific Criticism?* Minneapolis: Fortress Press, 1993. A comprehensive effort to map the methodology of social science criticism.

Ferguson, Everett. *Backgrounds of Christianity.* 3d ed. Grand Rapids: Eerdmans, 2003. A wealth of information about the history, literature, groups, structures, and daily life of the New Testament world.

Hanson, K. C., and Douglas Oakman. *Palestine in the Time of Jesus: Social Structures and Social Conflicts.* Minneapolis: Fortress Press, 1998. Excellent resources on the social dynamics of first-century Palestine.

Horrell, David, ed. *Social-Scientific Approaches to New Testament Interpretation.* Herndon, Va.: T.&T. Clark, 2000. Collection of classic articles addressing the social world of early Christianity.

Horsley, Richard. *Archaeology, History, and Society in Galilee: The Social Context of Jesus and the Rabbis.* Harrisburg: Trinity Press International, 1996. A good example of the use of social description to construct the social world of ancient Palestine.

Malina, Bruce. *The New Testament World: Insights from Cultural Anthropology.* Atlanta: Westminster John Knox, 2003. Introductory text using models from cultural anthropology to map the framework of first-century Mediterranean cultures.

Malina, Bruce, and Richard Rohrbaugh. *Social-Science Commentary on the Synoptic Gospels.* 2d ed. Minneapolis: Fortress Press, 2003. Running commentary on the first three Gospels from the perspective of cultural anthropology. There are similar commentaries on the Gospel of John, the letters of Paul, and the book of Revelation.

Meeks, Wayne. *The First Urban Christians: The Social World of the Apostle Paul.* New Haven: Yale University Press, 1983. A description and analysis of the social dynamics of Pauline churches.

Neyrey, Jerome. *Paul, In Other Words.* Louisville: Westminster John Knox, 1990. A comprehensive treatment of Paul's authentic letters using models from cultural anthropology.

Neyrey, Jerome, ed. *The Social World of Luke-Acts: Models of Interpretation.* Peabody, Mass.: Hendrickson, 1991. Uses models from the social sciences to provide a comprehensive analysis of the social world in the narrative of Luke-Acts.

Osiek, Carolyn. *What Are They Saying about the Social Setting of the New Testament?* New York: Paulist, 1984. Accessible summary and analysis of this whole field of study.

Petersen, Norman. *Rediscovering Paul: Philemon and the Sociology of Paul's Narrative World.* Philadelphia: Fortress Press, 1985. An analysis of the cultural assumptions and social roles in Paul's letter to Philemon.

Pilch, John, and Bruce Malina, eds. *Biblical Social Values and Their Meaning: A Handbook.* Peabody, Mass.: Hendrickson, 1993. Brief explanations and reflections on many items relevant to the social life of the first century Mediterranean world.

Rohrbaugh, Richard, ed. *The Social Sciences and New Testament Interpretation.* Peabody, Mass.: Hendrickson, 1996. A helpful collection of "readers guides" to different facets of first-century society using models from cultural anthropology.

Schüssler Fiorenza, Elisabeth. *In Memory of Her: A Feminist Theological Reconstruction of Christian Origins.* New York: Crossroad, 1986. Exposes the oppressiveness of texts and interpreters to recover the presence and activity of women in the early Christian movement.

Stambaugh, John, and David Balch. *The New Testament in Its Social Environment.* Philadelphia: Westminster, 1986. Social description of many facets of daily life in the New Testament world.

Stegemann, Ekkehard, and Wolfgang Stegemann. *The Jesus Movement: A Social History of Its First Century.* Minneapolis: Fortress Press, 1995. A comprehensive social analysis of the development of the Jesus movement as it moved from Palestine into the larger Gentile world.

Stegemann, Wolfgang, Bruce Malina, and Gerd Theissen, eds. *The Social Setting of Jesus and the Gospels*. Minneapolis: Fortress Press, 2002. Interesting articles on social, political, and economic dynamics of the historical Jesus and the Gospels.

Theissen, Gerd. *The Sociology of Early Palestinian Christianity*. Philadelphia: Fortress Press, 1978. Social analysis of the Jesus movement in the context of first-century Palestine.

7

CULTURAL STUDIES

Making Mark

ABRAHAM SMITH

Since the Enlightenment, biblical scholars have usually focused on the sources lying behind a biblical text, its stages of production, or its final form. In recent years, however, a shift has occurred. Many biblical scholars now primarily explore the perspectives shaping readers, and indeed the diversity of readers.[1] Fernando F. Segovia's plotting of the evolution of biblical criticism puts this recent shift in historical perspective. According to Segovia, biblical studies has evolved in three stages with historical criticism as its first stage, literary criticism and (socio)cultural criticism as its second stage and cultural studies as its present and third stage.[2] Within the third stage of cultural studies, biblical criticism takes on a multitude of voices and directions.[3] The voices are multiple and the directions varied because of the growth of non-male and non-Western individuals in the biblical profession, individuals who have pushed biblical criticism to consider the "situated and interested nature of all reading and interpretation."[4]

So, what is cultural studies? Though resistant to a single definition, cultural studies typically embraces a variety of methods to examine *any* or *all* parts of culture. Given this interest, which is also known as cultural studies' democratization of culture, cultural studies does not assign more value to what some may deem "high" (professional or refined) culture over "low" (folk or popular or everyday) culture. Indeed, cultural studies often critiques altogether the distinction between "high" and "low" cultures or it seeks to open up more space for the latter, which is largely marginalized in many societies.

More specifically, cultural studies seeks to analyze "the cultural formations of any historical period or cultural context."[5] The cultural formations could include, for example, *cultural practices* (any or all of a given culture's typical, customary activities such as eating, writing, working, or interpreting texts) and *cultural products* (any or all of what a given culture produces, from simple artifacts to more complex institutions such as works of art, literature, religious institutions, and professional societies). Thus, for example, the *cultural practice* of searching for the history behind texts or for the meanings of texts is itself a cultural formation. Professional biblical scholars have practiced this search since the eighteenth century within a specific cultural context. Although they have presented their approach as natural and timeless, such an approach has not always been important for those who hear, read, or are moved by biblical texts.

Likewise, the *cultural product* we now know as detective fiction arose within a specific cultural context, one in which it gained popular appeal and acceptance. That is, Anglo-American detective fiction (for example, Arthur Conan Doyle's *Sherlock Holmes* series), a spin-off from the mystery form, did not become popular until the late nineteenth and early twentieth centuries. Its popularity and acceptance arose then—and not in the mid-nineteenth century when Edgar Allan Poe, the originator of the mystery form, wrote his tales—because only in that later period did the Enlightenment's worship of reasoning and deductive detection gain popular appeal.[6]

Thus proponents of cultural studies say that all cultural practices and cultural products, whether texts or readings of texts by readers/hearers or the theories supporting those readings, make sense or come about because of larger historical cultural forces. Even discourses or those common and seemingly natural ways to depict or represent someone or something are not timeless, neutral, and natural. They appear neutral, rather, because various institutions—such as educational, economic, political, or ecclesiastical institutions—over time have persuaded those who use the discourses to think of them as natural. When Europeans first traveled to Africa, for example, they "interpreted African women's sparse dress—dress appropriate to the climate of Africa—as a sign of . . . lewdness and lack of chastity."[7] Europeans continued to think of African women (and men) in this way, moreover, to support slave trading, that is, to justify the sale and exploitation of black labor based on a presumed inherent inferiority in the morals of black persons.

Therefore, as Fernando F. Segovia writes, cultural studies is an "ideological mode of discourse."[8] Cultural studies uses a variety of methods to unmask what appears to be natural or innocent, to reveal the ideologies or systems of thought that make otherwise historical constructions appear as timeless and neutral givens. Moreover, the task of unmasking sometimes requires such a variety of methods because the ideologies are often complex and thus require multiple angles of examination. Using a single method is simply not sufficient.

This chapter, then, is necessarily interdisciplinary in orientation and, while it consistently focuses on Mark,[9] the emphasis is not solely on Mark. Rather, the chapter features Mark as a *site* for understanding a variety of cultural practices and products and the ideologies or patterns of thought behind them.[10] Mark, then, is like a website with links to other sites. Some of the sites treat the work of professional biblical scholars and others do not. Again, cultural studies democratizes culture and seeks to retrieve some perspectives that have been marginalized over time.

Using cultural studies, the chapter has three objectives. Part 1 provides a brief overview of the "origins" and development of cultural studies. In part 2 I explore how Mark has been (re-)produced through various *cultural practices* since its initial receptions in the first century C.E. In part 3 I analyze Mark as a literary *cultural product* received in its own time. To do so, we read Mark as a response to the tyranny and abusive power of the Roman Empire in which Mark's audiences lived. We also explore how the Gospel itself *reinscribes* tyrannical powers, that is, it *reinforces* the tyrannical powers through the adoption of the very literary strategies that the Empire used. Admittedly, for all three parts of the chapter my discursive pictures of the cultural productions and practices are acts of historical imagination. These acts require hard work and a careful sifting of evidence, but they are still *constructions*. They are provisional models for understanding the making of Mark's Gospel from the ancient period to today.

1. THE "ORIGINS" AND DEVELOPMENT OF CULTURAL STUDIES

Cultural studies in the West has its origins in sociological theory, French literary theory, and certain forms of Marxist thought. It is not a theory unifying all of these, but rather a conglomerate or stew of theories and perspectives giving attention to various cultural patternings, practices, and products from around the globe. Nonetheless, given its Western emergence, cultural studies began with at least two central forms: one British and the other North American.[11]

In its British variety, cultural studies evolved in three phases: (1) the initial "culturalist" phase, (2) the French theory phase, and (3) the radical plurality and internationalization phase. In the "culturalist" phase, roughly from 1958 to the late 1960s, Raymond Williams, Edward P. Thompson, and Richard Hoggart criticized elitist views of culture in post–World War II Britain.[12] These sociologists of culture maintained that "culture" must not be understood as the so-called "best that has been known and thought."[13] They thus criticized the elitist view of culture that Matthew Arnold defined in his *Culture and Anarchy*.[14] For Williams, to the contrary, culture included *all* the ways of life that affected ordinary people. Thus, he defined "the theory of culture as the study of relationships between elements in a whole way of life."[15] These critics also considered working class persons to be culture producers and not simply mass culture consumers.[16] Likewise, they deemed the culture that working class individuals produced worthy of study. They also insisted on examining all cultural products within a larger network of interlocking processes related to the "production, distribution, and consumption of said products."[17] This new view of culture, moreover, would continue to prevail with the founding of the Centre for Contemporary Cultural Studies within the University of Birmingham (the BCCCS) in 1964.[18]

In the second phase of British culture studies, roughly from the late 1960s and throughout the 1970s, after the Centre's leadership was passed on from Richard Hoggart, its first director, to Stuart Hall, cultural studies conducted a series of raids on French theory. From the French Marxist philosopher Louis Althusser, for example, cultural studies developed some important ideas about ideology. Cultural studies no longer understood ideology, as had some earlier Marxists, simply as false consciousness or a distorted view of reality that conceals the way power works in the relations between the dominating and dominated classes of a society.[19] Rather, ideology, like a large force-field, shapes the full constellation of possible social relations including but also going beyond class relations.[20] Moreover, according to Althusser, through a system of relatively autonomous yet interlocking structures in this force-field, individuals and collective groups are forced to relate to each other in accordance with certain "ideological state apparatuses." These systems or structures (for example, the family system, educational systems, and ecclesiastical systems) produce "ideologies of authority, hierarchy, and conformity."[21]

In the third phase, roughly from the 1980s to the present, cultural studies has undergone a radical multiplication of methods, a Gramscian turn, and internationalization. Ground for the radical pluralization had already been laid by important "interruptions," from feminist circles in the 1970s and ethnicity studies in the 1980s,[22] and the radical pluralization would continue in the 1990s and beyond. To respond to questions about gender and ethnicity, though, cultural studies had to shift from or alter Althusserian theory because it did not presuppose the actual agency of human subjects. The switch was made to the theory of an Italian Marxist, Antonio Gramsci. How did his theory help? Gramsci argued that a vanguard of intellectuals, what he called "organic intellectuals," could actually work against a repressive ideology, that is, a set of strategies designed to support the dominant group's conception or view of life as commonsensical and natural over that of other groups in a society. The organic intellectuals, moreover, could help subalterns—dominated groups such as women and citizens of former colonies—overcome hegemony or domination by exposing that very hegemony and offering a counter.[23] Thus, ideology is not a single force-field that decrees what human beings must do in society. Rather, people have choices and dominated groups can expose hegemony and offer a counterhegemony.

As early as the 1980s, cultural studies also saw an internationalization. This was brought about in part through typical avenues of institutionalization/professionalization: university curricula in Britain, conferences in the United States and eventually outside of the English-speaking world, and a veritable explosion of journal articles and books. Internationalization of a different sort also occurred as one or more non-Western groups looked internally on their own homegrown forms of cultural studies.[24]

The feminist cultural criticism of bell hooks and the philosophical cultural criticism of Cornel West are key examples of cultural studies in North America. bell hooks is a feminist literary critic, teacher, student of theory on liberative educational practices (for example, as illustrated in the work of the Brazilian educator Paulo Freire), and a prolific writer. hooks criticizes the way women or certain ethnic/racial groups are represented in the writing and visual art of dominant groups.[25] Like the French philosopher Michel Foucault, she advocates the "insurrection of subjugated knowledge," that is, the retrieval of knowledge content or ways of knowing produced by a subjugated or dominated group.[26] Furthermore, and very helpful for analyzing ideology in the cultural products and cultural practices of biblical studies, she analyzes the "gaze" or perspective by which persons are represented or portrayed. Does the "gaze" in a book, a film, or other works of art support the domination of one group by another (as with some medieval paintings that depicted Arabs as the torturers of Christ during his passion or as with television westerns that portrayed Native Americans as "uncivilized" and expendable)?[27] Does the "gaze" reflect internalized oppression (as with the character Pecola, a little black girl who longs to be white in Toni Morrison's novel *The Bluest Eye*)?[28] Is the gaze resistant to the dominant society and thus an attempt to retrieve the perspective of dominated groups (which, I think, is at least one of the reasons for the production of the Gospel of Mark)? hooks also insists on a critique of binary opposites (for example, "superior/inferior, good/bad, white/black") because they lead to simplistic depictions of groups as if representatives of particular groups are altogether superior or altogether inferior, altogether good or altogether bad, and so on.[29]

Cornel West is a philosopher, teacher, lay preacher, student of Gramsci's Marxist thought about the elite intellectual's role in social movements, and also a prolific writer. West demystifies or exposes the politics or ideology behind the representations of dominated groups by dominating groups. He often reveals the historical conditions that made certain myths of representation possible. He also exposes the intersection among several different types of domination, including class, gender, sexual orientation, and racial/ethnic background.[30] Furthermore, West astutely recognizes the operations of power that perennially have allowed some persons to bully, berate, and butcher others all in the name of texts deemed authoritative. Among those so-called authoritative texts, of course, is the Bible itself, about which West says, "Without the addition of modern interpretations of racial and gender equality, tolerance, and democracy, much of the [biblical] tradition warrants rejection."[31]

2. EXPLORING CULTURAL PRODUCTIONS AND PRACTICES IN THE MAKING OF MARK

So, what can biblical scholars and students do with cultural studies? We can certainly still use traditional biblical studies methods, but now interwoven with other methods to explore a variety of cultural products from ancient times to the present. Thus, first, I explore early church dogma as an ideological product and then move on to see how translations of Mark also are ideological products. Second, I look at Markan scholarship as a set of cultural practices, that is, as practices that are not objective but ones that bear a distinctive ideological force. Third, I examine the reception of Mark in visual art or how visual artists have shaped Mark in accordance with the theological or political influences of their times. In the end, my explorations should help us to see how our cultural reading practices are not natural and how they limit how Mark is constructed.

Mark, Textual Manuscripts, and Dogma as a Cultural Product

To begin to understand Mark as a cultural product, we must first know that no Markan autograph (original manuscript) exists. Scholars literally construct what we now know as the Gospel of Mark from different versions in what were once hand-written manuscripts. With no printing presses, scribes copied manuscripts by hand, sometimes introducing changes accidentally and sometimes on purpose. Thus, manuscripts or textual "witnesses" exhibit what scholars call "variants" that range from slightly different wordings of a text to the addition or subtraction of a number of verses. The most notable example in Mark is the existence of different versions of the Gospel's ending. A whole sub-discipline of biblical studies, textual criticism, tries to determine the "best" and most original wording of Mark and other texts. Textual critics evaluate the reliability of the manuscripts or witnesses themselves as well as internal evidence such as the author's style in order to reconstruct the earliest possible version.

Yet, text criticism need not be seen as an end in itself or with the single goal of determining the ever-elusive final form of Mark's Gospel. Considering text criticism in an interdisciplinary way with larger sociohistorical goals, the very presence of the variants could provide a site for detecting the cultural productions of some of Mark's earliest interpreters. As Bradly S. Billings has noted, "It has not always been readily appreciated by theologians and historians that individual manuscripts constitute primary source documents in understanding the sociohistorical situation of early Christianity and are, therefore, worthy of critical examination in their own right."[32] Billings argues that although critics often try to read a biblical text in its original social and historical context, they do not do the same for the individual manuscripts and textual variants within them.[33] Hence, in a cultural studies mode, I am suggesting that text criticism, when combined with other disciplines such as history, could expose how scribal transmission is a cultural product. Such analysis would show how a text's construction involves conflicts over knowledge and power.

In a compelling example Bart Erhman analyzes the theological motivation for the scribal alteration of Jesus' last words in the closing scenes of Mark's Gospel.[34] In the closing scenes, where Jesus rarely speaks, human opposition has proceeded apace with trumped-up charges, witnesses who do not agree, and failure in Jesus' own fellowship. Not even his closest comrades—ones (like Simon, James and John) earlier graced to see more than the others—remain faithful. And now, as the human opposition climaxes with Jesus' crucifixion (15:21-37), the narrative landscape or textual arrangement and development is bleak and arid. Nearing the end alone, and without a human companion, the previously rather silent Jesus now emits a loud, plaintive prayer to God. Narrated with both a transliteration (the representation of a letter in one alphabet with the corresponding letter from another alphabet) and a translation (the representation of a word from one language to its equivalent in another) of the Aramaic of Psalm 22:1, these last words of Jesus, "My God, my God, why have you forsaken me?" (15:34) capture Jesus' utter abject state.

The sense of Jesus' abandonment by God, however, was a problem for some early Christians. These "proto-orthodox" Christians, as we might call them, were Christians whose beliefs won out over time and thus their beliefs were established as correct or orthodox beliefs. The proto-orthodox Christians battled with other Christians, like the Gnostics who assumed that a divine being temporarily dwelt within the human being Jesus and had abandoned him just before his death. The proto-orthodox scribes found it difficult to accept the word "forsake/abandon" (Greek: *enkatelipes*) even though this was an appropriate translation of the Aramaic of Psalm 22:1.[35] Assuming that the Greek word *enkatelipes* could also be understood as "left . . . behind" and that the Gnostics would favor that rendering for their christological purposes,[36] the proto-orthodox scribes established a variant of 15:34 that used an altogether different word to replace *enkatelipes*, namely *ōneidisas* ("reviled," "reproached" or "taunted").[37]

Though the proto-orthodox variant makes sense when one considers the mockery that attends Jesus' trial and crucifixion, the "reviled" translation does not capture the Aramaic cry, nor does it find support in the best external evidence for the verse.[38] Thus, Mark was *made* to cohere with proto-orthodox Christology for fear that the Gnostics would use what is likely the most original wording to support their own Christology.[39] Moreover, given this example, the task of cultural studies is to "insurrect the subjugated knowledge" of those whose voices sometimes are not heard.[40] Thus a cultural critic's task here is to make sure the Gnostic voices are heard (even if we disagree with them). This also exposes some of the conflict involved in the making of Mark as a cultural product.

Mark, Translations, and Re-Presentation as Cultural Identity Formations

The declaration that Mark is *made* presupposes more than carefully sifting variants to create a text that approximates Mark's original wording. As we are learning from recent translation studies, translations of a foreign text often domesticate foreign cultures, that is, they make foreign cultures appear to be more familiar. Translations also may radically re-create domestic subjects, that is, the persons who want in some way to benefit from such domestication for their own purposes.[41] Thus, on the one hand, translations of Mark could re-present or reshape the cultural identities of Mark's world and characters in ways palatable and ideologically meaningful to translators and their audiences. On the other hand, with certain translations, domestic subjects, once held under the sway of existing ideological positions in their own society, may begin to look at themselves differently. That is, the translations may grant them the ideological justification to re-present or re-create their identities apart from the images by which the dominant groups in their society had once represented them.[42]

Domestication of Foreign Cultures

One need not look to the current Bible boom to see obvious examples of translations or paraphrases that have domesticated Mark's world and cultures, though certainly the Bible's recent popularization, marked by commodification (growth in the value of something only because it makes money), radical harmonization (the adaptation of an earlier culture's ideas to fit the new target culture), and a-politicization (the erasure of the otherwise political dimensions of a product or of ideas), has virtually decreed the domestication of Bibles altogether.[43] As the following example from William

Tyndale's English translation of 1525–26 makes clear, though, the domestication of Mark is not a recent phenomenon.

Between the written production of the English Wyclif Bible translation in the fourteenth century, on the one hand, and the printed productions of the Coverdale, Matthew, and Great Bible translations in the sixteenth century, on the other hand, several important events occurred: Johann Gutenberg invented the printing press,[44] Desiderius Erasmus became influential in England, and the books of the German Protestant reformer Martin Luther influenced powerful figures everywhere, including England.[45] In addition, William Tyndale published the first printed English Bible translation in 1525–26, a Bible consisting of the New Testament and a partially completed Old Testament. Tyndale's translation of Mark 14:1-16 persistently domesticates these verses, however, by substituting the word "ester" (Easter) for Passover (14:1, 12, 14, 16), even referring to the Passover Lamb (14:12) as the "ester lambe" (Easter Lamb). This re-presentation or reconfiguration of the Passover, much in accord with Luther's own German translation, which was available to Tyndale, and clearly distinct from Erasmus's version, which uses the term *pascha* for the Passover lamb, conveyed a view of Passover Tyndale's Christian audiences could easily digest. At the same time, Tyndale's translation virtually erased the *Jewish* cultural setting of Jesus' meal with his disciples.[46] As bell hooks might put it, we can read Tyndale's gaze or perspective in his translation.[47]

Re-Creation of Domestic Subjects
Yet, the re-production of the foreign cultures of Mark's world and characters are not the only ideological results of translation. The domestic subjects (flesh-and-blood readers and hearers from Mark's more recent audiences) change as well, as another example from Tyndale's translation will make clear. The wording selected by Tyndale for his translation evinced his ideological preferences. Accordingly, Tyndale, who translated directly from the original languages, made "substitutions of simple words for the technical and Latinized vocabulary idolized by the theologians of the day."[48] More critical for this chapter, Tyndale places John in the wilderness not proclaiming a "baptism of penance" (based on the Latin word *poenitentiam*), but a "baptism of repentance" in Mark 1:4. Tyndale understood the word *poenitentiam*, however, to imply "paying a penalty or fine," which seemed to distract from the Greek idea of changing one's mind that lay behind the word *metanoeō*.[49] Moreover, penance at the time was a practice by which believers sought restitution based on acts prescribed by a priest. Tyndale thus repeatedly used cognates or words with related meanings for the word "repentance" (1:4, 15; 6:12). Similarly, Tyndale changed "confess" to "acknowledge" when he translated the Greek word *exomologeō*, thus avoiding the Roman Catholic view of "confession," for which a priest would be required for absolution (1:5).[50] These vocabulary choices, with several others—such as "priest" and "church" becoming respectively "elder" and "congregation" and "charity" (based on the

Latin Vulgate's *caritas*) becoming "love"—had the net effect of helping to produce "a different religious identity, the English Protestant."[51] This provided one of the bases for English nationalism in the face of the international presence and power of the Roman Catholic Church in the sixteenth century.

Mark, Biblical Studies, and Cultural Practices of Modern Reading

All professional societies, whether the American Medical Association, American Historical Association, Modern Language Association, or the Society of Biblical Literature, practice certain ways of reading that grant them authority. These reading conventions organize knowledge in ways that create professional experts.[52] The disciplines and methodologies of professions, moreover, are, in effect, power arrangements, embracing the acceptable patterns of the dominant discourse.[53]

Understanding how reading involves ideological and cultural constraints and power relations helps us to think of biblical studies itself as a battleground over reading practices. Indeed, a key feature of current biblical studies is a move from simply (or only) determining the "meaning" of texts to analyses of the "political conceptual frameworks" that give shape to biblical studies itself.[54] Over time, these frameworks have virtually become invisible to biblical scholars. They are hidden from view and yet they are a part of the philosophical and cultural discourses of modernity that mostly Christian-centered (and then mostly Protestant) Westerners have simply assumed. Thus, an important directive in cultural studies could be to investigate the political frameworks of biblical studies, that is, to use Cornel West's language, to demystify the discourses of biblical studies or to demystify the discourse formations (or assumptions) that systematically ground the questions that biblical studies asks and the categories out of which biblical studies is construed.

What, therefore, are some of the political conceptions that have shaped Markan scholarship since the dawn of biblical studies? One conception, as Mary Ann Tolbert notes, was a deep-seated need to find the historical Jesus, a conception that sometimes stood in the way of addressing some of Mark's literary riddles. According to Tolbert, two types of criticism—despite their otherwise valuable contributions—impeded calls for a narrative approach to Mark. One was source criticism, which sought to determine written sources lying behind the Gospels. Another was form criticism, which saw the Gospels as made of small, independent units that originally circulated orally (see chapter 1 above). Both approaches emphasized stages behind the Gospel of Mark. In the interest of the quest for the historical Jesus, moreover, both approaches relegated the author behind the Gospel of Mark to the role of a compiler, a rather unartful one at that. Only then through the transitional discipline of redaction criticism (in its composition criticism mode) would a full literary approach to Mark see the light of day.[55] Thus, the literary insights that could have helped scholars solve various literary riddles of Mark, such as its negative portrayal of the disciples or its apparently enigmatic ending, had to wait until a much later period, as late as the last third of the twentieth century.[56]

Yet another conception, also one that Tolbert notes, was a deep-seated need to make the New Testament "Gospel" genre or overall form unique.[57] We can see this conception in biblical studies in two ways. First, the aforementioned form critics attempted to make a Gospel, the genre that the Markan editor began, "unique" in a *negative* way.[58] That is, they simply assumed that Mark was totally different from any other first-century-C.E. writing, despite the difficulty of arguing that any "form" can be totally "new." As literary theorist Alastair Fowler has asserted, "No work, however avant-garde, is intelligible without some context of familiar tropes [that is, distinctively fashioned words or phrases]."[59] Second, more *positively*, other New Testament scholars adopted language "from the later philosophical work of Martin Heidegger" to make Mark appear unique.[60] Heidegger himself viewed language as a "house of being," that is, as a vehicle that could uniquely express the essence of a person or a culture.[61] New Testament scholars, particularly advocates of an approach called the "New Hermeneutic," considered then that the genre in which the apparent essence of Jesus was expressed must also be unique.[62] In truth, as many scholars would now concede, Mark and the other Gospels are not unique. Instead, they draw on a variety of literary conventions from the first-century C.E. Scholars thus read and constructed Mark yet again to serve the interests of their own cultures.

Mark, Traditions of Representation, and the Politics of Visual Art

Cultural studies does not seek to understand Mark solely as examined by professional biblical scholars. Toward the goal of democratizing cultures, cultural studies recognizes a diversity of receptions or appropriations of biblical texts. These receptions, moreover, may themselves be related to various "cultures" or "traditions" of appropriating the Bible. So, just as there is a culture of reception among professional biblical scholars with the scholars more or less interpreting texts in similar ways, various other communities of interpreters appropriate texts in ways that are acceptable to their respective communities. When cultural studies proponents analyze visual biblical art, therefore, they do so not to determine which work of art is more historically accurate than other works according to the decrees of professional biblical scholarship. Indeed, if one's interest is in historical accuracy so defined, one may be sorely disappointed. Moreover, as the following examples illustrate, other ideological frameworks—whether artistic, theological, or political— shape how the artist depicts a biblical character or event.

When the sixteenth century Flemish artist Joachim Patinir painted the scene of Jesus' baptism, he certainly depicted the heavens as if they had been ripped apart, which corresponds to Mark's depiction of the heavens "tearing

Baptism of Christ (ca. 1515) by Joachim Patinir
Photo © Erich Lessing / Art Resource, NY

apart" (*schizomenous*, 1:10). This image stands in contrast to the Lukan and Matthean depictions of the event, for both Matthew and Luke suggest that the heavens simply *opened* (Matt 3:16, *ēneōchthēsan*; Luke 3:21, *aneōchthēnai*). Yet, several critical aspects of Patinir's painting "Baptism of Christ" take Mark's rather simple depiction of the scene in different directions altogether.

First, Patinir, who may be seen as an early landscape artist, broadens the scope of the scene to include vivid details about the setting: groves of trees, distant mountains, and huge rock formations carved out for human inhabitants. Mark does not appear to dwell on such details but most of Patinir's other paintings also show an interest in landscapes. Second, as with many artists who painted the baptism of Jesus, Patinir portrays God in the heavens pointing a finger and thus directing the gaze of the observers toward Jesus. More importantly, Patinir positions the dove that is just below God on the same axis with God and with Jesus who appears below the dove. Although theories about Jesus as fully divine developed after Mark, it appears that Patinir here is influenced by the later church's doctrine of the Trinity. As art critic Steffano Zuffi has asserted, "The perfect axis down the center of the painting signifies the unity of the three persons of the Trinity."[63]

A more recent example of traditions of representation reveals the complexity of the issue of representation, especially when one looks beyond simply the visual artists' representations of biblical figures or events to the ways in which the shapers of cultural periods or the historians of those periods have depicted the artists themselves.

The example, one about two artists, comes from the Harlem Renaissance period, a cultural flowering of black arts and letters mostly in Harlem, New York from the mid-1920s to the mid-1930s. Both artists, whose names I will mention later, were well trained. Both artists apprenticed under the German artist Weinold Reiss. Both artists depicted biblical scenes. One of them, for example, depicted Simon of Cyrene (Mark 15:21). The other depicted John the Baptist in Herod's prison (Mark 6:14-29). The two worked together on murals in New York. Both were also illustrators for the single issue of the magazine *Fire*, an issue intended to spotlight the accomplishments of a small cadre of young Harlem Renaissance figures including the novelist Zora Neale Hurston and the poet Langston Hughes.[64]

Yet, students of the Harlem Renaissance period likely know well only Aaron Douglas, who depicted Simon of Cyrene as black.[65] The cultural shapers of the period and subsequent historians of the period have canonized Douglas because his art portrays black people in what may be regarded as straightforwardly positive ways.[66] Given the negative stereotypes of black people in the first third of the twentieth century, Douglas's work was welcomed by Alain Locke and W. E. B. Du Bois, the cultural "fathers" or advisors of the Harlem Renaissance artists. As an illustration for one of the poems in James Weldon Johnson's *God's Trombones*, Douglas's "The Crucifixion" (1927) positions Simon as the largest figure in the illustration, thus giving central attention not to Jesus but to Simon. As Douglas's biographer Amy Kirschke notes, "Although Christ appears in brighter colors at the base of the composition, it is the dark body of Simon, the flat, broad shoulders of the black figure, that dominates."[67] Furthermore, the cross that Simon bears is huge. One even wonders how the little Jesus who walks closer to the foreground with his disciples could ever have carried the cross. Still, despite the three spears that seem to come from every side of the painting except the top to depict the Romans compelling Simon to bear the cross, Douglas depicts Simon as strong. One can only imagine that the illustration spoke volumes to blacks in the early twentieth century as they themselves faced multiple assaults on their bodies and often through compulsion. Hence, Douglas's art was embraced and many identified with it, and many still do.

***Crucifixion* (1927) by Aaron Douglas**
From *God's Trombones* by James Weldon Johnson, © 1927 The Viking
Press, Inc., renewed © 1955 by Grace Nail Johnson. Used by permission
of Viking Penguin, a division of Penguin Group (USA) Inc.

Only in recent years, however, have historians appreciated Richard Bruce
Nugent, whose depiction of John the Baptist in his *Salomé* series is patently
erotic and some would say also homosexual. The realities of black homosexual life were profusely present in Harlem during this period and were a part

of the identity of some closeted black artists like the poet Countee Cullen and the Harlem Renaissance advisor Alain Locke himself. Yet Nugent, who was openly gay, has virtually been excluded from the canons of black history because his work did not conform to the culture shapers' views of what was respectable, especially in response to the negative depictions of black life then and now. The tradition that assigned the name Salome to the dancing daughter influenced Nugent as did the tradition that saw the dancing daughter as erotically linked to John the Baptist (see chapter 5 on Feminist Criticism, above). Nugent's John the Baptist, moreover, has "pink-stained lips," "a meticulously groomed golden beard," and his long hair is "well-coifed."[68] On the one hand, cultural studies would critique Nugent's depiction of John the Baptist to the extent that it fosters negative depictions of females. Likewise, cultural studies would critique the stereotypical images he associated with gay males to the extent that these images seem to limit the options of gay males themselves. On the other hand, it would also question the politics of exclusion that essentialized blackness as if black life came only in one stripe. Cultural studies would also question the black-white binary that virtually dictates the terms of the discussion and thus erases from consideration all

Untitled (1930) detail of John the Baptist by Richard Bruce Nugent
Photo © 1998 Thomas H. Wirth. Used by permission.

other ethnic/racial groups that do not fit this so-called normative gaze of social relations in the United States. Thus cultural studies would ask us to explore how the making of Mark affects the making of history and how history includes some persons while it excludes others.

Altogether, moreover, these observations on Markan studies, though brief, suggest—in a cultural studies' vein—that Markan scholarship and reception are not simply about *meaning* but, if examined carefully, they reveal larger discourse formations shaping the questions and issues raised in the scholarship and reception. Yet, cultural studies does not simply seek to expose the larger ideological discourse formations shaping the perspectives of interpreters, be they Markan translators, Markan specialists, or popular artists depicting Markan characters. As well, it seeks to expose the cultural formations shaping texts in their own time. To see these issues, I turn to part 3.

3. Mark as a Cultural Product of Its Time: Resisting Empire and Tracing Tyranny

As shown in part 2, cultural studies helps us to see the pre-reading ideological constraints we bring to readings of texts, whether those constraints are related to religious dogma, ethnocentric values, reading theories, or popular traditions. Yet, cultural studies also helps us to examine the ideological forces shaping the reception and even the production of texts in the first century as well. Again, I will feature a variety of texts from Mark. I will seek to determine, as best we can, how Mark would have been received by audiences in the first century C.E. We will also try to determine how the production of Mark would have both resisted and reinscribed some of the typical literary/ideological strategies of the Roman world.

Resisting Empire

Few Markan critics would doubt that Mark's audiences heard the Gospel at some level as resistance literature.[69] Wherever they lived, the early audiences of the Gospel of Mark likely felt the coercive pressures of Rome with its massive military forces and its extraction of taxes from colonized nations.[70] They likely also felt the ideological pressure of Rome's divine expansionist claims with its attendant auto-ethnographic literary strategies, i.e., its discursive ordering of its own ethnic group over all others. Mark certainly is interested in issues of authority and power, as such issues echo throughout the aural narrative landscape or the repetitive textual arrangement and development of Mark's Gospel.[71] And Mark's apocalyptic perspective decidedly *resists* the claim that the world is under the rule of anyone besides God. This perspective is true in the narrative's first scriptural echoes about God's reign having already drawn near (Mark 1:1-15)[72] And the perspective remains throughout the Gospel, including in the climactic framing of Jesus' role as the last messenger sent by God in reclaiming that reign (à la the parable of the tenants in Mark 12)[73] and in the "little apocalypse" of Mark 13 on the future consummation of the reign.

In a recent article, "Tyranny Exposed," I, too, have joined the wave of scholars seeing Mark as resistance literature.[74] In that work, I argued that Mark's apparently disjunctive account about John the Baptist (6:14-29), when cast in the larger narrative context of a prophet's rejection, depicts Herod Antipas as a tyrant. Moreover, the depiction of Herod as a tyrant is presented in ways that would have seemed fairly conventional and stylized in the light of the political invective of that day.[75] This is certainly a possible—and, I think, even plausible—reading given my estimation of the overall narrative acoustical development of Mark's Gospel, as spelled out below.

That is, in many circles of biblical scholarship, a plausible reading of Mark's Gospel would appear as follows. Beyond a brief introduction, the Gospel of Mark is constructed with a series of calls, commissions, and corrections through which Jesus prepares his disciples for a crucible (the narrative's most intense scenes of opposition). Accordingly, one could construe the Gospel of Mark as having three major parts: a prologue (1:1-15) and two large units (1:16—10:52 and 11:1—16:8). Thus, after Mark's introduction of Jesus, John the Baptist, God's dominion, and the prophetic way (1:1-15), Mark presents two major divisions. In the first division (1:16—10:52), Mark presents a series of call episodes, commissions, and corrections. The call episodes (1:16-20; 2:13-14) organize two other blocks of episodes about the growth of Jesus' prophetic fame and the growth of the opposition to his work (1:21—2:12; 2:15—3:6).[76] The commission scenes (3:7-19; 6:7b-30) reveal the potential fate of discipleship as death (6:14-29) and anticipate the unreadiness of the disciples to face the crucible. The correction scenes (chaps. 6 and 7, and more especially chaps. 8, 9, and 10) both *reveal* the lack of perception and misperception of the disciples and *depict* Jesus repeatedly at work to correct the disciples' thinking and their wills in preparation for the crucible.

In the second division, i.e., the crucible (or the intense closing scenes of the Gospel, 11:1—16:8), Mark fully shifts the setting of Jesus' ministry from Galilee to Jerusalem, where Jesus demonstrates his knowledge of Scripture and of the future *and* he provides "an example of faithful, watchful endurance through suffering, persecution, and even death."[77] With an overall presentation of "mounting opposition," a fracturing fellowship, and recognition (or misrecognition), moreover, the closing scenes of the Gospel present the climactic testing moments for Jesus and his disciples.[78] Thus, these scenes show the drastic difference between the readiness of Jesus and the unreadiness of the disciples for the growing opposition. During the testing periods, Jesus—as example—is watchful and ready; the disciples are not. Because of his knowledge, Jesus is able to *endure* the crucible before Jewish and Roman authorities, the very request he made to his disciples in the Olivet apocalyptic discourse (13:9-13).[79] His disciples, however, fail miserably and are no longer "*with* him."[80] They cannot commit themselves fully because they have not become rooted strongly in their beliefs about God's ability to see them through trials.

All three parts—prologue and two major divisions—presumably serve to model what is necessary for persons facing crucibles in their own times. Thus, Markan audiences, whenever they heard the Gospel in the late 60s or early 70s of the first century c.e., likely learned readiness for the endurance of pressure-filled circumstances before Jewish and Gentile authorities, both through the positive portrait of Jesus and the negative portrait of the disciples.

Given that reconstruction of Mark's narrative development, Mark 6:14-29, which occurs between two parts of a commissioning scene, has at least two roles. The most straightforward role is criticism of Herod Antipas's tyrannical, abusive power.[81] Mark 6:14-29 also provides, though, a basis or framework for first-century audiences' assessment of tyranny wherever it is found, whether later in the narrative or in their own lives.

Tracing Tyranny

Admittedly, the plausible reading of Mark 6:14-29 and indeed of the entire Gospel I have just offered may obscure as much as it makes clear. On the one hand, it presents a rather straightforward audience-oriented literary-critical reading of Mark. The reading is not detached from ancient historical moorings but emanates from a basic historical reconstruction of Mark's audiences. That is, Mark's audiences were first-century persons facing persecution or its threat. Thus, they needed to hear the beginning of the good news (1:1) in pressure-filled circumstances. This reading, moreover, yields a thematic and climactic upshot. In accordance with the likely plot-driven nature of ancient characterization, Mark historically places characters in the service of the Gospel's plot. The reading does not assume that the characters are figures on the order of autonomous selves or historically accurate selves, as may be the case with typical modern or postmodern biographies.[82]

On the other hand, this plausible reading may obscure an important power dimension. Not exposed in this reading, at least as presented, is the extent to which the composition of the Gospel of Mark does not solely *respond to* the cultural products of dominant cultural formations. Mark also, perhaps in unwitting ways to its author or initial audiences, participates in the *reinscription of* such cultural formations and their products. To use the words of bell hooks, this erstwhile plausible reading then does not acknowledge "the ways power as domination reproduces itself in different locations employing similar apparatuses, strategies, and mechanisms of control."[83] Accordingly, a cultural studies approach to Mark must not only trace the tyranny that the author of Mark appears to reject but also the tyranny that the Gospel of Mark appears to have inscribed in its rhetoric.

Indeed, this is the sterling challenge Tat-siong Benny Liew has made in his article, "Tyranny, Boundary and Might: Colonial Mimicry in Mark's

Gospel" (see also chapter 8 below, "Postcolonial Criticism," by Liew). He has challenged us to expose Mark's "colonial mimicry," that is, Mark's duplication of colonial ideology.[84] In this part of the chapter, then, I sketch a few instances of Mark's colonial mimicry, as Liew exposes, before going on to see one further, more extended example of the same phenomenon.

Tyrannical Strategies of Colonial Mimicry

Liew argues that Mark's colonial mimicry is expressed in at least three ways. First, Mark "attributes absolute authority to Jesus."[85] That is, Mark is not critical of the "constitution" of authority itself, only of certain types of authority.[86] Accordingly, for Liew, Jesus' authority is noted in several ways. In word and deed, he is *the* (my emphasis) authoritative interpreter and embodiment of Scripture.[87] He is "God's last authorized agent."[88] And, notwithstanding Jesus' previous examples of "egalitarian ideals," his own re-constituted family (those who do the will of God rather than literal mother, brother, and sister, cf. 3:35) itself displays "authoritarian politics."[89] This occurs in its "infantilization" of believers, its demonization of Peter for his inappropriate rebuke of Jesus, and its assignment of menial work roles to the Twelve.[90] Second, Mark maintains binary opposites that were also used by Rome, for example, the insider/outside rhetoric, with its attendant sociopolitical end-time realignment of power and its "interest-recurring" retributive justice system.[91] Third, Mark construes authority as the right to wield power, which means, in the context of the politics of the parousia or "second coming," that one (in this case, Jesus) would have the "the ability to have one's commands obeyed and followed or the power to wipe out those who do not."[92]

Neo-Colonial Tyranny Again: The Pursuit of Pilate

In one of its most recent forms, cultural studies has profited substantially through a coalition with feminist critics and postcolonial critics. Particularly, these critics have provided ideological critiques of those parts of culture that appear relatively benign until the underlying ethos of those products is exposed.[93] Feminist critics have questioned how women are presented. Postcolonial critics, among other things, have exposed the power of neocolonialism or the ways that colonized subjects maintain the strategies of their colonizers through the discourse through which the colonized depict their world. In biblical studies this means that texts may often appear to be relatively benign—even helpful in the struggle of resistance to oppression. Under close examination, however, the texts actually harbor destructive and damaging images.

In light of both the helpful and destructive character of the biblical texts, let us now look at the construction of Pilate in Mark 15:1-15 to show how Mark's otherwise resistant tenor actually supports an ideology of domination. To do so in a brief space, however, three discussions are necessary: (1) a brief review of the scholarship on Pilate as presented in Mark 15:1-15, (2) an examination of the larger narrative frames of resistance in which Mark characterizes Pilate, and (3) an exploration of the underlying ideology of domination of those narrative frames.

Review of Scholarship on Pilate in Mark 15:1-15

What we know about Pilate, the governor of Judea from 26 to 36/37 C.E., is limited. However, sources outside the New Testament do portray him as a despot.[94] According to the Hellenistic Jewish author Philo in his *Embassy to Gaius*, Pilate's dedication of some "golden shields" to the emperor Tiberius in Herod's Jerusalem palace was motivated by a desire to "annoy the multitude."[95] In relating Pilate's obstinacy toward removing the golden shields when requested to do so by the Jews, Philo's criticism of Pilate receives considerable amplification (*The Embassy to Gaius*, 302-3).[96] The Jewish historian Josephus likewise shows Pilate's disregard for Judean sensibilities when he relates Pilate's introduction of the battle standards into Jerusalem *by night*. The standards were offensive because they included images of the Roman emperor. Pilate only removed the standards in response to the relentless protest of Jewish dissenters (Josephus, *Jewish Antiquities* 18.3.1; *Jewish War* 2.9.2-3).[97] Pilate's confiscation of funds from the temple's sacred treasury to build an aqueduct likewise shows his insensitivity along with his violent character. Many of the Judean dissenters were bloodily beaten by soldiers attired in civilian clothing (Josephus, *Antiquities* 18.3.2; *Jewish War* 2.9.4).[98] Furthermore, Pilate's order for the capture and murder of armed Samaritans who made an ascent on Mt. Gerizim (where Samaritans worshiped) was considered so egregious that it essentially led to the loss of his governorship (Josephus *Antiquities* 18.4.1-2).[99]

Notwithstanding the generally negative portraits of Pilate given in Philo and Josephus, until recently many scholars have argued that Mark portrays Pilate in a favorable—if not altogether positive—light.[100] Pilate certainly does not receive Mark's most explicit harsh criticism. This is reserved for the sociopolitical/religious authorities and Jesus' disciples.[101] Mark's criticism of these two groups, however, may be strong because they appear so frequently on his narrative stage. And, their frequent appearance may itself be a result of Mark's desire to teach the Gospel's audiences.

Recent scholarship has shown, however, that Mark's presentation of Pilate is not one of a relatively harmless figure who vacillated under pressure. That is, when one reads Mark's Gospel in the light of the power dimensions of the first-century C.E. Roman Empire, as Warren Carter and Albert de Mingo Kaminouchi have done, one is nudged strongly to view Pilate as "a governor with enormous power."[102] Thus, Mark's construction of Pilate is one of many instances in which Mark seeks to resist abusive power.

Narrative Frames of Resistance in Mark's Characterization of Pilate

Aiding Mark in the presentation of Pilate as abusive are three narrative frames of resistance. First, the episode on Pilate in Mark 15:1-15 cannot be read apart from the staged mockeries of Jesus as the *brigand/king*. The staged mockeries, all given on Jesus' last day on the Markan narrative stage, present Jesus as the Romans would likely have viewed him.[103] That is, many of the closing scenes of Mark's Gospel are replete with the mockery of Jesus as a king-pretender. These scenes include Pilate's repeated use of kingship language ("King of the Jews," 15:2, 9, 12)[104] and the purple-robe mockery that follows when Jesus is handed over to the soldiers (15:16-20). The scenes also include the mockery that will attend the actual crucifixion itself when the words "King of the Jews" are used on the superscription (15:26) and Jesus is hoisted up between two brigands (15:25-32), so-called criminals often associated with royal pretensions.[105] Furthermore, scaffolding for the construction of the mockery begins at least as early as the arrest scene on the day before, where Jesus depicts his capture as if the arresting party had come to arrest a brigand (14:43-52, esp. v. 48).

The force of the narrative's repeated mockeries, though, is resistant because the last of a series of passion prediction units has already prepared Markan audiences for this inevitable "mocking and flogging" conclusion (10:34). The net effect then is that someone else is in control of events—not those who now, like pawns, are fated to carry them out. Notably, moreover, with the last "delivery" of Jesus (14:10, 11, 18, 21, 41-42, 44; 15:1, 10, 15), now into the hands of the soldiers (15:15), both Pilate and the soldiers are swept together under the general description of mere "human hands" (9:31) and "Gentiles" (10:33). Mark's audiences, moreover, would likely view these hands in moral alignment with the "hands of sinners," the description Jesus used for the hands of his captors in Gethsemane (14:41). Read in this way, the narrative does not draw Pilate favorably. He is one with other humans and sinners all placed within a *show of hands*, with all the hands strung together by the voice of the one who now remains virtually silent as his predictions at last find resolution.

Second, the episode on Pilate is also a part of the "trial" sequence that begins with the high priest's interrogation of Jesus (14:53-65) and culminates with Pilate's delivery of Jesus to the soldiers (15:15). Whatever the historical merits of the "trial/interrogation" before the council as presented by Mark,[106] Mark's presentation appears to have several goals. Mark's presentation characterizes the involvement of the whole council in the "trial/interrogation" just as the deliberation of the whole council would lead to the binding and handing of Jesus over to Pilate (14:55; cf. 15:15). Mark also ridicules the "trial/interrogation" as a travesty of justice (for example, a decision is reached using false witnesses, and worse, witnesses whose false testimonies "did not agree," 14:55-59). This travesty is not unlike Pilate's release of Barabbas and his delivery of Jesus for crucifixion (15:15).[107] Mark also highlights the virtual silence of Jesus, which also characterizes his appearance before Pilate (14:61-62; 15:2-5). Finally, Mark highlights the mockery and violence that attended the "trial/interrogation," which was likewise present when Jesus appeared before Pilate (14:65; 15:1-15). That Jesus predicts both the "handling" of Jesus by the council and by Pilate, moreover, suggests that the trial sequence connections are also read as events in another person's control, though carried out through the agency in part of the council and in part of Pilate.

So, what is the net effect of the parallels between the two parts of the trial sequence? Among other things, the parallels could well have led Markan audiences to judge Pilate's abuse of justice in the same way that these audiences would have judged the council's abuse. This judgment is probable, moreover, despite the narrative aside on Pilate's knowledge of the jealousy that prompted the chief priests to hand Jesus over (15:10). That is, the information in the aside need not be viewed as excusing Pilate, but as reinforcing the gravity of Pilate's mishandling of justice.[108] Thus, Mark again is resistant here, and Mark again does not paint Pilate in a favorable light.

Perhaps, though, in yet a third way, Mark provides a narrative frame of resistance that significantly shapes the way in which Pilate would be read, namely, in the parallels Mark makes between this episode and a previous episode about tyranny in 6:14-29. The most striking parallels, as I have shown in "Tyranny Exposed," relate to power relations and the problem of the will clarified through those power relations. That is, Herod Antipas and Pilate are drawn similarly in terms of what they know, what they can do, and in their regard for the human *will*. Both Herod Antipas and Pilate recognize the righteousness or innocence of John and Jesus, respectively (6:20; 15:14), with Herod Antipas being greatly perplexed (6:20) and Pilate marveling (*thaumazein*, 15:5) at Jesus' silence. Both obviously also have the power to release their prisoners. That is, the decision is not in the hands of Herodias who bears a grudge (6:19) or the chief priests who deliver Jesus out of envy (15:10). The decision rests squarely with the ruling authorities. Yet, both Herod Antipas and Pilate shift from what appears to be a more positive encounter to one that is wholly negative and deadly because they submit their wills/wishes/wants to others. That is, Herod Antipas submits his will to the dancing daughter to whom he has made a pledge to do whatever she "wishes" (*thelēs*, 6:22). Herod does so because he does not "wish" (*ēthelēsen*, 6:26) to refuse her, though the daughter's "wish" (*thelō*, 6:25) is informed by Herodias who "wanted" (*ēthelen*) to kill John. Pilate submits his will to the crowd he desired to please. What the crowd "wishes" (*thelete*, 15:9, 12[?]), though, is manipulated by the chief priests as stylized by Mark.[109] Altogether, then, the repetition of the will/wish/want language in Greek produces a thematic echo that links Herod Antipas and Pilate together. Both men submit their wills to human beings whose desires lead respectively to the deaths of John and Jesus.

Both episodes also vindicate or legitimize the prophets. Though John's endurance is not palpably highlighted (because the greater narrative focus is on Herod Antipas's response, not John's actions), John's only narrated action is described in the imperfect tense ("John *was telling* [elegen] Herod. . .," 6:18), indicating that the action was continuous. The greater vindication, though, is ironic. That is, the account of the encounter is a part of a series of reception episodes all of which speak about possible positive receptions of a prophet *and* lamentably and increasingly more negative ones.[110] What happened to John in the narrative's past is then interpreted in the light of what has happened to Jesus in one of the immediately preceding episodes (6:1-6a) and what will happen to the disciples as sent ones (6:6b-13) in the most immediately preceding episode. The eventualities of John's encounter are thus less in Herod's control and constructed more so in the context of an ongoing narrative pattern. Rejection, even horrific rejection, is often subsequent to an initial, more positive acceptance.[111]

In the case of Jesus, the vindication is clear. His silence alone (15:5) could be vindication. The vindication is even clearer when one notes the recurrence of the positive/negative reception along with the repeating predictions Jesus has made of his own death. The predictions place the eventualities of Jesus' trial before Pilate squarely in the context of realities for which Jesus is already prepared. They also allow Jesus to become the example of that endurance to which he has already called his disciples much earlier (13:9-13, esp. v. 13).

Thus, it may be that Mark has designed the confrontation between Herod Antipas and John the Baptist (6:14-29) to forecast the one between Pilate and Jesus, with similarities of format or language confirming the link. Accordingly, if Markan audiences would have been able to see a *synkrisis* (comparison or contrast) between John the Baptist and Jesus, it is likely that they would also see a *synkrisis* between Herod Antipas and Pilate. So, perhaps the initial tyrant vs. philosopher typology that formed the backdrop for Mark 6:14-29 provides the scaffolding for the construction of the later scene when yet another tyrant type (now, a governor) will meet another philosopher type. Thus, what happens between Herod Antipas and John the Baptist *establishes the pattern* for what will happen between Pilate and Jesus. Again, then, Mark does not portray Pilate favorably.

Mark's Ideology of Moral Superiority

If Markan audiences could have heard Mark 15:1-15 in the light of the narrative frames mentioned above, the price of admission would likely have been to consent to a certain ideology of domination. That is, Mark 15:1-15 seems constructed on a code of moral superiority based on the ability to endure in the face of a captor whose morals are weak or altogether absent. Such a code is found both in smaller tales and even larger narratives in the ancient world.

For example, the faithful endurance of a Jew in a foreign court (or before a foreign ruler) was characteristically used as a vindication story to highlight the superiority of the Jew before the foreign ruler. The best example of this vindication story appears in 4 Maccabees, an apocryphal text designed to prove that reason is superior to the passions. In 4 Maccabees, all of the protagonists, Eleazar (an aged priest), seven brothers, and their mother all use reason to maintain their devotion to God despite the taunts and torturous schemes of the tyrant Antiochus IV, the king of Syria.[112]

Without assigning a genetic link, there certainly are a number of parallels found between the experiences of Jesus in Mark and that of Eleazar (or the seven brothers and their mother) before Antiochus IV in 4 Maccabees. Just as Jesus is bound (*dēsantes*, 15:1)[113] in Mark's Gospel to highlight the brutality of his handlers, the language of bringing and binding exposes the tyrannical force of Antiochus IV and his henchmen in 4 Maccabees. Persons are "rounded up" (*synarpasthentōn*, 5:4); seized (*syllambanesthai*,17:1); brought (*agagein*, 8:2; *agomenoi*, 8:3; *ēgeto*, 10:1); and bound (*diedēsan*, 9:11; *prosedēsan*, 9:26; *dēsantes*, 11:9).

Also, in both narratives, an initial antithetical typological construction is the basis for a later one. That is, one confrontation between a tyrant type and a philosopher type becomes the basis for yet another confrontation between these antithetical types. Notice has already been given to this feature in Mark. In the case of 4 Maccabees, the initial confrontation between Antiochus IV and Eleazar (5:1—7:23), between a tyrant and a sage, becomes the basic template on which the subsequent tyrant vs. philosopher encounters are based, whether that of the encounters between Antiochus IV and the seven brothers (8:1—14:10), or that of the encounter between Antiochus IV and the mother of the seven (14:11—17:6).[114]

Likewise, just as Pilate reacts with amazement at Jesus' silence (*thaumazein*, 15:5), Antiochus IV and his council marvel (*ethaumasan*) at the endurance of Eleazar, the seven, and the mother of the seven (4 Macc 17:17; cf. 9:26; 17:16; 18:3). Relatedly, within the whole of the mockery charade in Mark 15, onlookers request that Jesus save himself (15:30-31), a request on a par with Pilate's request for Jesus to answer charges brought against him, though Jesus refuses to answer (15:3-5). In 4 Maccabees as well, the offer to save oneself is made repeatedly: to Eleazar (*sōzoio*, 5:6; *sōthēti*, 6:15; cf. 6:27); and to the seven (*sōzoito*, 10:1; *sōze seauton*, 10:13; *sōtērion*, 12:6; cf. 15:26-27).

In both narratives, moreover, what matters is endurance. In 4 Maccabees, endurance is featured repeatedly to indicate the faithfulness and resolve of Eleazar, the seven sons, and their mother (5:23; 6:9; 7:22; 9:6, 22; 15:31, 32; 16:1, 8, 17, 19, 21; 17:7, 10). Though Mark only uses the word once (13:13) to describe the faithfulness expected of Jesus' disciples, Jesus' whole tenor during his last days casts him also as the faithful example of endurance.

Yet, if Mark is similar to 4 Maccabees in featuring the moral superiority of Jesus before Pilate, the inherent politics of difference in both narratives does not erase social hierarchies; it simply replaces them.[115] Those who would follow the Jesus described in Mark's Gospel would see themselves, in the light of their relations with Jesus, as morally superior to their oppressors (all *Pilate* types) even if not superior in military force. And lest one be seduced to rally for such rhetoric, we must be reminded that this posture of moral superiority would then endorse the apocalyptic realignment of power authorized in Mark 13.[116] As Tolbert notes, "The apocalyptic vision described in Mark 13 calls for the utter destruction of the world and everyone in it who is not among the elect. Under what circumstances is such a vengeful, bloodthirsty, and pitiless view of one's enemies morally justified? Should any group who see themselves as marginalized and powerless be encouraged to appropriate this passionate hope for the divine annihilation of their oppressors?"[117]

Mark, though, was not alone in constructing this kind of ideology. Many of the Jewish novels, like other popular indigenous genres of this period (for example, the ancient Greek novel and the *Life of Aesop*, and ancient Greek novel fragments), were produced to "capture a sense of ethnic pride and competitiveness," a likely feature for once independent and presently colonized native populations.[118] Indeed, this literature may be described as propaganda literature that allows the lowly, whether the slave of a master or the wealthier but subjugated elite of an ethnic group, to triumph over the more powerful.[119]

If Mark does, in fact, resonate with many of these ancient popular propagandistic narratives, perhaps one function of Mark's Gospel is to communicate the great power and prestige of Jesus' network of followers in a narrative world over against presumably superior power complexes in the real world. Perhaps persecuted audiences found such a narrative supportive, but it is no less ideological in advancing the claim to moral superiority. Pilate's strings thus are not only moved by Jesus' voice but by a typological tyrant-philosopher construction and a larger genre with propagandistic import and fatal ultimate consequences.

We must also note, though, that the Romans too considered themselves morally superior, and on that basis they thought themselves fit to rule the world. Crucial for the propagation of Rome's imperialistic influence from Augustus on was a discursive effort, namely, as noted earlier, an ethnic superiority campaign that included divine expansionist claims. With Virgil's epic *The Aeneid* (written between 31 and 19 B.C.E.), Rome justified its right to rule the world.[120] That is, Virgil's *Aeneid* does not simply portray the main character Aeneas as a wanderer like Odysseus, one of the heroes of the Trojan War in Homer's epic *The Odyssey*. *The Aeneid* also places the protagonist in a war to win Latium, the city from which Rome was established. Furthermore, *The Aeneid* makes Aeneas "the executor of a divine universal plan which did not become visible until Virgil's time," namely, in the reign of Augustus.[121] Thus, in *The Aeneid*, Rome is depicted as divinely ordained to be ruler of the world[122] and Augustus is depicted as a long-awaited restorer of peace.[123]

Mark thus emulates strategies that the Roman Empire used, strategies that the colonized also used to strike back. Mark's clear resistance against Pilate and those of his ilk, then, is a cultural production of the marginalized at least at some level. It is also a production that paints oppressors in the worst of moral colors in order to make palatable their destruction in the overall narrative sweep of the politics of the Markan parousia. The tyranny of Herod and of Pilate then continues beyond the narrative to those who would embrace the narrative's own reinscription of tyrannical postures.

CONCLUSION

So what have we learned from this chapter? We have learned that cultural studies examines a variety of cultural products and cultural practices to discover how they work within larger cultural frameworks in history. Using a variety of disciplines, not just one, cultural studies moves us from *mere* textual analysis to examinations of power that are constituted by the pre-reading ideological constraints that we bring to texts, whether we do so with expert reading theories or not. In part 1 we saw how various theorists helped to shape the history of cultural studies, both from Britain and from North America. We also gave notice to the radical plurality and internationalization of cultural studies, which makes it a rich stew of methods that must be adapted in each larger geopolitical context. That also means that it would be impossible for me as a black North American to represent cultural studies in every context. So, a different story would be told by others in a different country and with a different set of historical circumstances shaping how they think about life.

In part 2 we moved from the development of cultural studies to look at particular examples of how it would be used in Markan studies. Cultural studies helped us to see the ideological force in the history of the development of Mark's textual manuscript traditions. Cultural studies exposed the links between cultural identity formation and translations of Mark. It also exposed the discursive frameworks that have shaped Markan scholarship. Likewise, with cultural studies, we saw how visual artists have made Mark to suit their agendas and how history has included or excluded visual artists themselves to some extent on the basis of their biblical art.

What we have seen then is how there are larger ideological forces governing our readings and receptions of the Bible; indeed there are whole theories of reading and larger cultural currents working within the various dimensions of our society. Our readings and receptions of the Bible then are never innocent and our ways of appropriating the Bible are not natural as if they represent a consistent set of practices from dawn to eternity.

Thankfully, while cultural studies aids us in seeing our own ideological constraints, it also does not dismiss altogether the ideological cultural products and practices of the texts we examine. Rather, as part 3 revealed, cultural studies also raises questions about the likely reception of older texts, the degree to which those texts resisted empire, and the degree to which the same texts seductively reinforced empire through certain ideological codes of domination reinscribed on the very heart of the stories we read. In the end, then, cultural studies asks us to pay close attention to the "other," whether we ourselves take up that role or we design it for someone else.

FURTHER READING

General

During, Simon, ed. *The Cultural Studies Reader*. New York: Routledge, 1999. This reader begins with an accessible general introduction that charts the evolution and promise of cultural studies. Then, the reader features representative essays by the leading contributors to cultural studies. An editorial introduction summarizes each essay and assesses the relevance of the essay for contemporary cultural studies work. While the initial essays treat general theoretical matters in cultural studies, subsequent sections of the reader focus more on specific cultural studies topics such as space and time, nationalism and postcolonialism, ethnicity and multiculturalism, and sexuality and gender.

Grossberg, Lawrence, Cary Nelson, and Paula Treichler, eds. *Cultural Studies*. New York: Routledge, 1992. An invaluable reader that includes a general introduction to cultural studies, a reader's guide, and thirty-nine essays by leading cultural theorists, including works by Stuart Hall, bell hooks, and Cornel West. Most of the essays were presented at an important international conference on cultural studies held at the University of Illinois at Urbana-Champaign in 1990. The conference and essays treated not only the history and theoretical heritage of the field. It also interrogated the contemporary uses of cultural studies, questioning whether it had been co-opted away from its initial commitments to making a difference in society.

hooks, bell. *Black Looks: Race and Representation*. Boston, Mass.: South End, 1992. A virtual storehouse of illustrations on key concepts in cultural studies such as gaze, representation, and domination.

Storey, John, ed. and intro. *Cultural Theory and Popular Art: An Introduction*. 2d ed. Athens, Ga.: University of Georgia Press, 1998. A clear, helpful introduction to cultural studies, it defines some of the key terms such as culture, ideology, and popular culture. The work's best feature is its use of examples from culture to illustrate important concepts in cultural studies such as Althusser's view of ideology. Another important feature of the work is that it also offers chapters on the major influences on cultural studies such as Marxism and feminism.

West, Cornel. *Keeping Faith: Philosophy and Race in America*. New York: Routledge, 1994. While this work is a good collection of West's essays altogether, "The New Cultural Politics of Difference" is the most relevant of the essays for cultural studies. That essay places cultural studies in historical perspective and explains important concepts in cultural studies such as hegemony, representation, binary opposites, and demystification.

Biblical

The Bible and Culture Collective. *The Postmodern Bible.* New Haven: Yale University Press, 1995. Like other proponents of cultural studies, the authors of the *Postmodern Bible* worked collaboratively (in the Bible and Culture Collective) to offset the politics of exclusion. In the cultural studies tradition of critique, they offered solid critiques of contemporary biblical practices of interpretation, particularly on the questions of suppressed meaning, the formation of identities, and the use of the Bible to legitimate the status quo. The work's chapter on ideological criticism provides stellar discussions of Althusser's concept of ideology and of Marxist criticism in general.

Blount, Brian K. *Cultural Interpretation: Reorienting New Testament Criticism.* Minneapolis: Fortress Press, 1995. Although Blount does not explicitly draw on the cultural studies tradition here, he certainly seeks to democratize the cultural practice of biblical interpretation. The work persuasively demonstrates the influence of context on biblical interpretation. Particularly, Blount exposes the influence of historically conditioned methods and prevailing theological models on interpretations of Mark 14:55-64 and Mark 15:2-15. Blount also highlights the ideological biases in all interpretations, whether that of well-known biblical critics, that of Nicaraguan campesinos (or farm workers) in *The Gospel in Solentiname*, or that of North American blacks in their spirituals and sermons.

———. *Can I Get a Witness? Reading Revelation through African American Culture.* Louisville: Westminster John Knox, 2005. Blount explicitly links this work to British cultural studies, for which he offers a short history. The work then compares the apparently counter-cultural speech of rap (particularly that of Tupac Shakur) to the resistance hymns in the Apocalypse of John.

Exum Cheryl J., and Stephen D. Moore, eds. *Biblical Studies/Cultural Studies.* Edited by Stephen D. Moore and Cheryl J. Exum. This collection of nineteen essays grew out of an international conference at the University of Sheffield in 1997. Although most of the essays do not draw deeply from the wells of the cultural studies tradition, they at least explore the multiple popular venues (such as art and music) through which the Bible has been appropriated and thus they democratize interpretive practices.

Guardiola-Sáenz, Leticia A. "Borderless Women and Borderless Texts: A Cultural Reading of Matthew 15:21-28." *Semeia* 78 (1997): 69–81. In this article, Guardiola-Sáenz draws on cultural studies in two ways. First, she democratizes the cultural practice of biblical interpretation. That is, she explicitly acknowledges her reading of the story of the Canaanite woman in Matt 15:21-28 in the light of her own experience of dispossession as a Mexican-American. Second, she critiques the text's implicit ideology of chosenness for some persons and dispossession for others.

Moore, Stephen D., ed. *In Search of the Present: The Bible through Cultural Studies.* *Semeia* 82 (1998). A collection of articles that investigates the role of the Bible as a popular cultural product in the contemporary world. Several of the essays draw explicitly on the cultural studies tradition, especially the introductory article by Stephen Moore and Ralph Broadbent's ideological critique of select British New Testament commentaries.

Segovia, Fernando F. *Decolonizing Biblical Studies: A View from the Margins.* Maryknoll, N. Y.: Orbis, 2000. This collection of previously published essays examines the shifts in the development of biblical studies and it positions present biblical scholarship under the rubric of cultural studies. Largely intended as a theoretical work, the essays help to show how deeply embedded ideology is in all cultural products and practices, including the biblical texts, their worlds, and all forms of biblical interpretation.

————. "Cultural Studies and Contemporary Biblical Criticism as a Mode of Discourse." Pages 1–17 of *Reading from this Place.* Volume 2 of *Social Location and Biblical Interpretation in Global Perspective.* Edited by Fernando F. Segovia and Mary Ann Tolbert. Minneapolis: Fortress Press, 1995. Segovia traces the evolution of biblical criticism and thus puts biblical cultural studies in perspective. He asserts that biblical studies has evolved in three stages with historical criticism as its first stage, literary criticism and (socio)cultural criticism as its second stage, and cultural studies as its present and third stage.

Smith, Abraham. "'I Saw the Book Talk': A Cultural Studies Approach to the Ethics of an African American Biblical Hermeneutics." *Semeia* 77 (1997): 115–38. The work charts the history of cultural studies in Britain and in North America. In its exposure of the alluring yet misogynistic codes of Luke-Acts, moreover, the work evokes bell hooks' critique of textual constructions of gender.

8

POSTCOLONIAL CRITICISM

Echoes of a Subaltern's Contribution and Exclusion[1]

TAT-SIONG BENNY LIEW

COMMENTING ON THE STATE OF EUROPEAN colonialism in 1916, Vladimir Ilich Lenin stated that "the world is completely divided up, so that in the future *only* redivision is possible."[2] The first part of Lenin's statement certainly rang true. One has to think only of the "Scramble for Africa" in the last quarter of the nineteenth century.[3] Literally "racing" to colonize and redraw the map of Africa, European imperialists gave little attention to indigenous cartography or native traditions and ties, and simply superimposed their own borders and boundaries on the continent. The best-known example is arguably the creation of "Rhodesia," named after the British-born Cecil Rhodes, whose profits from his British South Africa Company also became the funding source of the world-renowned Rhodes Scholarship. One can see the fulfillment of the second part of Lenin's statement in the early 1920s, when the Ottoman Empire was defeated, dismembered, and redistributed. Claiming a mandate from the League of Nations, British and French colonizers "invented" various nation-states in the Middle East under

their respective charge. Among these newly invented nation-states were
Iraq, Jordan, and Lebanon.[4]

The scope and speed of decolonization since the conclusion of the Second
World War merely two decades or so later are thus nothing less than stun-
ning. The English word "postcolonialism" supposedly made its first appearance in 1959, when a British newspaper used it to refer to what had happened
in India after its independence in 1947.[5] In many ways, therefore, the term
is linked not only to independence movements of the twentieth century, but
also to relations between people inside and outside the geopolitical West, the
West in which politics and geography are linked. That is why, for example,
Robert J. C. Young connects what he calls the "theoretical and political position" of postcolonialism with two conferences. First, at the Bandung Conference in 1955, twenty-nine African and Asian countries that had recently
gained political independence met to form an alliance against both the geopolitical West and the Soviet bloc. Second, recently or newly independent
nations from Africa, Asia, and Latin America gathered as a transnational
body at the Tricontinental Conference in Havana in 1966 to resist and seek
liberation from imperialism.[6] Young's connection brings out three important
aspects of postcolonialism. First, postcolonialism involves a combination
of—for lack of better terms—academics and activism. Second, postcolonialism often entails an international or global frame. Third, postcolonialism
does not mean the end of, but the continual struggle against, imperialism.

This last point calls for some clarification of terms. "Imperialism" refers
to various ideologies and practices by which one nation may extend itself to
exert control and domination over other nations and territories for its own
interests. "Colonialism" is a narrower term. It describes only one specific
form of imperialist expansion and exploitation: the occupation of land and
setting up of colonies. The difference between imperialism and colonialism
explains, for example, why many former colonies still find themselves under
the indirect or informal rule of others, including but not restricted to their
former colonial masters. This continual or new hegemony over former colonies or colonized nations is most often carried out through economic and/or
cultural means. The evolution of the United States from being a "new empire"
in the nineteenth century to being the sole superpower today is undoubtedly
the best illustration of this process, though one must keep in mind that the
threat and the practice of U.S. military occupation is not yet and perhaps
will never be entirely absent.[7] Some have chosen to call this different form or
phase of imperialism—that is, one without direct acquisition and occupation
of colonies—"neocolonialism."

Understanding colonialism as a specific stage or form within the larger
frame of imperialism will also help us differentiate between postcolonialism
with and without a hyphen. What the hyphenated term "post-colonialism"
emphasizes is the temporal aspect (incidentally, it is also the earlier of the
two terms). It was first used by social scientists to indicate the period after

political independence has taken place; its focus is therefore chronological. In contrast, "postcolonialism," without a hyphen, gives more attention to the cultural aspects, particularly the ongoing cultural legacies of colonization. This difference is, of course, a matter of emphasis. An unhyphenated postcolonialism does not in any way dismiss or deny the place or the point of political or national independence. In fact, both the chronological and cultural dimensions are important in distinguishing postcolonialism from anti-colonialism. Anti-colonialism is as old as colonialism itself. The age of colonialism is a significant issue that I will discuss later. A post-independence chronology for postcolonialism is important because neocolonialism, or the difference between colonialism and imperialism, is in many ways based on the experience of having political independence without economic and cultural autonomy. In other words, if anti-colonialism strives to end colonialism, postcolonialism comes to the realization that ending colonialism is not enough. As a way to talk about the cultural dimension of postcolonialism, I will examine how postcolonial studies have emerged by not only interrogating the connection between culture and (neo)colonialism but also integrating all kinds of theoretical and philosophical discourse into the struggle against imperialism.

MAPPING POSTCOLONIAL STUDIES

While postcolonialism's transnational frame separates it from the narrower nationalism of anti-colonialism, the cultural or theoretical/philosophical aspects of postcolonialism go back to the coupling of academic and activist politics. To give an overview of and orientation to postcolonial studies, I will feature four pioneering publications: (1) the late Edward W. Said's *Orientalism*,[8] (2) Gayatri Chakravorty Spivak's "Can the Subaltern Speak?"[9] (3) Abdul R. JanMohamed and David Lloyd's *The Nature and Context of Minority Discourse*,[10] and (4) Homi K. Bhabha's *The Location of Culture*.[11]

Most scholars mark the beginning of postcolonial studies with the publication of Said's *Orientalism* in 1978. In this groundbreaking text, Said uses Michel Foucault's understanding of discourse as a network of power and knowledge. He points out how the geopolitical West has been able to subject the Orient or the Arab world through discourse, making the Orient the object of all kinds of study since the eighteenth century. In other words, colonization involves cultural and cognitive work as well as military or physical violence. Critiquing how the geopolitical West dominates and colonizes people whom it defines as the "Other" by "learning," "knowing," and constructing them, Orientalism leads to the development of colonial discourse analysis. Such analysis stresses and scrutinizes how texts, meanings, knowledge, and power are all intertwined and implicated in the colonial enterprise. Of particular interest is how colonial discourse creates subjection through culture and representation, especially how subjection is related to constructions of both colonizing and colonized subjects. The label "Oriental" itself, for example, functions simultaneously to identify and homogenize all Arabs in distinction from everything and everyone that is "Occidental," Western, or white European. The ongoing significance of Said's study can be readily seen in the cultural and political imaginations of the geopolitical West after 9/11, particularly in the so-called "war on terror" of the U.S. empire. Representing Arabs as "terrorists" justifies not only U.S. imperialism abroad, but also a particular state identity for the U.S. nation at home.

Said presents Orientalism as mainly a colonizing and racializing discourse over the Arabs—or how colonialism is related to racism—but he offers few if any alternatives for or accounts of resistance. Gayatri Chakravorty Spivak, on the other hand, in a densely packed and painfully dense essay—published almost a decade later—registers another foundational point in the development of postcolonial studies. While her "Can the Subaltern Speak?" can be—and has been—read as not only endorsing but also exacerbating Said's silence on or denial of colonized people's agency, Spivak's essay actually changes the direction of postcolonial studies on several important fronts. It does this with a heavy and heady dose of Derridean deconstruction (see chapter 4 above). First, instead of pondering colonial discourse that functions to colonize as Said did, Spivak probes discourse from the geopolitical West that ends up silencing and further subjugating the colonized *despite* its benevolent intention to speak for and help rescue them. She suggests, for example, that white men and women, in their enthusiasm to "save brown women from brown men," have misread a young Indian woman's suicide in 1926. While the woman committed suicide to avoid being captured for attempting a political assassination and thus to cover up an insurgency for India's independence, her "benevolent" white interpreters read her suicide as nothing but another tragedy of *sati*, or the ancient patriarchal practice of Hindu widow sacrifice. Second, with the word "subaltern," Spivak challenges a practice of Marxist historiography known as Subaltern Studies. Subaltern Studies rewrite previous histories of India done by both colonial British and elite Indian scholars. They do so to recover the agency and resistance of the rural peasantry in India against British colonialism. Spivak, however, challenges Subaltern Studies by pointing to the general invisibility of Indian women in subaltern histories. This, in turn, leads to the third contribution of Spivak's essay to postcolonial studies. It greatly nuances colonial dynamics by simultaneously questioning two assumptions. The first is that the colonized are a unified and undifferentiated group of people, and the second that racial difference is the primary base or even sole basis of colonialism. Finally, in contrast to Said, Spivak does begin to look at the cultural productions of the colonized, such as the ancient Hindu religious texts on *sati*. This is helpful even if her conclusion on the effects of such productions, especially those by subaltern "third world women," remains guarded.

In a way that both parallels and protests the two beginnings represented by Said and Spivak, respectively, the next two beginnings of postcolonial studies share a common concern to show the vulnerability of empire, whether by highlighting the articulation of the colonized or the anxiety of the colonizers. The third beginning, like the first, has a recognizable label or title. Unlike Said's "colonial discourse analysis," however, "minority discourse" looks at—as its adjective announces—the discourse of the less powerful. While "minority discourse," like Spivak's work, is interested in the cultural work of the subordinate, it—as its noun notifies—refuses Spivak's conclusion about the dismissal, if not the impossibility, of subaltern speech. Two of the most representative champions for "minority discourse" are Abdul R. JanMohamed and David Lloyd. Not only do they work to retrieve texts and voices of the marginalized who spoke and continue to speak back to the imperial center, but they also promote dialogues and hence collaboration among different minority cultures and groups. Their edited volume, *The Nature and Context of Minority Discourse*, puts together contributions from not only women and various racial/ethnic minority groups in the United States, but also an Israeli scholar who is committed to the rights and well-being of Arabs as well as a feminist scholar who is located in India. In other words, while JanMohamed and Lloyd recognize—like Spivak—that differences exist among the colonized, they—perhaps, again, unlike Spivak—reaffirm the possibility of solidarity across differences because of the shared experience of domination.

If "minority discourse" focuses on the articulation of and conversation among colonized groups, Homi K. Bhabha's emphasis is back on the colonial center of power and the colonial texts it creates. *The Location of Culture*, which is a collection of Bhabha's many influential essays, reveals two important characteristics of his work in relation to those that we have discussed thus far. First, Bhabha's object of analysis is comparable to Said's, but his almost impenetrable style is closer to that of Spivak. Second, unlike both Said and Spivak, Bhabha does not critique colonialism and imperialism by delineating the pervasiveness of their destructive power (even or especially for those who have benevolent intentions). Instead, Bhabha carries out his criticism by disclosing the cracks in the incoherence, insecurity, and incompleteness of empire. Using psychoanalytic theory and its emphasis on the unconscious, Bhabha reads the records and treats the ills of colonialism by stressing its repressed distresses, contradictions, and uncertainties. As we will see in greater detail below, Bhabha sees the colonial practice of cultural indoctrination in a way that is very different from that of, say, the Nobel-prize winning novelist of Indo-Trinidadian heritage, V. S. Naipaul.[12] In contrast to Naipaul's emphasis that cultural indoctrination leads to a sense of inferiority on the part of the colonized, Bhabha focuses instead on how the practice might have negative implications on and for the colonizers.[13]

READING SENSIBILITIES AND READING STRATEGIES

My goal in highlighting these admittedly arbitrary beginning points is to bring out the wide scope of and internal differences within postcolonial studies and also to make clear that postcolonial studies does not belong to any single person or even school of thought. Further, it is important to explain that these multiple beginnings are but benchmarks or mileposts of postcolonial studies. Just as there have been continuous developments since these beginnings with each new generation of critics, there were thinkers who had already targeted colonialism before Said. Someone like Frantz Fanon, the Algerian author of *The Wretched of the Earth* and other insightful texts, is cited as often and as much as any recognized postcolonial scholar.[14] However, Fanon is often considered a harbinger or forerunner rather than an originator of postcolonial studies. This is because he did not live long enough to see Algeria achieve independence. Aside from the contribution of harbingers and the "criterion" of having experienced independence, there is little question that postcolonial studies became a recognized field only because of the combined cogency or force of its multiple beginnings.

These four beginnings also help to give a sense of the sensibilities of postcolonial criticism. Of no small significance is that all five scholars I have mentioned were or are professors of literature. For good and/or ill, this means that postcolonial studies are always already fitted for literary analysis.

The World(ing) of a Text

Postcolonial criticism is clearly an oppositional reading practice that challenges colonial culture and control in terms both material and discursive. Perhaps this is why Bhabha says in an interview that he understands "reading as ravishment, reading as being ravished."[15] Reading can be a powerful force both on and by the reader. One of the basic assumptions of postcolonial criticism is that textual practice, both reading and writing, is inseparable from the realities—particularly imperial realities—of the world in which such practice takes place. A postcolonial critic thus seeks to read a text in light not only of the text's entanglement in and engagement with a colonial world, but also the critic's own involvement and investment in a different and/or related world of empire. Critics committed to challenging imperialism in all its forms and disguises have examined, for example, both the context and the content of Shakespeare's writings to tease out the sharp, subtle, and/or sweeping inflection of colonial dynamics. Precisely when English colonialism was in its critical infancy in the late sixteenth and early seventeenth centuries, Shakespeare wrote about not only a "civilizing mission" in *The Tempest*, but also the isolating or marooning experience of a dark-skinned Moor in Venice in *Othello*.[16] Said refers to this as the "worldliness" of both text and critic.[17]

Perhaps coincidentally, Spivak uses the term "worlding" to talk about how writing or textuality might serve both to justify and implement imperialism in general and colonialism in particular.[18] What both of the terms, "worldliness" and "worlding," insist on is the connection between culture and colonialism, or the link between literary studies and liberation struggles against imperialism.

With this understanding, Said has suggested what he calls a "contrapuntal" strategy for reading the literary canon of "English literature."[19] This practice keeps in mind more than the content and context of one canonical text. The point is to establish a counterpoint, whether this is a counter-narrative by a non-canonical writer, or a context covered up or written over. According to Said, one should never read, for example, the European author Joseph Conrad's *Heart of Darkness* by itself. Rather, one should read it alongside something like the Nigerian novelist Chinua Achebe's *Things Fall Apart.* Such a "contrapuntal" reading is helpful because both texts concern the "Scramble for Africa" at the end of the nineteenth century, but they are written from a European's and an African's perspective, respectively.[20] Likewise, one must not read the overwhelming maleness of Rudyard Kipling's *Kim* in isolation from the ideology of the British Empire as a form of manly sport and competition. Bringing thus into one's reading both what an author includes and excludes, one can bring into focus not just how this canonical text relies on and invests in imperial ideology and dynamics (like *Kim*), but also how imperialism is always met by resistance (like the existence of *Things Fall Apart* alongside *Heart of Darkness*). For Said, the "worldliness" of the text and the critic leads to an interpretive move that juxtaposes various visions and revisions. This affirms for him a larger humanistic vision of the intertwined and overlapping nature of even disparate histories. "Contrapuntal reading" reads across and bridges differing, even conflicting perspectives.

Across Time, Space, and Disciplines

Attempts by postcolonial critics to connect their own imperial condition with that of a literary text from the past—whether Shakespeare, Kipling, or Conrad—are clearly cross-temporal if not necessarily cross-cultural endeavors. Nevertheless, one should remember that one main difference between a postcolonial and an anti-colonial undertaking is the former's transnational frame. Perhaps the international frame of postcolonialism signals something about its move beyond an anti-colonial nativism, or beyond a desire to return to a pre-colonial and indigenous past that is free of impurity or intermixing. One can be sure, however, that the international frame of postcolonialism involves not only a political alliance but also a syncretic or mixed form of knowledge-politics. This is clear in Said's use of Foucault, Spivak's use of Derrida and Marxism, as well as Bhabha's use of psychoanalysis. This syncretic or hybrid use of knowledge as politics is in some sense not surprising, given colonialism's history as a cross-continental, and thus cross-cultural—though admittedly conflictual and often violent—interaction.

Postcolonial criticism's interdisciplinary bent also becomes understandable if one considers how colonialism is, as Said's *Orientalism* points out, also a racializing discourse. In other words, one cannot make sense of colonialism without knowing something about how knowledge and power work together to create and categorize experience in racial terms. Yet, as Spivak's featuring of the subaltern as "third world women" reminds us, colonialism also takes place at the intersection of race and gender. Such an intersection tells us that categories like race and gender do not exist in isolation. Colonial domination takes place therefore not only in intersections between but also along the elision of race, gender, sexuality, and class. Put differently, those who are categorized as racially inferior and thus "deserving" or "in need of" colonization can find themselves sliding smoothly along a scale made up of these intersecting and interrelated categories. The "basis" of their subordination can easily be changed from their racial inferiority to their feminization to their sexual deviance, and their lower-class status or lack of class distinction. Precisely because of this colonial flexibility, postcolonial criticism has to engage with issues that preoccupy racial/ethnic, gender, sexuality, and/ or Marxist studies. These diverse fields of studies provide, of course, fertile ground for multilateral cultivation and interruption.[21]

Alternative Knowledge and Agency

Yet another reason for the interdisciplinary emphasis of postcolonial criticism is its commitment to contest colonial knowledge by bringing to light subordinated perspectives and/or creating alternative knowledge.[22] This is also why postcolonial criticism insists on not only reassessing the literary and cultural productions of the colonizers, but also on retrieving and resourcing those of the colonized. Spivak, for example, critiques previous scholarship—including feminist scholarship—for failing to question how the white, bourgeois protagonist of Charlotte Brontë's *Jane Eyre* achieves freedom and happiness at the expense of Bertha Mason, a captive woman from the West Indies. Spivak also shows how Jean Rhys drew from her Caribbean upbringing to rewrite or provide a prequel to *Jane Eyre*. In *Wide Sargasso Sea*, Rhys writes from the perspective of a Jamaican Creole (that is, culturally mixed) woman as well as from the perspective of her husband, Rochester.[23] In a delightfully ironic fashion, Spivak's attentiveness to the limits and liabilities of representing a subaltern is also accompanied by her almost endless effort to introduce—through both translations and commentaries—the Bengali writings of Mahasweta Devi to the English-speaking world.[24]

The attempt to preserve and produce cultural traditions and works that are alternative to those of the geopolitical West is connected to the issue of agency within postcolonial criticism. By agency, I mean particularly the ability of the colonized to act and speak in resistance to or subversion of imperial power. As noted above with respect to the four beginning points of postcolonial studies, agency has been one of the most central and controversial questions for postcolonial critics. For example, can a subaltern achieve a voice and represent herself? What does it say about agency if the only change that accompanies political independence is the transformation from colonialism to neocolonialism? What does it say if those who have "successfully" championed for and/or ruled after independence turn out to be, wittingly or unwittingly, agents or brokers of and for an ever-present if behind-the-scene empire?[25] The perplexing and knotty question of agency is in many ways inseparable from another critical concept of postcolonial criticism: ambivalence.

Ambivalence

Before discussing the postcolonial emphasis on ambivalence, let me reiterate the purpose of postcolonial criticism. Postcolonial criticism studies discourses and literary texts to look for as well as look at the complexities of colonial rule and resistance. It seeks to confront and contest not only past devices and dynamics of domination but also their legacies. This includes their covert continuations into the present, even in the very aspiration for and act of resistance. Think again of those who not only lead the struggles for independence but also rule afterwards. They are, more often than not, elites who have been educated in and/or by the imperial center. As a result, it is likely that they at least partly identify with or have internalized some colonial ideas or ideals. Theoretically or psychoanalytically, in *Black Skin, White Masks*, Fanon has written insightfully about the colonized person's simultaneous attraction to and repulsion by the colonizer. Literarily, Jean Rhys again provides an example in her short story, "The Day They Burned the Books." There one finds another Creole on a Caribbean island. This one is torn between his hatred of his white, abusive father and his love for that same father's library of European books.[26]

Ambivalence refers then to the messy relations and blurring line between colonial domination and resistance against it. Bhabha is, generally speaking, most tightly associated with this concept of and sensitivity to ambivalence. For Bhabha, ambivalence or the inability to separate cleanly and neatly the colonizer from the colonized implies, first and foremost, the vulnerability of empire. In other words, Bhabha is adamant about the agency of the colonized, even or especially as he emphasizes the incompleteness or inconsistency of colonial control. His related concept of "mimicry" points to the colonizers' desire that the colonized become like them. This desire not only invites the colonized to turn mimicry into mockery, but also creates a tremendous amount of anxiety for the colonizers. The colonizers' anxiety has much to do with their need to acknowledge and disavow simultaneously the sameness and the difference that they see between themselves and those whom they colonize. Since the presence and the *potential* removal of difference that separates the colonizer and the colonized serve to justify colonization, removing difference and achieving sameness will make colonization indefensible. For the colonizers, mimicry further means that all identities—even their own identity as colonizers—may change. This movement or mutation from mimicry to both mockery and menace is key to Bhabha's concept of ambivalence. Mimicry also points to cross-cultural fusion or transcultural creation, like the creolization that Rhys experienced and wrote about. Bhabha also has a special term for this transgressive, transfiguring, and hence transformative mingling; he calls it "hybridity." While all of these terms have their own particular focus and emphasis and so should not be collapsed into one another, they do also converge on the impossibility of "purity." Just as there is no "pure" colonizer and colonized, resistance mingles with complicity, and domination with its own disruption.

Whether a postcolonial critic is reading a text produced by a colonizer or a colonized person, an emphasis on ambivalence will lead her to avoid clean-cut binary oppositions. For example, she will be reluctant to present a total or one-sided condemnation or absolution of a text's complicity with a colonial project. Instead, she will accentuate the differences, contradictions, and tensions within a text. Such an emphasis is consistent with the realization that liberation from colonial and imperial ideology and practice is, as Spivak suggests, "incredibly slow and time-consuming work, with no guarantees."[27] Whether one understands it in terms of internalization and/or mimicry, the story of "colonized-turning-into-colonizers" is well known. Given the Arab American Said's place within the story of postcolonial studies, one only has to think about how Arabs or Palestinians are often displaced by Jews, arguably one of the most displaced peoples in human history. Similarly, returning to Spivak's criticism of Subaltern Studies, when she points out the erasure of subaltern as "third world women," she shows how the very people who work against colonial oppression may duplicate it. Again, the relation between colonizer and colonized—or the relation between disruption and domination—is fluctuating and ambivalent. Spivak's critique or ambivalence further nuances the place of colonialism or where colonialism takes place. The power differential between the Subaltern Studies historians and Spivak's subalterns as "third world women" shows that "there is a first world in every third world."[28] Similarly, scholars of "minority discourse" who are often "minorities" themselves demonstrate that "there is [also] a third world in every first world."[29] In other words, colonialism can be "internal" as well as "external." Postcolonial criticism must then pay attention not only to the presence of fissures within both the colonial and the colonized sides, but also the possibility of connection between or across the colonizer-and-colonized divides. In one sense, what ambivalence calls for is a refusal to simplify. Instead, postcolonial criticism inclines toward an acknowledgment of complexity. One expression of this acknowledgment is that it, as Spivak says, "does not perceive acknowledgment of complicity as an inconvenience."[30]

WHAT DOES MARK HAVE TO DO WITH IT?

I have already mentioned Spivak's use of Derridean deconstruction in her postcolonial work. Let me now add that what Jacques Derrida once said about deconstruction is also applicable to postcolonial criticism. According to Derrida, "Deconstruction is not a method and cannot be transformed into one."[31] It should be clear, I hope, from my emphasis on sensibilities and strategies that postcolonial criticism does not involve and has not developed a number of mechanical steps that one can simply follow to approach any given text. What it does offer is a set of conceptual resources and a specific objective to interrogate and oppose imperialism.

An important question is what postcolonial criticism has to do with the Bible in general and with Mark in particular. Let me make four suggestions, although they admittedly overlap and cannot be separated neatly or considered in isolation. The first two are more general and historical. The first has to do with the contexts in which the Bible initially came into being. The second concerns the ways in which people have used the Bible to justify and support colonialism. My last two suggestions are actually similar, but also more particular to the current situation of the U.S. empire. They point respectively to how the Bible has become a resource book for the Bush administration, and how "our" current empire is akin to the Roman Empire of the New Testament times.

Original Contexts

Turning to my first suggestion, one reason for postcolonial biblical criticism is that the various books that make up the Bible, including Mark, were all collected and/or written in the context of colonization. I mentioned earlier that the Jewish people have had a long history of displacement. They were colonized by the Assyrians, the Babylonians, the Persians, and the Greeks in the Hebrew Bible period and by the Romans in New Testament times. While neither Mark nor any of his fellow canonical writers witnessed the achievement of independence and hence, like Fanon, none could claim a postcolonial status, they also, like Fanon, can provide insights for postcolonial criticism. In fact, I will suggest that the practice of postcolonial *biblical* criticism might help postcolonial criticism as a whole to rethink the chronology, geography, and the diversity of colonialism. In response to the tendency of some postcolonial theorists and critics—particularly in the initial stage of the field's development—to focus on the French and British empires in Africa and Asia and hence implicitly or unintentionally communicating that colonization was a post-eighteenth-century phenomenon, others have helpfully recognized the need to address the colonial legacies of the Spanish and Portuguese empires in the Americas since the fifteenth or the sixteenth century.[32] One need not extend the logic very far to see the legitimacy and the benefit of examining colonialism of an even earlier time by a different empire in a different area.[33] During the time of the New Testament, the Roman Empire had colonized both lands and peoples as far as North Africa and West Asia. The argument becomes even more persuasive if one considers that Said's seminal work targets the same area of the world as the New Testament: the eastern Mediterranean and especially Palestine. Similarly, Orientalism as a colonizing and racializing discourse involves an elision of or a connection between race and religion (Arabs as Muslim).

Using the Bible for Colonial Ends

The elision of race and religion points to a second reason for postcolonial biblical criticism: the long tradition of using the Bible for colonial ends. Walter Mignolo, in arguing for the need to look at the "five hundred years" of colonization of the Americas, proposes that the basis of colonization shifted from religion (or, more specifically, the dominance of Christian imagery) to race with the outbreak of the U.S.-Spanish War in 1898.[34] The so-called "discovery of America" funded by Spanish royalty also coincided with their last crusade against Islam.[35] Religion has, however, never been completely replaced by race as a basis for colonization, even if Mignolo is correct that race has become more important. Both are—along with gender, sexuality, and class—terms that slide and elide into one another within the scale and scope of colonization. Religion in general and the Bible in particular have long been, and continue to be, used for the justification and the implementation of colonization.[36] In Spivak's reading of Brontë's *Jane Eyre*, she insightfully points out how the text ends with a justification of imperialism in terms of not only a civilizing mission but also a Christian soul-making enterprise through a missionary character, St. John Rivers.[37] Derrida is well justified, then, to call capitalist globalization, or the continuation of the *religiously* implicated imperial project that started from the old Roman Empire, "globalatinization."[38]

Contemporary Use of the Bible

In addition to the colonial context of the Bible and the use of the Bible for colonial ends, there is a third and more contemporary reason. This suggestion may also serve as a preventive not to over-read Mignolo's suggestion about shifting colonial justification from religion to race in the nineteenth century. R. S. Sugirtharajah makes a timely intervention in pointing out that the U.S.

empire has returned to the Bible as a "textual motor" for its imperial opera-
tion.[39] More specifically, Erin Runions has pointed to a link between certain
"evangelical biblical interpretation," contemporary wars in Afghanistan and
Iraq, and Muslim women.[40] The Hebrew Bible not only often portrays Israel
as a woman, but also as constantly in need of God's rescues, and at times,
"justifiable" punishments. God, however, will work tirelessly on her behalf so
that she will fulfill her God-given destiny to rule over all other nations. In like
manner, Runions proposed that some have understood President George W.
Bush to be a divinely appointed leader who would rescue both the nation of
the United States *and* the women of Islam from evil, even or especially as he
has worked to establish the "new world order" of U.S. hegemony. In addition,
Runions suggested that the confidence that the Bush administration has had
about the imperial destiny of the United States and the assured victory of its
imperial warfare is based on an apocalyptic interpretation of the Bible.[41] Such
an interpretation presents history not only as a cosmic struggle between God
and evil but also as moving toward God's preordained mastery, supremacy,
or conquest. Of course, apocalyptic interpretation of the Bible is itself partly
a product of the apocalyptic traditions that exist in parts of both the Hebrew
Scripture and the New Testament. Given the role that the Bible plays in the
imperial pursuits of the United States today, biblical criticism becomes inevitably a critical site of postcolonial struggles.

Empire Then and Now

The connection that Sugirtharajah and Runions make between the Bible and
our current time leads, in turn, to a fourth reason for postcolonial biblical
criticism. This final reason will not only circle us back to the imperial context of the Bible but also contribute a corrective to the refusal to consider
colonialisms before the fifteenth century. A consistent thesis in the massive
study on empire by Michael Hardt and Antonio Negri is that empire has
gone full circle. The global empire of the United States today is actually most
like the ancient Roman Empire in, for instance, its "horizontal" or dispersed
and decentered character.[42] Allow me to generalize a bit to make a point.
If—using Said's vocabulary—the world of the text (Mark, in this case) and
the world of the critic (we who live at the beginning of the twenty-first century) resemble each other, then a postcolonial criticism or reading of Mark
becomes both understandable and potentially useful. I am not saying that
the work of interpretation requires some kind of contextual correlation. Nor
am I implying that some "original" context of the text must have priority and
thus functions as a kind of interpretive control. Keeping in mind the desire to
read across time in postcolonial criticism in general and Said's "contrapuntal"
reading in particular, I am only suggesting that a corresponding context does
facilitate a critic's interpretive endeavor.

DO YOU HEAR WHAT I HEAR?

What then would a postcolonial reading of Mark look like? Given the presence of and references to Roman colonizers in general and the death of
Jesus by Roman crucifixion in particular, numerous readings have presented
Mark as an anti-colonial document, even if the adjective "postcolonial" is
not explicitly employed.[43] A couple of readings that self-identify as "postcolonial" have, in contrast, tended to read Mark as not only anti-Roman, but
also against the local ruling elites and institutions of Palestine. Both Richard
A. Horsley and David Joy interpret Mark as a narrative from a subordinated
social group or peasantry.[44] Horsley does so through the distinction anthropologists make between the "great tradition" (represented by the local elites)
and the "little tradition" (represented by the peasantries, including Mark).
Joy does so by comparing or equating Mark with the historiography of Subaltern Studies. Strikingly, both make a point to include and present women as
part of the subjected peasantries or subalterns in ways that end up reinforcing and condoning women's subordination within these already subordinate
groups. In spite or perhaps even because of Horsley's attempt to argue that
the women followers of Jesus in Mark are "representative and exemplary"
(since they continue to follow and serve Jesus *after* the disastrous failings of
the male disciples, 14:17-72; 16:1-8), his comfort in identifying the women's
stories as a "subplot"—that is, one that is subordinate to another main or
major plot within Mark—is itself most telling.[45] Somewhat similarly, while
Joy specifically mentions three women (the hemorrhaging woman, 5:25-34;
the Syrophoenician woman, 7:24-30; and the poor widow, 12:41-44) as part of
the crowd or subaltern in Mark, he sees no problem in stating—immediately
following the listing of the women and on the same page—that the twelve
(male!) disciples "were the crowd's true representatives."[46] What I am getting
at is how Spivak's call and challenge to the Subaltern Studies historians that
attention be paid to gender within the term "subaltern" has generally fallen
on deaf ears, even if Spivak is mentioned in Joy and women disciples are specifically mentioned by both Horsley and Joy.[47] Echoing Laura E. Donaldson's
recent complaint that questions of gender remain peripheral to postcolonial
criticism,[48] I will begin with a subaltern (as) woman in Mark.

My choice of this particular subaltern (as) woman has yet another echo.
In Stephen D. Moore's essay, "Mark and Empire," Moore sees the poor widow
of 12:41-44 as representing a breakthrough in Mark's ambivalence towards
empire that also falls on deaf ears (including those of Mark's Jesus).[49] Although
Moore does not mention this explicitly, talking about the poor widow's offering in Mark has the added advantage of highlighting the material conditions
of colonialism, particularly since neocolonialism tends to operate precisely
on both cultural and economic fronts. Mark, for Moore, is disgusted by the
Roman Empire but delighted in Jesus' empire. For example, Jesus' exorcism of

the unclean spirit, "Legion" (itself an echo of the Roman legion or army), out of the demoniac and "out of the country" (5:10) is coupled with Jesus' own future return "with great power and glory" (13:26). Within Markan studies, Moore shows that the episode of the poor widow has been read in two opposing ways. On the one hand, her act has been seen as a model of self-sacrifice that is lauded and will be copied by Jesus himself. On the other hand, she has also been read as a negative example to substantiate Jesus' condemnation of the local elites who "devour widows' houses" (12:40), and justify Jesus' proclamation of the temple's destruction (13:1-2). It is to move beyond both of these impasses (Mark's view of empire and the widow's function in Mark) that Moore reads the poor widow in terms of a "self-divestment." With her gift of two small copper coins that amount to everything she has to live on, the poor widow has, according to Moore, gone beyond reciprocity, pay back, and economic exchange. In contrast, then, to Jesus who is promised "power and glory" in return for his crucifixion, the poor widow realizes Derrida's philosophical ruminations and definition of what constitutes a true gift.

While Moore shares with Horsley and Joy a desire to oppose imperialism—and from that, a commitment to oppose previous readings of Mark—Moore's postcolonial reading distinguishes itself from those of Horsley and Joy in at least two related ways. First, it does not read Mark single-dimensionally as an anti-imperial protest but demonstrates how "ambivalence" can be a helpful concept to read and emphasize in Mark. Second, with ambivalence, Moore opposes not only previous readings that fail to bring out Mark's context in and contest with imperialism, but also Mark's own imperial textual "worlding" and so in a sense Mark itself.

If Horsley's well-meaning reading is meant to trump the male disciples of Jesus with the women disciples, Moore's reading will have the poor widow trump even Jesus himself. Like Horsley's reading, however, Moore's reading also ends up defeating itself. I have already mentioned how Horsley fails to heed the power differential signified by his own identification of the women stories in Mark as a "subplot." The inadequacy of Moore's postcolonial reading is that he does not specify what the poor widow's gift is for. It is one thing to say that she gives for the sake of giving in terms of not looking for or expecting a return. It is quite another if this "absolute gift" becomes a gift without any purpose or reason. Put differently, Moore is clear that the widow does not give her gift at the temple with a selfish purpose, but his silence on the purpose behind the widow's gift also renders her gift meaningless. This is especially problematic since Moore, like Horsley and Joy, not only links the temple with the local or indigenous elites, but also presents these elites as "compradors" who collaborate with the Romans and hence become the prime target of Mark's protest.[50] In other words, the poor widow ends up giving a true gift voluntarily and selflessly—without hope or expectation of returns or repayments for herself—to support accomplices and abettors of imperialism. How can this meaningless—no, mindless—gift be understood as "encapsulating, or at least adumbrating, a *counter-imperial* . . . ethic"?[51] And what does this selfless but mindless giving imply about the agency of this subaltern (as) woman?

Seong Hee Kim, in an interesting twist, suggests that what we are dealing with here is not a gift without reciprocity, but refuse.[52] Reading with what she calls "dialogical imagination" and "*Salim* interpretation" (the practice among Korean women to make things alive with their daily household chores), Kim reads the widow's act as a realization of Jesus' statement in response to the question about paying taxes to the Roman Empire (12:13-15a). With a denarius in his hand, Jesus proclaims that one should "give to Caesar what is Caesar's and to God what is God's" (12:15b-17). According to Kim, the widow is giving *everything* back to the imperial power, just as Jesus suggests. In other words, with this act she is declaring her refusal to participate or have anything to do with the temple cult and the Roman Empire. While this reading gives the widow agency, there are three main problems.

First, this reading collapses too quickly the local elites and the Roman imperialists. Instead of a denarius with the emperor's image, Mark is specific that the two copper coins given by the widow (literally, *lepta* or *leptas*, 12:42) are those that were first minted during the Maccabean period; that is, a time of Israel's revolt against the Seleucid kingdom and its achievement of a century-long self-governance before being occupied by the Romans. As if he is afraid that one will not make that distinction, Mark adds the comment to compute the insignificant value of the coins in not only Roman terms but also with a transliteration of Latin (again, literally, "which is a *kodrantes*" 12:42). While it is tempting to read this as the widow's refusal of *both* nationalist movement and Roman imperialism, as Kim does, there is a second problem. Read in light of the coins' association with the Maccabean period, Kim's reading puts Mark close to members of the Qumran community who separated themselves from the rest of Jewish society in protest against the "evil" Hasmonean dynasty that resulted from the Maccabean revolt and prepared for the cosmic struggle against evil. In itself, this is not a problem. In fact, it could be an example of Said's "contrapuntal reading," and it would further highlight the apocalyptic dimension that many Markan scholars have found in the Gospel.[53] The problem has to do with the politics of geography that Mark's Jesus communicates. Instead of moving *away* from the centers of power and refusing to participate, Jesus makes his way intentionally *toward* Jerusalem, even if he knows ahead of time that doing so will cost his very life. This becomes even more problematic when Kim states that the widow's act plays the function of "impelling and embarrassing Jesus to continue on his suffering journey."[54] Jesus' journey seems to be one of engagement and protest—even confrontational challenge, as shown by his assuming of the interrogator's role in the immediately preceding passage (12:35-40)—not a refusal to participate.

Finally, Kim's suggestion that the widow's "in-between" space—her life between the Roman and the divine empire—threatens the worldly systems of power loses its force if the widow refuses to participate, "giving up everything which belonged to the worldly empire." If the widow chooses "radically . . . to live on the side of the kingdom of God" alone,[55] her threatening, ambiguous position "in-between" disappears.

My dissatisfaction with these readings means that I must return to re-read and reassess Mark, but I hope my reference to these readings will also help communicate how postcolonial readings of Mark may be pursued in very diverse ways. If the Mishnah (a key Jewish rabbinic text) is correct that there were thirteen trumpet-shaped receptacles in the temple's Court of Women for contributions, is there yet a different echo that one might "contrapuntally" hear out of the widow's falling coins? Following up on Kim's reading, I return to the ambivalent feelings about local elites prevalent within postcolonial studies. For many postcolonial critics, the local ruling elites represent both emancipation *and* oppression. On the one hand, they champion the end of colonialism; on the other, they embody a continuation of colonialism in new forms. Presenting the local elites as *solely* compradors and collaborators of the Romans—as Horsley, Joy, Moore, and Kim do—is to flatten or lessen the complexity of the situation. In contrast, Ashis Nandy provides a much more helpful and nuanced term by calling the elite nationalists "ornamental dissenters."[56]

While it is easy to see the local ruling elites as "compradors" given their many conflicts with Jesus and their role in Jesus' crucifixion by the Romans, it is also easy to skip the tensions that exist between these elites and the Roman authorities, particularly in the episode on Jesus' trial and sentencing in 15:1-39.[57] Such tensions do nevertheless reverberate out of Moore's own musings on this episode, when he asks if the local elites out-maneuver Pilate or if Pilate manipulates them.[58] Moore's own language shows, in other words, there is something else going on between the local elites and the Romans besides or alongside collaboration. This becomes even clearer if we go back to Mark's other coin story, as Kim does. In Mark 12:13-17, the local elites try to trap Jesus with a trick question about whether Jews should pay taxes to Caesar. It is a trick question precisely because the elites are playing the role of "double agents"; they represent simultaneously Roman eyes on the lookout for potential tax-objectors (hence troublemakers) and Jewish hearts that oppose colonial domination. Their ties to Israel's traditions can also be seen by the frequency with which they refer to these traditions, scriptural and otherwise (2:1—3:6; 7:1-23; 10:2-12; 12:13-27; 14:55-64). Regardless of whether these references are ornamental and/or indications of perspectival interpretation (12:35-40), the ties between the local elites and the Jewish people—and hence the elites' role as double agents—can clearly be seen not only in the narrator's attribution of their murder of Jesus to "jealousy" (15:10), but also in the narrator's comments on their fear of or concern with the crowd (11:15-18, 27-33; 14:1-2).

What I am getting at is that the local elites also present themselves as leaders of and champions for Israel's nationalism. Thus, the poor widow's gift may be her way of supporting this protest movement against Roman colonization. After all, as Mark's specific terminology on the coins reminds us, the Jewish temple was rededicated as a symbol of and for nationalist independence at the conclusion of the Maccabean revolt (167–164 B.C.E.). Since the extra-canonical book 4 Maccabees centers on the praiseworthy martyrdom of Eleazar, seven brothers, and their mother during the Maccabean revolt, one may read it "contrapuntally" with this episode in Mark.[59] If so, as 4 Maccabees would show with its mother-as-martyr figure, albeit problematically,[60] that women have been part of Israel's struggles against colonization. Put differently, the poor widow is making a political statement against imperialism and about her agency with her gift, even if she is silent.[61] In the same way that women must be acknowledged as agents in colonial expansion and exploitation,[62] women must also be viewed as active participants in anti-colonial struggles.

This statement by the poor widow in Mark, however, remains problematic on several fronts. Both her politics and agency not only are subsumed under the nationalism the elites champion, but also are signified and singularized in the form of self-renunciation. Self-emptying or self-divestiture, including selfless giving, is great if one is *not* giving up one's livelihood, and hence one's very life. Mark's Jesus seems to be speaking up precisely against this as a form of exploitation and victimization, if or especially when the episode is read in light of what goes before and after it, as we have already discussed. However, Jesus' protest is gravely undercut when, as Moore suggests, one remembers that two chapters later, there will be another woman who "did what she could" or "did with whatever she had" by breaking open and pouring an alabaster jar of expensive pure nard ointment on Jesus (14:3-9). When some around them suggest that the jar could have been exchanged for money to help the poor rather than "wasted" this way, Jesus defends the woman's act as a "good work" that will be remembered wherever his gospel is proclaimed. In other words, while Jesus sees a problem in the local elites' exploitation of the poor widow, he is quite ready to affirm another woman's extravagant gesture to support his cause.

In an ironic way that actually parallels Horsley's identification of the women's stories as a "subplot" in Mark, Mark's women are limited to playing supportive roles in anti-imperial movements, whether the movement in question is championed by the local elites or by Jesus. By "supportive" here, I mean the way women characters are not only denied speech but also included in Mark when they are needed but dismissed or disappear as soon as they have performed their function. In contrast, major characters with recurring and speaking roles in Mark are all male.[63] Regardless of the economic status of the woman or the symbolic status of her "anointing" act,[64] the anonymous woman of Mark 14, like the poor widow of Mark 12, never appears again in Mark's narrative. Her anointing of Jesus is never explicitly brought up again within Mark's narrative; not even when some other women, on the first Easter morning, bring spices to the tomb with the hope to anoint Jesus' body, and are asked to retell the good news of Jesus' resurrection (16:1-8). If Spivak is correct that the Rani, the widow of the royal Raja in Sirmur of India, "emerges [only] in the colonial archives because of the commercial/territorial interests of [Britain's] East India Company,"[65] one can add—on the basis of Mark—that women are treated the same way by their own anti-colonial "heroes," both elite and subaltern. Women in Mark, after providing the resources or playing particular roles for the "manly" struggle against colonialism, are erased with only a trace. They are, as Donaldson suggests, a "ghostly" presence that will, hopefully, continue to haunt Mark's readers.[66]

These ambivalent or self-contradictory dimensions should not be surprising when we keep in mind that in the long history of colonialism and imperialism, the Bible—of which Mark is a part—has also played the role of a double agent. While the Bible contains writings by a colonized people, colonizers have also used it to rationalize and realize imperialism's projects. That is to say, when it comes to the Bible and Mark, the line between "colonial" and "minority" discourse is seriously blurred. Rather than reading Mark in a single dimension (Horsley and Joy) or hoping too much or too quickly for a third way out (Moore and Kim), postcolonialism must heed Spivak's advice that it does not in any way—or via any book—signify that a clean break from colonial legacies is in sight.[67] Since Spivak suggests that Derridean deconstruction is helpful for keeping postcolonial ambitions or reasoning in check, let me conclude by quickly and briefly blurring or bringing together two more echoes: one from Derrida and the other from yet another subaltern (as) woman in Mark.

Like the first two, this third subaltern (as) woman also spends or depletes her economic resources. She does so, we are told, in a long but unsuccessful attempt to find a cure for her bleeding problem (5:25-26). Fortunately for her, she has faith in Jesus and manages to have her bleeding stopped by touching Jesus' garment, and hence tapping into his miraculous healing power (5:27-29). Unfortunately for her, Jesus is adamant about keeping track of where his resources have gone, so he demands that the woman come forth to acknowledge her debt (5:30-34). Reading this in continuation and conjunction with Jesus' exorcism of "Legion" from the Gerasene demoniac as a gesture of kicking out or removing Rome's military occupation (5:1-20), Horsley suggests that the woman's bleeding condition and her economic destitution can also be read symbolically as her being sucked or bled dry by the Romans.[68] While Horsley proposes this—in light of the healing effected for the woman by Jesus—as yet another unmistakable gesture of Mark's anti-imperialism, this blurring or mixing of blood and currency—or blood as currency—is precisely what Derrida critiques as not only a feature of "globalatinization," but also one that is tied up with the Christian traditions.[69] While Derrida himself

seems to put the blame for this mutation and combination of Christian traditions, blood, and money—and the Christian-sanctioned capitalist globalization that results—on the Roman Empire and its deployment of Christianity,
I suggest that what has been happening is a "reasonable" though inexcusable
echo or ripple out of Mark's Gospel. Instead of dismissing Horsley' reading
as an idiosyncratic reading of an isolated incident in Mark, one finds other
echoes within the Gospel of this entanglement or transmutation among
Christ, blood, and money. Mark's Jesus, in affirming a life of self-sacrifice for
himself and his followers, states that he will "give his life [as] a ransom for
many" (10:45). The missing ingredient that will help turn or transform his
life into a ransom or a form of currency turns out to be, of course, his blood.
As part of the menu of his Passover meal with his disciples, Jesus will take the
cup and say to them—in the words of Mark 14:24—"This is my blood of the
covenant, which is being poured out for many." To oppose this imperial phenomenon of "globalatinization"—a form of Trinitarian transmutation involving religious, economic, and colonial violence, if you will—it will take not
only more than the postcolonial "Holy Trinity" of Said, Bhabha, and Spivak,[70]
but also many more postcolonial readings of the Bible, Mark and otherwise.

FURTHER READING

General

Bhabha, Homi K. *The Location of Culture.* New York: Routledge, 1994. A collection
    of Bhabha's original and difficult essays where he explicates and works out
    some of his influential concepts of "mimicry," "hybridity," and "ambivalence."
Harrison, Nicholas. *Postcolonial Criticism.* Malden: Polity, 2003. This volume
    focuses on literature, and is helpful in showing how postcolonial studies may
    contribute to the work and practice of literary criticism, and vice versa.
JanMohamed, Abdul R., and David Lloyd, eds. *The Nature and Context of Minority
    Discourse.* New York: Oxford University Press, 1990. An important collection
    that not only bridges racial/ethnic minority studies and postcolonial studies,
    but also features the reality of "internal colonization."
Loomba, Ania. *Colonialism/Postcolonialism.* New York: Routledge, 1998. An acces-
    sible introduction to the history and theory associated with colonial/postco-
    lonial studies.
McClintock, Anne. *Imperial Leather: Race, Gender, and Sexuality in the Colonial
    Contest.* New York: Routledge, 1995. One of the earlier texts that explore the
    intersecting and interlocking factors of colonialism.
Said, Edward. *Orientalism.* New York: Pantheon, 1978. The groundbreaking study
    of Orientalism as a colonizing and racializing discourse that marks the begin-
    ning of "colonial discourse analysis."

Spivak, Gayatri Chakravorty. *The Post-Colonial Critic: Interviews, Strategies, Dialogues*. Edited by Sarah Harasym. New York: Routledge, 1990. A collection of interviews that is still one of the best ways to get a sense of a very significant and complex postcolonial thinker and writer.

Biblical

Donaldson, Laura E., ed. *Postcolonialism and Scriptural Reading. Semeia* 75. Atlanta: Society of Biblical Literature, 1996. One of the earliest collections of essays on postcolonial biblical criticism.

Dube, Musa W. *Postcolonial Feminist Interpretation of the Bible*. St. Louis: Chalice, 2000. With a focus on Matthew's Gospel, this is a pioneering text that seeks to highlight and address the need for bringing together feminist and postcolonial criticism of the Bible.

Horsley, Richard A. *Hearing the Whole Story: The Politics of Plot in Mark's Gospel*. Louisville: Westminster John Knox, 2001. A liberating reading of Mark as an anti-Roman protest by imperially subjected peasantries.

Liew, Tat-siong Benny. *Politics of Parousia: Reading Mark Inter(con)textually*. Leiden: Brill, 1999. Looks at the apocalyptic emphasis in the Gospel of Mark within its Roman imperial context, particularly how Mark presents matters of authority, agency, and gender.

Moore, Stephen D., and Fernando F. Segovia, eds. *Postcolonial Biblical Criticism: Interdisciplinary Intersections*. New York: T & T Clark International, 2005. A collection of essays exploring how postcolonial biblical criticism intersects with other contemporary currents of biblical studies.

Sugirtharajah, R. S., ed. *The Postcolonial Biblical Reader*. Malden: Blackwell, 2006. A recent reader on both the theory and the practice of postcolonial biblical criticism, and edited by arguably the most prominent and prolific postcolonial biblical critic of this generation.

GLOSSARY

Allegory—a text that has hidden, often spiritual, meanings lying behind its literal sense.

Ambivalence—in postcolonial studies, particularly in Homi Bhabha's theoretical vocabulary, this term refers to the contradictory relationship between the colonizer and the colonized. For Bhabha, this relationship involves both repulsion and attraction, resistance and cooperation.

Anachronism—reading the Gospels through the lenses of one's own time, ignoring the historical gap between "then" and "now," e.g., reading Mark as a twenty-first century text.

Anagogy—the spiritual or mystical level of interpretation in the fourfold levels of meaning sought by interpreters in the Middle Ages. The other levels were the literal, the allegorical, and the moral. Anagogy is often related to the heavenly, transcendent realm.

Analepsis—the narration of an event *after* its ordinary chronological order in the narrative world; a flashback. A term introduced by Gérard Genette in his book *Narrative Discourse*.

Androcentrism—treating males as the universal human norm; a male-centered worldview.

Binary opposition—pairs of concepts placed in opposition to one another. One of the pair is often considered to be superior to the other. Key binary oppositions in Western culture include male/female, reason/emotion, active/passive, heterosexual/homosexual, and white/nonwhite. The dismantling of binary oppositions is especially associated with deconstructive criticism.

Canon—a list of works accepted as authoritative and normative by a particular group—the canon of English literary classics, for example. The New Testament canon consists of twenty-seven early Christian writings accepted as authoritative by all Christian traditions.

Characters—the persons in a narrative, the participants in its action or plot. In *Aspects of the Novel*, E. M. Forster distinguished "flat" and "round" characters. Flat characters are simple, constructed around a single idea or trait, and static. Round characters are complex. They cannot be summed up in a single sentence, and sometimes develop over the course of a narrative. Two methods of characterization are sometimes also distinguished: showing and telling. The narrator may "show" a character through the character's words and actions; the narrator may also "tell" about the character, describing and evaluating him or her directly.

Colonial discourse analysis—examines how colonialism produces and is produced by fields of knowledge that simultaneously represent and constitute "reality" and relations of power. Such analysis owes much to Edward W. Said's extension of Michel Foucault's understanding of "discourse" to the study of colonial power. Discourse shapes how knowledge and power come into existence in and through relation to each other. See *discourse formation*.

Compradors—local elites who not only mediate between the colonizers above them and the colonized below them, but also retain their relatively privileged position in the "middle" by compromising or even identifying with the colonizers.

Creole/creolization—people, language, and/or process of racial, ethnic, and cultural intermixing, particularly as a result of European colonization of the Caribbean and South America.

Cultural anthropology—in Gospel studies, the use of anthropological models that organize information about a culture, such as a model of a kinship structure, to illuminate the cultural context of the Gospels.

Cultural studies—a multidisciplinary approach that both investigates the cultural products and cultural practices of a given society and determines the ideology or notion of reality that supports the power relations in that society. As a multidisciplinary approach, cultural studies is not a single method. It may thus use traditional methods like source and form criticism and more contemporary approaches such as feminist criticism and postcolonial criticism to expose ideology in culture.

Deconstructive criticism—a flexible and inventive strategy of reading that seeks to highlight troubling aspects of texts that more traditional readings have tended to repress (e.g., logical or ethical contradictions), or that highlights seemingly unimportant details of texts that traditional readings have ignored or failed to notice but that can yield important insights into the workings of the text. Deconstruction is associated with the work of such philosophers and critics as Jacques Derrida and Gayatri Spivak. It is part of the larger phenomenon of *poststructuralism*.

Demystification—the unraveling of the strategies of representation that support the dominance of one group or over others. Thus, demystification critiques the myths that support the present relations of power in a society.

Demythologizing—Rudolf Bultmann's attempt to translate the myths of the New Testament into existentialist expressions about the truth of what it means to live as an authentic human being in this world.

Discourse formation—a term developed by French philosopher Michel Foucault. It refers to a worldview, a mix of ideas and assumptions that shape how people think and talk about a given topic. These ideas and assumptions develop over time and thus they appear natural though they are not. For example, the scientific discourse formation or worldview shapes how many biblical experts interpret the bible, but this is not the worldview that has always shaped biblical interpretation.

Endogamy—the practice of marrying within one's family or clan. It preserves or advances the wealth, status, and power of the group and of individuals within the group.

Ethnocentrism—reading a Gospel through the lenses of one's own culture and imposing those categories on a text from a different culture.

Evangelist—the writer of a Gospel. The term comes from the Greek *euangelion* or "good news," which was translated into Old English as "gospel."

Exogamy—the practice of marrying outside one's primary family or clan as defined by one's culture. It is often used to prevent conflict and cement alliances between groups.

Feminism—a term that probably should appear in the plural, "feminisms." There are liberal, cultural, socialist, existentialist, radical, psychoanalytic, postmodern, and other forms of feminism. What most feminists share is resolute opposition to the various forms of male domination faced by women. They also share the conviction that women can and should create their own gendered identities and take responsibility for their own choices, political and personal. See the definitions of Alcott and hooks in chapter 5.

Feminist criticism—in Gospel studies, any approach to the text that begins with a commitment to feminism. It can involve a critique of previous interpretations of a text; it can seek to reconstruct the history of women in the cultural context of the text; or it can offer a feminist reader-response analysis, among other perspectives.

Focalization—a technical term some narrative theorists use to refer to the perspective from which a narrative event (scene or speech) is presented, that is, who sees and hears. In the Gospels that narrator may present a scene from his or her own perspective or from the perspective of a character. See *point of view.*

Form criticism—a scholarly method that traces the history of the Gospels to an oral stage lying behind the written Gospels. It seeks to classify small units of tradition, of which the Gospels were thought to be composed, into categories or "forms," such as controversy story, parable, legend, and so on. It assigns each of these units a *Sitz im Leben,* a setting and function in the life of the early Christian communities, such as preaching, teaching, or baptismal ceremony.

Gaze—a term drawn from film criticism and feminist criticism. It refers to the ways in which a viewer or reader is directed to see a character or event with a particular perspective or in a certain distinctive way.

Gender—the social construction of persons as male or female. Often contrasted with *sex,* which is considered as a biological designation for men and women distinguished in terms of genetic structure and reproductive organs. Gender may be pictured as a sliding scale between male and female. Some have proposed the category of a third gender to designate persons who are seen as neither fully male nor fully female.

Genre—a form or type of writing or work of art. Specific genres usually include a set of basic conventions that distinguish them as a type of work from other types. Thus, fairy tales typically begin ("Once upon a time") and end ("And they lived happily ever after") in the same way. Likewise, mysteries typically involve a sleuth or detective, a puzzle to be solved, and red herrings that may throw the reader off track, while apocalypses typically involve otherworldly visions, symbolic beasts, and angelic interpreters.

Geopolitical West—the adjective serves to indicate that "the West" is not only a politically interested construction but also that such political interests and power are highly invested in and inseparably linked to matters of geography.

Globalatinization—a term coined by Jacques Derrida to refer to the current phenomenon of globalized capitalism as a continuation of a religiously implicated imperial project that got started with the ancient Roman Empire. The term, in other words, refers to a complex and historical mingling in which religion, economics, and colonialism replicate and reinforce each other.

Hegemony—the Italian Marxist Antonio Gramsci developed this term. It refers to a set of assumptions that allows one group to have dominance over one or more dominated groups until the dominated groups counter the old hegemony with a new, more compelling one. Moreover, hegemony often works through the institutions of everyday life. The dominated groups accept their present place in society not primarily through force but because the dominant group in society has used basic civic institutions such as schools, homes, and churches to convince these groups to concede to the dominated group's notion of reality.

Hybridity—most closely associated with Homi Bhabha's postcolonial theory, this term indicates that cultures are always already mixed or impure, and renders problematic any idea of or desire for a pre-existing "purity" or "original."

Ideology—in Marxist thought, this term originally meant false consciousness or a distorted view of reality that conceals the way power works in the relations between the dominating and dominated classes of a society. Subsequently, the scope of the term broadened beyond class. Many contemporary critics see ideology as a basic constitutive framework of the everyday world by which individuals are shaped, formed, and compelled to act.

Immasculation—a term coined by Judith Fetterley in *The Resisting Reader*. It refers to what can happen when a female reads an androcentric or patriarchal text: she reads and identifies as male, identifying against herself.

Implied author—the author implied by the totality of a work. The implied author is distinguished from the flesh-and-blood real author. The implied author is the persona and the set of values that the reader experiences as the implicit creator and controller of the work. Wayne Booth coined and popularized this term in *The Rhetoric of Fiction*.

Implied reader—this term was originally coined by Wolfgang Iser in *The Implied Reader*. Iser defined the concept as one that "incorporates both the prestructuring of the potential meaning by the text, and the reader's actualization of this potential through the reading process."

Intentional fallacy—seeking to interpret a text by imagining what the real author's intentions might have been.

Intercalation—inserting or sandwiching one story inside another.

Intertextual—between texts.

Intratextual—within a text.

Irony—incongruity between the literal meaning and another meaning. Verbal irony involves an utterance that cannot be taken at face value. Dramatic irony is an ironic incongruity in situations or events in a narrative. In theater, dramatic irony occurs when the audience recognizes something that a character or characters in the play do not. In Mark, the readers often understand something that characters, such as the disciples, do not.

Kyriarchy—Elisabeth Schüssler Fiorenza coined this term to capture the nature of multiple systems of domination and subordination. Kyriarchy comes from the Greek word for "lord" or "master," *kyrios*, and the Greek word for "rule," *archein*. It describes an interlocking pyramid involving gender, race, class, age, education, and other factors. In such a pyramid, elite males are dominant. Some interpreters prefer the term kyriarchy to the term *patriarchy* which is thought to focus too much on gender as the key element of domination. Other interpreters may prefer the term patriarchy either because they believe gender is the primary matrix of dominance or because they believe it captures the same system of interlocking forms of domination.

Markan hypothesis—the hypothesis that Mark is the earliest Gospel. Proponents of the hypothesis often argue that Mark, therefore, preserves the most accurate historical record of the life of Jesus. They view Mark as the most realistic and least theological Gospel. These views were strongly challenged by Wilhelm Wrede in *The Messianic Secret*.

Marxist criticism—though more than one form exists, this type of criticism examines all literature or works of art as products of labor. Such labor, moreover, is one of a variety of possible responses to class struggle. The response may simply reflect the ideology or point of view of the dominant class or it may seek to alter or resist that ideology. Some Marxist critics view literature and other works of art as responses solely to class struggle while others see struggle occurring in multiple ways, for example, in gender relations, ethnic relations, and so on.

Mimicry—a key word in the postcolonial theory of Homi Bhabha, it signifies both the desire and the anxiety involved in colonial relations. Colonial mimicry occurs when the colonized is lured into imitating the culture of the colonizer. Such mimicry is never perfect, however. It can slide over into mockery, and thereby threaten the authority of the colonizer.

Minority discourse—self-expressions by and conversations among minority or colonized groups, especially in response to their experiences of marginalization.

Narratee—the persona in the text to whom the story is addressed (e.g. Theophilus in Luke 1:1-4; Acts 1:1). In some narratives the narratee is a character. In others, as in the Gospels, it is difficult to distinguish the narratee from the aspect of the implied reader that is internal to the text.

Narrative criticism—a term coined by New Testament critics to refer to analysis of each Gospel as a literary whole. Deeply influenced by secular narratology, it focuses on character, plot, setting, and point of view.

Narratology—narrative theory. Typically, narratology searches for the general principles that manifest themselves in individual narratives.

Narrator—the person who tells the story. In some works this is a character (e.g., John in Revelation). In the Gospels, the narrator is not a character. The reliable third-person omniscient narrator of each Gospel is the voice of the implied author.

New Criticism—the dominant mode of Anglo-American literary criticism in the 1940s and 1950s. It focused on the literary work itself (its language and internal structures) rather than on the historical background of the text, the biography of the author, or the effect on the reader.

Parousia—the Greek word for "coming" or "presence," it refers to the second coming or return of Jesus clothed with power to judge and redeem.

Passion—when used of Jesus, this term refers to his suffering and death. The passion narrative in a Gospel consists of those portions of the Gospel that narrate the crucifixion and the events leading up to it.

Plot—the arrangement of the episodes of a story; the structure and relations between its actions. Often motivation and conflict are considered central elements of plot.

Point of view—the perspective from which a story is told. It includes both visual and aural perspectives as well as evaluative or ideological perspective. The size of a character may be presented through a child's eyes, for example. A character may be viewed as wicked, a servant of Satan. Narrators tell the story from their own perspectives and may incorporate the perspectives of characters within their perspectives. Traditionally, a distinction has been made between first- and third-person point of view. A first-person narrator is an "I" who is also a character in the story. A third-person narrator stands outside the story and refers to characters as "he" or "she." Point of view is further classified according to the degree of knowledge possessed and reliability. An omniscient point of view, for example, knows everything about characters and events. It has privileged access to the minds of characters. A reliable point of view is aligned with the point of view of the implied author. In the Gospels, Jesus' point of view is aligned with that of the implied author, whereas that of the Jewish authorities is not.

Politics of exclusion—the set of ideologies or frameworks that justify or legitimate the actions of persons in a given society. Thus, in examining the politics of exclusion in a text, one examines the set of assumptions that appear to justify the hierarchical positioning of one group over others.

Post-colonial/postcolonial—the hyphenated form of the term was first used in the post–World War II era to refer to the newly independent nation-states and/or the time after European colonies achieved political independence. The emphasis was thus on the temporal dividing line between what was before and what is after independence. Contemporary postcolonial studies, however (the hyphenated form of the term has largely dropped out of use), tends to emphasize the blurred nature of this dividing line. For example, the former colonial powers continue to control the former colonies, albeit through indirect means such as globalization. The term *postcolonial* generally refers today to the ongoing legacies of colonization. More specifically, it refers to a range of assumptions and practices used to understand and/or resist various colonial histories and ideologies.

Poststructuralism—developed within or in reaction to structuralism in such fields as philosophy, literary studies, history, and psychology. As its name suggests, structuralism is preoccupied with structures and systems. Faced with a collection of Gospels, for example, the structuralist tendency is to ask what the underlying structures and rules of production are that all Gospels share in common. The poststructuralist tendency of theorists like Jacques Derrida or Roland Barthes is to ask instead why literature eludes all such attempts to fix its meaning or contain its complexity. Poststructuralists also target many of the basic enabling assumptions of Western culture and society. For example, they argue that "foundational" concepts such as being, presence, essence, center, identity, self, or nature are neither as stable nor as reliable as they seem to be. To give a further example, Michel Foucault argues that heterosexuality and homosexuality are specifically Western constructions whose origins lie in the medical science of late nineteenth-century Europe. See *deconstructive criticism*; *structuralism*.

Prolepsis—the narration of an event *before* its logical order in the narrative world; foreshadowing. A term introduced by Gérard Genette in his book *Narrative Discourse*.

Reader-response criticism—a pragmatic approach to criticism that focuses on the role of the reader. It privileges the reader over the author and the text in the creation of meaning. Some versions of reader-response criticism focus more on the "reader-in-the-text"—the role of the reader encoded or implied in the text—and others emphasize the various responses of actual readers as individuals or as members of interpretive communities.

Reception history—a form of criticism that describes and analyses various responses to texts and other cultural products through time. Within biblical studies, reception history may track the history of the interpretation of a biblical text in art, hymns, poems, sermons, and other forms of expression as well as in scholarly readings. Reception history is closely related to reader-response criticism.

Redaction criticism—a scholarly method that treats each evangelist as an editor or redactor of traditional material. It seeks to separate tradition (materials the evangelist inherited) from redaction (how the evangelist edited and shaped tradition). It uses editorial material to reconstruct the evangelist's community—the situation he (or she?) sought to address—and unique theology.

Representation—a term drawn from art criticism to indicate the depiction or representation of a reality by a visual or verbal image of that reality. Representations are neither natural nor neutral. They do not solely reflect reality; they help to constitute or make reality. That is, representations have an ideology or a point of view. Thus, analyzing the perspectives of representation in a work is critical if one wants to see the ways in which the work supports, alters, or radically resists dominant notions of what is true about society.

Self-consuming artifact—Stanley Fish's term for literature that says something and then takes it back or does something to the reader and then undoes it in the course of the temporal experience of reading.

Septuagint—the Greek version of the Hebrew Scriptures. It contains Greek translations of Hebrew and Aramaic texts as well as some material composed originally in Greek.

Settings—temporal, spatial, and social locations of narrative events. In the Gospels, location may have important symbolic significance. In Matthew, for instance, Galilee is associated with the Gentiles. The events of the passion take place in a social setting where a Roman governor has the final say over Jesus' fate.

Social criticism—an umbrella term we have chosen to cover approaches to the Gospels influenced by sociology, anthropology, and social history. The focus is "social," that is, less on the individual and the unique than on the group and the general.

Social description—the reconstruction of the material culture, customs, and everyday life of the first-century Mediterranean world.

Social history—the history of groups, movements, and institutions. It charts broad historical changes.

Social location—refers to the position in a society a group of people shares. Establishing the social location of a group helps to identify the political, economic, religious, and cultural place of that group in society. It also helps to clarify the power dynamics of that group in relation to other groups.

Sociology of knowledge—the study of the relationship between a group's worldview and its social organization.

Source criticism—in the context of Gospel studies, this is a scholarly method that seeks to determine the sources of the Gospels and especially to explain the literary relationships between them. The majority explanation is the *two-source hypothesis.*

Story and discourse—terms introduced to Gospel critics by Seymour Chatman. Story is the *what* of the narrative, its plot, characters, setting, and the like. Discourse is *how* the narrative is told, including the ordering of the events in the plot, comments by the narrator to the narratee, point of view, and so on. Story and discourse are separable only in theory; what we have in narrative is the story-as-discourse.

Structuralism—a multidisciplinary approach arising out of linguistics. It views language as a system of signs that have meaning only in relation to other signs. It tends to analyze texts in terms of the systems of rules, codes, and conventions that govern their production. It may view the text as a complex communication between a sender and a receiver. Bracketing historical questions, it studies the text "synchronically," that is, as it appears at a given point in time. It may seek to uncover the "deep structures" of the text. These structures are often seen in terms of binary oppositions such as good and evil, order and chaos, and light and dark and mediations between these oppositions.

Subaltern—member of any subordinated group in a society, whether those of the working class, women, the colonized of an empire, sexually oppressed individuals, or an underrepresented racial/ethnic group. Often subalterns, such as colonized women, are members of more than one subordinated group.

Syncretic—merging or fusing of what used to be diverse and disparate, with something that is distinctly new and different coming about as a result.

Synkrisis—an ancient form of amplification or elaboration. It is a literary technique that compares or contrasts two or more items.

Synoptic Gospels—the Gospels of Matthew, Mark, and Luke. They are called synoptic (from the Greek word *synopsis,* meaning "a viewing together") because of the similarities between them in wording and content, in contrast to the Gospel of John.

Textual criticism—a subdiscipline of New Testament criticism that tries to determine the "best" and most "original" wording of a biblical text. Scribes copied biblical manuscripts by hand, sometimes introducing changes accidentally and sometimes on purpose. Thus, manuscripts or textual "witnesses" exhibit "variants" that range from slightly different wordings to the addition or subtraction of a number of verses. Textual critics evaluate the reliability of manuscript witnesses as well as internal evidence, such as the author's style in order to reconstruct the earliest possible version.

Translation studies—a scholarly approach that studies both the actual practice of translation as well as theories about how translators should produce translations.

Two-source hypothesis—the hypothesis that Mark was the first written Gospel and that Matthew and Luke used Mark and a second source called Q (from the German word for source, *Quelle*) to compose their Gospels. It attributes passages common to all three Gospels to Mark and passages common only to Matthew and Luke to Q. To round things out, scholars often label material peculiar to Matthew as *M* and material peculiar to Luke as *L*.

Worldliness and worlding—Edward W. Said uses "worldliness" to talk about how the practice of writing/reading texts is inevitably embedded in the (imperial) conditions of the world in which such practice takes place. "Worlding" is Gayatri Chakravorty Spivak's term for the process through which colonialism redraws and renames the world, especially, though not exclusively, through textual practices like mapping and writing.

NOTES

PREFACE

1. Influential early examples of Markan narrative and/or reader-response criticism included: Robert C. Tannehill, "The Disciples in Mark: The Function of a Narrative Role," *Journal of Religion* 57 (1977): 386–405; idem, "The Gospel of Mark as Narrative Christology," *Semeia* 16 (1979): 57–95; Norman R. Petersen, "'Point of View' in Mark's Narrative," *Semeia* 12 (1978): 97–121; idem, *Literary Criticism for New Testament Critics* (Philadelphia: Fortress Press, 1978); David Rhoads, "Narrative Criticism and the Gospel of Mark," *Journal of the American Academy of Religion* 50 (1982): 411–34; David Rhoads and Donald Michie, *Mark as Story: An Introduction to the Narrative of a Gospel* (Philadelphia: Fortress Press, 1982); Robert M. Fowler, *Loaves and Fishes: The Function of the Feeding Stories in the Gospel of Mark* (Chico, Calif.: Scholars Press, 1981).

2. See, for example, Janice Capel Anderson, "Matthew: Gender and Reading," *Semeia* 28 (1983): 3–28; Elizabeth Struthers Malbon, "Fallible Followers: Women and Men in the Gospel of Mark," *Semeia* 28 (1983): 29–48; Mary Ann Tolbert, "Defining the Problem: The Bible and Feminist Hermeneutics, *Semeia* 28 (1983): 113–26.

3. See, for example, Gary A. Phillips, "History and Text: The Reader in Context in Matthew's Parables Discourse," *Semeia* 31 (1985): 111–38; Stephen D. Moore, "Are the Gospels Unified Narratives?" in *Society of Biblical Literature 1987 Seminar Papers*, ed. Kent Harold Richards (Chico, Calif.: Scholars Press, 1987), 443–58; idem, *Literary Criticism and the Gospels: The Theoretical Challenge* (New Haven: Yale University Press, 1989).

1. INTRODUCTION

1. Willi Marxsen, *Mark the Evangelist: Studies in the Redaction History of the Gospel*; trans. James Boyce et al. (Nashville: Abingdon, 1959), 15–22.

2. See further Norman Perrin, *What Is Redaction Criticism?* (Philadelphia: Fortress Press, 1969).

3. Marxsen, *Mark the Evangelist*, 18.

4. Eusebius, *Ecclesiastical History* 3.39.15; LCL, quoting from Papias, *Expositions of the Words of the Lord*. The latter work, which we know only through Eusebius, seems to date from about 140 C.E.

5. Augustine, *On the Agreement of the Evangelists* 1.2.4; Seán P. Kealy's translation in *Mark's Gospel: A History of Its Interpretation* (Ramsey, N.J.: Paulist, 1982), 27.

6. Origen, *Commentary on John*; *Ante-Nicene Fathers*, Vol. 9, ed. Allan Menzies (Grand Rapids: Eerdmans, n.d.), 10.2, p. 382.

7. Ibid., 10.16, pp. 393–94.

8. Ibid., 10.2, p. 382.

9. Origen, *On First Principles*; trans. Karlfried Froelich, in *Biblical Interpretation in the Early Church*, ed. Karlfried Froelich (Philadelphia: Fortress Press, 1984), 4.3.1, p. 64.

10. Ibid., 4.2.3, p. 57.

11. John Calvin, *Commentary on a Harmony of the Evangelists Matthew, Mark, and Luke*; trans. William Pringle (Grand Rapids: Eerdmans, 1949), 1:xxxviii.

12. Irenaeus, *Against Heresies*; *Ante-Nicene Fathers*, Vol. 1, ed. Alexander Roberts and James Donaldson (Grand Rapids: Eerdmans, n.d.), 3.11.8.

13. William Wrede, *The Messianic Secret*; trans. J. C. Greig (Greenwood, S.C.: Attic Press, 1971), 129.

14. Ibid., 129.

15. Ibid., 125–26.

16. Ibid., 69.

17. Ibid., 72, 215.

18. Ibid., 229.

19. Ibid., 229.

20. Ibid., 145.

21. Quoted in Stephen Neill and Tom Wright, *The Interpretation of the New Testament 1861–1986*; 2d ed. (Oxford: Oxford University Press, 1988), 258. This translation is from the 3d German edition, 1959, of *Die Formgeschichte des Evangeliums*.

22. Rudolf Bultmann, *The History of the Synoptic Tradition*; trans. John Marsh (New York: Harper & Row, 1965), 372. Karl Ludwig Schmidt, the third figure most often associated with the form-critical study of the Gospels, pronounces a judgment similar to Bultmann's, but with particular reference to Mark (*Der Rahmen der Geschichte Jesu* [Berlin: Trowitzsch, 1919]).

23. Marxsen, *Mark the Evangelist*, 18.

24. Ibid., 17.

25. Ibid., 18.

26. Ibid., 19.

27. Ibid., 25.

28. Ibid., 25.

29. Origen, *On First Principles* 4.2.3.

30. Quoted in Kealy, *Mark's Gospel*, 33. The verse is attributed to Augustine of Dacia (d. 1282).

31. Kealy, *Mark's Gospel*, 36.

32. Marxsen, *Mark the Evangelist*, 37–38.

33. Ibid., 92; cf. 54–116 et passim. Kealy, too, notes that "symbolic exegesis . . . has become popular among several modern interpreters of Mark's gospel" (*Mark's Gospel*, 36).

34. Theodore J. Weeden, *Mark: Traditions in Conflict* (Philadelphia: Fortress Press, 1971).

35. W. D. Davies and Dale C. Allison, *Critical and Exegetical Commentary on the Gospel according to Saint Matthew*, vol. 1: *Introduction and Commentary on Matthew I–VII* (Edinburgh: T&T Clark, 1988), reviewed by Jack Dean Kingsbury in *Journal of Biblical Literature* 110 (1991): 344–46.

36. Kingsbury, review of Davies and Allison, 344.

37. Ibid., 344.

38. Ibid.

39. Ibid., 346.

40. See, for example, Norman Perrin, "The Evangelist as Author: Reflections on Method in the Study and Interpretation of the Synoptic Gospels and Acts," *Biblical Research* 17 (1972): 5–18, reprinted in Norman Perrin, *Parable and Gospel*, ed. K. C. Hanson (Minneapolis: Fortress Press, 2003), 51–63; and "The Interpretation of the Gospel of Mark," also reprinted in *Parable and Gospel*, 64–72. In the latter Perrin argued that, following Marxsen, it was necessary to take account of the evangelist as a literary author and to move to an appreciation of the Gospel text as a whole. Perrin wrote, "It was necessary for redaction criticism to mutate into a genuine literary criticism" (69). He credits Dan Via for the vivid expression.

41. Mary Ann Tolbert, "Reading the Bible with Authority: Feminist Interrogation of the Canon," in *Escaping Eden: New Feminist Perspectives on the Bible*, ed. Harold C. Washington, Susan Lochrie Graham, and Pamela Thimmes (Sheffield: Sheffield Academic Press, 1998), 150.

42. Davies and Allison, *Critical and Exegetical Commentary*, xi.

43. See Jane P. Tompkins, "An Introduction to Reader-Response Criticism," in *Reader-Response Criticism: From Formalism to Post-Structuralism*, ed. Jane P. Tompkins (Baltimore: Johns Hopkins University Press, 1980), xvi–xvii.

44. The same is true of the performer and audience when considering the aural experience of a Gospel performed or read aloud. Both performer and hearers engage in creative activity in part through the interplay between them. Hearing a Gospel was the norm prior to printed bibles and still occurs today. See, for example, Joanna Dewey, "The Gospel of Mark as an Oral-Aural Event: Implications for Interpretation," in *The New Literary Criticism and the New Testament*, ed. Elizabeth Struthers, Malbon and Edgar V. McKnight (New York: Continuum, 1994), 145–63; and David Rhoads, "Performing the Gospel of Mark," in *Reading Mark, Engaging the Gospel* (Minneapolis: Fortress Press, 2004), 176–201.

45. Patriarchy sanctions male authority over women and children, especially the authority of males of dominant races and classes. Some biblical scholars prefer to use the term "kyriarchy," from the Greek word for lord (*kyrios*). Elisabeth Schüssler Fiorenza coined the term to describe an interlocking pyramid of structures of oppression involving gender, race, class, age, etc. In such a pyramid, elite males are dominant, but elite females may have power over some men. See *Wisdom Ways: Introducing Feminist Biblical Interpretation* (Maryknoll, N.Y.: Orbis, 2001), 118–22, 211.

46. See Rudolf Bultmann, "New Testament and Mythology," in *Kerygma and Myth*; ed. Hans Werner Bartsch; trans. R. H. Fuller (New York: Harper & Row, 1961), 1–44.

47. See Steve Ross, *Marked* (New York: Seabury, 2005).

48. Cf. James W. Carey, "Overcoming Resistance to Cultural Studies," in *What Is Cultural Studies? A Reader*, ed. John Storey (London: Arnold, 1996), 65: "British cultural studies could be described just as easily and perhaps more accurately as ideological studies." On ideological criticism in biblical studies, see The Bible and Culture Collective, *The Postmodern Bible*, ed. George Aichele et al. (New Haven: Yale University Press, 1995), 272–308.

49. This function, covertly at least, extended down into the modern period. Symptomatic in this regard is Ralph Broadbent's study of late nineteenth and early twentieth century British biblical commentaries, which finds them to be almost invariably accommodated to the imperial status quo ("Ideology, Culture, and British New Testament Studies: The Challenge of Cultural Studies," *Semeia* 82 [1998]: 33–61).

50. Indicative of such integration is the extent to which narrative criticism is painlessly combined with redaction criticism in such widely used commentaries on Mark as Francis J. Moloney, *The Gospel of Mark: A Commentary* (Peabody, Mass.: Hendrickson, 2002), and John R. Donahue and Daniel J. Harrington, *The Gospel of Mark* (Collegeville, Minn.: Liturgical, 2005).

51. In marked contrast, deconstruction, and the larger phenomenon of post-structuralism in which it participates, has exerted formative influence in the neighboring field of literary studies.

52. This is catalyzed in particular by the work of Richard Horsley; see his *Hearing the Whole Story: The Politics of Plot in Mark's Gospel* (Louisville: Westminster John Knox, 2001), and *Jesus and Empire: The Kingdom of God and the New World Disorder* (Minneapolis: Fortress Press, 2003).

2. NARRATIVE CRITICISM

1. Archibald MacLeish, "Ars Poetica," in *Collected Poems 1917–1954* (Boston: Houghton Mifflin, 1962), 50–51.

2. Robert C. Tannehill, *The Sword of His Mouth*; Semeia Supplements 1 (Philadelphia: Fortress Press, and Missoula, Mont.: Scholars, 1975).

3. Robert W. Funk, *Language, Hermeneutic, and the Word of God: The Problem of Language in the New Testament and Contemporary Theology* (New York: Harper & Row, 1966).

4. Dan O. Via Jr., *The Parables: Their Literary and Existential Dimension* (Philadelphia: Fortress Press, 1967).

5. John Dominic Crossan, *In Parables: The Challenge of the Historical Jesus* (New York: Harper & Row, 1973); Crossan, *The Dark Interval: Towards a Theology of Story* (Niles, Ill.: Argus Communications, 1975; reprint, Sonoma, Calif.: Polebridge, 1988).

6. A. J. Greimas, "Elements of a Narrative Grammar," trans. Catherine Porter, *Diacritics* 7 (1977): 23–40. For an explanation, see Daniel Patte, *What Is Structural Exegesis?* Guides to Biblical Scholarship (Philadelphia: Fortress Press, 1976), 41–43. For an adaptation and application to the parables, see Crossan, *Dark Interval*.

7. Claude Lévi-Strauss, "The Structural Study of Myth," *Journal of American Folklore* 68 (1955): 428–44; Lévi-Strauss, "The Story of Asdiwal," trans. Nicholas Mann, in *The Structural Study of Myth and Totemism*, ed. Edmund Leach, Association of Social Anthropologists Monographs 5 (London: Tavistock, 1967), 1–47. Elizabeth Struthers Malbon, *Narrative Space and Mythic Meaning in Mark*; New Voices in Biblical Studies (San Francisco: Harper & Row, 1986; repr., The Biblical Seminar 13, Sheffield: Sheffield Academic Press, 1991).

8. Daniel Patte, *Paul's Faith and the Power of the Gospel: A Structural Introduction to the Pauline Letters* (Philadelphia: Fortress Press, 1983); Patte, *The Gospel according to Matthew: A Structural Commentary on Matthew's Faith* (Philadelphia: Fortress Press, 1987). See also Patte, *Structural Exegesis for New Testament Critics*; Guides to Biblical Scholarship (Minneapolis: Fortress Press, 1990).

9. This diagram is based on that of Seymour Chatman, *Story and Discourse: Narrative Structure in Fiction and Film* (Ithaca: Cornell University Press, 1978), 151.

10. For example, Stephen H. Smith, in *A Lion with Wings: A Narrative-Critical Approach to Mark's Gospel* (Sheffield: Sheffield Academic Press, 1996), states: "As it so happens, however, there is essentially no difference between implied author and narrator in the Gospel of Mark, and there is thus no problem in treating them as one" (23 n. 28; see also 39).

11. Mark Allan Powell, *What Is Narrative Criticism?* Guides to Biblical Scholarship (Minneapolis: Fortress Press, 1990), 27.

12. See, e.g., Jack Dean Kingsbury, *The Christology of Mark's Gospel* (Philadelphia: Fortress Press, 1983).

13. Elizabeth Struthers Malbon, "The Christology of Mark's Gospel: Narrative Christology and the Markan Jesus," in *Who Do You Say that I Am? Essays on Christology in Honor of Jack Dean Kingsbury*, ed. Mark Allan Powell and David R. Bauer (Louisville: Westminster John Knox, 1999), 33–48, see esp. 43.

14. Elizabeth Struthers Malbon, "Narrative Christology and the Son of Man: What the Markan Jesus Says Instead," *Biblical Interpretation* 11 (2003): 373–85, see especially 384.

15. E. M. Forster, *Aspects of the Novel* (New York: Harcourt, Brace & World, 1927; reprint, 1954), 103–18.

16. Norman R. Petersen, "'Point of View' in Mark's Narrative," *Semeia* 12 (1978): 97–121.

17. For the now-classic exposition of the disciples as failed followers, see Theodore J. Weeden, Sr., *Mark: Traditions in Conflict* (Philadelphia: Fortress Press, 1971). See also Werner H. Kelber, *Mark's Story of Jesus* (Philadelphia: Fortress Press, 1979). For the view of the disciples as "fallible followers," see Robert C. Tannehill, "The Disciples in Mark: The Function of a Narrative Role," *Journal of Religion* 57 (1977): 386–405, and Elizabeth Struthers Malbon, "Fallible Followers: Women and Men in the Gospel of Mark," *Semeia* 28 (1983): 29–48, reprinted as chapter 2 of Malbon, *In the Company of Jesus: Characters in Mark's Gospel* (Louisville: Westminster John Knox, 2000).

18. Vernon K. Robbins, *Jesus the Teacher: A Socio-Rhetorical Interpretation of Mark*, rev. ed. (Philadelphia: Fortress Press, 1992).

19. Elizabeth Struthers Malbon, "The Jewish Leaders in the Gospel of Mark: A Literary Study of Marcan Characterization," *Journal of Biblical Literature* 108 (1989): 259–81, esp. 275–81, rep. as chapter 5 of *In the Company of Jesus*.

20. Elizabeth Struthers Malbon, "New Literary Criticism and Jesus Research," in *The Handbook of the Study of the Historical Jesus*, vol. 1: *How to Study the Historical Jesus*, ed. Tom Holmén and Stanley E. Porter (Leiden: E. J. Brill, forthcoming).

21. Elizabeth Struthers Malbon, "Galilee and Jerusalem: History and Literature in Marcan Interpretation," *Catholic Biblical Quarterly* 44 (1982): 242–55; repr. in *The Interpretation of Mark*, ed. William R. Telford (London: T.&T. Clark, 1995), 253–68.

22. Willi Marxsen, *Mark the Evangelist: Studies on the Redaction History of the Gospel*, trans. James Boyce et al. (Nashville: Abingdon, 1969). Werner H. Kelber, *The Kingdom in Mark: A New Place and a New Time* (Philadelphia: Fortress Press, 1974).

23. On the larger issues of apocalyptic and temporality in relation to Mark's plot, see Dan O. Via Jr., *The Ethics of Mark's Gospel: In the Middle of Time* (Philadelphia: Fortress Press, 1985), esp. 27–66.

24. Norman R. Petersen, *Literary Criticism for New Testament Critics*; Guides to Biblical Scholarship (Philadelphia: Fortress Press, 1978), 49–50.

25. Gérard Genette, *Narrative Discourse: An Essay in Method*, trans. Jane E. Lewin (Ithaca: Cornell University Press, 1980).

26. For a brief definition of the term and a synopsis of the scholarly debate surrounding it, see M. H. Abrams, *A Glossary of Literary Terms*, 6th ed. (New York: Harcourt Brace, 1993), 90.

27. For a fuller narrative critical discussion of chapters 4–8, see Elizabeth Struthers Malbon, "Echoes and Foreshadowings in Mark 4–8: Reading and Rereading," *Journal of Biblical Literature* 113 (1993): 211–30.

3. READER-RESPONSE CRITICISM

1. John 6:25-59 explicitly compares Jesus' feeding of the multitude with Moses' providing manna for the Israelites during their wilderness wanderings. Many interpreters of Mark have suggested that a similar allusion, however vague, is present also in Mark.

2. George Steiner, "'Critic'/'Reader,'" *New Literary History* 10 (1979): 423–52.

3. That is, it is more a matter of mind than heart, more cognitive than emotive. However, we must not draw too sharply the distinction between religious and academic communities or between matters of the mind and the heart. Presumably, using one's intellect does not preclude being religious, and vice versa.

4. Stanley Fish, *Is There a Text in This Class? The Authority of Interpretive Communities* (Cambridge and London: Harvard University Press, 1980), 26.

5. Ibid., 27.

6. A good way to gain insight into first-century oral performance of the Gospel is to perform it orally today. For a performance of Mark's Gospel using a contemporary American English translation, see the videotaped performance by David Rhoads (available from SELECT, 2199 E. Main St., Columbus, OH 43209). Rhoads performs the entire Gospel of Mark from memory, an astonishing feat today, but commonplace in antiquity.

7. Wolfgang Iser, "The Reading Process: A Phenomenological Approach," *New Literary History* 3 (1972): 293.

8. RSV.

9. Frans Neirynck, with Theo Hansen and Frans Van Segbroeck, has counted twenty-eight instances of *palin* in Mark, nearly all of which point back clearly to an antecedent moment in the reading experience; see *The Minor Agreements of Matthew and Luke against Mark with a Cumulative List*; Bibliotheca ephemeridum theologicarum lovaniesium 37 (Leuven: Leuven University Press, 1974), 276–77.

10. NRSV, emphasis added.

11. Wolfgang Iser, *The Act of Reading: A Theory of Aesthetic Response* (Baltimore and London: Johns Hopkins University Press, 1978), 167–72.

12. Neirynck, *Minor Agreements*, 261–72.

13. Wayne C. Booth, *A Rhetoric of Irony* (Chicago: University of Chicago Press, 1974).

14. Ibid., 10–14, 33–44.

15. Ibid., 10.

16. Ibid., 11.

17. Ibid.

18. Ibid., 12.

19. Ibid., 28–29.

20. Stanley E. Fish, *Self-Consuming Artifacts: The Experience of Seventeenth-Century Literature* (Berkeley, Los Angeles, and London: University of California Press, 1972).

21. This list has remarkable affinities with what Stephen Moore has to say about the deconstructive interpretation of the Gospel of Mark.

22. The word *parable* in 4:11 and elsewhere in Mark seems to have the sense of "puzzle" or "riddle."

23. RSV, emphasis added.

24. My translation.

25. Judith Fetterley, *The Resisting Reader: A Feminist Approach to American Fiction* (Bloomington and London: Indiana University Press, 1978); idem, "Reading about Reading: 'A Jury of Her Peers,' 'The Murders on the Rue Morgue,' and 'The Yellow Wallpaper,'" in *Gender and Reading: Essays on Readers, Texts, and Contexts*, ed. Elizabeth A. Flynn and Patrocinio P. Schweickart (Baltimore and London: Johns Hopkins University Press, 1986), 147–64. For a discussion of the basics of feminist criticism and for an application of feminist reader-response criticism, see chapter 5, Feminist Criticism: The Dancing Daughter.

26. Fetterley, *The Resisting Reader*, xii, xx.

27. Fetterley, "Reading about Reading," 164.

28. Fetterley, *The Resisting Reader*, viii.

29. Ibid., xxii.

30. Although some ancient manuscripts of the Gospel of Mark include additional verses at the end of the Gospel, the oldest and most accurate manuscripts end at Mark 16:8. The manuscript copies of Mark that tack on extra verses beyond 16:8 themselves represent resisting readings of Mark's ending. Certain copyists did not want Mark to end at 16:8, so they took it upon themselves to supplement the ending.

31. In making this identification, I am in agreement with Werner H. Kelber, John Dominic Crossan, and Thomas Boomershine; see Kelber's discussion in *The Oral and the Written Gospel: The Hermeneutics of Speaking and Writing in the Synoptic Tradition, Mark, Paul and Q* (Philadelphia: Fortress Press, 1983), 103–4.

32. Some clues: in Mark 3:21, Jesus' family comes to take him home because they think he "has gone out of his mind." When his mother and brothers arrive to take him away, Jesus acknowledges that he is estranged from his family (Mark 3:33-35). This estrangement is alluded to again in 6:4. Altogether this suggests that Mark avoids calling Mary "the mother of Jesus" in 15:40, 47, and 16:1 in order to imply to the reader that Jesus is still alienated from his mother and his brothers.

33. A common historical solution for the puzzle of Mark 14:51-52 is that the young man is the author himself, which would make Mark an eyewitness of the scene in Gethsemane. A common literary-theological solution to the puzzle of Mark 16:5 is that the young man is really an angel (as in Matthew). Both of these solutions are ingenious, but the Gospel of Mark explicitly authorizes neither. Mark likes to give us puzzles without obvious solutions.

34. Elisabeth Schüssler Fiorenza, *In Memory of Her: A Feminist Theological Reconstruction of Christian Origins* (New York: Crossroad, 1983), 138–9, 321–23; Elizabeth Struthers Malbon, "Fallible Followers: Women and Men in the Gospel of Mark," *Semeia* 28 (1983): 29–48 [repr. in Elizabeth Struthers Malbon, *In the Company of Jesus: Characters in Mark's Gospel* (Louisville: Westminster John Knox, 2000), 41–69].

35. A feminist critic who also has problems with this reading is Mary Ann Tolbert, *Sowing the Gospel: Mark's World in Literary-Historical Perspective* (Minneapolis: Fortress Press, 1989), 291–99.

36. Regarding the impact of the ending of Mark on the reader, see Tolbert, *Sowing the Gospel*; regarding the entire Gospel's orientation toward the reader, see Robert M. Fowler, *Let the Reader Understand: Reader-Response Criticism and the Gospel of Mark* (Harrisburg, Pa.: Trinity Press International, 2001).

37. Tolbert, *Sowing the Gospel*, 292–93.

38. Mary Ann Tolbert also seems to be asking this question, but does not go far in pursuing an answer (*Sowing the Gospel*, 274, 292–93). On the minor characters of "little people" in Mark, see David Rhoads, Joanna Dewey, and Donald Michie, *Mark as Story: An Introduction to the Narrative of a Gospel*, 2d ed. (Minneapolis: Fortress Press, 1999), 129–35.

4. DECONSTRUCTIVE CRITICISM

1. By "early" I mean the period 1967–1972. Derrida published three books in French in 1967 and a further three in 1972, all of which were eventually translated into English: Jacques Derrida, *Speech and Phenomena and Other Essays on Husserl's Theory of Signs*, trans. David B. Allison (Evanston: Northwestern University Press, 1973); idem, *Of Grammatology*, trans. Gayatri Chakravorty Spivak (Baltimore: Johns Hopkins University Press, 1976); idem, *Writing and Difference*, trans. Alan Bass (Chicago: University of Chicago Press, 1978); idem, *Dissemination*, trans. Barbara Johnson (Chicago: University of Chicago Press, 1981); idem, *Posi-*

tions, trans. Alan Bass (Chicago: University of Chicago Press, 1981); idem, *Margins of Philosophy,* trans. Alan Bass (Chicago: University of Chicago Press, 1982). The year 1974 saw the publication of Derrida's *Glas* (which appeared in English under the same title; trans. John P. Leavey Jr., and Richard Rand [Lincoln: University of Nebraska Press, 1986]). *Glas* ushered in what I would regard as Derrida's "middle period." My book *Mark and Luke in Poststructuralist Perspectives: Jesus Begins to Write* (New Haven: Yale University Press, 1992) is primarily inspired by Derrida's principal work from this period. The expression "later Derrida" refers to the last fifteen or twenty years of his career. For a brief introduction to the later work, see Catherine Keller and Stephen D. Moore, "Derridapocalypse," in *Derrida and Religion: Other Testaments,* ed. Yvonne Sherwood and Kevin Hart (Chicago: University of Chicago Press, 2005), 189–207; and for full-scale introductions, see John D. Caputo, *The Prayers and Tears of Jacques Derrida: Religion without Religion* (Bloomington: Indiana University Press, 1997), or Herman Rapaport, *Later Derrida: Reading the Recent Work* (London and New York: Routledge, 2002).

2. To deconstruct is to dismantle, to take something apart so as to examine how it functions.

3. As the literary critic Frank Kermode recognized in a reading of the Markan parables that was itself influenced by deconstruction; see his *The Genesis of Secrecy: On the Interpretation of Narrative* (Cambridge: Harvard University Press, 1979), 27, 46–47.

4. Not that Derrida himself reflects explicitly on Christian theology in this fashion.

5. Derrida, *Glas,* 189b.

6. His argument is complex and its details need not concern us here. I have summarized it more fully in my *Poststructuralism and the New Testament: Derrida and Foucault at the Foot of the Cross* (Minneapolis: Fortress Press, 1994), 25–36.

7. Note the passive constructions ("hardened" [*pepōrōmenē*]) in 6:52 and 8:17c, which seem, as has often been suggested, to imply divine agency, especially in light of such texts as Exod 4:21ff.; Luke 9:45; 18:34; and Rom 11:7-8.

8. Plato, *Phaedrus,* in *The Collected Dialogues of Plato,* ed. Edith Hamilton and Huntington Cairns, trans. R. Hackforth (Princeton, N.J.: Princeton University Press, 1961), 275d-275e.

9. Derrida, "Plato's Pharmacy," in *Dissemination,* 77.

10. Ibid.

11. Derrida reads Rousseau in *Of Grammatology* and Plato and Mallarmé in *Dissemination.*

12. Derrida, *Positions,* his emphasis.

13. As Robert Fowler pithily puts it, Mark trails off before narrating "circumstances in which one could imagine something like the Gospel of Mark being narrated. The story *in* Mark's Gospel seems to preclude the telling *of* Mark's Gospel" (*Let the Reader Understand: Reader-Response Criticism and the Gospel of Mark,* 2d ed. [Harrisburg, Pa.: Trinity Press International, 2001], 250, his emphasis).

14. Barbara Johnson, *A World of Difference* (Baltimore: Johns Hopkins University Press, 1987), 2.

15. Derrida, *Positions,* 41.

16. At least one feminist deconstructive reading of Mark has already been ventured: see Susan Lochrie Graham, "Silent Voices: Women in the Gospel of Mark," *Semeia* 54 (1991): 145–58. In my *Poststructuralism and the New Testament*, 43–64, I attempt to bring deconstruction and feminism into dialogue around the Johannine Jesus' encounter with the Samaritan woman.

17. For the concept of the implied reader, see Elizabeth Struthers Malbon's and Robert Fowler's chapters in the present volume.

18. The Gentile/Jew opposition maps particularly neatly onto the Christian/Jew opposition in Mark, then (see further n. 26 below). This is not the case in other early Christian texts. In the Jewish-Christian Gospel of Matthew, for instance (to take Mark's nearest neighbor), Judaism and Christianity have a more complex, overlapping relationship.

19. For earlier work on Mark in a post-Holocaust register by two Jewish scholars, see George M. Smiga, *Pain and Polemic: Anti-Judaism in the Gospels* (Mahwah, N.J.: Paulist, 1992), 25–51; Amy-Jill Levine, "Matthew, Mark, and Luke: Good News or Bad?" in *Jesus, Judaism, and Christian Anti-Judaism*, ed. Paula Fredriksen and Adele Reinhartz (Louisville: Westminster John Knox, 2002), 77–98.

20. See further William R. Telford, *The Barren Temple and the Withered Fig Tree* (Sheffield: JSOT Press, 1980). For more recent engagement with these issues, see *The Temple Theme in Mark*, a thematic issue of the journal *Biblical Interpretation* (15:3, 2007), ed. Tom Shepherd.

21. The carnage is described at length in Josephus, *Jewish War* 6.8.5ff., and even though Josephus is no stranger to exaggeration, there is no reason to doubt that a massacre occurred.

22. A theme subsequently picked up and made more explicit by Matthew and Luke; see, for example, Matt 22:7; 27:25; Luke 13:34-35; 19:41-44.

23. The Gospels being no exception; they are organized around such megametaphors as "kingdom of God," "Son of God," and so on.

24. A suggestion made in passing by Richard A. Horsley; see his *Hearing the Whole Story: The Politics of Plot in Mark's Gospel* (Minneapolis: Fortress Press, 2001), 252.

25. Recall Derrida's interest in what he labeled "undecidables," terms or formulations that cannot be comfortably included in hierarchical binary oppositions, but which resist and disrupt them instead. I am arguing that the centurion's utterance is such an undecidable, which places him "inside" and "outside" at one and the same time, thereby sabotaging that opposition.

26. Scholars have long argued that the Gentile character of the Markan community is suggested by details such as Mark 7:3-4 ("For the Pharisees, and all the Jews, do not eat unless they wash their hands . . ."), which explanation would not be necessary if the community were predominantly Jewish.

5. FEMINIST CRITICISM

1. Given the environment and the content, the Gospels were probably written by men. I take no position here on whether each evangelist deliberately addressed a specific community or had a more general audience in mind.

2. Quoted in bell hooks, *Ain't I A Woman: Black Women and Feminism* (Boston: South End Press, 1981), 160.

3. The term *womanist* is the self-designation of many black women following Alice Walker in *In Search of Our Mothers' Gardens* (New York: Harcourt Brace Jovanovich, 1974).

4. See the autobiographical reflections by David Gunn, "Reflections on David," in *A Feminist Companion to Reading the Bible*, ed. Athalya Brenner and Carole Fontaine (Sheffield: Sheffield Academic Press, 1997), 548–66, and F. Scott Spencer's introduction to his *Dancing Girls, Loose Ladies, and Women of the Cloth: The Women in Jesus' Life* (New York: Continuum, 2004).

5. Quoted in Sandra Harding, "Conclusion: Epistemological Questions," in *Feminism and Methodology*, ed. Sandra Harding (Bloomington: Indiana University Press, 1987), 188.

6. Linda Alcoff, "Cultural Feminism Versus Post-structuralism: The Identity Crisis in Feminist Theory," *Signs* 13 (1988): 432.

7. See Elisabeth Schüssler Fiorenza, *Wisdom Ways: Introducing Feminist Biblical Interpretation* (Maryknoll, N.Y.: Orbis, 2001), 118–22, 211. Because Schüssler Fiorenza is a biblical scholar, the term has the most currency in that field. Some interpreters prefer the term "kyriarchy" to "patriarchy," which is thought to focus too much on gender as the key element of domination. Other interpreters may prefer the term patriarchy either because they believe gender is the primary matrix of dominance or because they believe it captures the same system of interlocking forms of domination.

8. The view of humans as central and superior, anthropocentrism, is itself the subject of challenges from environmental thinkers who prefer biocentrism with all elements of ecosystems as important and interdependent. Some religious environmentalists now interpret Genesis 1 in the light of Genesis 2, advocating a theocentric environmental ethic where humans are accountable to God for their environmental stewardship or care.

9. In contrast, see Phyllis Trible's interpretation of Genesis 2–3 in "Depatriarchalizing in Biblical Interpretation," *Journal of the American Academy of Religion* 41 (1973): 30–48, esp. 35–36.

10. Elisabeth Schüssler Fiorenza, *In Memory of Her* (New York: Crossroad, 1983), 47, citing Bernadette Brooten, "Junia . . . Outstanding among the Apostles," in *Women Priests: A Catholic Commentary on the Vatican Declaration*, ed. L. Swidler and A. Swidler (New York: Paulist, 1977), 141–44. See also the thorough discussion in Eldon J. Epp, *Junia, The First Woman Apostle* (Minneapolis: Fortress Press, 2005).

11. Schüssler Fiorenza, *In Memory of Her*, 47. The NRSV does call Phoebe a deacon in Rom 16:1.

12. Carol Meyers, *Discovering Eve: Ancient Israelite Women in Context* (New York: Oxford University Press, 1988), 16–19.

13. Meyers, *Discovering Eve*, 95–121.

14. Virginia Ramey Mollenkott, *The Divine Feminine: The Biblical Imagery of God as Female* (New York: Crossroad, 1983); Fiorenza, *In Memory of Her*, 130ff.

15. Phyllis Trible, *God and the Rhetoric of Sexuality* (Philadelphia: Fortress Press, 1978), chap. 2.

16. Elsa Tamez, "Women and the Bible," *Lucha* 9 (1985): 54–64.

17. For a discussion of the work of feminist historians, see Patricia Crawford and Jane Long, "History, feminist," in *Encyclopedia of Feminist Theories*, ed. Lorraine Code (London: Routledge, 2000), 252–54.

18. To find examples, see Catherine A. Brekus, *Strangers and Pilgrims: Female Preaching in America, 1740–1845* (Chapel Hill: University of North Carolina Press, 1998); Caroline Walker Bynum, *Fragmentation and Redemption: Essays on Gender and the Human Body in Medieval Religion* (New York: Zone Books, 1991); Caroline Walker Bynum, *Jesus as Mother* (Berkeley: University of California Press, 1982); Christiana de Groot and Marion Ann Taylor, eds., *Recovering Nineteenth-Century Women Interpreters of the Bible* (Atlanta: Society of Biblical Literature, 2007); Bettye Collier-Thomas, *Daughters of Thunder: Black Women Preachers and Their Sermons, 1850–1979* (John Wiley and Sons, 1997); Patricia Demer, *Women as Interpreters of the Bible* (New York: Paulist, 1992); Chanta M. Haywood, *Prophesying Daughters: Black Women Preachers and the Word, 1823–1913* (University of Missouri Press, 2003); Ronald Kastner and Patricia Wilson Kastner, *A Lost Tradition: Women Writers of the Early Church* (Lanham, Md.: University Press of America, 1981); Gerda Lerner, *The Creation of Feminist Consciousness: From the Middle Ages to Eighteen-seventy* (New York: Oxford University Press, 1993); Alice Rossi, ed., *The Feminist Papers: From Adams to de Beauvoir* (Boston: Northeastern University Press, 1988); Marla J. Selvidge, *Notorious Voices: Feminist Biblical Criticism, 1500–1920* (New York: Continuum International Publishing Group, 1996); Elizabeth Cady Stanton et al., *The Women's Bible* (1895; reprint, Salem, N.H.: Ayer Company, 1988); Marion Ann Taylor and Heather E. Weir, eds., *Let Her Speak for Herself: Nineteenth-Century Women Writing on the Women of Genesis* (Waco, Tex.: Baylor University Press, 2006).

19. My discussion depends on many of the works on gender and reading cited in Diana Fuss, "Reading Like a Feminist," *differences* 1 (1989): 77–92, and Patrocinio P. Schweickart, "Reading Ourselves: Toward a Feminist Theory of Reading," in *Gender and Reading: Essays on Readers, Texts, and Contexts*, ed. Elizabeth A. Flynn and Patrocinio P. Schweickart (Baltimore: Johns Hopkins University Press, 1986), 31–62.

20. Judith Fetterley coined this term in *The Resisting Reader: A Feminist Approach to American Fiction* (Bloomington: Indiana University Press, 1978).

21. Elaine Showalter, "Critical Cross-Dressing" in *Men in Feminism*, ed. Alice Jardine and Paul Smith (New York: Methuen, 1987), 124–27.

22. Audre Lorde, "Age, Race, Class and Sex: Women Redefining Difference" in *Sister Outsider* (Freedom, Calif.: Crossing, 1984), 119.

23. English language concordances are often keyed to a particular translation. An example of a concordance keyed to the NRSV is John R. Kohlenberger, ed., *The Concise Concordance to the New Revised Standard Version* (Oxford: Oxford University Press, 1993). Online Bible sites often allow you to search multiple English translations and sometimes Greek texts. One example is the E Canon site with a persistent web address of http://purl.org/ECanon.

24. One place to identify such passages is *Religion Index One* under the headings "Women in Christianity" and "Women in the Bible" for the years 1970 to the present. You may also search online databases available through a library such

as ATLA Religion Database or the EBSCO Religion and Philosophy Collection. Another source is Stanton, *The Women's Bible*, which confronted passages used to justify oppression.

25. One way to spot these is to check databases under the heading Bible. N. T. name of Gospel. What passages are repeatedly the subjects of articles? Another way to find them is to leaf through the indexes, tables of content, and bibliographies of several standard commentaries on the Gospel, such as Vincent Taylor's *The Gospel according to St. Mark*, 2d ed. (New York: St. Martin's, 1966); Robert A. Guelich's *Mark 1—8:26*; Word Biblical Commentary, 34a (Dallas: Word, 1989); or Joel Marcus, *Mark 1–8: A New Translation with Introduction and Commentary*, Anchor Bible 27 (New York: Doubleday, 2000). Which passages do the authors single out for special comments or notes? Which passages provoke the longest bibliographies and the longest comments?

26. One place to start is with Bruce J. Malina's *The New Testament World: Insights from Cultural Anthropology*, 3d ed. (Louisville: Westminster/John Knox, 2001). Two others are Carolyn Osiek, Margaret Y. MacDonald with Janet H. Tulloch, *A Woman's Place: House Churches in Earliest Christianity* (Minneapolis: Fortress Press, 2006). and Tal Ilan, *Integrating Women into Second Temple History* (Peabody, Mass.: Hendrickson, 2001). You will always have to keep in mind the presuppositions and ideology shaping any reconstruction.

27. I have changed very little in this section from the first edition of *Mark and Method*. I found little I wish to change and hope readers will read more recent interpretations, some of which respond to my interpretation, and learn from multiple perspectives. Some articles or chapters treating the story since 1992 include Alice Bach, "Calling the Shots: Directing Salome's Dance of Death," *Semeia* 74 (1996): 103–26; Nicole Wilkinson Duran, "Return of the Disembodied or How John the Baptist Lost His Head," in *Reading Communities Reading Scripture: Essays in Honor of Daniel Patte*, ed. Gary A. Phillips and Nicole Wilkinson Duran (New York: Continuum, 2002), 277–91; Jennifer A. Glancy, "Unveiling Masculinity: The Construction of Masculinity in Mark 6:17-29," *Biblical Interpretation* 2 (1994): 34–50; Regina Janes, "Why the Daughter of Herodias Must Dance (Mark 6.14-29)," *Journal for the Study of the New Testament* 28 (2006): 443–67; Ross S. Kraemer, "Implicating Herodias and Her Daughter in the Death of John the Baptizer: A (Christian) Theological Strategy?" *Journal of Biblical Literature* 125 (2006): 321–49; Abraham Smith, "Tyranny Exposed: Mark's Typological Characterization of Herod Antipas (Mark 6:14-29)," *Biblical Interpretation* 14 (2006): 259–93; and F. Scott Spencer, "Shall We Dance? Women Leading Men in Mark 5–7," *Dancing Girls, Loose Ladies, and Women of the Cloth: The Women in Jesus' Life*. (New York: Continuum, 2004), 47–75. One book, Florence Morgan Gillman's *Herodias: At Home in That Fox's Den* (Collegeville, Minn.: Liturgical Press, 2003), treats Herodias including the Markan story. I have changed most instances of patriarchy to patriarchy/kyriarchy. I have also removed references to the hemorhaging woman as "unclean" and to her flow of blood as "polluting." Amy-Jill Levine convincingly argues that the text does not point to purity issues nor would first-century Jews likely have seen the woman in this way. See Levine, "Mark 5:25-34: Woman with a Twelve-Year Hemorrhage," in *Women in Scripture: A Dictionary of Named and Unnamed Women in the Hebrew Bible, the Apocryphal/Deuterocanonical Books, and the New Testament*, ed. Carol Meyers, Tony Craven, and Ross S. Kraemer (Grand Rapids: Eerdmans, 2001),

424–25, and "Discharging Responsibility: Matthean Jesus, Biblical Law, and Hemorrhaging Woman," in *A Feminist Companion to Matthew*, ed. Amy-Jill Levine with Maryanne Blickenstaff (Sheffield: Sheffield Academic Press, 2001), 70–87. I have also changed race to ethnicity once, added references to films and DVDs, updated/added notes, and made minor corrections and changes.

28. Works that discuss the use of the story in culture include Hugo Daffner, *Salome: Ihre Gestalt in Geschichte und Kunst* (Munich: Schmidt, 1912); Rana Kabbani, *Europe's Myths of Orient* (Bloomington: Indiana University Press, 1986); Blaise Hospodar de Kornitz, *Salome: Virgin or Prostitute?* (New York: Pageant, 1953); Ewa Kuryluk, *Salome and Judas in the Cave of Sex* (Evanston: Northwestern University Press, 1987), 189–258; Françoise Meltzer, *Salome and the Dance of Writing* (Chicago: University of Chicago Press, 1987), 13–46; Mario Praz, *The Romantic Agony*, 2d ed. (New York: Oxford University Press, 1970); Linda Seidel, "Salome and the Canons," *Women's Studies* 2 (1984): 26–66; and Helen Grace Zagona, *The Legend of Salome and the Principle of Art for Art's Sake* (Geneva: Librairie E. Droz, 1960).

29. Examples of DVD productions of the Strauss opera are *Strauss—Salome* (1974); Director: Götz Friedrich; Deutsche Grammophon; DVD Release 2007 and Petr Weigl's production *Strauss—Salome* (1990); Deutsche Oper Berlin; Kultur Video; DVD Release 2005. Among films released on DVD that encompass Wilde's Salome are director Ken Russell's *Salome's Last Dance* (1988), offering a play within a film; and director Steven Berkoff's *Oscar Wilde's: Salome* (1995). Alice Bach, "Calling the Shots: Directing Salome's Dance of Death," *Semeia* 74 (1996): 103–26, discusses some of the films.

30. Heinrich Heine, "Atta Troll," excerpt from Caput 19, in *The Complete Poems of Heinrich Heine: A Modern English Version*, trans. Hal Draper (Boston: Suhrkamp/Insel, 1982), 458–59.

31. Blaise Hospodar de Kornitz, *Salome: Virgin or Prostitute?* (New York: Pageant, 1953).

32. This and the following translations of Mark are the author's.

33. Lev 18:16; 20:21 forbid marriage to a brother's wife. It is not clear whether and which first-century hearers would apply this to halfbrothers. Leviticus does not prohibit uncle-niece marriages. See Josephus, *Antiquities* 18.5.1–4; K. C. Hanson, "The Herodians and Mediterranean Kinship," parts 1 and 2, *Biblical Theology Bulletin* 19 (1989): 75–84, 142–51.

34. Various manuscripts read *autou* (of him) or *autas* (of her) in 6:22. If the original read *autou*, the little girl is Herod's daughter and her name is Herodias, like her mother's. If the original read *autas*, the girl is Herodias's daughter and Herod's niece. This relationship is further complicated by the extra-Markan information from Josephus that Herodias (the mother) was Herod Antipas's niece: and that Philip the tetrarch was not Herod Antipas's brother. Philip the tetrarch married Salome, Herodias's daughter.

35. The traditional age for marriage for females in Greco-Roman Palestine was probably about twelve. See Leonie J. Archer, *Her Price Is Beyond Rubies: The Jewish Woman in Greco-Roman Palestine*, JSOT Supp. 60 (Sheffield: JSOT Press, 1990); Harold W. Hoehner, *Herod Antipas* (Cambridge: Cambridge University Press, 1972), 154–56.

36. Taylor, *The Gospel according to St. Mark*, 315.

37. Kabbani, *Europe's Myths of Orient*, 68–69. For more on Orientalism, see Benny Tat-siong Liew's discussion of Edward Said's *Orientalism* in chap. 8 on postcolonial criticism.

38. Chrysostom, "Homily XLVIII," in vol. 10 of *A Select Library of the Nicene and Post-Nicene Fathers of the Christian Church*, ed. Philip Schaff, trans. George Prevost and M. B. Riddle (Grand Rapids: Eerdmans, 1956), 299.

39. Calvin, *A Commentary on a Harmony of the Evangelists*, vol. 1; trans. William Pringle (Grand Rapids: Eerdmans, 1949), 222–24, 228.

40. Kabbani, *Europe's Myths of Orient*, 76.

41. Sandol Stoddard, *The Doubleday Illustrated Children's Bible* (Garden City, N.Y.: Doubleday, 1983), 278.

42. Origen, *Commentary on Matthew, Book X*, in *The Ante-Nicene Fathers* 10; ed. Alan Menzies (Grand Rapids: Eerdmans, n.d.), 428–29.

43. Isabel Combs Stube, "The Johannisschüssel: From Narrative to Reliquary to *Andachtsbild*," *Marsyas* 14 (1968–69): 1–16; Seidel, "Salome and the Canons," 47.

44. Caroline Walker Bynum in *Fragmentation and Redemption*, 79–117 and 151–65, describes males and females who used this imagery; Christ, like a woman, bled and fed. See also her *Jesus as Mother*, 110–69.

45. Roger Aus, *Water into Wine and the Beheading of John the Baptist*, Brown Judaic Studies 150 (Atlanta: Scholars Press, 1988), and Brenda Deen Schildgen, "A Blind Promise: Mark's Retrieval of Esther," *Poetics Today* 15 (1994): 115–31, discuss connections between Esther and Mark 6:14-29.

46. Margarita Stocker, "Biblical Story and the Heroine," in *The Bible as Rhetoric*, ed. Martin Warner (London: Routledge, 1990), 94–95.

47. Calvin, *A Commentary on a Harmony of the Evangelists*, 223.

48. Hospodar de Kornitz, *Salome*, 49–50.

49. Or, as Liew suggests in chapter 8, the poor widow may be making "a political statement against imperialism and about her agency with her gift, even if she is silent" (p. 228). See also his discussion of other readings of this widow.

50. See page 134 above and notes 43 and 44 for references to discussions of relevant medieval readings tying John and Jesus to food.

6. SOCIAL CRITICISM

1. The term *Ioudaios* in the New Testament has traditionally been translated as "Jew." In recent years, however, some New Testament scholars have been questioning that translation. For most contemporary readers, the term *Jew* is primarily a religious designation. For many Christian readers, moreover, *Jew* acquires its precise meaning in contrast to "Christian." At the time in which Mark was writing, however, what would later be termed *Christianity* had not yet separated from what would later be termed *Judaism*. In Mark's context, *Ioudaios* was not yet a religious designation. Rather, it was an ethnic designation for people of the nation of Israel living in or originating from the territory of Judea. As such, it is better translated "Judean." Hence, I am using the term *Judean* to refer to anyone in the ancient Mediterranean world

who belonged ethnically to the people of Israel, whether inside or outside the land of Israel. Throughout the chapter, the term *Judean* will be used rather than *Jew* or *Jewish* in reference to the first century. In the first century, the designation "Judeans" could refer to Israelite residents of Judea in southern Palestine, Israelite residents within the larger territory of the (Roman) Province of Judea, people living in dispersion who originated from Judea, or all of the above together. The particular usage of this term throughout the chapter should be obvious from its context, the predominant usage being to Israelite residents within the larger territory of the (Roman) Province of Judea. It is important to note that Jesus, his disciples, and the non-Gentile authorities in Mark's narrative were all Judeans belonging to the people of Israel. As readers, we are called to read the New Testament so that we do not universalize the particular controversies among Judean groups in the first century and so that we thereby avoid making them into a clash between religions in our very different context.

2. Peter Berger and Thomas Luckman, *The Social Construction of Reality: A Treatise in the Sociology of Knowledge* (Garden City, N.Y.: Doubleday, 1963). On worldviews, see Michael Kearney, *World View* (Novato, Calif.: Chandler & Sharp, 1984).

3. See Berger and Luckmann, *The Social Construction of Reality*, 142–73.

4. Beverly Gaventa, *From Darkness to Light: Aspects of Conversion in the New Testament* (Philadelphia: Fortress Press, 1986).

5. All translations from Mark in this chapter are the author's. See David Rhoads, Joanna Dewey, and Donald Michie, *Mark as Story: An Introduction to the Narrative of a Gospel* (Minneapolis: Fortress Press, 1999), 10–38.

6. Wayne Meeks, "The Man from Heaven in Johannine Sectarianism," *Journal of Biblical Literature* 91 (1972): 44–72.

7. See Howard Kee, *Community of the New Age: Studies in Mark's Gospel* (Philadelphia: Westminster, 1977), and David Rhoads, "Network for Mission: The Social System of the Jesus Network in Mark," in *Reading Mark, Engaging the Gospel* (Minneapolis: Fortress Press, 2004): 95–139.

8. Robin Scroggs, "The Earliest Christian Communities as Sectarian Movement," in *Christianity, Judaism, and Other Greco-Roman Cults: Studies for Morton Smith at Sixty*. Part 2: *Early Christianity*, ed. Jacob Neusner (Leiden: Brill, 1975), 1–23.

9. J. G. Gager, *Kingdom and Community: The Social World of Early Christianity* (Englewood Cliffs, N.J.: Prentice Hall, 1975).

10. Bruce Malina, *The New Testament World: Insights from Cultural Anthropology*, rev. ed. (Atlanta: John Knox, 2003).

11. Bruce Malina, "The Social Sciences and Biblical Interpretation," *Interpretation* 37 (1982): 229–42.

12. Vernon Robbins, *Jesus the Teacher: A Socio-Rhetorical Interpretation of Mark* (Philadelphia: Fortress Press, 1984).

13. John Pilch, "Healing in Mark: A Social Science Analysis," *Biblical Theology Bulletin* 15 (1985): 142–50.

14. Herman Waetjen, *A Reordering of Power: A Socio-Political Reading of Mark's Gospel* (Philadelphia: Fortress Press, 1989).

15. Jerome Neyrey, "The Idea of Purity in Mark's Gospel," in *Social Scientific Criticism of the New Testament*, ed. John Elliott. *Semeia* 35 (1986): 91–128.

16. On social location, see the introduction and the bibliography on intercultural criticism in *From Every People and Nation: The Book of Revelation in Intercultural Perspective*, ed. David Rhoads (Minneapolis, Minn.: Fortress Press, 2005.

17. John Elliott, *What Is Social Scientific Criticism?* (Minneapolis: Fortress, 1993). See also his *A Home for the Homeless: A Sociological Exegesis of 1 Peter, Its Situation and Strategy*, 2d ed. (Minneapolis: Fortress Press, 1990).

18. See Kristen De Troyer et al., eds., *Wholly Woman, Holy Blood: A Feminist Critique of Purity and Impurity* (Harrisburg, Penn.: Trinity Press International, 2003).

19. On differing perspectives regarding the prevalence of purity/defilement dynamics in first-century Israel, see Paula Fredriksen, "Did Jesus Oppose the Purity Laws?" *Bible Review* 11 (1995): 18–25, 42–47, and John Poirer, "Purity beyond the Temple in the Second Temple Era," *Journal of Biblical Literature* 122 (2003): 247–65.

20. In addition to Neyrey's work, I am especially indebted in this section to the following works: Jacob Neusner, *The Idea of Purity in Ancient Israel* (Leiden: Brill, 1973); Jacob Milgrom, "Purity and Impurity," *Encyclopedia Judaica* (Jerusalem: Keter, 1971): 1405–14; idem, "Israel's Sanctuary: The Priestly Picture of Dorian Grey," *Revue Biblique* 93 (1976): 370–99; Philip Peter Jensen, *Graded Holiness: A Key to the Priestly Conception of the World* (Sheffield: JSOT Press, 1992); Tikva Frymer-Kensky, "Pollution, Purification, and Purgation in Biblical Israel," in *The Word of the Lord Shall Go Forth*, ed. Carol Meyers and M. O'Conner (Winona Lake, Wis.: Eisenbrauns, 1983): 399–414; and Jonathan Klawans, *Impurity and Sin in Ancient Israel* (Oxford: Oxford University Press, 2000). For further bibliography, see Jerome Neyrey, "Clean/Unclean, Pure/Polluted, and Holy/Profane: The Idea and the System of Purity," in *The Social Sciences and New Testament Interpretation*, ed. Richard Rohrbaugh (Peabody, Mass.: Hendrickson, 1996): 80–104.

21. On holiness, see John Gammie, *Holiness in Israel* (Minneapolis: Fortress Press, 1989), and Hannah Harrington, *Holiness: Rabbinic Judaism and the Greco-Roman World* (New York, N.Y.: Routledge, 2001).

22. Klawans, *Impurity and Sin*, 137.

23. Jerome Neyrey, "The Idea of Purity in Mark's Gospel," 91–128. See also idem, "A Symbolic Approach to Mark 7," *Foundations and Facets Forum* 4 (1988): 63–91; John Pilch, "Biblical Leprosy and Body Symbolism," *Biblical Theology Bulletin* 11 (1981): 102–6.

24. On the Pharisees and Sadducees, see Jacob Neusner, *The Traditions about the Pharisees before 70*. 3 vols. (Leiden: Brill, 1971), and Anthony Saldarini, *Pharisees, Scribes and Sadducees in Palestinian Society: A Sociological Approach* (Wilmington, Del.: Glazier, 1988).

25. On hand washing before meals, see Roger Booth, *Jesus and the Laws of Purity: Tradition History and Legal History in Mark 7* (Sheffield: JSOT Press, 1986): 155–202.

26. On the Essenes at Qumran, see Michael Newton, *The Concept of Purity at Qumran and in the Letters of Paul* (Cambridge: Cambridge University Press, 1985); Hannah Harrington, *The Impurity Systems of Qumran and the Rabbis: Biblical Foundations* (Atlanta: Scholars Press, 1993); and Jonathan Klawans, *Impurity and Sin*, 48–56, 67–91.

27. See especially Mary Douglas, *Purity and Danger: An Analysis of the Concepts of Pollution and Taboo* (London: Routledge & Kegan Paul, 1966); idem, "Pollution,"

The International Encyclopedia of the Social Sciences 12, ed. David Stills (New York: Macmillan, 1968), 336–42; idem, *Implicit Meanings: Essays in Anthropology* (London: Routledge & Kegan Paul, 1975); idem, *Natural Symbols: Explorations in Cosmology* (New York: Pantheon, 1982).

28. Mary Douglas, *Purity and Danger*, passim.

29. On animals, see Walter Houston, *Purity and Monotheism: Clean and Unclean Animals in Biblical Law* (Sheffield: JSOT Press, 1993).

30. Jonathan Z. Smith, "Animals and Plants," *Encyclopedia Britannica*, 15th ed., 1:911–18; idem, "The Influence of Symbols upon Social Change: A Place on Which to Stand," *Worship* 44 (1970): 457–74; idem, "The Wobbling Point," *Journal of Religion* 52 (1972): 134–9.

31. Smith, "Animals and Plants," 914.

32. Smith, "Influence of Symbols," 467.

33. Smith, "Animals and Plants," 914.

34. Smith, "Influence of Symbols," 467.

35. Douglas, *Natural Symbols*, 70.

36. Douglas, *Implicit Meanings*, 269.

37. Malina, Bruce and Jerome Neyrey, *Calling Jesus Names: The Social Value of Labels in Matthew* (Sonoma, Calif.: Polebridge, 1988).

38. See Neyrey, "The Idea of Purity," 15. For the idea that the Markan Jesus does not eliminate ritual impurity in this passage but simply prioritizes moral purity over ritual purity, see Klawans, *Impurity and Sin*, 146–50.

39. Klawans, *Impurity and Sin*, 149–50.

40. See Marcus Borg, *Conflict, Holiness, and Politics in the Teaching of Jesus* (New York: Edwin Mellon, 1984), and Craig Blomberg, *Contagious Holiness: Jesus Meal's with Sinners* (Downers Grove, Ill.: InterVarsity, 2005).

41. I am grateful for a summer grant from the National Endowment for the Humanities that enabled me to do the initial research for this article. I am grateful to the following people for reacting to a draft of the manuscript: Joanna Dewey, Edgar Krentz, Wilhelm Linss, Jerome Neyrey, John Pilch, Jonathan Z. Smith, and Herman Waetjen. Carolyn Osiek and students in her graduate seminar at Brite Divinity School offered valuable suggestions for the revised version.

7. CULTURAL STUDIES

1. See, for example, Mary Ann Tolbert, "The Politics and Poetics of Location," in *Social Location and Biblical Interpretation in the United States*, vol. 1 of *Reading from this Place*, ed. Fernando F. Segovia and Mary Ann Tolbert (Minneapolis: Fortress Press, 1995), 332.

2. Fernando F. Segovia, "Cultural Studies and Contemporary Biblical Criticism as a Mode of Discourse," in *Social Location and Biblical Interpretation in Global Perspective*, vol. 2 of *Reading from this Place*, ed. Fernando F. Segovia and Mary Ann Tolbert (Minneapolis: Fortress Press, 1995), 2, 3.

3. Ibid., 5.

4. Ibid.

5. Paul Smith, "A Course in 'Cultural Studies,'" *Journal of the Midwestern Language Association* 24 (1991): 39–49, esp. 40.

6. Poe's tales such as "The Purloined Letter," "The Mystery of Marie Rogêt," and "The Rue Morgue" were all written between 1841 and 1845. On Poe as the originator of the mystery form, see Helen Mary Lock, "A Case of Mistaken Identity: Detective Undercurrents in recent African-American Fiction," Ph.D. diss., University of Virginia, 1991), 26, and Julia Symons, *Bloody Murder: From the Detective Story to the Crime Novel* (New York: Viking, 1985), 35–41.

7. Kelly Brown Douglas, *Sexuality and the Black Church* (Maryknoll, N.Y.: Orbis, 1999), 36.

8. On cultural studies as deploying an "ideological mode of discourse," see Fernando F. Segovia, "Methods for Studying the New Testament," in *The New Testament Today*, ed. Mark Allan Powell (Louisville: Westminster John Knox, 1999), 7.

9. In using the term *Mark*, this chapter does not assume a perspective on the flesh-and-blood author, about whom there is not a scholarly consensus. Nor does this chapter presuppose the idea of an identifiable Markan community. For a critique of the latter, see Dwight N. Peterson, *The Origins of Mark: The Markan Community in Current Debate* (Leiden: Brill, 2000).

10. For this wide-angle approach, I am indebted to Mary Ann Tolbert, "The Politics and Poetics of Location," 314, who has challenged biblical studies to analyze "each site of writing, reading, or theorizing by carefully investigating the specific historical, cultural, political and social matrix that grounds it."

11. On the debate about the "origins" of British cultural studies, see Stuart Hall, "The Emergence of Cultural Studies and the Crisis of the Humanities," *October* 53 (1990): 11–23; idem, "Cultural Studies and its Theoretical Legacies," in *Cultural Studies*, ed. L. Grossberg, C. Nelson, and P. Treichler (London: Routledge, 1992), 277–294; H. K. Wright, "Dare We De-centre Birmingham? Troubling the 'Origin' and Trajectories of Cultural Studies," *European Journal of Cultural Studies* 1 (1998): 33–56. See also the warnings of Walter D. Mignolo about the "coloniality of power" that concentrating on British cultural studies might involve in *Local Histories/Global Designs: Coloniality, Subaltern Knowledges, and Border Thinking* (Princeton, N.J.: Princeton University, 2000), 91–126; 172–214.

12. On the term "culturalist," see Vincent B. Leitch, "Birmingham Cultural Studies: Popular Arts, Poststructuralism, Radical Critique," *Cultural Studies and New Historicism* 24 (1991): 74.

13. *The Columbia Dictionary of Modern Literary and Cultural Criticism*, ed. Joseph Childers and Gary Hentzi (New York: Columbia University, 1995), 67.

14. Although Arnold's view of culture was not necessarily tied to *belles letters* but also sought the incorporation of the world outside of literature "in the name of a higher or larger [and therefore transformative and stabilizing] vision," that world simply did not include "popular or working-class culture." For the quoted material, see respectively Robert J. C. Young, *Colonial Desire: Hybridity in Theory, Culture and Race* (London: Routledge, 1995), 58, 56.

15. See Raymond Williams, *The Long Revolution* (Harmondsworth: Penguin, 1965), 63. Also, see Williams's *Culture and Society, 1780–1950* (New York: Columbia University Press, 1958), 576, in which he defines culture as: "a whole way of life, not only as a scale of integrity, but as a mode of interpreting all our common experience and, in this new interpretation, changing it."

16. Dwight N. Hopkins, "Introduction," in *Changing Conversations: Religious Reflection and Cultural Analysis*, ed. Hopkins and Sheila Greeve Davaney (New York: Routledge, 1996), 3.

17. Leitch, "Birmingham Cultural Studies," 74–75.

18. Cary Nelson, Paula A. Treichler, and Lawrence Grossberg, "Cultural Studies: An Introduction," in *Cultural Studies*, ed. Lawrence Grossberg, Cary Nelson, and Paula A. Treichler (New York: Routledge, 1992), 9.

19. For a critique of ideology as false consciousness, and a general accounting of different concepts of ideology, see The Bible and Culture Collective, *The Postmodern Bible* (New Haven: Yale University Press, 1995), 272–27.

20. Terry Eagleton, *Literary Theory: An Introduction* (Oxford: Basil Blackwell, 1983), 87.

21. Louis Althusser, *Essays on Ideology* (London: Verso, 1984), 127; Douglas Kellner, "Ideology, Marxism and Advanced Capitalism," *Socialist Review* 8 (1978): 53.

22. On these "interruptions," a term used by Stuart Hall, see Stephen D. Moore, "Between Birmingham and Jerusalem: Cultural Studies and Biblical Studies," *Semeia* 82 (1998): 11–12.

23. See Antonio Gramsci, *Selections from the Prison Notebooks of Antonio Gramsci*, ed. and trans. Quintin Hoare and Geoffrey Nowell Smith (New York: Harper & Row, 1973), 231–33.

24. I owe these insights and much of the language to Moore, "Between Birmingham and Jerusalem," 14–18. Also, see J. Cheryl Exum and Stephen D. Moore, "Biblical Studies/Cultural Studies," in *Biblical Studies/Cultural Studies: The Third Sheffield Colloquium*, ed. J. Cheryl Exum and Stephen D. Moore (Sheffield: Sheffield Academic Press, 1998), 19–45, esp., 20, 29–32. In all honesty, cultural studies not only underwent an internationalization, but persons living outside the West could also tell a different story about the "origins" of cultural studies. On these matters, see Robert Stam and Ella Shohat, "De-Eurocentricizing Cultural Studies: Some Proposals," in *Internationalizing Cultural Studies: An Anthology*, ed. Ackbar Abbas and John Nguyet Erni (Oxford/Malden, Mass.: Blackwell, 2005), 481–98. Also, see the journal *Inter-Asia Cultural Studies*.

25. bell hooks is the author of more than twenty books. See, for example, bell hooks, *Ain't I A Woman* (Boston: South End, 1981); *Outlaw Culture: Resisting Representations* (New York: Routledge, 1994). On domination and representation, see bell hooks, *Black Looks: Race and Representation* (Boston: South End, 1992), 3.

26. On Foucault's "insurrection of subjugated knowledge," see Michel Foucault, *Power/Knowledge: Selected Interviews and Other Writings*, ed. Colin Gordon (New York: Pantheon, 1980), 82.

27. On the depiction of Arabs in medieval art, see Jan N. Pieterse, *White on Black: Images of Africa and Blacks in Western Popular Culture* (New Haven: Yale University, 1992), 24. On the negative depictions of Native Americans, see hooks, *Black Looks*, 186.

28. On this example, see hooks, *Black Looks*, 6.

29. bell hooks, *Killing Rage: Ending Racism* (New York: Henry Holt and Company, 1995), 202.

30. West is the author of twenty books and hundreds of articles. See, for example, *Prophesy Deliverance: An Afro-Revolutionary Christianity* (Philadelphia: West-

minster, 1982); *The American Evasion of Philosophy: A Genealogy of Pragmatism* (London: University of Wisconsin, 1989); *Race Matters* (Boston: Beacon, 1993); and *Democracy Matters: Winning the Fight against American Imperialism* (New York: Penguin, 2004). On Gramsci's influence on West, West writes: "For him [Gramsci], the aim of philosophy is not only to become worldly by imposing its elite intellectual views upon people, but to become part of a social movement by nourishing and being nourished by the philosophical views of oppressed people themselves for the aims of social change and personal meaning" (*American Evasion*, 231). On the intersection of various types of domination, see Cornel West, *Keeping Faith: Philosophy and Race in America* (New York: Routledge, 1994), 20.

31. West, *American Evasion*, 233.

32. Bradly S. Billings, "The Disputed Words in the Lukan Institution Narrative (Luke 22:19b-20): A Sociological Answer to a Textual Problem," *Journal of Biblical Literature* 125 (2006): 507–26, 525.

33. Ibid., 507.

34. What follows emanates from Bart Ehrman, *Misquoting Jesus: The Story behind Who Changed the Bible and Why* (San Francisco: HarperSanFrancisco, 2005), 170–73.

35. Ibid., 170.

36. The assumption is that the redeemer's Spirit left him at the cross, as if the body were negative and the Spirit returned to the *pleroma*, i.e., the world of eternal powers. See Bart Ehrman, "The Text of Mark in the Hands of the Orthodox," in *Biblical Hermeneutics in Historical Perspective: Studies in Honor of Karlfried Froehlich on his Sixtieth Birthday*, ed. Mark S. Burrows and Paul Rorem (Grand Rapids: Eerdmans, 1991), 24.

37. On the translation of *ōneidisas*, see the fuller account of the problem in Bruce M. Metzger's *Textual Commentary on the Greek New Testament* (London: United Bible Societies, 1975), 120.

38. Ehrman, *Misquoting Jesus*, 173.

39. Ibid., 173.

40. Again, see Foucault, *Power/Knowledge*, 82.

41. Lawrence Venuti, *The Scandals of Translation: Toward an Ethics of Difference* (London: Routledge, 1998), 67–87.

42. Ehrman, *Misquoting Jesus*, 173.

43. See the critique of the Bible boom in R. S. Sugirtharajah, "Scripture, Scholarship, Empire: Putting the Discipline in its Place," *Expository Times* 117 (2005): 2–11.

44. William E. Nix, "Theological Presuppositions and Sixteenth Century English Bible Translation," *Bibliotheca Sacra* 124 (1967): 44.

45. Abraham Smith, "The Productive Role of English Bible Translators," *Semeia* 76 (1996): 60.

46. On the similarities between Luther and Tyndale, see Morna D. Hooker, "Tyndale's 'Heretical' Translation," *Reformation* 2 (1997): 136.

47. On reading the gaze from which interpretation is made, see hooks, *Black Looks*, 115–31.

48. Harold L. Phillips, *Translators and Translations: A Brief History of the Making of the English Bible* (Anderson, Ind.: Warner, 1958), 26.

49. Nix, "Theological Presuppositions," 48.

50. M. Ellsworth Olsen, *The Prose of Our King James Version: Its Origin and Course of Development* (Washington, D.C. Review and Herald, 1947), 59.

51. Venuti, *Scandals*, 83. Tyndale initially translated *presbyteros* as "senior"; his later editions, however, used "elder." See Nix, "Theological Presuppositions," 48.

52. Wai-Chee Dimock, "Feminism, New Historicism, and the Reader," *American Literature* 63 (1991): 604–5; Emile Durkheim, *Professional Ethics and Civic Morals*, trans. Cornelia Brookfield (Glencoe, Ill.: Free, 1958); Talcott Parsons, "The Professions and Social Structure," in *Essays in Sociological Theory* (Glencoe, Ill.: Free, 1954), 34–39.

53. Mark Seltzer, *Henry James and the Art of Power* (Ithaca, N.Y.: Cornell University Press, 1984), 4.

54. Elisabeth Schüssler Fiorenza, *Jesus and the Politics of Interpretation* (New York: Continuum, 2000), 3.

55. Mary Ann Tolbert, "The Gospel of Mark," in *The New Testament Today*, 47.

56. Ibid., 47.

57. Ibid., 50.

58. Ibid.

59. See Alastair Fowler, *Kinds of Literature: An Introduction to the Theory of Genres and Modes* (Cambridge: Harvard University Press, 1982), 259. As Christopher Bryan has asserted, moreover, the notion of a writer proceeding without genre, or creating a totally new genre (*sui generis*), is (even if theoretically possible) akin to the notion of a writer choosing to write in an unknown language. . . . In fact, the wildest artistic experimentation invariably has some connection, either by adaptation or reaction, to what has preceded it. See *A Preface to Mark: Notes on the Gospel in its Literary and Cultural Settings* (Oxford: Oxford University Press, 1993), 12.

60. Tolbert, "The Gospel of Mark," 50.

61. Ibid.

62. Ibid.

63. Steffano Zuffi, *Gospel Figures in Art*, trans. Thomas Michael Hartmann (Los Angeles: J. Paul Getty Museum, 2002), 149.

64. For general information on the Harlem Renaissance period, see Nathan Irvin Huggins, *Harlem Renaissance* (London: Oxford, 1971); Steven Watson, *The Harlem Renaissance: Hub of African-American Culture, 1920–1930* (New York: Pantheon Books, 1995); and Cary D. Wintz, *Harlem Speaks: A Living History of the Harlem Renaissance* (Naperville, Ill.: Sourcebooks, 2007).

65. One can see this depiction as early as George Washington Williams's *History of the Negro Race in America (1619–1880)* (orig. published in 1883; New York: Arno, 1968), 6, and in the writing of the black political thinker and educator Anna Julia Cooper, *The Voice of Anna Julia Cooper: Including a Voice from the South and Other Important Essays, Papers, and Letters*, ed. Charles Lemert and Esme Bhan (Lanham: Rowman & Littlefield, 1998), 316–17. For a thoughtful analysis of Simon of Cyrene, and one that seeks to critique the impression that the episode on Simon does not really matter, see Brian Blount, "A Socio-Rhetorical Analysis of Simon of Cyrene: Mark 15:21 and Its Parallels," *Semeia* 64 (1993): 171–98.

66. Indeed, I have contributed to that canonization. See my "Aaron Douglas, the Harlem Renaissance, and Biblical Art: Toward a Radical Politics of Identity," in

African Americans and the Bible: An Interdisciplinary Project, ed. Vincent Wimbush (New York: Continuum, 2000), 682–95.

67. Amy Kirschke, *Aaron Douglas: Art, Race, and the Harlem Renaissance* (Jackson, Miss.: University Press of Mississippi, 1995), 100.

68. Ellen McBreen, "Biblical Gender Bending in Harlem: The Queer Performance of Nugent's Salome," *Art Journal* 57 (1998): 22–28, esp. 25.

69. See, e.g., Mary Ann Tolbert, "When Resistance Becomes Repression," in *Reading from This Place*; Vol. 2: in *Social Location and Biblical Interpretation in Global Perspective*, eds. Fernando F. Segovia and Mary Ann Tolbert (Minneapolis: Fortress Press, 1995), 331–46; Musa Dube, "Talitha Cum! A Postcolonial Feminist & HIV/AIDS Reading of Mark 5:21-43," in *Grant Me Justice! HIV/AIDS & Gender Readings of the Bible*, ed. Musa W. Dube and Musimbi Kanyoro (New York: Orbis, 2004), 115–40; Richard A. Horsley, *Hearing the Whole Story: The Politics of Plot in Mark's Gospel* (Louisville: Westminster John Knox, 2001), 121–48; and Tat-siong Benny Liew, *The Politics of Parousia: Reading Mark Inter(con)textually* (Leiden: Brill, 1999).

70. Susan P. Mattern, *Rome and the Enemy: Imperial Strategy in the Principate* (Berkeley: University of California Press, 1999), 157.

71. On Mark's "critique of abusive power," see Donald Senior, "'With Swords and Clubs . . .': The Setting of Mark's Community and His Critique of Abusive Power," *Biblical Theology Bulletin* 17 (1987): 10–20.

72. On the scriptural allusions and the apocalyptic nature of Mark 1:1-15, see Joel Marcus, *The Gospel of Mark 1-8*, Anchor Bible 27 (Garden City, N.Y.: Doubleday, 1999), 149.

73. Mark's framing of Jesus' death within the context of the second longest parable of the narrative, the parable of the tenants (12:1-12), suggests that the death is a signal of the immediacy of God's final consummation of divine reigning. Indeed, some scholars (not all) may have missed an insight offered by the parable, for the "beloved" son is the *last* one sent, a climactic act.

74. Abraham Smith, "Tyranny Exposed: The Characterization of Herod Antipas in Mark 6:14-29," *Biblical Interpretation* 14 (2006): 259–93.

75. Ibid., 259–93.

76. On the increased fame and opposition, see Mary Ann Tolbert, *Sowing the Gospel* (Minneapolis: Fortress Press, 1989), 131–42.

77. Ibid., 275. On Jesus' knowledge of Scripture, John R. Donahue writes: "In these pericopes [12:13-17; 12:18-27; 12:28-34], Jesus is portrayed as instructing official Judaism on the true meaning of the Jewish scripture and beliefs." See John R. Donahue, "A Neglected Factor in the Theology of Mark," *Journal of Biblical Literature* 101 (1982): 580.

78. On the "mounting opposition" of the closing chapter of Mark's Gospel, see Donahue, "A Neglected Factor," 570. On the "recognition sequences," see Tolbert, *Sowing the Gospel*, 272.

79. It is critical to note that the disciples are expected to face Jewish *and* Gentile authorities.

80. Mark uses the word "with" (*meta*) to mark the shift in Jesus' fellowship from its seeming cohesion to its fracturing. Although the Twelve were commissioned to be "with" Jesus (*meta*, 3:14), the narrative later describes Judas as "one of the twelve" who brings "with [*meta*] him" a crowd with swords and clubs, from the chief priests,

the scribes, and the elders (14:43). Likewise, when the high priest's servant says to Peter, "You also were with [*meta*] him [Jesus]" (14:67), Peter denies it.

81. Senior, "With Swords and Clubs . . .", 10–20.

82. For Aristotle, plot is characterized by wholeness (a comprehensive concept which refers to a process of change from good to bad or otherwise, though Aristotle prefers good to bad), magnitude (a size that is sufficient for the efficient development of the plot), and unity (a completeness that is forfeited by the omission or replacement of any episode). Aristotle, *Poetics*, 7, 8.

83. bell hooks, *Black Looks*, 115.

84. Tat-siong Benny Liew, "Tyranny, Boundary and Might: Colonial Mimicry in Mark's Gospel," *Journal for the Study of the New Testament* 73 (1999): 13.

85. Ibid.

86. Ibid. On colonial mimicry in Mark, also see Eric Thurman, "Looking for a Few Good Men: Mark and Masculinity," in *New Testament Masculinities*, Semeia Studies, ed. Stephen D. Moore and Janice Capel Anderson (Atlanta: Society of Biblical Literature, 2003), 139ff. On the term itself, see Homi Bhabha, *Location of Cultures* (New York: Routledge, 1994), 86.

87. Liew, "Tyranny, Boundary," 13–15.

88. Ibid., 16.

89. Ibid., 8–21.

90. Ibid.

91. Ibid., 22–23.

92. Ibid., 24–27. For a longer examination of Mark's colonial mimicry, see Liew, *Politics of Parousia*.

93. In this regard, I am most influenced by bell hooks.

94. Admittedly, the earliest information we have about Pilate within or outside of the New Testament is limited. Pilate is mentioned in all four canonical Gospel accounts (Mark 15:1-15, 43-45; Matt 27:2-26, 58, 62-65; Luke 3:1; 13:1; 23:1-25, 52; John 18:28—19:16, 38); in Acts (3:13; 4:27; 13:28); and in 1 Tim (6:13). As we will see later in the body of this chapter, he is likewise featured in Philo and Josephus.

95. Philo, *The Embassy to Gaius*, in *Philo*, trans. F. H. Colson (Cambridge, Mass.: Harvard University, 1962), 299.

96. For example, Philo speaks of Pilate as "naturally inflexible, a blend of self-will and relentlessness" (*The Embassy*, 301) and of his customary "outrages and wanton injuries . . . [his] executions without trial . . . [his] ceaseless and supremely grievous cruelty" (*The Embassy*, 302).

97. Cf. See Richard A. Horsley and Neil Asher Silberman, *The Messiah and the Kingdom* (Minneapolis: Fortress Press, 2002), 66–67.

98. Horsley and Silberman, *The Messiah*, 67.

99. According to William Riley Wilson, as a result of the Mt. Gerizim incident, "the Samaritan senate sent an embassy to Vitellius, the legate of Syria, accusing Pilate of murder and claiming that the gathering had been peaceful and nonpolitical. Vitellius appointed an emissary to take charge of the government in Judea, then he ordered Pilate to Rome to answer charges before the emperor. This marked the end of Pilate's procuratorship [actually his prefecture]." William Riley Wilson, *The Execution of Jesus: A Judicial, Literary and Historical Investigation* (New York: Scribner's, 1970), 19–20.

100. On this traditional view, see the list cited by Helen K. Bond, *Pontius Pilate in History and Interpretation* (New York: Cambridge University Press, 1998), 103 n. 43. For a schematic on the various reconstructions of Pilate by modern interpreters, see Warren Carter, *Pontius Pilate: Portraits of a Roman Governor* (Collegeville, Minn.: Liturgical, 2003), 3–11.

101. The expression "sociopolitical/religious authorities" reveals a now-common assumption, namely, that these authorities were not simply religious authorities but persons wielding sociopolitical power at some level. On this matter, see Carter, *Pontius Pilate*, 30. Cf. Alberto de Mingo Kaminouchi, *"'But It Is Not So among You': Echoes of Power in Mark 10:32-45,"* JSNT Supplement Series (New York: T&T Clark International, 2003), 202.

102. Carter, *Pontius Pilate*, 56.

103. Again, as noted earlier, the mockery of Jesus as a kind of brigand begins as early as Gethsemane (cf. 14:48).

104. What Warren Carter has stated about the term "king" with respect to Matthew applies for Mark as well: "The noun 'king' (*basileus*) commonly denotes Rome's emperors, the most central, important, and powerful figure in the imperial world." See Warren Carter, "Resisting and Imitating the Empire: Imperial Paradigms in Two Matthean Parables," *Interpretation* 56 (2006): 263.

105. On the staged mockery that preceded Roman executions, see K. M. Coleman, "Fatal Charades: Roman Executions Staged as Mythological Enactments," *Journal of Roman Studies* 80 (1990): 44–73. Cf. Joel Marcus, "Crucifixion as Parodic Exaltation," *Journal of Biblical Literature* 125 (2006): 73–87. On the associations between royal pretenders and brigandage, see Josephus's description of the royal aspirant Judas (son of Ezechias) who was also a brigand chief (*War* 1.56; cf. *Antiquities* 18.271). Likewise, Josephus speaks of a certain Simon as a king-pretender who had a band of brigands (*War* 2.56; cf. *Antiquities* 18.273).

106. On the trial/interrogation debate, see Donald Senior, *The Passion of Jesus in the Gospel of Mark* (Collegeville, Minn.: Liturgical, 1991), 88–91; John R. Donahue and Daniel J. Harrington, *The Gospel of Mark*; Sacra Pagina (Collegeville, Minn.: Liturgical, 2002), 426–27.

107. On the unlikelihood of the "history of the custom of releasing prisoners on Passover," see Kaminouchi, *"But It Is Not So among You,"* 194. Cf. C. S. Mann, *Mark: A New Translation with Introduction and Commentary*; Anchor Bible, 27 (Garden City, N.Y.: Doubleday, 1986), 634. Also, Eduard Schweizer, *The Good News According to Mark: A Commentary on the Gospel* (London: SPCK, 1981), 335, notes the stylized character of the whole of 15:1-15, i.e., that the upshot is not history but a presentation of the "defenseless silence of Jesus in the face of all the questioning by his interrogators. . . ."

108. Admittedly, here, I read *de* not as an adversative conjunction (which would then be translated, in accordance with the NRSV, as "but") but as a simple coordinating one (which would be translated as "and").

109. Smith, "Tyranny Exposed," 282–83. Several scholars have noted, independently from me and in varying degrees, some of the parallels listed. Cf. Kaminouchi, *"But It Is Not So among You"*; Tolbert, *Sowing the Gospel*, 273; Liew, *Politics of Parousia*, 82.

110. See Smith, "Tyranny Exposed," 280–81.

111. Independent of my own work, Timothy J. Geddert, *Watchwords: Mark 13 in Markan Eschatology* (Sheffield: Sheffield Academic Press, 1989), 157, has essentially said the same.

112. See Lawrence Wills, *The Jew in the Court of the Foreign King: Ancient Jewish Court Legends* (Minneapolis: Fortress Press, 1990).

113. Note also that Mark 15:16 speaks of Jesus as having been led away (*apēgagon*; cf. 14:53).

114. Cf. Ramsay MacMullen, *Enemies of the Roman Order: Treason, Unrest, and Alienation in the Empire* (Cambridge: Harvard University, 1966), 83–84.

115. On the dangers of a politics of difference, see Renita Weems, "The Hebrew Women Are Not Like the Egyptian Women: The Ideology of Race, Gender and Sexual Reproduction in Exodus 1," *Semeia* 59 (1994): 25–34.

116. Again, see Liew's warning about the politics of the parousia. Liew, "Tyranny, Boundary," 22–23.

117. Tolbert, "When Resistance Becomes Repression," 344.

118. Laurence Wills, "Jewish Novellas," in *Greek Fiction: The Greek Novel in Context*, ed. J. R. Morgan and Richard Stoneman (London: Routledge, 1994), 224.

119. On the fragments as nationalistic propaganda, see *Ancient Greek Novels: The Fragments (Introduction, Text, Translation, and Commentary)*, ed. Susan A. Stephens and John Winkler (Princeton, N.J.: Princeton University Press, 1995), 8.

120. See *Aeneid* 1.279. On the date for the composition, see Musa W. Dube, *Postcolonial Feminist Interpretation of the Bible* (St. Louis: Chalice, 2000), 81.

121. Albrecht Dihle, *Greek and Latin Literature of the Roman Empire: From Augustus to Justinian*, trans. Manfred Malzahn (London: Routledge, 1994), 32.

122. Dionysius of Halicarnassus gives a similar portrait of Rome as divinely ordained to rule the world. See John T. Squires, *The Plan of God in Luke-Acts* (Cambridge: Cambridge University, 1993), 41.

123. See Virgil, *Aeneid* 3; Livy 1.1—2.6.

8. POSTCOLONIAL CRITICISM

1. "Subaltern" here refers to a minority person who is marginalized and disempowered, particularly because of her gender and race/ethnicity.

2. V. I. Lenin, "Imperialism, the Highest Stage of Capitalism," in *Selected Works: One-Volume Edition* (New York: International, 1971), 223; emphasis original.

3. See, for example, G. N. Uzoigwe, "European Partition and Conquest of Africa: An Overview," in *General History of Africa*; Vol. 7: *Africa under Colonial Domination 1880-1935*, ed. A. Adu Boahen (Berkeley: University of California Press, 1985), 19–44.

4. See, for example, Russell E. Lucas, *Institutions and the Politics of Survival in Jordan: Domestic Responses to External Challenges, 1988-2001* (Albany: State University of New York Press, 2005), 13–16; and Eliezer Tauber, *The Formation of Modern Syria and Iraq* (Portland: Frank Cass, 1995).

5. R. S. Sugirtharajah, *Postcolonial Criticism and Biblical Interpretation* (New York: Oxford University Press, 2002), 2.

6. Robert J. C. Young, *Postcolonialism: An Historical Introduction* (Malden: Blackwell, 2001), 57, 211–13.

7. See, for example, Walter LaFeber, *The New Empire: An Interpretation of American Expansion, 1860–1898* (Ithaca: Cornell University Press, 1963); and David Ray Griffin, John B. Cobb Jr., Richard A. Falk, and Catherine Keller, *The American Empire and the Commonwealth of God: A Political, Economic, Religious Statement* (Louisville: Westminster John Knox, 2006).

8. Edward W. Said, *Orientalism* (New York: Pantheon, 1978).

9. Gayatri Chakravorty Spivak, "Can the Subaltern Speak?" in *Marxism and the Interpretation of Culture*, ed. Cary Nelson and Larry Grossberg (Urbana: University of Illinois Press, 1988), 271–313. This essay has an earlier incarnation as "Can the Subaltern Speak? Speculations on Widow-Sacrifice," in *Wedge* 7/8 (1985): 120–30.

10. Abdul R. JanMohamed and David Lloyd, eds., *The Nature and Context of Minority Discourse* (New York: Oxford University Press, 1990).

11. Homi K. Bhabha, *The Location of Culture* (New York: Routledge, 1994).

12. See, for example, V. S. Naipaul, *The Mimic Men* (London: Penguin, 1967).

13. See, for example, Bhabha, "Of Mimicry and Man: The Ambivalence of Colonial Discourse," *Location of Culture*, 85–92.

14. Fanon's most important publications are arguably *The Wretched of the Earth*, trans. Constance Farrington (New York: Grove, 1963), *A Dying Colonialism*, trans. Haakon Cheveliar (New York: Grove, 1965), and *Black Skin, White Masks*, trans. Charles Lam Markmann (New York: Grove, 1967). For samples of how Fanon occupies or preoccupies much of postcolonial theory and studies, see, for example, Renate Zahar, *Frantz Fanon: Colonialism and Alienation* (New York: Monthly Review, 1974); Homi K. Bhabha, "Interrogating Identity: Frantz Fanon and the Postcolonial Prerogative," *Location of Culture*, 40–65; and Anthony C. Alessandrini, ed., *Frantz Fanon: Critical Perspectives* (New York: Routledge, 1999).

15. Kalpana Seshadri-Crooks, "Surviving Theory: A Conversation with Homi K. Bhabha," in *The Pre-Occupation of Postcolonial Studies*, ed. Fawzia Afzal-Khan and Kalpana Seshadri-Crooks (Durham: Duke University Press, 2000), 373.

16. See, for example the collection of essays in Ania Loomba and Martin Orkin, eds., *Post-Colonial Shakespeares* (New York: Routledge, 1998).

17. Edward Said, *The World, the Text, and the Critic* (Cambridge: Harvard University Press, 1983), 1–16.

18. See, for example, Gayatri Chakravorty Spivak, *The Post-Colonial Critic: Interviews, Strategies, Dialogues*, ed. Sarah Harasym (New York: Routledge, 1990), 1–2.

19. Edward Said, *Culture and Imperialism* (New York: Alfred A. Knopf, 1993), 1–19, 31–43, 51, 66–67, 76, 136–43.

20. For those who may not be familiar with these texts, Conrad's is a "canonical" text of "English literature" detailing the experiences of a European named Marlow in the African Congo. Achebe's is written from the perspective of an African who struggled to hold on to the histories and cultures of his traditional Ibo society with the advent of British colonization.

21. A good example is Anne McClintock, *Imperial Leather: Race, Gender, and Sexuality in the Colonial Contest* (New York: Routledge, 1995). The inter- or trans-disciplinary nature of postcolonial criticism may also partly account for the density of Spivak's and Bhabha's writings.

22. See, for example, Valentin Y. Mudimbe, *The Invention of Africa: Philosophy and the Order of Knowledge* (Bloomington: Indiana University Press, 1988).

23. Gayatri Chakravorty Spivak, "Three Women's Texts and a Critique of Imperialism," *Critical Inquiry* 12 (1985): 243–61.

24. See, for example, Gayatri Chakravorty Spivak, *Imaginary Maps* (New York: Routledge, 1995); Spivak, *Old Women* (Calcutta: Seagull, 1997); and Spivak, *The Breast Stories* (Calcutta: Seagull, 1997).

25. On nationalism in postcolonial criticism, a good place to start is Partha Chatterjee, *Nationalist Thought and the Colonial World* (Minneapolis: University of Minnesota Press, 1993).

26. Jean Rhys, "The Day They Burned the Books," in *The Collected Short Stories* (New York: Norton, 1987), 151–57.

27. Gayatri Chakravorty Spivak, "A Note on the New International," *Parallax* 7 (2001): 15.

28. This memorable turn of phrase belongs to Trinh T. Minh-ha; see, for example, her *When the Moon Waxes Red: Representation, Gender and Cultural Politics* (New York: Routledge, 1991).

29. This is the second half of Trinh's turn of phrase.

30. Gayatri Chakravorty Spivak, *A Critique of Postcolonial Reason: Toward a History of the Vanishing Present* (Cambridge: Harvard University Press, 1999), xii.

31. Jacques Derrida, "Letter to a Japanese Friend," in *A Derrida Reader: Between the Blinds*, ed. Peggy Kamuf (New York: Columbia University Press, 1991), 273.

32. See, for example, Walter D. Mignolo, *Local Histories/Global Designs: Coloniality, Subaltern Knowledges, and Border Thinking* (Princeton: Princeton University Press, 2000).

33. Young has argued for limiting postcolonialism to European empires since the fifteenth or sixteenth century because of the ability of these empires to expand beyond a single and coherent land mass with the developments in navigational technologies and skills (*Postcolonialism*, 15–16). The irony is that Young himself begins this defense by acknowledging how many imperialists of the nineteenth century invoked the Roman empire as both "guiding model and moral justification" (*Postcolonialism*, 15–16, 33). One should also remember that the Romans did have a navy to help secure and control the Mediterranean coast.

34. Mignolo, *Local Histories*, 21–33.

35. Young, *Postcolonialism*, 21.

36. For a detailed account of the Bible and colonization, see Michael Prior, *The Bible and Colonialism: A Moral Critique* (Sheffield: Sheffield Academic Press, 1997).

37. Spivak, "Three Women's Texts," 249.

38. Jacques Derrida, "Faith and Knowledge: The Two Sources of 'Religion' at the Limits of Reason Alone," trans. Samuel Weber, in *Religion*, ed. Jacques Derrida and Gianni Vattimo (Stanford: Stanford University Press, 1998), 29–30.

39. R. S. Sugirtharajah, "Introduction," in *The Postcolonial Biblical Reader*, ed. R. S. Sugirtharajah (Malden: Blackwell, 2006), 1–2.

40. Erin Runions, "Biblical Promise and Threat in U.S. Imperial Rhetoric, Before and After 9/11," in *Interventions: Activists and Academics Respond to Violence*, ed. Elizabeth A. Castelli and Janet R. Jakobsen (New York: Palgrave Macmillan, 2004), 71–88.

41. See also Erin Runions, "Desiring War: Apocalypse, Commodity Fetish, and the End of History," *The Bible and Critical Theory* 1 (2004). Accessible online at http://publications.epress.monash.edu/tou/bc/2004/1/1.

42. Michael Hardt and Antonio Negri, *Empire* (Cambridge: Harvard University Press, 2000), 20, 163, 166, 314–16.

43. See, for instance, Ched Myers, *Binding the Strong Man: A Political Reading of Mark's Story of Jesus* (Maryknoll: Orbis, 1992), and Herman C. Waetjen, *A Reordering of Power: A Socio-Political Reading of Mark's Gospel* (Minneapolis: Fortress Press, 1989).

44. Richard A. Horsley, *Hearing the Whole Story: The Politics of Plot in Mark's Gospel* (Louisville: Westminster John Knox, 2001); and David Joy, "Markan Subalterns/The Crowd and Their Strategies of Resistance: A Postcolonial Critique," *Black Theology* 3 (2005): 55–74.

45. Horsley, *Hearing*, 203–29.

46. Joy, "Markan Subalterns," 65.

47. Ibid., 57. Joy refers here to the introductory comments provided by Donna Landry and Gerald MacLean (*The Spivak Reader* [New York: Routledge, 1996], 203), but stops right before the editors cite from Spivak's essay, "Can the Subaltern Speak?"

48. Laura E. Donaldson, "Gospel Hauntings: The Postcolonial Demons of New Testament Criticism," in *Postcolonial Biblical Criticism: Interdisciplinary Intersections*, ed. Stephen D. Moore and Fernando F. Segovia (New York: T.&T. Clark, 2005), 97–98.

49. Stephen D. Moore, "Mark and Empire: 'Zealot' and 'Postcolonial' Readings," in *Postcolonial Theologies: Divinity and Empire*, ed. Catherine Keller, Michael Nausner, and Mayra Rivera (St. Louis: Chalice, 2004), 134–48.

50. Moore, "Mark and Empire," 138, 142.

51. Ibid., 146; emphasis mine. I cannot relate this episode really to Joy's reading, since he does not do anything beyond listing it to enlist the poor widow as part of the subaltern. The episode does not present a similar problem for Horsley because he reads it in terms of the widow's victimization or exploitation by the local elites (*Hearing*, 216–17).

52. Seong Hee Kim, "Rupturing the Empire: Reading the Poor Widow as a Postcolonial Female Subject (Mark 12:41-44)," *lectio difficilior* 1 (2006), http://www.lectio.unibe.ch/06_1/kim_rupturing.htm.

53. For example, Dennis Duling gives the Gospel the subtitle, "A Mysterious Apocalyptic Drama," in *The New Testament: History, Literature, and Social Context*; 4th ed. (Belmont: Wadsworth, 2003), 293. Mark's apocalyptic emphasis has much to do not only with the apocalyptic discourse by Jesus in chap. 13, but also the promised reappearance of the risen Christ and his reunion with the disciples at the end of the Gospel (16:7).

54. Kim, "Rupturing the Empire."

55. Ibid.

56. Ashis Nandy, *The Intimate Enemy: Loss and Recovery of Self under Colonialism* (Delhi: Oxford University Press, 1983), xiv.

57. The severity of this oversight can be seen, for example, in Jack Dean Kingsbury's book, *Conflict in Mark: Jesus, Authorities, Disciples* (Minneapolis: Fortress

Press, 1989). In this book the conflicts between the Judean and Roman authorities are all but absent.

58. Moore, "Mark and Empire," 140.

59. See David A. deSilva, "4 Maccabees," in *Eerdman's Commentary on the Bible,* ed. James D. G. Dunn and John W. Rogerson (Grand Rapids: Eerdmans, 2003), 888–901, for information about this book.

60. See, for example, Stephen D. Moore and Janice Capel Anderson, "Taking It like a Man: Masculinity in 4 Maccabees," *Journal of Biblical Literature* 117 (1998): 249–73, on how the woman martyr is used to exemplify masculinity and thus entrench a masculinist ideology.

61. It is worth pondering if the way Spivak premises agency on speech is not itself problematic. Women from cultures outside of the geopolitical West have understood, for example, the power of silence in resistance; see, for example, King-kok Cheung, *Articulate Silences: Hisaye Yamamoto, Maxine Hong Kingston, Joy Kogawa* (Ithaca, N.Y.: Cornell University Press, 1993). To be fair to Spivak, one should read "Can the Subaltern Speak?" in light of her concern about the limit of representing or speaking *for* a subaltern. In other places, such as "Versions of the Margin: J. M. Coetzee's *Foe* Reading of Defoe's *Crusoe/Roxana,*" Spivak certainly understands the power of silence, as in her argument that Friday is "an agent of withholding" or one who refuses to yield an authentic native voice (in *Consequences of Theory: Selected Papers of the English Institute, 1987–88,* ed. Jonathan Arac and Barbara Johnson [Baltimore: Johns Hopkins University Press, 1991], 172).

62. Reina Lewis, *Gendering Orientalism: Race, Femininity and Representation* (New York: Routledge, 1995).

63. Despite my earlier questioning of agency as speech, let me note that the only woman who actually speaks in Mark is the Syrophoenician woman (7:24-30). This woman's story is no less material. Not only is her debate with Jesus carried on in material terms (food and crumbs), the focus of their debate also centers on the woman's motherly love and care for her demon-possessed daughter. To use the vocabulary of Hardt and Negri, the woman is given both speech and victory because she is debating Jesus in terms of her "affective labor," or what has generally been called "women's work" (*Empire,* 292–93).

64. Some suggest that the woman's act should be read as her performance of a "prophetic" role. She is anointing God's "anointed" for the liberation of God's people. Hence the woman is comparable to Samuel (who anointed Saul and David), Ahijah (who anointed Jeremiah), and/or Elijah (who anointed Jehu). See, for example, Horsley, *Hearing,* 217–18.

65. Gayatri Chakravorty Spivak, "The Rani of Sirmur: An Essay in Reading the Archives," *History and Theory* 24 (1985): 263.

66. Donaldson, "Gospel Hauntings," 97–113.

67. Spivak, *Critique,* 1–2.

68. Horsley, *Hearing,* 212.

69. Derrida, "Faith and Knowledge," 49–56.

70. Robert J. C. Young, *Colonial Desire: Hybridity in Theory, Culture and Race* (New York: Routledge, 1995), 163.

INDEXES

Ancient Sources

Names